HANDBOOK of ACCOUNTING PRACTICE

Jay Ruben, M.S., C.M.A., C.P.A.

PRENTICE HALL
Englewood Cliffs, New Jersey 07632

Prentice-Hall International (UK) Limited, *London*
Prentice-Hall of Australia Pty. Limited, *Sydney*
Prentice-Hall Canada, Inc., *Toronto*
Prentice-Hall Hispanoamericana, S.A., *Mexico*
Prentice-Hall of India Private Limited, *New Delhi*
Prentice-Hall of Japan, Inc., *Tokyo*
Simon & Schuster Asia Pte. Ltd., *Singapore*
Editora Prentice-Hall do Brasil, Ltda., *Rio de Janeiro*

10 9 8 7 6 5 4 3 2 1

Library of Congress Cataloging-in-Publication Data

Ruben, Jay.
Handbook of accounting practice / by Jay Ruben.
p. cm.
Includes index.
ISBN 0-13-376112-6
1. Accounting. 2. Auditing. 3. Accounting—Data processing.
I. Title.
HF5635.R894 1992
657—dc20 92-16992
CIP

ISBN 0-13-376112-6

90000>
9 780133 761122

PRENTICE HALL
Professional Publishing
Englewood Cliffs, NJ 07632
Simon & Schuster, A Paramount Communications Company

Printed in the United States of America

To Janice, my wife and best pal, who has been there every step of the way.

To Carrie and Brad whom I'll never be able to repay for being my kids.

and

My mom who got me started.

About the Author

Jay Ruben, MS, CMA, CPA is Vice President/Director of Training for AccountEd International, a company that performs instructional design and financial/accounting training programs for executives of large corporations here and abroad.

Mr. Ruben is a member of the faculty at California State University, Northridge, where he teaches accounting at the undergraduate level. Prior to that he practiced accounting for over thirty years.

He has published books on *"How to Increase Your Fees by Preparing your Clients' Business Plans" and "How to Get and Keep your Growing Clients"*. His work has also appeared in many industry related journals over the years. In addition, he has created and successfully applied his ideas as a frequent lecturer both in United States and in the Pacific Rim countries.

Mr. Ruben is currently V.P. Director of Professional Education for the West Los Angeles Chapter of IMA (Institute of Management Accountants), and is a former member of: UCLA Management Alumni Association Board of Directors; California Society of CPA's Chairman of San Fernando Valley Discussion Group; Southern California Society of Real Estate Investors Board of Directors and facilitated as a Tutor for the Minority Business Program for California State University, Northridge.

What This Book Will Do for You

This book is to be used as a problem solving tool. It will help you when you have a quandary about

Financial accounting

Auditing

Statement analysis

Cost accounting

Managerial accounting

Electronic data processing.

As an accountant, you must wear many hats: You must collect data, process it, evaluate the results and then present these results in financial reports that are meaningful, understandable, and in conformity with generally accepted accounting principles and pronouncements.

In addition, you must communicate to a variety of users, an expression of responsibility on the information that is presented. And, this is dictated by the nature of the work performed and the characteristics of the company issuing the statements.

The results are only as good as the procedures and controls utilized to collect them. Therefore, you may need to analyze and design financial and cost accounting systems.

Accounting is an interpretation of an organization's resources and results of operations and, is, by this nature, historical. However, the information presented is used to make predictions about the organization's future resources and its potential for financial returns. Thus, you must not only be able to apply various techniques to forecast future results, but, you should be able to show management how to make decisions among alternatives.

There is no shortage of written information to help you solve the myriad of problems that you face each and every day. But, unfortunately, this data is scattered in bits and pieces among an almost infinite array of publications, hard to find and assimilate.

The book addresses this issue by presenting, in one handy volume, the answers to many of the questions and dilemmas that you have to solve.

The *Handbook of Accounting Practice* is organized to ease the job of locating information through a combination of detailed chapter listings, indexes and an information retrieval device constructed in financial statement format.

How This Book Is Organized

The book is divided into seven sections.

Section 1—Financial Accounting

The first section presents an overview of GAAP and how they can be applied to a variety of financial statements and reports. The material is then expanded into an exposition of official pronouncements, computation methods, examples, and disclosure requirements. There is also help for the reader who has questions about specific operating areas including partnerships, consolidated statements, not for profit organizations, oil and gas, rate regulated industries, governmental organizations, insolvencies and bankruptcies and financial statement defeasance.
SEE CHAPTERS 1–5.

Section 2—Auditing

This section discusses Generally Accepted Auditing Standards and describes how these standards affect the accountant's ability to plan and conduct audits, analyze, review and test internal controls, test procedures, and gather evidence. Sample engagement letters and report formats are presented in this section. Statistical sampling methods, and other techniques to enhance the audit process, are described. There are also chapters on SEC procedures, special reports and internal accounting and auditing functions.
SEE CHAPTERS 6–15.

Section 3—Financial Statement Analysis

Along with the major ratios and trend investigations, we present the concept of "Top Down Analysis" in which environmental, industry and finally, company factors are examined.
SEE CHAPTERS 15 and 16.

Section 4—Cost Accounting

Cost accounting is defined as the collecting, recording, summarizing and analyzing of the cost of products sold. Section 4 begins with an overview (including terminology) then describes job order, process, and standard cost systems. It then explains variable versus full absorption methods, activities

based costing, joint and by product accounting, and service department allocation.
SEE CHAPTERS 17–23.

Section 5—Managerial Accounting

This section describes the scientific approach to analysis for management. Methods to determine cost behavior, prepare forecasts and budgets, build deterministic models, and make decisions under conditions of uncertainty are explained. In addition, there is a chapter about business plan preparation.
SEE CHAPTERS 18–29.

Section 6—Systems Analysis and Design

This section presents methods to analyze and design systems. It includes traditional as well as structured approaches, implementation and prototyping.
SEE CHAPTERS 29 and 30.

Section 7—Using Electronic Data Processing

This section describes EDP analysis procedures including hardware and software selection, and accountant's workstations. It also describes a way of adding computer consulting to your practice.
SEE CHAPTERS 31 and 32.

How to Use This Book

This book has been organized to help you locate the information you need to solve problems as quickly and accurately as possible.

As you look for information on a particular subject, you will be helped by the following aids:

1. *A detailed table of contents.*
2. *Chapter overview.*
3. *A detailed index* at the end of the book.
4. *The formatted financial statements finding tools.*
   Located at the beginning of pertinent chapters, these formats show where to find answers to financial accounting questions you may have.

In addition, we have provided many exhibits to help you easily analyze or structure your particular situation.

Jay Ruben

Contents

CHAPTER 1

How a Better Understanding of Generally Accepted Accounting Principles Can Improve Your Accounting Practice

Introduction

This chapter will help you wade through the morass of theory to find the best way to solve your financial accounting problems. To do this, we have organized the material to help you integrate this "cumbersome" body of generally acceptable alternative accounting principles into a framework that can be easily applied. What follows emphasizes the following:

- How accounting theory is derived
- Where it can be found
- How you can find the "best" GAAPs to use

The material is divided into the following sections:

- A New Look at GAAP
- When you Can Deviate from GAAP to Prepare Small Business Financial Statements
- How to Use the Conceptual Framework
- Converting the Structural Framework into Specifics
- Finding, Justifying and Documenting Your Approach
- Accounting Treatment Selection Worksheet and Questions
- Accounting Theory Finding Guide

A New Look at GAAP

An accountant who doesn't understand GAAP is like a surgeon who cannot figure out the body's circulatory system. GAAP is the glue that binds all of the tasks of identifying, gathering, and reporting accounting data so it can be communicated and understood by its users.

The Accounting Principles Board, in its Statement #4, expresses the following:

> Generally Accepted Accounting Principles encompass the conventions, rules, and procedures necessary to define accepted accounting principles at a particular time. The standards of GAAP include not only broad guidelines or general applications but also detailed practices and procedures.

From this, we can easily infer that GAAP is used for two purposes:

1. To identify alternatives
2. and, then, to narrow alternatives

Note: The term, *Generally Accepted* does not describe a formal body of laws that practitioners have to consult before they make any entry or adjustment.

On the contrary GAAP is applied by agreement, rather than by mandate. GAAP, as it exists today, has resulted from "Substantial Authoritative Support," which is derived from the following:

- Pronouncements of authoritative bodies of the American Institute of Certified Public Accountants (APB, FASB)
- Special research committees
- Industry practices
- Accounting publications

Be Aware: You have the choice to *not* be governed by the above. But, if you choose to deviate, you must be able to justify and explain your rationale.

When You Can Deviate from GAAP to Prepare Small Business Financial Statements

Many smaller organizations find a complete application of GAAP to their particular firms is costly, difficult and, quite often, just not very pertinent.

Example: APB and FASB pronouncements on Earnings per Share, Accounting for Leases, Accounting for Pension Plans, and Accounting for Income Taxes are not only burdensome to follow, but, don't present information that is of much use to a small firm.

The Solution: As a result of the lobbying of groups representing smaller CPA firms, the AICPA has adopted Other Consistent Bases of Accounting (OCBOA).

OCBOA applies to certain types of financial reports that are *not* prepared in accordance with GAAP, but, instead, present a more useful representation of the firm's net worth and results of operations for the purposes intended. The following financial statement formats are acceptable substitutions:

1. Cash Basis
2. Modified Cash Basis
3. Income Tax Basis

How to Use the Conceptual Framework to Solve Your Particular Problems

The conceptual framework describes the organization of GAAP. By moving through the hierarchal structure, you'll find it much easier to

- Find the most pertinent accounting treatment
- Justify your presentations

NOTE: It is the FASB's intention to continue to develop this framework and, to improve its usefulness in our continually changing financial and accounting environment.

Definition per FASB Discussion Memorandum #4:

A coherent system of interrelated objectives and fundamentals that can lead to consistent standards that prescribe the nature, function, and limits of financial accounting and financial statements.

The framework is constructed on three levels:

LEVEL 1: What are the basic objectives of financial accounting?

LEVEL 2: What are the basic concepts (qualitative characteristics) of accounting that contribute to its objectives?

LEVEL 3: How is accounting information to be recognized and measured?

1. *Objectives of Financial Reporting*

The major objective of financial reporting is to be *useful*. This is further expanded to the following:

- To *whom* should these statements be useful? The FASB has listed three categories of users:

  External Users

  Investors

  Creditors

  Internal Users

  Internal management.

Internal management collects, prepares and controls the quality and accuracy of financial information. *External* users must rely on that management to provide the financial information that they need.

Observation: Financial accounting theory is written for the benefit of the external user who is not privy to the activities of the corporation.

Caution: When you are involved in preparing statements, be sure to consider the external user first.

How is that useful information to be utilized?

The FASB has identified three major purposes:

- *To provide information that is understandable.* While the statements may be technically accurate and provide full disclosure, if they cannot be understood by the creditors, investors, or management, whatever information they reveal has no practical value and is literally worthless.
- *To predict cash flow.* Although financial statements are employed to measure past activity, their true value lies in their ability to foretell whether trends will continue into the future. And, future cash flow is of prime importance.
- *To provide information about an enterprise's financial resources*, which is what the balance sheet shows.
- *To evaluate the organization and its management*. Investors and lenders try to get the best return for their financial resources, subject to acceptable risk. The information contained in the financial statements must be clear, concise, and useful in order to help the outsiders make informed decisions.

2. Qualitative Characteristics of Financial Statements

These define the attributes of the information presented in the financial statements.

Examples:

- Does the information change or reinforce the user's opinions about the income, cash flows, and financial resources of the company?
- Is it believable?
- Can it be compared to prior operations of the firm and financial reports of other entities?

These are divided into the following:

a. Primary Characteristics
   i. Relevance
   ii. Reliability
b. Secondary Characteristics
   i. Comparability
   ii. Consistency
c. Classification as a Financial Statement Element

a. *Primary Characteristics:*

i. *Relevance.* To be relevant, information must be capable of changing a person's behavior, or course of action. It must be generated early enough to give the users a chance to act quick enough to benefit from what they learn.

Example: A company's statement of income reports a profit of $3,000,000. How much would that number have to change in order to be relevant and alter the user's opinion about the company?

ii. *Reliability.* To be acceptable, financial statements must be believable, dependable, or reliable. The following are necessary to ensure reliability:

(a) The statements must be verifiable and capable of being checked, reviewed, or audited.

(b) The financial reports must be prepared without bias. Avoiding partiality requires objectivity and independence by both management and the accountants.

How one achieves a bias free state is a philosophical question beyond the scope of this book. But, when financial statements lose their objectivity they, likewise, lose their reliability.

(c) The reports must be faithful representations of the resources and operations of the company. Just as a symphony is only an expression of a mood created by its composer; financial statements, likewise, are only impressions of the financial position and results of operations of a company prepared in accordance with GAAP. Their goal is the "truest" depiction of the information within that framework.

NOTE: Relevance versus Reliability: In order for financial information to be relevant, it must reinforce or change a user's behavior. Furthermore, it must be presented as soon as possible after the event took place. However, to be reliable, the information contained therein must be verifiable. But, financial statements contain a variety of estimates and assumptions about future events that will not be positively known for some time after the report has been prepared and published.

EXAMPLE: The Alpha Corporation's year-end financial statements present accounts receivable of $585,000 minus an allowance for uncollectible accounts of $58,500. How do we know that this allowance is reliable? or, if it is sufficient? On the other hand, if we wait until we determine the *exact* amount of receivables that will be ultimately collected, the statements will lose their timeliness and, of course, their relevance.

b. *Secondary Characteristics:*

Secondary characteristics provide an additional layer of detail to further define and enhance the utility of accounting information.

i. *Consistency.* The same accounting principles should be applied to similar events from period to period. If, however, there is a good reason to employ different measurement alternatives, the reasons and the results must be disclosed.

NOTE: The consistency requirement makes it easier for the user to make comparisons and analyze trends.

ii. *Comparability.* When financial information is recorded and reported in a similar manner by different organizations, it is easier for the reader to make comparisons between different companies and, dissimilar industries.

However: Comparability is a goal worth pursuing. But, it shouldn't be taken as a requirement that all accounting principles be uniformly applied. In the United States, we have successfully employed and modified GAAP to develop a reporting framework which has gained widespread acceptance. Uniformity carries with it, the need of a body of accounting legislation and the various "joys" of the governmental regulatory apparatus.

Furthermore: The ability to compare different companies is further reduced when applied to diverse industries.

Example: A meaningful comparison between an auto manufacturer and a public utility is not very likely.

c. *Financial Statement Elements:*

Since these are the building blocks of financial reporting, a brief review is pertinent:

1. *Assets:* Economic resources which have been acquired by the enterprise as a result of past transactions. They should provide future benefit and be under the control of the organization.
2. *Liabilities:* Economic obligations that have arisen from past economic events or transactions, and will be settled by future transfers of assets or performances of services.
3. *Equity:* The residual interest of the owners or shareholders in the business.
4. *Comprehensive Income:* All changes in net equity that do not include transactions with the owners.
5. *Revenues:* Gross inflows to the business as a result of delivering or producing goods or rendering services to customers.
6. *Expenses:* Outlays during a period that support the company's business operations.
7. *Gains and Losses:* Gross receipts or outlays from activities from peripheral or incidental transactions. They are usually not connected with the company's major business operations.

d. *Recognition and Measurement Concepts:*

By applying these concepts you can determine the rational alternatives when you need to solve specific accounting theory or procedural problems. These concepts are subdivided into three segments:

1. Assumptions
    a. Going concern
    b. Entity
    c. Stable measuring unit
    d. Periodicity

2. Principles
   a. Full disclosure
   b. Historical cost
   c. Revenue recognition
   d. Matching

3. Constraints
   a. Materiality
   b. Industry practices
   c. Cost/Benefit equation
   d. Conservatism

1. *Assumptions.* An assumption is roughly defined as an idea which is taken for granted.

Example: Everyone assumes that the stars come out at night. We don't need proof.

In accounting, assumptions are those principles that are known to underlay the entire measurement and reporting process. These are:

a. *Going Concern.* GAAP assume that an organization has a relatively long life; a time frame long enough to see its plans materialize. Therefore, financial statment components are valued at their continuing use in the business, instead of what they would bring on liquidation.

Example: The inventory valuation, as portrayed on the balance sheet, makes the assumption that the goods will be sold in the ordinary course of business, instead of under forced sale conditions which would, of course, yield less.

b. *Entity.* Whether the accounting books are kept for individuals, large corporations, the U.S. Government, or the economy in general, they are maintained for specific *entities.* An accounting entity is a separate organism, which has its reporting mechanism, and maintains an existence distinct from its respective constituencies.

Example: Joe Smith forms a company, "Joe's Fish." Joe and the fish business are distinct entities.

c. *Stable Monetary Unit.* In the U.S. we assume that the dollar is stable and can be relied upon as a standard of measurement. Therefore, we presuppose that fluctuations in its value will be minor.

However over time, increases in price and resulting reductions in our currency's value have tended to diminish the usefulness of historical costs. Since these increases have not been significant, the dollar has functioned as the stable currency of choice.

Those countries that have experienced hyper-inflation have found that the resulting rapid declines of their currencies have negated any usefulness of the stable money concept.

d. *Periodicity.* Accounting measures economic activity in short, finite time periods, which are usually portioned into current operating cycles.

What is an operating cycle? The time span needed to convert cash into inventories, then to sales, then back to cash.

In most organizations, the normal period is a year, if that time frame is greater than the current operating cycle.

NOTE: As the reporting duration becomes shorter, we are forced to rely more on estimates and assumptions to place items in the appropriate time period and provide useful data to the reader.

2. *Principles.* These principles define the standards which guide the application and use of GAAP.

a. *Full Disclosure.* The primary purpose of accounting is to provide pertinent details about the assets, liabilities, resources, revenues, and expenses of an entity. While full disclosure is required, you have to walk a fine line of providing sufficient useful data, while, avoiding the tendency to provide too much information. Too much data may lead to information overload.

NOTE: In the absence of information to the contrary, it is generally assumed that the financial statements, by themselves, provide everything the reader will need. Additional details, that are found in the footnotes, are intended to enhance and simplify the basic data.

b. *Historical Cost.* Because historical cost can be verified, and, hence, reliable, it has been chosen to be the acceptable valuation system in the United States.

c. *Revenue Recognition.* Under GAAP, revenue is usually recognized when it is *realized.* Realization usually occurs when an exchange takes place and title passes. When this happens we assume that the company has done everything needed to ensure passage of title and the buyer has given his or her acceptance.

However, in accounting theory, the economic substance of a transaction is more important than form. Therefore, regardless of the passage of title, some (generally acceptable) other methods recognize income at different times. These include the following:

- The installment sales method

- The percentage of completion method

NOTE: We have previously discussed OCBOA which may recognize revenues upon collection. While these alternatives do not report income in accordance with GAAP, they have been found useful for the purposes intended.

d. *Matching.* Expenses are matched to applicable revenues. This is part of the systematic and rational allocation process. While many of the numbers determined by this process depend on estimates, matching has been found to produce useful, timely data.

Example 1. A company sells 100 units at $90 each. These had been originally purchased at $60. This principle asserts that $6,000 (100 units at $60) be matched to the sale.

Example 2. When a firm acquires property and equipment, its cost will be systematically and rationally allocated to those future periods which we expect to benefit from the purchase.

3. *Constraints.* Accounting is a social art; it is affected and must exist amongst the other arts, subject to the environment. Therefore, its principles and procedures are continually redefined by an ever changing world of social, political, and economic circumstances.

a. *Materiality.* The accounting perception of materiality states, "If it doesn't matter, don't worry about it." But, the definition of just how small something has to be to not matter is purely judgmental.

Furthermore, materiality is dependent upon an item's significance as well as its magnitude.

QUESTION: Is a distortion of 10% material? To answer this we have to ask ourselves the following:

- Will it turn a profit into a loss?
- Will it turn stockholders' equity into a deficit?
- Or, will it affect the firm's cash balances?

SUGGESTION: Keep track of the cumulative effects of all adjustments that *are not* going to be recorded by preparing a *score sheet*. This is a workpaper schedule that will show the results of the adjustments *not* made on the following:

- Working capital
- Stockholders' equity
- Gross profit
- Net income

After you've completed your work, the totals in each category will portray the cumulative outcome and allow you to decide if adjustments may, after all, have to be made. Exhibit 1-1 provides an example of a score sheet.

XYZ COMPANY
SCORE SHEET—ITEMS PASSED
Year Ended December 31, 1988
Increase (Decrease)

	Total	Working Capital	Equity	Gross Profit	Net Income
Inventory	(4,445)	(4,445)	(4,445)	(4,445)	(4,445)
Equipment	(865)		(865)		(865)
Accounts Payable	(1,234)	(1,234)	(1,234)	(1,234)	(1,234)
Accounts Receivable	149	149	149		149
Prepaid Insurance	4	4	4		4
Total	(6,391)	(5,526)	(6,391)	(5,679)	(6,391)
Total before AJE		324,578	129,544	118,555	55,444
Percentage		1.70%	4.93%	4.79%	11.53%

Exhibit 1-1—***Score Sheet***

b. *Industry Practices.* The accounting procedures of many industries (e.g. oil, banking, insurance) cannot always be found within an all encompassing set of GAAP. Accordingly techniques have to be modified to provide useful information.

c. *Cost Benefit Equation.* Information is not free. All too often, the benefits of acquiring more definitive data do not equal the costs required to obtain it. Deciding how to measure the value of additional information versus the cost to obtain it is a difficult question at best. Fortunately, *information economics* techniques provide solutions. These procedures will be described in Chapter 29.

d. *Conservatism.* Accountants are told, "When in doubt, choose the accounting treatment that will avoid overstating assets or income."

CAUTION: Unfortunately, conservatism is often improperly used. An accountant may think it is safer to present a bleaker picture than necessary because investors will not be taken in by overly optimistic financial information. However, this practice may distort trend measurement. As a consequence, overzealous expensing or write downs may mislead the user about probable future income or cash flow of the company.

Example: A company carries inventory on its books at the end of 1988 at a historical cost of $1,000,000. Management decides to use the conservative approach and reduce this cost to a hypothetical market value of $800,000, thereby, lowering the inventory and the resulting profit for that year by $200,000. However, if this proposed adjustment is inaccurate, the following year's income will be overstated.

How the FASB Translates the Conceptual Framework into Specifics

The structural framework presents the basic ground rules. But, more is needed. That's where the Financial Accounting Standards Board (FASB) comes in.

FASB rulings, which are issued as *pronouncements*, have substantial authority. Therefore, any deviation requires an auditor to either explain, qualify, or disclaim his or her opinion and explain the reasons and impact of any departures.

There are three major forms of pronouncements:

1. *Statements of Financial Accounting Standards (SFASs)* which institute new GAAPs or amend existing ones.
2. *Interpretations* to explain existing SFASs, Accounting Principles Bulletins (APBs) and Accounting Research Bulletins (ARBs).
3. *Statements of Financial Accounting Concepts (SFACs)* which present the objectives and concepts upon which GAPP is based.

The FASB continues to narrow differences between alternatives by publishing additional pronouncements.

NOTE: Previous opinions of the APB and the CAP remain in force unless specifically superseded by action of the FASB.

How to Theoretically Justify and Document Your Treatment of a Specific Accounting Matter

Use the following worksheet to help you determine which way to go when you come up against a controversial subject. As you will see, it takes you through the various components of the conceptual framework model and allows you to document your thought process.

Note: An alphabetical finding list to ARBs, APBs, FASB, FASB Interpretations, and Financial Accounting Standards Bulletins is at the end of Chapter 1.

Accounting Treatment Selection Worksheet

Client ____
Financial Statement Date ____________________________
Accounts Involved __________________________________

Brief Description of Proposed Treatment

____

____

____

____

Note: It is assumed that the subject will have a material effect on the financial statements.

Answer every question. Explain all No answers.

Objectives

1. Will it improve the users' understanding of the financial statements? ___
2. Will it improve their ability to assess future cash flows? ___
3. Will it provide better information about enterprise resources, claims and changes in them? ___

Qualitative Characteristics

1. Can it be presented in a timely matter in order to help the users make a decision about the company's financial position, net income and cash flows? ___
2. If it changes their previously held views about the company, can these changes be supported? ___
3. Can the basis and estimates used in its computation be verified? ___
4. Will the resulting financial statements be as free from management manipulation and bias? ___
5. Is it consistent with prior reporting practices? ___

(Continued on next page)

6. Will it help users compare the company to other firms? ___

Assumptions

1. Are elements valued in accordance with the going concern concept? ___
2. Will income and expense items be recorded in the proper time period? ___

Principles

1. Will historical cost be used as a valuation method? ___
2. Will revenue be recognized under the realization principle or another acceptable method (e.g. percentage of completion, installment basis)? ___
3. Will expenses be recognized in accordance with the matching, or systematic and rational allocation principles? If not, will they be immediately recognized? ___
4. Will the principles of full disclosure be adhered to? ___

Constraints

1. Will the benefits of the new information exceed the costs of providing it? ___
2. Does the proposed treatment agree with current industry practice? ___
3. Will it lead to a conservative presentation? ___

List the Applicable ARBs, APBs, FASBs.

____

____

____

If the proposed accounting practice is not supported by the above opinions and pronouncements, list other authoritative support:

____

____

____

When you've completed your work, and the above checklist, be sure you can answer the following:

1. *Do the statements support your understanding of the dynamics of the organization?*

A company is much more than its journals, ledgers, and financial reports. It is a product of its management, products, facilities, and all the other elements that make up the soul of the business. Make every effort to feel that soul *before* classifying, recording, and communicating financial data.

2. *Do the company's financial statements and its components conform to the Structural Framework?*

a. Will the statements, as presented, serve the users' needs? ___
b. Are they useful? Are they understandable? ___
c. Is the information presented relevant? ___
d. Have the reports been prepared soon enough to facilitate informed decisions? ___
e. Is the information displayed reliable? Can it be verified?
f. Have the GAAPs been applied consistently from period to period? ___
g. Has the conceptual framework been followed with regard to asset valuation, and income and expense recognition? ___

3. *Have you sufficiently researched FASB literature to satisfy specific questions?*

NOTE: To obtain information directly from the FASB, write to:
Publications Office
Financial Accounting Standards Board
High Ridge Park
P.O. Box 3821
Stamford, Connecticut 06903-0821.

SUGGESTION: To obtain intelligence about practically any accounting subject the Accountant's Index, published by the AICPA, is most helpful.

4. *Have you tried to anticipate changes in accounting principles that may have a future impact on the financial statements?*
The FASB derives its authority and is influenced by government regulators, influential users, various trade and professional groups, academia, and the accounting profession itself. The Emerging Issues Task Force (EITF) of the FASB studies problems and proposes solutions and publishes its own literature. Also, The Journal of Accountancy publishes exposure drafts, and articles that highlight particular problems.

5. *Can you stand back and ask yourself, "Do the statements, as prepared, make sense?"* ___

Finding List of Official Opinions and Pronouncements of the CAP, APB, and FASB

Key to Symbols

APB—Accounting Principles Bulletin
ARB—Accounting Research Bulletin
FASB—Financial Accounting Standards Bulletin
I—Interpretations of the FASB
T—Technical Bulletins

Topic	Sub Heading	Source	#	Sub
Accounting Changes		APB	20	
	Interim Statements	FASB	3	
		FASB	32	
	Hospitals	FASB	56	
	Railroad Track Structures	FASB	73	
		FASB	83	
	Inventory	I	1	
Accounting Policies	Disclosure	APB	22	
	Sold/Purchased Tax Benefits	T	82	1
Banks & Thrift Institutions	Industry Reporting	FASB	72	
Broadcasters	Industry Reporting	FASB	63	
Business Combinations		APB	16	
		FASB	10	
	Banks & Thrift Institutions	FASB	72	
	Elimination of Disclosure	FASB	79	
	Savings & Loans	I	9	
	Leases	I	21	
		T	84	1
		T	85	5
Cable Television Companies	Industry Reporting	FASB	51	
Changing Prices		FASB	89	
	Security Brokers/Dealers	T	79	8
		T	79	13
Compensated Absences	Current Assets/Liabilities	FASB	43	
Consolidated Statements		ARB	51	
		ARB	43	1-A
	Comparative Statements	ARB	43	2-A
		FASB	94	
Contingencies		FASB	5	
		FASB	11	
	Purchased Enterprises	FASB	38	

Topic	Sub Heading	Source	#	Sub
		I	14	
	Indirect Guaranties	I	34	
Convertible Debt		APB	14	
		FASB	84	
Current Asset/Liabilities		APB	6	
	Officers/Employees Loans	ARB	43	1-A
		ARB	43	3-A
	Debt Refinancing	FASB	6	
	Compensated Absences	FASB	43	
	Callable Obligations	FASB	78	
	Refinanced Short Term Debt	I	8	
		T	79	3
	Life Insurance	T	85	4
	Right of Setoff	T	88	2
Debt Extinguishment		APB	26	
	Gains and Losses	FASB	4	
Debt Refinancing	Current Assets/Liabilities	FASB	6	
Deferred Compensation		APB	12	
Depreciable Assets		APB	1	
		APB	6	
		APB	12	
	Depreciation & High Costs	ARB	43	9-A
	Emergency Facilities	ARB	43	9-C
	Declining Balance	ARB	44	
	Not-For-Profit Enterprises	FASB	93	
	Not-For-Profit Enterprises	FASB	99	
Development Stage Enterprises		FASB	7	
		I	7	
Disclosures	Related Parties	FASB	57	
Earnings per Share		APB	15	
	Non Public Suspension	FASB	21	
	Convertible Debt	FASB	55	
	Yield Test	FASB	85	
	Employee Stock Options	I	31	
Elimination of Disclosure	Business Combinations	FASB	79	
Employee Stock Options		APB	25	
	Compensation Involved	ARB	43	13-B
	Stock Appreciation Rights	I	28	
	Earnings per Share	I	31	
		I	38	
		T	82	2

(Continued on next page)

Topic	Sub Heading	Source	#	Sub
Equity Method		APB	18	
	Income Taxes	APB	24	
	Interest Costs Capitalized	FASB	58	
		I	35	
Extinguishment of Debt		FASB	64	
		FASB	76	
		T	80	1
	Defeasance	T	84	4
Financial Instruments		FASB	105	
Foreign Currency Translation		FASB	52	
		I	37	
Franchise Fee Revenue		FASB	45	
Futures Contracts	Marketable Securities	FASB	80	
Government Contracts	CPFF	ARB	43	11-A
	Renegotiations	ARB	43	11-B
	Terminated Defense	ARB	43	11-C
Hospitals	Accounting Changes	FASB	56	
Income Taxes		APB	10	
		APB	11	
	Special Areas	APB	23	
	Equity Method	APB	24	
	U.K. Tax Legislation	FASB	31	
		FASB	37	
		FASB	96	
		FASB	100	
		FASB	103	
	Interim Periods	I	18	
		I	22	
		I	29	
	Interim Periods	T	79	9
		T	83	1
		T	84	2
		T	86	1
Industry Reporting	Banks & Thrift Institutions	FASB	72	
	Broadcasters	FASB	63	
	Cable Television Companies	FASB	51	
	Insurance Enterprises	FASB	97	
	Insurance Enterprises	FASB	60	
	Insurance Enterprises	T	84	3
	Mortgage Banking	FASB	65	
	Mortgage Banking	T	87	3
	Motion Picture Producers	FASB	53	
	Record & Music Industry	FASB	50	
	Regulated Industries	FASB	71	

Topic	Sub Heading	Source	#	Sub
	Regulated Industries	FASB	90	
	Regulated Industries	FASB	101	
	Regulated Industries	T	87	2
	Title Plant	FASB	61	
Installment Method	Unrealized Profit	ARB	43	1-A
		APB	10	
Insurance Enterprises	Industry Reporting	FASB	60	
	Industry Reporting	FASB	97	
	Industry Reporting	T	84	3
Intangible Assets		APB	17	
	Motor Carrier	FASB	44	
	Banks & Thrift Institutions	FASB	72	
Interest Costs Capitalized		FASB	34	
		FASB	42	
	Equity Method	FASB	58	
		FASB	62	
Interest on Receivables/ Payables		APB	12	
		APB	21	
Interim Periods		APB	28	
	Segmental Reporting	FASB	18	
	Income Taxes	I	18	
	Income Taxes	T	79	9
Inventory	Pricing	ARB	43	4
Investment Tax Credit		APB	2	
		APB	4	
	Unused	I	25	
		I	32	
		T	81	2
Lease		FASB	13	
	Refunding Tax Exempt Debt	FASB	22	
	Inception	FASB	23	
	Renewals or Extensions	FASB	27	
	Sales with Leasebacks	FASB	28	
	Contingent Rentals	FASB	29	
	Nonrefundable Fees & Costs	FASB	91	
		FASB	98	
		I	19	
	Business Combination	I	21	
	From Government	I	23	
	Building Portion	I	24	
	Purchase of Leased Asset	I	26	

(Continued on next page)

Topic	Sub Heading	Source	#	Sub
	Loss on Sublease	I	27	
	Fiscal Funding Clauses	T	79	10
	Guaranteed Residual Values	T	79	14
	Loss on Sublease	T	79	15
	Interest Rate Used	T	79	12
		T	79	18
	Change in Income Tax Rate	T	79	16
		T	79	17
	Scheduled Rent Increases	T	85	3
	Residual Value of Leased Asset	T	86	2
		T	88	1
Long Term Construction		ARB	45	
Long Term Obligations		FASB	47	
Marketable Securities		FASB	12	
	Futures Contracts	FASB	80	
	Post Statement Changes	I	11	
		I	12	
		I	13	
		I	16	
		T	79	19
Mortgage Banking	Industry Reporting	FASB	65	
	Industry Reporting	T	85	2
	Industry Reporting	T	87	3
Motion Picture Producers	Industry Reporting	FASB	53	
Motor Carrier	Intangible Assets	FASB	44	
Nonmonetary Transactions		APB	29	
		I	30	
		T	85	1
Not-For-Profit Enterprises	Depreciable Assets	FASB	93	
	Depreciable Assets	FASB	99	
Oil & Gas		FASB	19	
		FASB	25	
	Full Cost Method	I	33	
		I	36	
Pension Plan Statements		FASB	35	
		FASB	75	
Pension Plans		FASB	87	
	Settlement	FASB	88	
	Other Post Retirement Benefits	FASB	106	
		T	81	3

Topic	Sub Heading	Source	#	Sub
Product Financing Arrangements		FASB	49	
Quasi Reorganizations	Dated Surplus	ARB	43	7-A
		ARB	43	
Real Estate Costs	Initial Rental Operations	FASB	67	
Real Estate Sales		FASB	66	
Receivables with Recourse	Transfer	FASB	77	
Record & Music Industry	Industry Reporting	FASB	50	
Regulated Enterprises	Industry Reporting	FASB	71	
	Industry Reporting	FASB	90	
	Phase in Plans	FASB	92	
	Industry Reporting	FASB	101	
	Industry Reporting	T	87	2
Research & Development		FASB	2	
		FASB	68	
	Software	FASB	86	
	Business Combinations	I	4	
	Software	I	6	
		T	84	1
Results of Operations		APB	9	
	Commercial Banks	APB	13	
		APB	30	
	Prior Period Adjustments	FASB	16	
Revenue Recognition	Right of Return	FASB	48	
	Warranty/Product Maintenance C	T	90	1
Segmental Reporting		FASB	14	
	Interim Financial Statements	FASB	18	
	Non Public Suspension	FASB	21	
		FASB	24	
	Major Customer Information	FASB	30	
	Health Care Facilities	T	79	5
	Puerto Rican Operations	T	79	4
Statement of Cash Flows		FASB	95	
		FASB	102	
		FASB	104	
Stockholders' Equity		APB	6	
		APB	10	
		APB	12	
	Profit/Loss Treasury Stock	ARB	43	1-B

(Continued on next page)

Topic	Sub Heading	Source	#	Sub
	Stock Dividends & Splits	ARB	43	7-B
	Donated Stock	ARB	43	1-A
	Treasury Stock	ARB	43	1-A
	Capital Surplus	ARB	43	1-A
	Treasury Stock	T	85	6
Taxes—Other	Real & Personal Property	ARB	43	10- A
Title Plant	Industry Reporting	FASB	61	
Troubled Debt Restructuring		FASB	15	
		T	79	6
		T	79	7
		T	80	2
		T	81	6

CHAPTER 2

Guidelines to Preparing Financial Statements and Reporting Financial Information

Introduction

The financial statements are the end result of most accounting activities. The information they contain helps the user perform the critical analyses so vital to an entity's well being. This chapter will describe the most frequently used financial statements and data.

We realize most of our readers are experienced financial-statement preparers. However, the ensuing computer shortcuts will speed your work.

The information presented here will focus on:

- The components of the information
- Its organization
- How to make your job easier
- How to improve the data's reporting usefulness

How to Prepare the Basic Financial Statement Package More Efficiently

The basic financial statement package consists of the following:

1. Balance Sheet
2. Income Statement
3. Statement of Cash Flows
4. Statement of Stockholders' Equity

Accountants have been preparing these statements, in one form or another, since the invention of the debit and credit. As needs and methods have changed, so have the processes to record the pertinent transactions. But, what each has had in common is that every transaction is found in multiple locations.

Example: An inventory change affects the assets, income tax liability, gross profit, net income and cash flows.

Furthermore, as errors were found, the corrections had to be entered many times; first, as journal enries, then, to the workpapers and, finally, to financial statements. The arrival of the personal computer, and its increasingly user friendly software and spreadsheets, has eased our tasks considerably, while exponentially expanding our powers of analysis.

There are many software products that will do these jobs. And, one of these, is, probably, just right for you.

Examples:*

- Lotus 1-2-3
- Quattro
- Excel

Flowchart of Spreadsheet Financial Statement Preparation Procedures:

1. Set up pre-established format
2. Enter the unadjusted trial balance
3. Prepare schedule and analyses
4. Prepare adjusting journal entries
5. Computer posting to adjusted trial balance
6. Income tax computation
7. Review adjusted trial balance
8. Review financial statements

Figure 2-1

NOTE: The examples in the body of the chapter have been shortened in order to demonstrate the significant components. Detailed analyses may be found in the appendix.

Step 1. *Set up a pre-established format.* This should layout the following:

- The financial statements to your specifications
- Worksheet trial balance.

The column settings for the worksheet trial balance follow:

Sample Company*
Worksheet Trial Balance
December 31, 1988

	Adjusted	Journal Entries	Unadjusted

Figure 2-2—*Worksheet Trial Balance Layout*

NOTE: We have placed the adjusted column *first* rather than in its customary location to ease future printing and data collection processes.

SUGGESTION: When you initialize your layout, try to generalize and consistently use cell locations.

For Example: Assume that the adjusted balance position for the account Cash is cell C-37. This reference should be used in the balance sheet layout. Then, any entry or change to cash, posted to the trial balance, will automatically alter that account on the balance sheet.

Step 2. *Enter the unadjusted account balances.* You can enter these amounts manually or your general ledger program may be capable of integration.

***NOTE:** A detailed analysis of the sample company is found in the Appendix to this chapter.

		C	D	E
	Sample Company			
	Worksheet Trial Balance			
	December 31, 1988			
		Adjusted	Journal Entries	Unadjusted
37	Cash			38,756
38	Accounts Receivable			597,317
39	Allow for Bad Debts			(20,000)
40	Inventories			16,463
41	Prepaid Expenses			2,850
42	Office Equipment			187,952
43	Accumulated Depreciation			(31,325)
44	Deposits			4,000

Figure 2-3—*Worksheet Trial Balance Unadjusted Entries*

NOTE: It is useful to display the resulting profit at the end of the balance sheet and the income statement sections. To enhance the information, a pre-tax income subtotal should be included in order to ease the calculation of income taxes.

	Adjusted	**Journal Entries**	**Unadjusted**
Retained Earnings	(398,575)		(398,575)
	49,255	(51,751)	101,006
Pre Tax Income	(82,092)	18,914	(101,006)
Income Tax	32,837	32,837	
Net Income	(49,255)	51,751	(101,006)

Figure 2-4—*Presentation of Pre-Tax and After-Tax Income*

Step 3. *Prepare necessary schedules and analyses.* These schedules, which will subsequently become a part of the client file, can be constructed within the body of the spreadsheet. They will serve as the basis for the necessary evidentiary support, as well as the resulting journal entries.

Step 4: *Prepare adjusting journal entries.* These entries should be constructed for two purposes:

a. To adjust the trial balance.

b. To update the relevant schedules.

For example: The allowance for doubtful accounts has been computed at 1% of sales. The following journal entry has calculated the provision based on this information. At the same time, the trial balance is adjusted.

Adjusting Journal Entry

Provision for Bad Debts		12,280
Allowance for Bad debts		(12,280)
To estimate bad debts @ 1% of sales		
Sales	1,227,957	
Provision	12,280	

Entries on Worksheet

	Adjusted	Journal Entries	Unadjusted
Accounts Receivable	597,317		597,317
Allow for Bad Debts	(32,280)	(12,280)	(20,000)
Provision for Bad Debt	12,280	12,280	

Figure 2-5—*Example of Adjusting Entry*

Step 5. *Compute posts adjustments.* The above procedures will produce the adjusted trial balance, which, in turn, generates the financial statements.

Example: In this format, adjusted accounts receivable will be calculated as follows:

+C38 = D38 + E38

Step 6. *Calculate income taxes.* The worksheet should be designed to figure the income tax provision. The resulting amount is then programmed to be carried over to both the worksheet trial balance and the financial statements.

SUGGESTION: Most spreadsheets allow you to build in income tax tables. These tables, if made a part of your analysis, should be designed to compute the following:

- Federal
- State income taxes
- Alternative minimum taxes

With this program, a change in the company's net pre-tax will also recompute the related taxes.

Income Tax		32,837
Income Tax Payable		(32,837)
To Record Provision		
Net Pre-Tax Income	82,092	
Tax Rate	40%	

Figure 2-6—***Income Tax Computation from Worksheet***

Step 7. *Review the adjusted trial balance.* Determine that the amounts included agree to the schedules.

Step 8. *Review the financial statements.*

- Do they make sense?
- Are they comparable to prior years?
- Are the amounts computed and presented in accordance with GAAP?

Refer to the following chapters:

- Chapter 1—Accounting Treatment Selection Worksheet
- Chapter 3—Details of the Statement of Income and Retained Earnings
- Chapter 4—Balance Sheet Components
- Chapter 11—Accountants Reports (compilations, reviews and opinions)
- Chapter 17—Financial Statement Analysis

How to Make the Statement of Income More Useful

This section will show you how to use spreadsheet techniques to improve your analysis of the information that has already been captured.

As you know, the Statement of Income presents the dynamics of the organization. By properly portraying and using the information already there, the user can analyze trends, project future cash flows, and discover abnormalities in the data presented.

While comparative income statements are most common for financial reporting purposes, the following supplementary data can be provided by your spreadsheet system.

This presentation will use the Income Statement shown in Figure 2-7.

Sample Company
Statement of Income
For the Year Ended December 31, 1988

		%
Sales	$1,227,957	100.00%
Cost of Goods Sold		
Inventory—Beginning	16,463	
Purchases	871,765	
	888,228	
Less: Ending Inventory	15,829	
Total Cost of Goods Sold	872,399	71.04%
Gross Profit	355,558	28.96%
Operating Expenses		
Advertising	3,110	0.25%
Accounting	6,225	0.51%
Automobile	7,282	0.59%
Depreciation	6,000	0.49%
Insurance	16,004	1.30%
Office	31,356	2.55%
Provision for Bad Debts	24,559	2.00%
Rent	30,000	2.44%
Repairs & Maintenance	28,462	2.32%
Salaries	73,100	5.95%
Taxes	8,661	0.71%
Telephone	2,531	0.21%
Utilities	36,176	2.95%
Total Operating Expenses	273,466	22.27%
Pre-Tax Income	82,092	6.69%
Provision for Income Taxes	32,837	2.67%
Net Income	$49,255	4.02%

Figure 2-7—***Statement of Income for Analysis Purposes***

We will now describe some ways the Sample Company Statement of Income may provide more useful information by:

1. Using broad versus detailed classifications.
2. Segregating components by function serviced.
3. Segregating components by product classification, geographic territory, or market group.
4. Comparing actual to forecast.
5. Presenting expenses in declining order.
6. Providing information about changes in income statement components.
7. Analyzing percentage changes in components.
8. Establishing an early warning system.

1. *Broad versus detailed information.* Computers are wonderful gadgets. With a few keystrokes, we can obtain reams of data about income, expenses, and practically anything we could conceivably desire. The trick is, however, to find the *relevant* information to make decisions.

Begin by studying revenues and expenses in order to group them into more meaningful segments.

Example: Telephone expense, which only constitutes 0.21% of sales could be combined with utilities.

2. *Segregate components by function serviced.* Most businesses make sales, acquire merchandise, market their products, and maintain administrative and plant facilities. By segregating the income statement's components into these functions and tasks you will produce a clearer picture about the firm's effectiveness in meeting its goals.

Note: Segment Accounting, an analysis usually required by GAAP for large companies, will be discussed later in this chapter.

3. *Segregate components by product classification, geographic territory, or market group.* Initially, this can be time consuming. However, once installed, it is an excellent way to quickly spot product winners and losers.

Caution: Be careful when you allocate expenses to various revenue categories. The wrong allocations can sink a profitable product, while, at the same time, support losing items.

4. *Compare actual to forecast.* Business forecasts are prepared as a result of management's planning function. Use the actual results to monitor the organization's adherence to plan.

5. *Present expenses in declining order.* This will easily portray their individual impact. It is a cumbersome job when done by hand. Fortunately, most electronic spreadsheets have a sorting function.

This results in The Sample Company, presentation shown in Figure 2-8.

Operating Expenses	
Salaries	$ 73,100
Utilities	36,176
Office	31,356
Rent	30,000
Repairs & Maintenance	28,462
Provision for Bad Debts	24,559
Insurance	16,004
Taxes	8,661
Automobile	7,282
Accounting	6,225
Depreciation	6,000
Advertising	3,110
Telephone	2,531
Total Operating Expenses	$273,466

Figure 2-8—***Operating Expenses in Declining Order***

It is now easy to see the significance of each of Sample Company's expenses. Often, information of this form will allow management to concentrate its efforts toward the more critical items.

6. *Provide information about changes in income statement components.* Comparative income statements, in condensed form, are shown in Figure 2-9.

	1988	1987	Change
Sales	$1,227,957	$1,124,495	$103,462
Cost of Goods Sold	872,399	808,904	63,495
Gross Profit	355,558	315,591	39,967
Operating Expenses	273,466	239,456	34,010
Pre-Tax Profit	82,092	76,135	5,957
Income Taxes	32,837	30,454	2,383
Net Income	$ 49,255	$ 45,681	$ 3,574

Figure 2-9—***Comparative Income Statements***

If we studied the information presented above, we might be dismayed to discover sales increases of $103,462 only added $5,957 to pre-tax net income. Why?

- Is it due to inefficient operations?
- Have there been accounting misclassifications?

7. *Analyze percentage changes in net income components.* Often, it is not the hard-dollar variations that affect the future well being of a company, but, instead, their percentage impact.

Figure 2-10 portrays the percentage impact of these changes on the major elements in the statement of income.

Sample Company
Percentage Changes in Statement of Income Components
For the Two Years Ended December 31, 1988
increase (decrease)

Sales	9.20%
Cost of Goods Sold	7.85%
Gross Profit	12.66%
Operating Expenses	14.20%
Pre-Tax Profit	7.82%
Income Taxes	7.82%
Net Income	7.82%

Figure 2-10—***Sample Company Percentage Changes in Net Income Components***

We now have some idea why an increase in sales did not produce a comparable expansion in net income.

Sales grew by 9%.

Operating expenses increased by over 14%.

CAUTION: Percentage change analysis, taken too literally, may be misleading.

For example rent is usually a relatively fixed expense. At any one point, a percentage relationship is easy to calculate. However, as sales increase, the percentage will decline.

8. *Establish an Early Warning System.* It takes time to prepare reliable income statements. Therefore, all too often, the critical information is received too late to help correct many potential problems.

Consider designing a financial reporting system that will spotlight certain crucial items;

- Shipments
- Labor hours and dollars
- Backlog
- Overtime
- Returns and rejections
- Cash balances

How often? It's up to you, the accountant, to determine the degree of criticality for each of these items—daily, weekly, monthly.

What You Should Consider When You Structure the Balance Sheet

Objectives

Investors, creditors, internal users, and other readers of this statement are principally interested in the following:

1. *Liquidity:* Can the organization pay its bills when due?
2. *Financial Flexibility:* Can the firm use its resources to adapt to internal as well as external changes?
3. *Operating Capability:* Does the company have the ability to operate at the same level of capacity in the future?

Basic Structure of the balance sheet.

ABC CORPORATION	
BALANCE SHEET	REFERENCE
Date	1
Assets	2
Current Assets	3
Long-Term Investments	4
Property, Plant, and Equipment	5
Intangible Assets	6
Total Assets	

Figure 2-11—*Balance Sheet Format*

(Continued on next page)

Liabilities & Stockholders' Equity	
Liabilities	7
Current Liabilities	8
Other Liabilities	9
Total Liabilities	
Commitments and Contingent Liabilities	10
Stockholders' Equity	11
Total Stockholders' Equity	
Total Liabilities and Stockholders' Equity	

Figure 2-11—*Continued*

NOTE: Detailed account analysis will be discussed in Chapter 3.

Explanation of Keyed Balance Sheet Items

1. *Date:* The date is at a point in time, normally the end of a month of the fiscal period.
2. *Assets:* In order for an item to be classified as an asset, it must:

a. have been acquired by some form of transaction
b. be under the control of the company
c. benefit future periods.

Example: Equipment is purchased by an entity to achieve its objectives over a future period of time. It is therefore classified as an asset. When it loses its usefulness, it must be written off to an expense or a loss account.

3. *Current Assets* include cash and those accounts that are expected to be converted into cash within the normal operating cycle. Assets in this class are reported in liquidity order.

For example, current assets would commence with cash and end with prepaid expenses (items that lack liquidity).

Note: The normal operating cycle is generally considered to be one year.

However, there are situations when the current operating cycle is greater than one year.

Examples: Wineries, lumber companies, tobacco growers. In these cases, the longer period should be used to classify current assets and liabilities.

4. *Long-Term Investments* are those securities that management does not intend to liquidate within the current period. These are generally acquired for their income earning capability or to obtain control of another entity.

5. *Property, Plant, and Equipment* contains those assets that have been acquired for the production of inventory, the sale of merchandise, or for general administrative purposes and operations of the business. They are expected to benefit future activities and, therefore, their cost is allocated to those future periods by charges to depreciation.

6. *Intangible Assets* are items whose value lies in their ability to help produce income in future periods. Their actual physical characteristics are unimportant. They include patents, trademarks, copyrights, licenses, franchises, and goodwill.

Intangible assets are amortized over the future periods expected to be benefitted.

7. *Liabilities* are present responsibilities that are to be settled in the future. In order to be recorded, they must obligate the company for a transaction that has already occurred and is *measurable.*

8. *Current Liabilities* are payable within one year or the current operating cycle, whichever is greater. They include the following:

Notes payable

Accounts payable

Accrued expenses

Taxes payable—payroll and sales

Income taxes payable

They are normally found on the balance sheet in the order of expected payment dates.

NOTE: How to Calculate the Current Portion of Long-Term Debt in an amortizing loan: The principal portion of each payment of an amortizing loan that is due in one year or less must be segregated from interest and reported as a current liability.

At any time, the amount owed on an amortizing loan is the present value of the remaining payments at the applicable interest rate.

For example, the present value of 25 years of monthly payments of $1,053.22 at an annual interest rate of 12% is $100,000.

Remember: If the loan amortizes monthly, the interest rate has to be divided by 12 and the number of years multiplied by 12.

Therefore: Continuing the above example, the following year by year schedule is derived:

Years Remaining	Months Remaining	Balance Due
25	300	100,000
24	288	99,325
23	276	98,564
22	264	97,707
21	252	96,741
20	240	95,653

Figure 2-12—*Loan Amortization*

The current portion is computed as follows:

Balance Due at Statement Date − Balance Due at End of Next Year = Payments on principal to be made next year or, the current portion of the long-term debt.

The following schedules results from the computations described above:

Years Remaining	Balance Due	Total Payment	Principal Payment	Interest	Long-Term Portion	Current Portion
25	100.000.00	12,638.69	675.02	11,963.67	99,239.38	760.62
24	99,324.98	12,638.69	760.62	11,878.07	98,467.89	857.09
23	98,564.36	12,638.69	857.09	11,781.60	97,598.57	965.79
22	97,707.27	12,638.69	965.79	11,672.90	96,618.99	1,088.28
21	96,741.48	12,638.69	1,088.28	11,550.41	95,515.18	1,226.30
20	95,653.20	12,638.69	1,226.30	11,412.39	94,271.38	1,381.82

Figure 2-13—*Current Portion of Long Term Debt*

In year 21, the following would be reported:

Current Liabilities	
Current portion of long-term debt	$1,226
Long-term debt	$95,515
Note payable	

9. *Other Liabilities* are the debts that are *not* payable in the current operating cycle (year). They include the following:

Notes payable

Bonds payable

Deferred income taxes

Deferred credits

10. *Commitments and Contingent Liabilities* are not fixed and determinable, and they may not obligate the company as a result of a past event. However, the doctrine of *conservatism* dictates that they be disclosed, if their impact is material, as follows:

Type A: Commitments include the following: Long-term leases, and other obligations which impose future obligations.

Type B: Contingent Liabilities can include many obligations that are neither fixed or determinable.

Examples: The firm may:

- Be the defendant in a lawsuit
- Be under audit by the Internal Revenue Service
- Have guaranteed another's obligations

If any of these are material, they must be divulged and the probable effect, if it can be estimated, stated.

Type C: Subsequent Events occur between the balance sheet date and the date when the statements are issued. They are roughly classified into two forms:

1. Those that provide additional data concerning conditions that *did exist* on the balance sheet date.

For example, additional information about the collection of an account is revealed after the balance sheet date. This might require financial statement adjustment.

2. Those that arise from conditions that *did not* exist on the date of the statements.

For example, the company has a serious fire that occurred after the balance sheet date. If significant, this should be disclosed by footnote.

11. *Stockholders' Equity* represents the claims by the owners on the resources of the business. Stockholders' Equity is divided into three sections:

A. *Contributed Capital:* Total proceeds from all classes of stock issued by the corporation.

B. *Unrealized Equity:* Unrealized losses on long-term investments or gains or losses on foreign currency translation.

C. *Earned Equity:* The history of the organization since inception, is usually reflected in retained earnings. It consists of the following:

Net after tax income

Dividends

Prior period adjustments

How to Prepare the Statement of Changes in Stockholders' Equity

A Statement of Changes in Stockholders' Equity is required as part of the basic financial statement package. It should present the following:

Investments by owners

Distributions to owners

Unrealized Capital

Earnings

	Number of Shares	Common Stock	Add'l Paid in	Retained Earnings
Beginning	2,500	$25,000	$15,000	$37,542
Stock Options	350	3,500	7,000	
Net Income				14,266
Dividends				(5,000)
Ending	2,850	$28,500	$22,000	$46,808

Figure 2-14—*Statement of Changes in Stockholders' Equity*

How to Construct the Statement of Cash Flows

Official Pronouncements:

APB #3. The Statement of Source and Application of Funds October, 1963

APB #21. Reporting Changes in Financial Position
March, 1971

FASB #95. Statement of Cash Flows
October, 1987

GAAP requires a Statement of Cash Flows to be included in the basic financial statement package, and presented in a format to help the user make decisions about the following questions:

1. Is the company able to generate future cash flows?
2. Can it meet its obligations?
3. Does it need external financing?
4. What are the reasons for the differences between net income and cash receipts and disbursements?
5. What are the cash and non-cash impacts of financial investments?

Organization of the Statement of Cash Flows:
The statement is divided into three major sections:

Operating Activities

Investing Activities

Financing Activities

The effect of various transactions on these activities is illustrated in the following matrix:

Cash Flow	Operating	Investing	Financing
In	Revenues	(−) Non-Current Assets Notes Rec Marketable Securities	(+) Non-Current Liabilities Equity
Out	Expenses	(+) Above	(−) Above

Figure 2-15—*Impact on Cash Flows*

Preparation Alternatives
According to FASB 95, cash flow may be presented by two alternative methods:

the indirect method

the direct method

The differences between these two is in the portrayal of net cash flow from *operating* activities. The bottom line is the same.

A. *Indirect Method.* The purpose of the indirect method is to convert net income to net cash flow from operations in the following order:

1. List net income
2. Eliminate non cash flow items
3. Include any changes in current assets and liabilities that do not change cash

B. *Direct Method.* The direct method provides details of operations by fragmenting the components of net income into various contributory factors.

For example, cash received from customers, or cash paid to suppliers.

Comment: While the direct method supplies more detail about each component of net income than the indirect method, it fails to reconcile the information presented in the analysis to net income.

How to Use Electronic Spreadsheets to Prepare the Statement of Cash Flows

Steps

1. Set up trial balance and worksheet formats.

2. Enter amounts from current and prior year balance sheets in the proper columns.

3. Subtract the prior amounts from current balances to obtain net changes.

4. Distribute these changes to the following columns:

a. Operating activities

b. Investing activities

c. Financing activities

5. Integrate additional scheduled information to properly classify the cash flows. The following examples show how various elements are distributed among the three activities:

Retained Earnings

Retained Earnings	
Net Income	$145,314
Dividends Paid	10,000
Net Change	135,314

Property & Equipment—Cost

Beginning	Purchases	Disposals	End
$375,094	$126,695	$(45,000)	$456,789

Accumulated Depreciation

Beginning	Expense	Disposals	End
$ (32,054)	$ (35,000)	$12,730	$ (54,324)

Notes Payable

Beginning	Loans	Payments	End
$(820,000)	$(100,000)	$45,000	$(875,000)

Example—Indirect Method

JCB Corporation
Statement of Cash Flows
For Year Ended December 31, 1988

Net Cash Flows from Operating Activities		
Net Income	$145,314	
Adjustments for differences between income and cash flows from operating activities		
Add: Depreciation	35,000	
Decrease—inventory	39,235	
Decrease—prepaid expenses	10,379	
Increase—in accounts payable	200,422	
Increase—income taxes payable	11,741	
Increase—deferred income taxes	5,064	
Increase—accounts receivable	(86,541)	
Net Cash Provided by Operating Activities		$360,614

Figure 2-16—*Statement of Cash Flows—Indirect Method*

(Continued on next page)

Cash Flows from Investing Activities		
Purchase of Marketable Securities	(362,986)	
Purchase of Equipment	(126,695)	
Proceeds from Equipment Sale	32,270	
Net Cash Used for Investing Activities		(457,411)
Cash Flows from Financing Activities		
Proceeds from issuance of Capital Stock	175,000	
Proceeds from issuance of notes payable	100,000	
Payment of notes payable	(45,000)	
Payment of dividends	(10,000)	
Net Cash from Financing Activities		220,000
Net increase in cash		123,203
Cash, January 1, 1988		86,452
Cash, December 31, 1988		$209,655

Figure 2-16—*Continued*

The Direct Method

The income statement portion of the trial balance is utilized to measure the changes in various asset components which contribute to the operating cash flow. For example:

1. *Schedule income statement components*

Sales	752,456
Cost of Goods Sold	(489,096)
Operating Expenses	(62,345)
Depreciation	(35,000)
Income Taxes	(20,701)
	145,314

2. *Combine income statement components with balance sheet changes:*

Collections from Customers		
Sales	752,456	
Receivable increase	(86,541)	665,915

Figure 2-17—*Details of Operating Cash Flows, Direct Method.*

Payments to suppliers		
Cost of Goods Sold	(489,096)	
Operating Expenses	(62,345)	
Inventory decrease	39,235	
Prepaid expense decrease	10,379	
Accounts payable increase	200,422	(301,405)
Income Tax payments		
Income tax expense	(20,701)	
Income tax payable increase	11,741	
Deferred income tax increase	5,064	(3,896)
Net Cash Provided by Operating Activities		360,614

Figure 2-17—*Continued*

3. *Prepare the "Cash Flows from Operating Activities" section of the Statement of Cash Flows.*

The net cash flow from operating activities is the same as that displayed when the indirect method was used. (Figure 2-17)

JCB Corporation
Cash Flows From Operating Activities
For Year Ended December 31, 1988

Cash Inflows		
Collections from customers		$665,915
Cash Outflows		
Payments to suppliers	($301,405)	
Income tax payments	(3,896)	
Total Cash Outflows		(305,301)
Net Cash Provided by Operating Activities		$360,614

Figure 2-18—*Statement of Cash Flow from Operating Activities, Direct Method*

How to Understand the Principles of Full Disclosure and Draft More Accurate and Readable Footnotes

Official Pronouncements:

SAS-1 Codification of Auditing Standards and Procedures—November, 1972

SAS-32 Adequacy of Disclosure in Financial
Statements—October, 1980

NOTE: See disclosure checklist in appendix to this chapter.

The Third Standard of Reporting

> Informative disclosures in the financial statements are to be regarded as reasonably adequate unless otherwise stated in the report.

NOTE: This is only intended to be an overview of the disclosure process. Detailed explanations of disclosures for specific accounts, will be explained in detail in Chapters 3 and 4.

Information Required to be Disclosed

See suggested footnote disclosures by topic in appendix to this chapter.

Under Generally Accepted Auditing Standards (GAAS) and GAAP, the reader has a right to assume that in the absence of information to the contrary, the data portrayed in the financial statements is complete.

For example, if accounts receivable are reported on the balance sheet at a net amount of $150,000, and nothing else is stated, the reader can assume that management believes these receivables are fully collectible.

Avoid Over-Writing: The purpose of the disclosure requirement is to provide the reader sufficient information to make decisions about the organization's financial resources, net income, and cash flows.

Too often, however, this information tends to become either too wordy or become so couched in "legalese" that it becomes virtually useless. Some suggestions for better footnote writing follow.

Generally, there are three forms of disclosure:

1. *By the information presented in the statements.*
2. *By parenthetical comments;* i.e., data included in the body of the statement to provide additional information about the account presented.

For example, Marketable securities at cost
(approximates market)

3. *By footnote* to provide the reader necessary additional information about the related statements.

Footnotes are usually drafted for the following:

Accounting Policies
Accounting Changes
Restatement of Financial Statements
Notes Regarding Specific Accounts
Discontinued Segments
Extraordinary Operations
Commitments
Contingencies
Earnings per Share

Whose Responsibility is it? Full disclosure is the duty of management. But, if you believe certain items, that could materially affect the fairness of the financial reports, have not been revealed, and, furthermore, management refuses to do so, you have a duty to present this information in your accountant's report.

How to Write Good Footnotes

In many cases, you'll probably be asked to draft the footnotes. We, therefore, recommend the following:

1. Try to put yourself into the shoes of the reader. Ask yourself "Do the statements, by themselves, present enough understandable information to allow that user to make informed decisions?"
2. Decide what disclosures can be made parenthetically without overly crowding the financial statements.

   Suggestion: A parenthetical comment should not take up more than three lines.
3. Write a brief outline of the footnote that you will need drafted.
4. Determine where that information should be placed. Use the newspaper approach. Put the most important material first.
5. Use short sentences and words that are understandable to the average reader.
6. Use a conversational style. Use the active tense, and avoid words like whereas and wherefore.
7. Review these notes to make sure they do not contradict the basic data contained in the financial statements or comments previously expressed.
8. Finally, when in doubt, disclose.

Examples of Footnote Disclosures

1. Accounting policies

Note: Information about the following should be included in the accounting policies section of the footnotes, when applicable:

Principles of consolidation
Revenue Recognition
Inventories
Property, Plant, and Equipment
Depreciation
Intangibles
Deferred Charges
Investment in Unconsolidated Companies
Income Taxes
Pension Plan

Examples of the Customary and Usual Descriptions About the Accounting Practices of the Company

Note: Any items that are significant enough to influence the reader should be referenced here.

1. *Accounting Policies.* The Company uses the following major accounting policies and practices:

a. *Consolidation*

The consolidated financial statements include the accounts of the company and its subsidiaries except as noted.

All significant intercompany accounts and transactions have been eliminated in consolidation.

b. *Inventories*

Inventories are valued at the lower of cost or market. In general, the inventories are valued on the basis of (e.g. FIFO, LIFO, Weighted Average, or some other method).

c. *Property, Plant, and Equipment*

Property, plant, and equipment is stated at cost, less accumulated depreciation. Depreciation is generally determined by the (describe method).

d. *Income Taxes Payable*

Income taxes have been provided on the various components of income as disclosed below. Deferred taxes exist primarily because there are timing differences between the financial statements and the corporate income tax returns in the reporting of the following: (Detail)

The Company conforms to the provisions of (APB 11, or FASB 96).

Note: Until FASB 96 is fully implemented, you have the option to continue to be governed by the provisions of APB 11.

2. *Commitments* (long-term leases, pension plans, employees' stock options)

a. *Long term leases*

The Company's premises are rented under operating leases expiring as follows: . . . . . . Minimum annual rents, under these leases are as follows:

3. *Contingent Liabilities:* (lawsuits, guaranties, income tax audit)

Remember: If a contingent liability can be accurately measured and is payable at the balance sheet date, it has to be recognized in the financial statements.

The company is a defendant in a lawsuit. The plaintiff states that the Company is liable for the following:
In management's opinion this lawsuit will not materially harm the company's financial position or operations.

Disclosure Guidelines for Internal Use Only Statements

Companies that prepare statements that are covered by OCBOA (other consistent bases of accounting) and/or are intended for the internal use of management only, may disregard many of the full disclosure guidelines.

CAUTION: Too often, the Internal Use Only statement is used by management as a convenient way to hide unfavorable financial information. But, if this information is known, it *must* be disclosed.

How to Prepare Interim Financial Statements

Official Pronouncements:

APB 28—Interim Financial Reporting—May, 1973

Interim financial statements are prepared by both public and private companies for the following reasons:

1. They are required by various governmental agencies (e.g., SEC).
2. To provide timely information before the year end audit is completed.

Because time is usually of the essence, various estimates are used. These may diminish the statements' reliability.

Minimum Summarized Information:

Statements are allowed to be prepared in short or summary form. However, the following must be revealed:

Gross Revenues

Provision for Income Taxes

Extraordinary Income or Loss

Accounting Changes

Earnings per Share (Primary and Fully Diluted)

Material Seasonal Variations

Effects of Disposal of Business Segment

Interim Versus Annual Statements

Interim financial statement reporting is different because:

1. The inventory can be computed or estimated.
2. Journal entries are for worksheet only.
3. Accounts are not closed.

These statements are prepared on a year-to-date basis first. Then the previous year-to-date results are subtracted.

For example, sales for the Quarter Ended June 30, 1989 are calculated as follows:

Sales, 9 months through September	$1,809,543
Less: Sales, 6 months through June	1,433,555
Sales for Quarter	$ 375,988

Procedures and Minimum Disclosure

Statement Format

• *Sales or gross revenues* are recorded in the same way as annual statements.

- *Costs.* When costs cannot be specifically identified with a specific interim period, they may be prorated.
- *Income taxes*
- *Extraordinary income* is recorded in the period when it occurs.
- *Cumulative effects of changes in accounting principle* are recorded in the first interim period, regardless of when the change was actually made.
- *Net income*
- *Primary and/or fully diluted earnings per share*
- *Other disclosures*

Seasonal revenues, costs, and expenses

Significant changes in income tax estimates

Effect of discontinued operations

Estimating inventory. Inventories may be approximated by applying the same gross profit percentage as used on the previous year's financial statements. If the inventory is computed, that fact, as well as the impact of significant adjustments, should be fully disclosed.

Example:

Cost of Goods Sold Percentage Prior Year	45.00%
Sales, interim	$1,809,543
Cost of goods sold	$ 814,294

Note: Permanent inventory declines should be recognized. Subsequent gains should be recorded, but, only up to the loss previously booked.

Annualizing income taxes. Inasmuch as income taxes increase as profits fall into higher brackets, they should be annualized as follows:

Example: Assume that the JMR Corporation has pre-tax income of $29,345 for the first quarter. Also, assume that income is not seasonal and there is no reason to think that it will not continue at the same rate for the remainder of the year.

Net income, first quarter	$ 29,345
Periods to annualize	4
Estimated income on an annual basis	117,380
State income taxes	(11,738)
Net income for federal income taxes	$105,642

Figure 2-19—*Interim Statements, Income Tax Annualization*

(Continued on next page)

Tax Brackets	Rate	
50,000	15.00%	$ 7,500
25,000	25.00%	6,250
25,000	34.00%	8,500
5,642	39.00%	2,200
Total Federal		24,450
Total Federal and State Taxes		36,188
Tax for Quarter (divided by 4)		$ 9,047

Figure 2-19—*Continued*

How to Gather Relevant Information to Prepare Personal Financial Statements

Official Pronouncements:

SOP 82-1 Accounting and Financial Reporting for Personal Financial Statements.

Accounting Standards Division of AICPA—Personal Financial Statements Guide

Objective

Provide accrual basis financial information for an individual, husband and wife, or family in the following formats:

Statement of Financial Condition

Statement of Changes in Net Worth

Disclosures Required

1. Description of the accounting entity
2. Accounting bases for presenting assets and liabilities
3. Methods used to measure assets and liabilities
4. Nature of joint ownership
5. Industry concentration of investments that are material to the total portfolio
6. Details regarding closely held businesses
7. Face amount of life insurance

Because SOP 82-1 requires fair market values to be used in preparing these statements, the valuation methods applied are acceptable deviations from the GAAP requirement to use historical cost.

What is the Right Market Value? There are a variety of alternatives. Unfortunately, the use of one over another can produce significantly different results.

Caution: You must be careful to disclose how you derived market value.

Fair market values are generally computed under one of the following alternative methods:

a. *Output values* measure the amount that would be received from the sale of the asset at arms length negotiated prices. The following are examples:

—Prices of current sales of comparable assets

—Sales prices in a regulated transaction (stock market quotations)

b. *Input values* measure how much it would cost to acquire a comparable asset, in today's market subject to its age, relevant technological changes, the asset's condition, and other considerations.

Example: A machine was purchased 5 years ago at a cost of $10,000. Comparable equipment can be purchased today for $22,500. However, the reported value should be adjusted for the asset's age, physical condition, and relevant technological changes.

Getting the Information you Need to Calculate Output and Input Values: Certified appraisers can perform valuations of practically anything, from real estate to equipment, or from jewelry to works of art.

Caveat: Get any appraisal in writing. Remember, appraising is an *art*. So, you may need to obtain more than one estimate.

c. *Present value of future cash flows.* This is known as the economic valuation method. Under this approach, an asset's worth is its future benefit to the owner discounted to its present value. While this method, theoretically, yields the best results, it is difficult to apply. When we use this approach we have to estimate the following three variables:

a. future cash flows
b. appropriate discount rate
c. number of periods into the future these cash flows will continue

Beware: The estimated discount rate may depend on a subjective evaluation of future economic and market conditions. A small deviation in the rate could materially distort the carrying value.

Valuing Specific Items on the Personal Financial Statement

The following personal financial statement formats (Figure 2-20) are keyed by line to specific account explanations:

King Tut
Statement of Financial Condition
Date

Assets

Cash	
Marketable Securities	1
Interest in Closed Corporation	2
Sole Proprietorship—King Tut Antiques	2
Residence	3
Real Property	3
Vested Interest in Pension Plans	4
Automobile	5
Personal Property	5

Liabilities

Accounts payable	
Income taxes payable	
Estimated income taxes on the difference between the estimated current values of assets and the estimated amounts of liabilities and their tax bases	6
Net Worth	

King Tut
Statement of Changes in Net Worth
For the Year Ended

Realized increases in net worth
- Salaries
- Dividends and interest
- Withdrawals from proprietorship

Realized decreases in net worth
- Personal expenditures
- Income taxes
- Other taxes

Figure 2-20—***Personal Financial Statement Formats***

(Continued on next page)

Loss on Sale of Marketable Securities
Net Increase in Net Worth
Unrealized increases in net worth

Figure 2-20—*Continued*

Note: Unrealized Increases in Net Worth is a separate section in the Statement of Changes in Net Worth and includes changes to current market value for the following:

- Marketable Securities
- Closed Corporations
- Sole Proprietorships
- Residence
- Real Property
- Vested Interest in Pension Plans
- Automobiles
- Personal Property

1. *Marketable Securities.* Their market values are readily available and can be easily obtained from the financial pages or various reporting services.

Note: For over-the-counter (OTC) securities, use the bid not the ask price.

Beware of dilution: Assume your client has a large, possibly controlling interest in a publicly held corporation. Also, assume his or her holdings were to be liquidated. The flooding of these additional shares onto the market would dilute, i.e., reduce the price of that interest. If this is the case, make sure you discount the price per share.

2. *Interest in closed corporations, partnerships, and sole proprietorships.* There are generally three valuation methods:

a. *Individual asset method:*

i. The fair market values (either calculated at input, output, or present values) of individual assets and liabilities are first estimated.

ii. Goodwill on excess earnings is then computed. (Methods of estimating goodwill will be discussed in Chapter 4).

b. *Multiple of earnings:* The average price earnings ratios of publicly held corporations in the same industry are derived. That multiple is then applied to the earnings of the privately held business to obtain a fair market value. Certain adjustments are required if this method is going to be used:

i. a discount in the multiple to compensate for loss in marketability because it is a closed corporation which is not publicly traded.

ii. adjustments for certain expenses and fringe benefits should be added back to net income before applying the multiple.

For example:
Auto Expense
Entertainment and Promotion
Officers' Salaries
Interest Expense

Computation of Value:

Net (Pre-Tax) Income	$ 65,000
Add back:	
Fringe benefits to stockholders	4,500
Excess officers' salary and pension plan	22,500
Adjusted Net Income	92,000
Less: Corporate income tax	(36,800)
Adjusted After Tax Income	$ 55,200
Public Company Multiple	12
Comparable Public Company Value	$662,400
Discount for Non-marketability	0.60
Market value of closed corporation	$264,960

Figure 2-21—***Calculation of Fair Market Value of Closed Corporation—Multiple of Earnings Method***

What About Officer/Stockholder Loans? Due to the entity theory, the value assigned to the business interests should include these loans. The offsetting amounts should then be separately disclosed on the personal financial statement.

Example: The Janoush Corporation has loaned $25,000 to its stockholder, John Doe. This loan is part of the valuation of his investment in the closed corporation. At the same time, that amount due to the corporation should be reported as a liability on Mr. Doe's personal financial statement.

Further valuation information:

AICPA: Valuation of a Closely Held Business—1987. Internal Revenue Service—Revenue Ruling 50-60

3. *Residence/Real Property.* While either the input, output, or the present value method may be used, the output procedure is usually applied because comparables and appraisals are easier to obtain than construction cost data.

Be aware: Comparable sales values do not tell the entire story. The owner may have added special improvements to the property, or there may be potential problems that might diminish its value (e.g., the building needs a new roof).

4. *Vested Interest in Pension Plans.* Included here are future payments that a stockholder will receive on his or her retirement. This amount is derived by computing the present value of the balance in the plan that is to be received in the future.

Example: The balance in Janice's corporate pension plan is $275,000. She will retire in 18 years, at which time, she'll receive her pension benefits. The estimated discount rate is 8%. This yields a financial statement carrying value of $68,818 computed as follows:

$$PV = 1/(1 + i)^n$$

$$PV = 275{,}000/(1.08)^{18}$$

5. *Automobile and Personal Property.* Their values can be estimated by the approaches discussed previously.

6. *Estimated Income Taxes on Unrealized Asset Appreciation.* SOP 82-1 assumes that all assets will be sold at the financial statement date. Income taxes are therefore, calculated on the difference between their fair market values and the owners' basis. An example of the calculation is shown below:

	Cost	Fair Mkt Value	Gain (Loss)
Marketable Securities	$ 13,550	$ 15,000	$ 1,450
Closed Corporation	1,000	87,500	86,500
Personal Residence(a)	15,000	225,000	210,000
Real Estate	125,000	145,000	20,000
Pension Plan		375,000	375,000
Personal Auto	12,000	4,000	*
			692,950
Tax Rate			35.00%
Estimated Taxes on Unrealized Asset Appreciation			$242,533

* Personal Asset. Loss not allowed.

Figure 2-22—***Personal Financial Statements, Cost versus Market Value***

(a) Consider the following example when you derive the basis to be used in computing estimated taxes on unrealized asset appreciation for the personal residence:

Original Residence	
Sales Price	$ 10,000
Improvements	5,000
Original Basis	$ 15,000
Sold for	$200,000
Original Basis	15,000
Total Gain	$185,000
Price of New Home	$200,000
Unrecognized Gain	(185,000)
Basis of new home	$ 15,000

Figure 2-23—*Estimated Income Taxes on Unrealized Asset Appreciation*

What You Should Know About Segment Reporting

Official Pronouncement:

FASB 14—Financial Reporting for Segments of a Business Enterprise—December, 1976

FASB 18—Financial Reporting for Segments of a Business Enterprise—Interim Financial Statements—November, 1977

FASB 24—Reporting Segment Information in Financial Statements that are Presented in Another Enterprise's Financial Reports—December, 1978

Definition of Segment: A component of an enterprise that provides a product or service or a group of related products or services primarily to unaffiliated customers for a profit.

Identifiable Segments present data about a company's operations:

(1) In different industries

(2) In foreign countries and export sales

(3) With major customers

Note: The FASB does not require segment information for non-public enterprises.

However, segment information, if presented clearly, is very useful information to management of a closed corporation.

Generally, the 10% test is used to decide which segments must be reported. Under that criterion, a segment must be reported separately if revenues, operating profits, *or* identifiable assets are at least 10% of company totals.

Example: ICE Enterprises reports the following sales by category:

		%
Vanilla	$ 87,500	39.35%
Chocolate	73,224	32.93%
Strawberry	43,650	19.63%
Rocky Road	12,543	5.64%
Pistachio	5,444	2.45%
	$222,361	100.00%

Therefore, vanilla, chocolate, and strawberry qualify as reportable segments. The segment information for ICE Enterprises are displayed as follows:

	Net Revenues	Income	Identifiable Assets
Vanilla	$ 87,500	$13,125	$350,000
Chocolate	73,224	8,055	292,896
Strawberry	43,650	7,857	174,600
Other	17,987	4,660	71,948
	$222,361	$33,697	$889,444

In addition to the above, the following other information should be reported by segment:

1. depreciation, depletion, and amortization
2. capital expenditures
3. accounting policies

CAREFUL: When dividing the statements into segments, be aware that serious distortions can occur as a result of improper transfer pricing and expense allocation. These subjects will be discussed in greater detail in Chapter 23.

How to Prepare Special Purpose Statements and Reports That Are Not in Accordance with GAAP

There are times when the strict application of GAAP is cumbersome, results in hardships, and is just not very useful. In these instances the use of Other Comprehensive Bases of Accounting (OCBOA) is approved. Under OCBOA, financial reports may be prepared in one or more of the following formats:

1. Pure Cash Basis
2. Modified Cash Basis
3. Tax Basis
4. Regulatory Basis

These reports are generally acceptable under the following situations when:

1. There use by third parties is limited.
2. Compliance with GAAP could be costly.
3. Operations are heavily influenced by cash flow and tax implications.
4. A certain format is proscribed by regulatory agencies.

Specifics for various OCBOA formats:

1. *Pure Cash Basis:*

a. When applicable
   i. The organization is not profit oriented (e.g. a club, or charitable association.)
   ii. Its operations are simplistic (e.g. it only collects and disburses cash.)
   iii. The entity and its accounting processes are relatively unsophisticated.
   iv. It had only one major activity.
   v. It has relatively little capital expenditures or other long term activities.

b. Statement titles
   i. Statement of Assets and Liabilities
   ii. Statement of Cash Receipts and Disbursements

2. *Modified Cash Basis.* The modified cash basis statement is generally prepared on the basis of cash receipts and disbursements, however, depreciation is recorded in the accounts.

a. When applicable
   i. The enterprise is organized for profit
   ii. Profits are distributed as collected
   iii. There is a major interest in minimizing taxes

b. Statement Titles

i. Statement of Assets and Liabilities Arising From Cash Transactions
ii. Statement of Revenues Collected and Expenses Paid

How You Can Identify and Report Accounting Changes

Official Pronouncements:

APB 20—Accounting Changes. Effective, July, 1971

FASB 16—Prior Period Adjustments. Effective June, 1977

There are four types of accounting changes:

A. *Changes in Accounting Principle* occur when a company goes from one GAAP to a different and *better* GAAP. When this is done, the total impact of the change, net of income taxes, is reported on the income statement right after net income.

Note: The effects are not difficult to calculate. Often these are valuations of the respective assets before and after the change.

Example: In 1988, The Bradley Corporation decided to change its method of calculating depreciation on assets acquired in 1985 from the declining balance to the straight line method. The calculation of the cumulative effect is shown below:

Cost of Asset	$100,000
Date Acquired	January 1, 1985
Life (in years)	8
Method	DDB
Accumulated Depreciation to December 31, 1987	
Double Declining Balance	$ 57,813
Straight Line	37,500
Cumulative Difference	20,313
Income Tax at 40%	8,125
Net After Tax Cumulative Change	$ 12,188

The above would be reported on the income statement as follows:

Cumulative effect on prior years' income of change in accounting principles	$12,188

Exceptions: The following changes in accounting principles require the retroactive restatement of prior financial statements:

1. Change in accounting for closely held corporations in connection with a public offering.
2. Change from LIFO to another method of inventory pricing.
3. Change in accounting for long term construction contracts.
4. Change to the full cost method of accounting in the extractive industries.
5. Change in accounting for railroad track structures (FASB 73).

B. *Change in Accounting Estimate:* Sometimes a company alters its reporting as a result of changes in economic or other conditions.

For example, the estimated lives of depreciable assets are changed.

When changes are made in accounting estimates, they are reported as a component of the affected expense. Their impact in that year is disclosed in the footnotes.

C. *Change in Reporting Entity:* When a corporation changes its investment reporting procedures from the cost method to the equity method, the cumulative effect of the change will be shown as an adjustment to retained earnings.

D. *Prior Period Adjustments:* Mathematical mistakes and other types of errors that were not discovered in previous years, and can be *definitively* identified with those years, are shown as adjustments to the retained earnings account.

Examples:

- Use of an accounting principle that is *not* generally accepted
- Use of an estimate that wasn't made in good faith
- Math errors
- Omission of a deferral or accrual

NOTE: A change that is required as a result of a new FASB pronouncement may be reported as a retroactive adjustment to prior years' income statements.

A Brief Overview of Financial Forecasts

This section presents the official pronouncements and reporting guidelines for financial forecasts. Further information will be covered as follows:

Auditing and Reporting Practices—Chapter 12

Forecasting Mechanics —Chapter 24

Official Pronouncements:

AICPA—Guide for Review of a Financial Forecast

Any forecast must, by necessity, depend upon assumptions of events that have not taken place, and, furthermore, may *never* occur. Therefore, it is imperative that the forecasting assumptions be well thought out and disclosed.

Use the guidelines promulgated by the AICPA to:

1. Try to determine the *single* most probable events based upon information known at the time.
2. Use accounting principles expected to be employed in the future.
3. Use the best information available.
4. Reflect enterprise plans.
5. Show support for reasonable assumptions.
6. Show relative effect of variations in assumptions.
7. Provide adequate documentation.

Exhibits

1. Sample Company

    Trial Balances
    Journal Entries
    Statement of Income
    Balance Sheet

2. Spreadsheet analysis for Statement of Cash Flows
3. Disclosure Guide

Exhibit 2-1

Sample Company
Worksheet Trial Balance
December 31, 1988

	Adjusted	Journal Entries	Unadjusted
Cash	38,756		38,756
Accounts Receivable	597,317		597,317
Allowance for Bad Debts	(32,280)	(12,280)	(20,000)
Inventories	15,829	(634)	16,463
Prepaid Expenses	2,850		2,850
Office Equipment	187,932		187,932
Accumulated Depreciation	(37,325)	(6,000)	(31,325)
Deposits	4,000		4,000
Accounts Payable	(126,412)		(126,412)
Notes Payable	(70,000)		(70,000)
Income Taxes Payable	(32,837)	(32,837)	
Common Stock	(100,000)		(100,000)
Retained Earnings	(398,575)		(398,575)
	49,255	(51,751)	101,006
Sales	(1,227,957)		(1,227,957)
Purchases	871,765		871,765
Inventory—Beginning	16,463	16,463	
Inventory—Ending	(15,829)	(15,829)	
Advertising	3,110		3,110
Accounting	6,225		6,225
Automobile	7,282		7,282
Depreciation	6,000	6,000	
Insurance	16,004		16,004
Office	31,356		31,356
Provision for Bad Debts	24,559	12,280	12,279
Rent	30,000		30,000
Repairs & Maintenance	28,462		28,462
Salaries	73,100		73,100
Taxes	8,661		8,661
Telephone	2,531		2,531
Utilities	36,176		36,176
Pre-Tax Income	(82,092)	18,914	(101,006)
Income Tax	32,837	32,837	
Net Income	(49,255)	51,751	(101,006)
Adjusting Entries			
Provision for Bad Debts		12,280	
Allowance for Bad Debts		(12,280)	
To Estimate Bad Debts			
Sales	(1,227,957)		
At	1%		
Beginning Inventory		16,463	
Inventory		(634)	
Ending Inventory		(15,829)	
To record ending inventory and close Beginning inventory			
Depreciation		6,000	
Accumulated Depreciation		(6,000)	
To record depreciation for 1988			
Income Tax		32,837	
Income Tax Payable		(32,837)	
To record provision			
Net Pre-Tax Income	82,092		
Tax Rate	40%		

Sample Company
Balance Sheet
December 31, 1988

Assets

Current Assets		
Cash		$ 38,756
Accounts Receivable	$597,317	
Less: Allowance for Bad Debts	32,280	565,037
Inventories		15,829
Prepaid Expenses		2,850
Total Current Assets		622,472
Property & Equipment		
Cost	187,932	
Less: Accumulated Depreciation	37,325	
Net Book Value		150,607
Deposits		4,000
		$777,079

Liabilities & Stockholders' Equity

Current Liabilities		
Accounts Payable		$126,412
Notes Payable		70,000
Income Taxes Payable		32,837
Total Current Liabilities		229,249
Stockholders' Equity		
Common Stock	$100,000	
Retained Earnings, Beginning	398,575	
Net Income to date	49,255	
Total Stockholders' Equity		547,830
		$777,079

Sample Company
Statement of Income
For the Year Ended December 31, 1988

		%
Sales	$1,227,957	100.00%
Cost of Goods Sold		
Inventory—beginning	16,463	
Purchases	871,765	
	888,228	
Less: Ending inventory	15,829	
Total Cost of Goods Sold	872,399	71.04%
Gross Profit	355,558	28.96%
Operating Expenses		
Advertising	3,110	0.25%
Accounting	6,225	0.51%
Automobile	7,282	0.59%
Depreciation	6,000	0.49%
Insurance	16,004	1.30%
Office	31,356	2.55%
Provision for bad debts	24,559	2.00%
Rent	30,000	2.44%
Repairs & Maintenance	28,462	2.32%
Salaries	73,100	5.95%
Taxes	8,661	0.71%
Telephone	2,531	0.21%
Utilities	36,176	2.95%
Total Operating Expenses	273,466	22.27%
Pre-Tax Income	82,092	6.69%
Provision for Income Taxes	32,837	2.67%
Net Income	$49,255	4.02%

Exhibit 2-2

JCB Corporation
Worksheet for Statement of Cash Flows
For the Year 1988

	Balances Beginning	Balances Ending	Operating	Investing	Financing
Cash	86,452	209,655			
Marketable Securities	187,014	550,000		(362,986)	
Accounts Receivable	199,135	285,676	(86,541)		
Inventory	234,667	195,432	39,235		
Prepaid Expenses	55,946	45,567	10,379		
Property/Equipment	375,094	456,789		(81,695)	
Accum Depreciation	(32,054)	(54,324)	35,000	(12,730)	
Accounts Payable	(197,022)	(397,444)	200,422		
Income Taxes Payable	(31,759)	(43,500)	11,741		
Notes Payable	(820,000)	(875,000)			55,000
Deferred Income Taxes	(7,436)	(12,500)	5,064		
Capital Stock	(25,000)	(200,000)			175,000
Retained Earnings	(25,037)	(160,351)	145,314		(10,000)
	0	0	360,614	(457,411)	220,000
Cash Change			$123,203		
Retained Earnings					
Net Income			$145,314		
Dividends Paid			10,000		
Net Change			$135,314		

Property & Equipment—Cost

Beginning	Purchases	Disposals	End
$375,094	$126,695	$(45,000)	$456,789

Accumulated Depreciation

Beginning	Expense	Disposals	End
$ (32,054)	$ (35,000)	$ 12,730	$ (54,324)

Notes Payable

Beginning	Loans	Payments	End
$(820,000)	$(100,000)	$ 45,000	$(875,000)

Exhibit 2-3

Financial Statement Disclosure Guidelines

Item	*Disclosure Guidelines*
Accounting Change	Nature of change Justification for change Effect of change on net income and EPS Explain why new treatment is better
Accounting Policies	Information that significantly affects the financial statements
Business Combinations	Name of companies involved Cost Method of accounting For purchases: cost, period of combination amortization methods, contingent payments, results of operations for current and immediately preceding period as though the enterprises had combined at the beginning of the period. For pooling: accounting adjustments to combining companies, previous revenues and expenses reported, description and number of shares issued, related retained earnings' increase or decrease, reconciliations of amounts of revenues and earnings previously reported
Capitalized Interest	Total amount of interest incurred and charged to expense Amount capitalized
Contingencies	Description of contingency Estimated amount of claim Probability or opinion of liability
Current Assets and	Valuation methods

(*Continued on next page*)

Exhibit 2-3—*Continued*

Item	*Disclosure Guidelines*
Current Liabilities	Inventory classifications Inventory valuation methods Asset restrictions Accounting policies
Debt Extinguishment	Description of the transaction Amount of debt outstanding Amount of debt considered extinguished Gain or loss net of income taxes Income tax effect
	Depreciable assets Expense for period Cost by major classes of assets Accumulated depreciation by major classes of assets Methods used Estimated lives
Discontinued Segment	Identification of segment Disposal date Gain or loss from disposal Income and loss from operations of segment before disposal (measurement) date
Earnings per Share	Restatement of prior period EPS Affect of stock splits and stock dividends Affect of warrants Adjustments to net income Affective warrants and options
Equity method investments	Name of investment Percentage owned Investor accounting policies Carrying value of investment versus underlying equity Market price quoted Summary of significant assets, liabilities, and results of operations, if material Carrying value of investment versus underlying equity and how the difference is being accounted for.

Item	*Disclosure Guidelines*
Income Taxes	Description of types of timing differences Deferred charges and credits from timing differences Unused carryovers and carrybacks Effect of FASB #96; Explanation of difference between expected and actual tax rates. Components of deferred tax expense Current and deferred between State and Federal taxes
Interest on receivables and payables	Description of accounts Effective interest rate Face amount of note
Inventories	Accounting principles used Methods of applying accounting principles Industry differences Classification (e.g. raw materials, and so on) Basis of pricing Inventory cost flow assumptions
Leases	Type of lease–capital versus operating Assets involved Amount carried in assets Interest rate used to capitalize Future minimum annual lease payments Term of lease Special terms or restrictions Rental expense for each period that an income statement is presented. Minimum, contingent and sublease rentals should be presented separately.
Long-Term Debt	Interest rate(s) Terms of payment Maturity of debt over next five years and thereafter Covenants Collateral

(Continued on next page)

Exhibit 2-3—*Continued*

Item	*Disclosure Guidelines*
Marketable Securities	Cost and market value Carrying value Unrealized gains and losses Realized gains and losses
Non-Monetary Transactions	Nature of transactions Basis of accounting Gains or losses
Pension Plans	Description of groups covered, benefit formula, funding methods, assets held, liabilities Unrecognized prior service cost and asset gains and losses Asset gains and losses Additional net pension asset or liability Discount rate used Amount of net pension cost for period Separate presentation of service, interest, actual return on assets
Research and Development	Amount charged to expenses
Stock Options	Number of shares covered Exercise price Number of shares that could be exercised Number of shares that have been exercised Option price(s)
Troubled Debt Restructuring (Debtors)	Description of terms Aggregate gain and tax effect Total net gain or loss on assets transferred Per share amounts
Troubled Debt Restructuring (Creditors)	Aggregate recorded investment Gross interest income that would have been earned Gross interest income included in net income Amount of commitment to lend additional funds

CHAPTER 3

How to Recognize and Report Revenues, Expenses and Net Income

Introduction

The major objective of the Statement of Income is to help the users distinguish between invested capital and income and be able to:

- Make decisions about the efficiency of management
- Predict the future of the business
- Evaluate how well management allocates resources

How the Chapter Is Organized

1. A income statement format is presented which is keyed to each of the major segments.
2. Each section contains the following:
   - Official pronouncements
   - Background
   - Computation rules and examples
   - Disclosure guidelines

Official Pronouncements Covering the Statement of Income in General

ARB #43 Chapter 2; June, 1953:

Form of Financial Statements

Accounting Terminology Bulletins #4, July, 1957

Costs, Expenses, and Losses

Accounting Principles Board (APB) #4, October, 1970

Basic Concepts and Accounting Principles Underlying Financial Statements of Business Enterprises

APB #10, December, 1966

Omnibus Opinion

Financial Accounting Standards Board (FASB), 1978–1985

Statements of Financial Accounting Concepts

Income Statement Format Guide and Finding Chart

ABC CORPORATION
Statement of Income and Retained Earnings
For the period ended

	Reference
Sales Revenue	A
Cost of Goods Sold	B
Gross Profit	
Operating Expenses	C
Selling and general and administrative expenses	
Research and Development expenses	D
Pension Expenses	E
Total Operating expenses	
Other Revenues and Expenses	F
Pre-tax income from continuing operations	
Income tax expense	G
Income from continuing operations	
Results from discontinued operations	H
Income from operations of discontinued segment (net of income taxes)	
Loss on disposal of segment	
Income (loss) from extraordinary operations	I
Gains and Losses from early debt extinguishment	J
Cumulative effect on prior years' income of change in accounting principles	K
Net income	
Earnings Per Share	L

Figure 3-1—***Income Statement Finding Guide***

A. Revenues

Official Pronouncement

FASB Statement of Financial Accounting Concepts #6
Elements of Financial Statements—December, 1985

1. *Definition*

Inflows or other enhancements of assets of a business entity or settlement of its liabilities (or a combination of both) during a period derived from delivering and/or producing goods, rendering services, or other activities that constitute the entity's ongoing major or central operations.

2. *When is income recognized?*

Revenue is usually recognized when:

a. *It is earned.* The entity has done everything necessary.
b. *It is realized.* Realization usually occurs when title passes.

Example: Assume a manufacturer sells a machine. Income is recognized when

i. the manufacturer completes the job
ii. title passes

3. *Four exceptions to the realization principle.*

a. *Before production is completed*

Example: Long term construction contracts when reasonably accurate estimates can be obtained.

b. *Before goods are sold*

Example: Certain commodities which have a guaranteed market.

c. *After the passage of title*

Examples: Installment method
Cost recovery method

d. *As allowed under other consistent bases of accounting—OCBOA*

4. *Long-term construction contracts*

a. *Alternatives*

i. *The percentage of completion method*: Used when a company has received a firm contract to provide products or services which are not scheduled to be completed until after the current fiscal year.

Although the work may not be finished for a number of years, and title has not passed, income is deemed to be earned as a result of efforts expended. Therefore, profit is recognized on each job by the proportion that the costs to date bear to the total expenses estimated to complete the work.

ii. *The completed contract method.* This technique delays recognition of income on long-term construction contracts until the job is complete. At that time, all revenues earned and expenses incurred are recorded.

b. *How to Use the Percentage of Completion Method*

i. *Reporting Income*

$$\text{Revenues To be recognized} = \frac{\textit{Expenses to Date}}{\text{Total Expenses}} \times \text{Total Revenues}$$

ii. *Income Statement Presentation*

Construction Revenues (A)
Less: Costs of Construction (B)
A = Costs in year + recognized profit
B = Costs in year

iii. *Journal Entries*

Construction in Progress xxx
Construction Revenues xxx

iv. *Balance Sheet Presentation*

If Construction in Process > Billings
Current Assets
Inventories
Construction in Process
Less: Billings to Date
Excess of construction costs plus recognized profit over billings

If Construction in Progress < Billings
Current Liabilities
Billings
Less: Construction in Process
Excess of billings over construction costs and recognized profits

v. *Footnote Disclosure*

The company uses the percentage of completion method of accounting for contracts that extend beyond one year. Accordingly, income is recognized in the ratio that costs incurred to date relate to estimated total costs. These costs are adjusted each reporting period, and the total of any losses expected to be incurred are immediately charged to income.

c. *Completed Contract Method*

i. *Reporting Income*—none until project completed

ii. *Income Statement Presentation*—none until project completed

At completion:

Construction Revenues
Construction Costs

Gross Profit

iii. *Journal Entries*—Construction in Progress—at cost only

Example

The following information applies to Terwilliger Construction Company:

Contract Amount			$5,000,000
Estimated Costs			4,000,000
Estimated Profit			$1,000,000
Profit Percentage			20%
Year	*1*	*2*	*3*
Construction Costs Incurred	$1,200,000	$2,000,000	$900,000
Partial Billings	200,000	4,000,000	800,000
Collections	40,000	900,000	4,060,000

Percentage of Completion Method

Construction Costs Incurred to Date	$1,200,000	$3,200,000	$4,100,000
Estimated Costs to Complete	2,800,000	800,000	
Total Estimated Costs	$4,000,000	$4,000,000	$4,100,000
Percent Complete			
(Cost to Date/Total Estimated Costs)	30%	80%	100%
Revenue to Date			
(% Complete X Contract Price)	1,500,000	4,000,000	5,000,000
Revenue to be Recognized this Year	1,500,000	2,500,000	1,000,000
Construction Costs Incurred This Year	1,200,000	2,000,000	900,000
Gross Profit to be Recognized	$300,000	$500,000	$100,000

Note: Assumes that company was not aware of additional costs in year 2. Otherwise, profit reduction would be required then.

(Continued on next page)

Figure 3-2—***Percentage of Completion***

Adjustments

Construction in Process	1,200,000	2,000,000	900,000
Accounts Payable	(1,200,000)	(2,000,000)	(900,000)
Construction in Process	300,000	500,000	100,000
Construction Expenses	1,200,000	2,000,000	900,000
Construction Revenues	(1,500,000)	(2,500,000)	(1,000,000)
Accounts Receivable	200,000	4,000,000	800,000
Partial Billings	(200,000)	(4,000,000)	(800,000)
Cash	40,000	900,000	4,060,000
Accounts Receivable	(40,000)	(900,000)	(4,060,000)
Partial Billings			5,000,000
Construction in Process			(5,000,000)

Figure 3-2—*Continued*

Presentation

Income Statement (Partial)

Construction Revenue	$1,500,000	$2,500,000	$1,000,000
Construction Expense	1,200,000	2,000,000	900,000
Gross Profit	$300,000	$500,000	$100,000

Balance Sheet (Partial)

Current Assets:		
Accounts Receivable	$160,000	$3,260,000
Inventories		
Construction in Process	1,500,000	
Less: Partial Billings	200,000	
Costs and Recognized Profit Not Yet Billed	$1,300,000	
Current Liabilities		
Partial Billings		4,200,000
Less: Construction in Process		4,000,000
Billings in Excess of Costs and Recognized Profit		$200,000

Figure 3-3—*Financial Statement for Percentage of Completion*

iv. *Balance Sheet Presentation*

If Construction in Process > Billings

Current Assets

Inventories

Construction in Process

Less: Billings to Date

Excess of Construction Costs over Billings

If Construction in Progress < Billings
Current Liabilities
Billings
Less: Construction in Progress
Excess of billings over construction costs

COMPLETED CONTRACT METHOD

Year	*1*	*2*	*3*
Adjustments:			
Construction in Process	1,200,000	2,000,000	900,000
Accounts Payable	(1,200,000)	(2,000,000)	(900,000)
Accounts Receivable	200,000	4,000,000	800,000
Partial Billings	(200,000)	(4,000,000)	(800,000)
Cash	40,000	900,000	4,060,000
Accounts Receivable	(40,000)	(900,000)	(4,060,000)
Partial Billings			5,000,000
Construction Revenue			(5,000,000)
Construction Expense			4,100,000
Construction in Process			(4,100,000)

Presentation
Income Statement (Partial)

Construction Revenue			$5,000,000
Construction Expense			4,100,000
Gross Profit			$ 900,000

Balance Sheet (Partial)

Current Assets:			
Accounts Receivable	$160,000	$3,260,000	0
Inventories			
Construction in Process	1,200,000		
Less: Partial Billings	200,000		
Costs and Recognized Profit Not Yet Billed	$1,000,000		
Current Liabilities			
Partial Billings	$4,200,000		
Less: Construction in Process	3,200,000		
Billings in Excess of Costs and Recognized Profit	1,000,000		

Figure 3-4—*Completed Contract Method*

vi. *Footnote Disclosure*

The company uses the completed contract method for long-term construction contracts. Under this method, revenues and costs of individual contracts are included in operations in the year in which they are completed. Losses expected to be incurred are charged to operations in the period such losses are determined.

d. *Recognizing losses on long-term construction contracts*

In accordance with the doctrine of conservatism, any estimated or actual losses are immediately recognized.

i. *Percentage of completion*

In year of loss, the following adjustments must be made:

- Credit construction in progress for profits previously recorded.
- Record provision for losses for any costs over revenues incurred in current year.

ii. *Completed Contract*

Dr	Loss of construction contract	XX	
Cr	Construction in process		XX

1. *Recording income before title passes*

Certain commodities including gold and various agricultural products have a guaranteed market. Since the difficult task is to extract or harvest them and get them ready for market, sales revenues may be recognized before sale.

2. *Accounting for revenues after title passes*

a. *Installment Method*

The installment method delays the recognition of income until the sales proceeds have been collected. This method is generally acceptable under the following conditions:

i. Revenues are received over a period of time which is greater than one year.

ii. The probability of collection is not reasonably assured.

In these cases, net income is computed as follows:

*Gross Profit Recognized = Gross Profit % * Collections*

Example: The Carrie Corporation is an installment sales dealer. The company normally earns a gross profit of 40% on sales. Therefore, it would recognize income on 40% of its collections, as shown below.

Figure 3-5—*Installment Method*

Sales on Installment	$100,000		
Cost of Goods Sold	60,000		
Gross Profit	40,000		
Gross Profit Percentage	40.00%		
Year	*1988*	*1989*	*1990*
Collections	$ 30,000	$60,000	$10,000
Profit Recognized	12,000	24,000	4,000
Entries—Assuming Recognition of Total Sales			
Sales	100,000		
Cost of Goods Sold	(60,000)		
Deferred Gross Profit	(40,000)		
Deferred Gross Profit	12,000	24,000	4,000
Gross Profit Realized on Installment Sales	(12,000)	(24,000)	(4,000)
Income Statement Presentation			
Gross Profit Realized on Installment Sales	12,000	24,000	4,000
Balance Sheet Presentation			
Installment Accounts Receivable	70,000	10,000	0
Less: Deferred Gross Profit	28,000	4,000	0
	42,000	6,000	

Figure 3-5—*Continued*

Disclosure

In the current year, the Company had $100,000 sales on installment. These sales are collectible over the next 3 years and collectibility is not reasonably assured. Therefore, it has elected to use the installment method with regard to these sales and record gross profit realized as these sales are collected.

Recording Repossessions

If complete payment is not made on an installment sale, the company should record a gain or loss on the repossession of merchandise.

Gain

Fair Market Value of Property Recovered	$>$	Accounts Receivable − Deferred Gross Profit

Loss

Fair Market Value of Property Recovered	$<$	Accounts Receivable − Deferred Gross Profit

Example: Assume customers in each example defaulted before making any payments in 1990.

	(A)	(B)
Fair Market Value of Repossessed Property	$8,000	5,000
Installment Accounts Receivable	10,000	10,000
Less: Deferred Gross Profit	4,000	4,000
Net	6,000	6,000
Gain (Loss)	$2,000	$(1,000)

Entry

	(A)	(B)
Accounts Receivable	(10,000)	(10,000)
Deferred Gross Profit	4,000	4,000
Inventory	8,000	5,000
Gain on Repossession	(2,000)	
Loss on Repossession		1,000

Cost Recovery Method

The cost recovery method does not require revenues until all direct costs required to produce those revenues have been recovered. It should only be used when the probability of collecting the accounts in full is extremely small.

Example

Sales	150,000
Cost of Sales	80,000
Gross Profit	70,000

	Collected	Recognized
1986	40,000	0
1987	30,000	0
1988	20,000	10,000
1989	60,000	60,000
Totals	150,000	70,000

Other Consistent Bases of Accounting (OCBOA)

The OCBOA method allows revenues to be recognized at times other than when realized, and, as such, is not in accordance with GAAP. As previously stated in Chapter 2, OCBOA are used when the accrual method is difficult to employ, cumbersome to utilize, or does not provide relevant information to the financial statement user.

How to Recognize Income from Franchise Fees

Official Pronouncement

FASB 45–Accounting for Franchise Fee Income
March, 1981

A franchise is a business interest which is sold by a franchiser to a franchisee. As the following matrix indicates, the recognition of income is dependent upon the following:

a. *Substantial performance.* The franchiser has done everything required to allow the franchisee to commence operations.
b. *No obligation to refund.* The franchiser is under no obligation to make any refunds to the franchisee.
c. *Operations have commenced.*

Franchise Income Recognition Matrix

	Substantial Performance	Refund Period Expired	Collection Assured	Recording
Substantial Performance?	Y	Y	Y	Income
	N	Y	Y	Unearned
Refund Period Expired?	Y	Y	Y	Income
	N	Y	Y	No entry
Collection Assured?	Y	Y	Y	Income
	Y	Y	N	Unearned for Amount Due

Figure 3-6—***Franchise Income Matrix***

How to Record Real Estate Sales

Official Pronouncement

FASB #66—Accounting for Sales of Real Estate
October, 1982

Note: FASB #66 was drafted to provide a better definition of how and when real estate sales are recorded. It was written to eliminate some of the confusion which had been caused by various forms of creative financing.

Caveat: FASB #66 does not apply to land sales.

Recognition criteria: All of the following criteria must be satisfied in order to use the accrual basis:

a. *The sale must be consummated.*

- All the contracting parties are legally bound.
- All consideration has been paid.
- The seller has performed all required acts.

Remember: The deal does not have to be all cash—financing also qualifies

b. Initial and continuing payments made by the buyer are adequate to show that he or she has enough at stake in the property to bear the risks of ownership.

c. The seller's mortgage or trust deed is not subject to subordination except to a primary or a future loan.

d. The risks and benefits of ownership are permanently transferred.

e. The seller must not have a substantial continued involvement in the property.

When to Recognize Income When a Right of Return Exists

Official Pronouncement

FASB #48. Revenue Recognition When Right of Return Exists—June, 1981

There are a number of industries (e.g. magazine publishing) that allow the customer to return any unsold merchandise. FASB #48 lists conditions that must be met before sales revenue can be recognized. These are:

a. The price is fixed or determinable.
b. The related indebtedness is not dependent on resale by the buyer.
c. Physical damage, theft, or destruction of the goods will not change the buyer's obligation to the seller.
d. The buyer has economic substance; i.e. not a front or strawman for the seller.
e. There are no significant obligations by the seller to help the buyer resell the merchandise.
f. A reasonable estimate can be made of the amount of future returns.

When Should Consignment Sales Income Be Recognized?

The seller/transferor does not record income until goods are sold by the transferee. Furthermore, the respective merchandise remains on the seller/transferor's books temporarily under the account title Consignment Out and is considered inventory for financial statement purposes.

B, C, D & E—Expenses

Official Pronouncement:

FASB Statement of Financial Accounting Concepts #5

Recognition and Measurement of Financial Statements of Business Enterprises—December, 1984

Definition

Outflows or other using up of assets of a business entity or incurrence of liabilities (or, a combination of both) during a period from delivering or producing goods, rendering services or carrying out other activities that constitute the entity's ongoing or major operations.

What Governs the Recording of Expenses?

a. *The Matching Principle*

Matching assumes a causal relationship between revenues and expenses.

For example, a company acquires 800 units at $50 each. It then sells 250 at $125. The costs would be matched to the sales as follows:

	Units	@	
Sales	250	125	$31,250
Cost of Goods Sold			
Purchases	800	50	40,000
Inventory	550	50	(27,500)
Total Cost of Goods Sold			12,500
Gross Profit	250	75	$18,750

2. *Systematic and Rational Allocation*

The principle of systematic and rational allocation apportions the cost of assets to future periods.

For example, the Troll company buys a main frame computer for $300,000. Management estimates that the computer will be used by the company for the next 10 years. Thus, $30,000 of its cost is systematically and rationally allocated to each of the next 10 fiscal periods.

3. *Immediate Recognition*

Many costs are expensed immediately because the amount of benefit to future years cannot be objectively calculated.

For example, Mr. Osband is the CEO of The Big Corporation. His salary is $1,000,000 per year. His job covers many tasks, which include defining Big's future policy and establishing long-range planning programs. It is obvious much of his efforts will benefit future periods. However, it is unfeasible to figure out how much. Therefore, his salary is expensed as incurred.

B. Cost of Goods Sold

The Three Components of Cost of Goods Sold

Purchases/Direct Materials

Direct Labor

Manufacturing Overhead

C. Operating Expenses

This classification generally includes selling, general and administrative, and all other expenses that contribute to the ordinary operations of the business.

D. Research and Development Expenses

Official Pronouncement:

FASB 2—Accounting for Research and Development Costs
October, 1974

1. *What Is Research and Development?*

a. *Research*: an activity devoted to discovering new information or techniques

b. *Development*: Takes these findings and uses them to improve profits or increase market share.

Immediate Expensing Required

While these costs are normally incurred to improve future profits, the FASB reasoned that it would be difficult to get a good handle on just which future periods would be benefitted. Therefore, R&D expenditures are required to be expensed immediately.

However: If the R&D expenditures will improve the use of existing machinery and equipment or facilities, they may be added to the related assets' bases.

2. *Software*

Software development costs may be capitalized under the following circumstances:

a. They improve existing general and administrative procedures.

b. They enhance existing software.

c. The software is developed for outsiders.

E. Pension Expenses

Official Pronouncements:

FASB #87—*Employers' Accounting for Pensions*
December, 1985

FASB 88—*Employers Accounting for Settlements and Curtailments of Defined Benefit Pension Plans for Termination Benefits*—
December, 1985

Definition: A pension plan is a contract between the company and its employees, where the employees' agree to work for the company and the company promises that it will fund a portion of their retirement.

1. *The three pension plan forms*

a. *Profit Sharing:* A profit sharing plan gives management the discretion to decide how much to contribute to the plan. This is subject, of course, to various government regulations.

b. *Defined Contribution:* The amount funded is a specified percentage of covered employees' salaries.

c. *Defined Contribution:* The amounts to be deposited by the employer are calculated to be sufficient to provide a minimum subsidy to covered employees after retirement.

2. *How to estimate the contributions required to estimate the fund to provide specified retirement benefits*

Consider the following time line:

```
A. - - - - - - - - - - - - R. - - - - - - - - - - - - C.
            t1                          t2
```

Where

A = Start of pension contributions

$t1$ = Period of contributions

R = Retirement date

$t2$ = Retirement period

C = Estimated date of death

i = interest rate or estimated return on assets invested

B = balance required to fund retirement

$Pt1$ = payment required to accumulate balance (B)

$Pt2$ = amount of each payment over retirement period

A company must provide enough funding in the period $t1$ to provide an annuity over the time frame $t2$. These funds will be invested at the interest rate = i.

Using an Electronic Spreadsheet to Compute Pension Plan Contributions

The following spreadsheet functions will help you perform the calculations:

B = @PV($Pt2$, i, $t2$)

$Pt1$ = @PMT(B, i, $t1$)

Caution: If accumulations and payments are to be made on a monthly basis,

If $t1$ and $t2$ are expressed in years, multiply each by 12

Divide i by 12 to obtain monthly interest rate

Example: Consider the following facts: An employee, age 25, will retire at 65 (in 40 years). At retirement, she will be entitled to a pension of $1,000 per month until her death, which is estimated to be age 80. The estimated annual rate of return on plan assets is 10%. The annual pension contribution is calculated as follows:

Estimated return on plan assets	10.00%
Monthly payment	$1,000.00
Years to contribute ($t1$)	40
Retirement time, months ($t2$)	180
Fund needed at retirement (B)	$93,057.44
Annual payment required in $t1$	$ 210.26

How to Compute Current Pension Expense

The current pension expense results from the following equation:

Service Cost

\+ Interest * Accumulated Benefit Obligations
\+ Amortization of Prior Service Costs
− Return on Plan Assets
− Gain
\+ Loss

Total Pension Plan Expense

The Components

Service Cost: The present value of future benefits attributed by the pension formula to services rendered by employees during the period.

For example, assume $50,000 per year is needed starting 10 years from today to fund all the covered employees' retirement, and the payment is expected to continue for 5 years. The service cost will be the present value of that future fund.

Discount Rate: The interest rate due on service cost required to be accumulated for employees' future benefits.

Why Figure a Discount Rate? The employees of the company have agreed to wait until retirement to receive any of their pension benefits.

Therefore, the discount rate is the interest rate the company has agreed to pay to the employees on these deferred payments.

Accumulated Benefit Obligation: The total present value of future benefits of all services rendered by employees before a specific data.

Return on Plan Assets: The amount earned on assets invested in the plan.

Gains or Losses: A change in value of the plan assets or the projected benefit obligation resulting from a difference between actual results and assumptions.

Prior Service Costs: The cost of retroactive benefits granted to employees prior to the institution of the plan. These are amortized over various periods to compute the annual pension expense.

What Are the Annual Contributions? Amounts contributed to the plan as required by government regulations.

Disclosure Requirements

FASB #87 requires the following:

- A description of the plan including:

  Groups covered
  Type of formula
  Funding policy
  Assets held
  Non-benefit liabilities

- The amount of pension plan expense showing the various components separately
- Reconciliation of the funded status of the plan with the amounts reported on the balance sheet. It should include:

  Fair value of assets
  Projected benefit obligation
  Amount of unrecognized past service cost
  Amount of unrecognized gains or losses
  Any additional liability recognized

- Weighted average discount rate
- Description and amounts of securities held in plan

Postretirement Benefits Other than Pensions

Official Pronouncement

FASB 106—Employers' Accounting for postretirement benefits other than Pensions—December, 1990.

Effective for fiscal years beginning on or after December 16, 1992.

FASB-106 requires an employer to estimate and accrue postretirement benefits other than income

What Is Included: All forms of benefits provided to retired workers and their dependents other than retirement income. They include health care, tuition assistance, and legal services.

If an employer has agreed to provide these benefits they must be accrued. The general form of the entry follows:

Net periodic postretirement benefit cost	XXX	
Accrued postretirement benefit payable		XXX

Calculating the Accrual: The amount to be accrued is the present value of funds required to be paid in the future after each employee's retirement. The methods of determining the discount rate and the accounting for the various other ingredients of the plan are similar to the provisions of FASB-87.

How to Estimate Future Health Care Costs: A great deal of subjectivity is involved here. You should attempt to develop information about cost projections for various forms of health care based on previous trends. Assume that government benefits will continue as provided by existing law.

Example:

Elvis Parsley has been employed by the company for the past 20 years. He is presently 57 and expects to retire at 65 and live to age 80. The expected rate of return on plan assets is 10%.

Employee Age	57
Expected Termination Age	65
Expected to Live to	80
Discount Rate	10%

(Continued on next page)

Age	Expected Future Claims	Present Value at Age 57	Present Value at Age 65
66	$ 2,500	1,060	2,273
67	2,625	1,012	2,169
68	2,756	966	2,071
69	2,894	922	1,977
70	3,039	880	1,887
71	3,191	840	1,801
72	3,351	802	1,720
73	3,519	766	1,642
74	3,695	731	1,567
75	3,880	698	1,496
76	4,074	666	1,428
77	4,278	636	1,363
78	4,492	607	1,301
79	4,717	579	1,242
80	4,953	553	1,186
	$53,964	$11,718	$25,123

The following entry would be made this year (when Elvis is 57)

Net periodic postretirement benefit cost	11,718	
Accrued postretirement benefit payable		11,718

At age 65, the obligation will total $25,123.

Disclosures: Generally the disclosures required are similar to those of FASB-87. In addition, disclosure should be provided about the nature of the benefits covered.

Pension Plan Calculation Advice: Don't Do It Yourself

The previous presentation discusses the general methods used to calculate pension plan expense. The derivation of the these formulas is a very complicated and time consuming process. Furthermore, the provisions of ERISA and other regulations are loaded with time bombs. Consider consulting an expert instead of doing the work yourself.

F. Other Revenues and Expenses

Alternative Presentations

1. Included in the operating revenues and expense section or 2. In a separate section of the income statement. See income statement illustration.

Author's opinion: Segregating other revenues and expenses in a separate section improves comparability between the firm and other similar but differently capitalized companies.

For example, if interest expense is buried in operating expenses, a company that receives most of its capital from investors will show better results than one that requires borrowed funds.

Classification Warning: Although the accounts discussed in this section, have been classified separately, they should not be categorized in the *extraordinary* revenues and expenses section. That section is reserved for items which are infrequent and unusual.

G. Provision for Income Taxes

Official Pronouncement:

FASB 96—Accounting for Income Taxes—December, 1987

Income taxes should be matched (i.e. allocated) to financial statement income and its various elements by applying the applicable income tax rates and regulations to that income.

Two Forms of Income Tax Allocation

- *Intraperiod tax allocation:* The procedure of distributing income tax expense to income from continuing operations, extraordinary income and expenses and other major segments.
- *Interperiod tax allocation:* Apportioning the income tax expense between periods.

How to Use Intraperiod Tax Allocation

Intraperiod income tax allocation apportions income tax expense among the following sections of the income statement:

Income from continuing operations
Results from discontinued operations
    Income from operations of discontinued segment
        Loss on disposal of segment
Income (loss) from extraordinary operations
Cumulative effect on prior years' income of change in
    accounting principles

Example: The following portrays the apportionment of income taxes assuming a single tax rate.

		Tax @ 40%
Income from continuing operations	$235,000	$ 94,000
Results from discontinued operations		
Income from operations	(34,500)	(13,800)
Loss on disposal of segment	(57,675)	(23,070)
Extraordinary Loss	(75,900)	(30,360)
Cumulative effect of change in Accounting Principles	49,500	19,800
Total	$116,425	$ 46,570

Figure 3-7—*Intraperiod Tax Allocation*

This will result in the following presentation:

Income from continuing operations		$ 235,000
Less income taxes		94,000
		141,000
Results from discontinued operations		
Income from operations	$(20,700)	
Loss on disposal of segment	(34,605)	(55,305)
Extraordinary Loss		(45,540)
Cumulative effect of change		29,700
		$ 69,855

Figure 3-8—*Intraperiod Income Tax Allocation Presentation*

How to Allocate Intra-Period Income Taxes Among Different Brackets

Intraperiod income tax allocation assumes that the income is earned in financial statement order.

Example: Assume the following:

	Net Income	Key
Income from continuing operations	35,600	a
Results from discontinued operations		
Income from operations	56,250	b
Loss on disposal of segment	(25,300)	c
Extraordinary Loss	(12,560)	d
Cumulative effect of change in accounting principles	62,450	e
Total	116,440	

Also, presume the following tax brackets

0–$50,000	15%
$50,000–$75,000	25%
$75,000–$100,000	34%
over $100,000	39%

Income taxes are therefore allocated as follows:

Code	Amount	0–50,000	–75,000	–100,000	100,000+
A	35,600	35,600			
B&C	30,950	14,400	16,550		
D	(12,560)		(12,560)		
E	62,450		21,010	25,000	16,440
TOTALS	116,440	50,000	25,000	25,000	16,440
TAX RATE		15.00%	25.00%	34.00%	39.00%
TAX	28,662	7,500	6,250	8,500	6,412

Figure 3-9—*Intraperiod Income Tax Allocation Computation*

This results in the following tax apportionment:

Code	Amount	0–50,000	–75,000	–100,000	100,000+
A	5,340	5,340			
B&C	6,298	2,160	4,138		
D	(3,140)		(3,140)		
E	20,164		5,253	8,500	6,412
TOTALS	28,662	7,500	6,250	8,500	6,412

Apportionment to discounted operations

Income from Operations	56,250)	11,445
Loss on disposal	(25,300)	(5,148)
	30,950	6,298

Income from continuing operations	35,600	
Less income taxes	5,340	
Net income from continuing operations		30,260
Results from discontinued operations		
Income from operations	44,805	
Loss on disposal of segment	(20,152)	24,653
Extraordinary loss		(9,420)
Cumulative effect of change		42,286
		87,779

How to Deal with Differences Between the Financial Statements and Tax Return Income

These result from dissimilarities between the definition of *income* per the Internal Revenue Service and GAAP.

For Example:

	Taxable income	Tax @ 40%
Per IRS regulations	$100,000	$40,000
Per GAAP	$150,000	$60,000

Thus, we see a $20,000 difference.

The Two Classes of Differences

a. *Permanent differences*

These are differences that are caused by diverse income tax regulations and GAAP. They are permanent because they will never reverse.

Income per GAAP but not taxable per the IRC:

- Interest on municipal bonds
- Life insurance proceeds to a corporation upon the death of an insured employee

Expenses according to GAAP but not tax deductible:

- Life insurance premiums on officers
- Amortization of goodwill
- Depreciation on stepped up basis from acquisition of assets

Deductions for tax purposes but not recognized as expenses under GAAP:

- Percentage depletion in excess of cost depletion
- Special divided deductions

Example: The JJR Corporation reports net income of $100,000, which includes $20,000 of municipal bond interest. The tax rate is 40%. Income tax is computed as follows:

Net Income	$100,000
Municipal Bond Interest	20,000
Taxable income	80,000
Income Tax Expense	$ 32,000

It is reported as follows:

Income before income taxes	$100,000
Less: Provision for income taxes	32,000
Net Income	$ 68,000

b. *Temporary differences:*

A difference in *when* an item will be recognized on the financial statement versus the tax return. These are supposed to reverse in future periods.

For example, a company recognizes income when a product is sold but uses the installment basis for tax purposes:

Sale	$10,000
Cost of Goods Sold	6,000
Gross Profit	$ 4,000
Gross Profit Percentage	40%

	Collections	Taxable	Financial Statement	Difference
1990	5,000	2,000	4,000	2,000
1991	3,000	1,200		(1,200)
1992	2,000	800		(800)
	10,000	4,000	4,000	0

Objective: The tax effect of the difference between the books and tax returns will reside in account called *deferred income taxes*. Inasmuch as any of these temporary differences are expected to reverse or vanish, so too will the deferred income taxes. The deferred taxes that are recognized should be the actual liability that is expected to be paid in the year that the reversals take place.

Note: Under the liability method described in FASB 96, the impact of different tax rates are considered.

Carrying on with the previous example, assume a 30% tax rate. The tax effects and the related adjustments are shown below.

Assuming a 30% tax rate, this results in the following:

	Taxable Income	Tax	Financial Income	Tax	Difference
1990	$2,000	$ 600	$4,000	1,200	(600)
1991	1,200	360			360
1992	800	240			240
	$4,000	$1,200	$4,000	1,200	0

Entries

	Provision for Taxes	Income Tax Payable	Deferred Income Taxes
1990	1,200	(600)	(600)
1991	0	(360)	360
1992	0	(240)	240
	1,200	(1,200)	0

Accounting for Temporary Differences—per FASB 96

Step 1: Schedule all temporary differences
This should include:

- Original amount of the temporary difference
- Origination date
- Future years in which each temporary difference is expected to reverse
- Amount of temporary difference that is expected to reverse

Step 2: Total differences by year
Step 3: If the expense adjustments exceed the income adjustments, carry them back and then forward
Step 4: Apply Estimated Tax Rates to the Resulting Amounts
Step 5: Total these amounts
This will be the deferred income tax liability or asset.
Example

	Current	**2**	**3**	**4**	**5**
Expected Tax Rates	50%	40%	40%	35%	30%
Taxable Income	$1,500				
Installment Sales		$2,000	$1,200	$800	
Depreciation		(4,000)	(2,000)		$2,000
Rent Income		3,000			
Bad Debt Expense				(2,000)	
	1,500	1,000	(800)	(1,200)	2,000
Carryback	(800)		800		
	700	1,000	0	(1,200)	2,000
Carryback	(700)	(500)		1,200	
Net Taxable	0	500	0	0	2,000
Deferred Income Tax	$ 0	$ 200	$ 0	$ 0	$ 600
Total	$ 800				

Figure 3-10—*Interperiod Tax Computation*

The Accounting for Net Operating Loss Carrybacks and Carryovers

Carrybacks: The amount of refund is limited to the taxes that were paid during the statutory period.

Example: A corporation has a net loss of $125,000 in 1988. The refund is calculated as follows:

Net Loss	$125,000

Prior Statutory Periods

	Net Income	Original Income Tax
1987	$35,430	$14,172
1986	25,965	10,386
1985	15,999	6,400
Total Net Income	$77,394	
Refund Available	30,958	
Loss Not Used	$47,606	

The unused loss of $47,606 can then be carried forward to future years, if available.

Loss carryforwards can only be used in the year(s) realized, and are realizable beyond a reasonable doubt. If we apply the above example, and, it turns out, that the company earned $130,000 in 1989, and the income tax is 40%, the loss carryforward is calculated and presented as follows:

		tax
Pre-tax operating income, 1989	130,000	52,000
Loss Carryforward	(47,606)	(19,042)
Net Tax		$ 32,958
Pre-tax operating income		$130,000
Less: income tax expense		52,000
Net operating income after taxes		$ 78,000
Extraordinary income		
Tax-benefit from carryover of net operating loss		19,042
Net income		$ 97,042

The tax benefit from the utilization of a net operating loss carryforward should be reflected as an extraordinary item.

Disclosure Guidelines

1. Income tax expense for components of the income statement.
2. Segments of income tax expenses including:
   a. current income tax expense or credit,
   b. deferred income tax expense or credit,
   c. investment tax credits,
   d. tax benefits of carryforward of operating losses,
   e. adjustment of a deferred tax liability related to a change in tax rates or the company's tax status.
3. Expiration dates of operating loss and tax credit carryforwards.

H. Results from Discontinued Operations

Official Pronouncements:

ABP-30 (as amended) Reporting the Results of Operations.

Reporting the effects of disposal of a segment of a business. June, 1973.

The reason for the segregation of discontinued operations is to provide separate information to the user about the continuing as well as discontinued operations of a business. If a segment is terminated and disposed, both its operating results and gain or loss on disposal should be reported.

Definition of a Segment

A component whose activities represent a single line or class of customer, and are measurable.

EXAMPLES: All activities of a specific industry
Wholesale versus Retail
International versus Domestic

What Should Be Measured?

1. Net income or loss resulting from the operations of that segment up to the measurement date.
2. Profit or loss incurred on disposal.

GAAP Requirements

1. All items of income and expense for the applicable segment, up to the *measurement date,* net of applicable income tax are to be reported separately. The measurement date is defined as the date when the company agreed to a formal plan to liquidate the division. If comparative statements are presented, these prior reports should segregate this information as "discontinued business operations."
2. The gain or loss on the disposal, net of tax effects, is computed and separately presented. The calculation performed is substantially equivalent to any computation of gain or loss on an asset sale.

Exception: All operating costs from the measurement date to the disposal date are added to the basis.

Example: On July 31, the Janice Corporation agreed in principle to liquidate its retail division. The date of disposal is September 30. The calculations of net income or loss from operating that segment up to the measurement date and profit or loss incurred from its disposal are presented below:

Sales	$195,443	
Expenses	200,525	
Loss	(5,082)	
Tax Effects (@ 40%)	2,033	
Net Loss from Segment Operations	($3,049)	
Loss from disposal		
Sales price of segment		$450,000
Equipment	$560,000	
Accum Depreciation	160,000	
Net Book Value	400,000	
Inventory, and so on	87,654	
Costs after measurement	19,698	
Total Costs		507,352
Net Loss		(57,352)
Less: Tax Effect		22,941
Net Loss From Disposal		$(34,411)

Figure 3-11—*Discontinuance of a Business Segment*

Income Statement Reporting

Results from discontinued operations	
Income from operations of discontinued segment (net of income taxes)	(3,049)
Loss on disposal of segment	(34,411)

CAUTION: A company that has decided to discontinue a segment may overallocate costs to that division, and improperly reduce expenses in its continuing operations.

I. Extraordinary Gains and Losses

Official Pronouncement

APB 30—Reporting the Results of Operations: Extraordinary, Unusual, and Infrequently Occurring Events and Transactions. Effective, June, 1973

Characteristics of Extraordinary Gains and Losses

These must have one or both of the following:

- Be infrequent
- Be unusual

Any of these events should be analyzed by referring to the specific facts and circumstances surrounding the firm and its industry. But, the burden is on the preparer to justify the classification as extraordinary.

Examples of Extraordinary Items

a. The tax benefit of an operating loss carryforward
b. Gains on restructuring payables
c. Most gains or losses on the extinguishment of debt
d. Most expropriations of property
e. Infrequent and unusual gains or losses resulting from wars and acts of God. What is extraordinary, of course, depends upon the company's geographic location.

How to Recognize Gains and Losses from Extinguishment of Debt

Official Pronouncements

FASB 4 Reporting Gains and Losses from the Extinguishment of Debt—March, 1975

FASB 64—Extinguishment of Debt made to Satisfy Sinking Fund Requirements—September, 1982

FASB 76—Extinguishment of Debt—November, 1983

A debt is extinguished when it is repaid prior to the maturity date. Gain or loss is recognized on the difference between reacquisition (repayment) costs and the carrying value of the liability on the company's books. If the gain or loss is material it should be reported as an extraordinary item.

Note: Defeasance provisions are covered as a Special Reporting Situation in Chapter 5.

All extraordinary gains and/or losses should be shown net of income tax effect.

K. Cumulative Effect of Changes in Accounting Principles

See Chapter 2 for coverage on this subject.

L. Earnings per Share

Official Pronouncements

APB 15—Earnings per share. Effective, May, 1969

APB 30—Reporting the Results of Operations.
Effective, June, 1973

FASB Statement No. 55—Deciding Whether a Security is a Common Stock Equivalent. Effective, February, 1982

FASB Statement No. 85—Yield Test for Deciding Whether a Security is a Common Stock Equivalent (Amendment to APB 15). Effective, March, 1985

NOTE: If a company does *not* sell its shares to the public, it generally is not required to report EPS data.

How to Present Earnings per Share Information

The following data is shown at the bottom of the income statement:

Earnings per share	*Primary*	*Fully Diluted*
Ordinary Income		
Results from discontinued operations		
Extraordinary income (loss)		
Cumulative effect on prior year's income of change in accounting principles		
Net income		

The primary as well as fully diluted EPS must be divided between these elements of income, if relevant.

Example:

Operating income	150,000.00
Extraordinary Loss	(12,000.00)
Net Income	138,000.00
Primary Earnings per share	1.50
Extraordinary items	(0.12)
Fully Diluted Earnings per Share	1.38

The Basic Equation to Compute EPS

$$\text{EPS} = \frac{\text{Net income to common stock}}{\text{Weighed average of common stock and common stock equivalents outstanding}}$$

The Components

1. *Net Income to Common Share*
   Income—Preferred Dividends

Note: If something is a common stock equivalent, any distribution or after tax expense attributed to it should be added back to income.

For example: convertible preferred stock dividends, after tax convertible bond interest

2. *Common Stock Equivalents*

Anything that is substantially comparable to common stock. This may include the following:

- Convertible debt
- Convertible preferred stock
- Stock options

Differentiating Between Primary vs. Fully Diluted EPS

Primary EPS: Net income divided by common stock and common stock equivalents. This is the basic EPS calculation.

Fully diluted EPS: EPS that results from converting all convertible securities (whether or not it would be reasonable to do so) into common stock. Presentation need not be made if the difference is less than 3% of the primary EPS.

Note: The fully diluted EPS calculation should only be made if it results in a *reduction* of EPS.

How to Compute Weighted Average of Shares Outstanding

The weighted average calculates the impact on the company's net assets of stock issued at various times during the year.

The Equation:

(1) List the cumulative number of shares issued at various times during the year:

For Example:

Date	Shares Issued	Cumulative
01-Jan	100,000	100,000
01-Apr	50,000	150,000
01-Oct	30,000	180,000

(2) Compute the weighted average shares outstanding by using the following equations:

	Cumulative Shares × Outstanding		Number of Months Outstanding / 12	
Date	**Cumulative**	**Months**	**% of Year**	**Weighted Shares**
01-Jan	100,000	3	25%	25,000
01-Apr	150,000	6	50%	75,000
01-Oct	180,000	3	25%	45,000
			100%	145,000

The impact of stock splits and stock dividends: Inasmuch as these do not provide any working capital, they are considered issued on the *first day of the fiscal year*.

Assume the following common stock issues:

		Cumulative Outstanding
January 1 outstanding	50,000	50,000
April 1st issued	15,000	65,000
July 1 issued	35,000	100,000
October 1, 2:1 split	100,000	200,000
December 31	200,000	

However, for these purposes, the stock split is considered to have been issued at the beginning of the year, multiply everything by 2.

Date	Cumulative		Months	% of Year	Weighted Shares
01-Jan	100,000	100,000	3	25%	25,000
01-Apr	30,000	130,000	3	25%	32,500
01-Jul	70,000	200,000	6	50%	100,000
			12	100%	157,500

Note: If comparative statements are to be presented, the stock splits are deemed to have taken place at the beginning of the first comparative period.

How to Segregate the Income That Belongs to Common Shareholders

If preferred stock is not convertible, dividends assigned to this security must be deducted from income before measuring EPS.

Example:

Preferred Stock issued at Par	500,000
Dividend Rate	10.00%
Net income	225,000
Amount to Preferred	(50,000)
Net income to Common	175,000
EPS	1.11*

* 175,000/157,500 = $1.11

How to Identify Stock Equivalents and Calculate Their Effect on Earnings per Share

Common stock equivalents are those securities that, by their very nature, have enough characteristics similar to common stock that they are *likely* to be converted.

Determining Which Securities Are Common Stock Equivalents

The following pass the muster to qualify as common stock equivalents:

- The yield, at issue date, on any convertible security should have been less than 66⅔% of the average Aa corporate bond yield at issuance.

Note: The yield is defined as the stated payment rate divided by the proceeds received.

Example: Company Z issues a $100,000 convertible bond bearing a coupon rate of 12% and receives $120,000. The yield is 10%.

- Stock options and warrants are *always* common stock equivalents.

Equivalency Test Example

Assume that the average corporate Aa bond rate is 10%. Test Securities A and B for equivalency

For example:	A	B
BOND YIELD	0.0600	0.0800
Ave Corp Bond Rate	0.1000	0.1000
X 66⅔%	0.0667	0.0667
Equivalent?	Y	N

Security A is a common stock equivalent because its yield is *less* than ⅔ of the average corporate bond rate.

Adjust Income for Impact of Equivalencies

If convertible securities are used in the EPS equation, any related distributions or expenses have to be added back to income as follows:

- Convertible preferred stock—dividends
- Convertible debt—after tax interest expense

Example:

Common Shares Outstanding		300,000
Net Income		$600,000
Tax Rate	40%	
Earnings per Share		$ 2.00
Convertible Securities		

Units	Description	Rate	Interest or Dividend Amount Outstanding	# of Shares Conversion Rate
1,000	Preferred Stock	4%	100,000	1
150	Bonds Payable	6%	150,000	100

Adjustment to Income	
Bonds Payable	9,000
Income Tax	(3,600)
Total	5,400
Unadjusted Income	600,000
Adjusted Income	605,400
Adjustments to Number of Shares	
Preferred Stock	1,000
Bonds Payable	15,000
	16,000
Unadjusted Shares Outstanding	300,000
	316,000
Adjusted EPS	1.92

Calculating the Effect of Stock Options on EPS

Stock options are always considered common stock equivalents. The computations assume the following:

(1) Any funds received from the exercise of the options are used to reacquire the company's shares at their average market price for the fiscal period. If the number of shares issued exceeds 20%, different guidelines apply. APB 15 requires a two step approach. It assumes that:

a. Any proceeds were used to first acquire up to 20% of the actual shares outstanding at year end at the market price
b. The remainder is to be used to retire long term debt, first, and what is left over to be invested in government bonds.

(2) The number derived as the difference between the shares issued and reacquired is used to compute the effect on EPS.

Different computations are used depending if they will affect the primary or fully diluted earnings per share:

Primary: The average market price of the applicable shares must be greater than the option price for a period of at least three months up to the option date.

Fully Diluted: As long as exercise of the options would reduce (dilute) the EPS, their impact would be shown.

Calculation Format

A. Shares	Number of stock options outstanding
B. Option Price	Price to recipient
C. Proceeds	A * B
D. Assumed Repurchase	C/market price
Increment	A − D

Example:

Shares Covered		30,000
Market price	15	
Option price	10	
Proceeds	300,000	
Shares purchased from treasury		20,000
Assumed Increment		10,000
Weighted Average shares o/s		157,500
Total shares o/s		167,500
EPS		1.04

Using a Worksheet to Compute EPS

Company

Earnings Per Share Calculation
Date

Key Information

Average Aa Corporate Bond Yield
Yield × 2/3
Marginal Income Tax Rate
Average Market Price per Share

Figure 3-12—***Earnings per Share Worksheet***

	Primary		Fully Diluted	
	Shares	Income	Shares	Income
A. Per Statement				
Less: Preferred Dividends		______		______
Net income to common		______		______
B. Options				
Warrants	______	______	______	______
	______	______	______	______
C. Convertible Securities				
Preferred Stock Bonds	______	______	______	______
Total	______	______	______	______

Options

Shares
Option Price
Proceeds ______ ______
Assumed Reacquired ______
Increment ______

Convertible Preferred Stock
Preferred Shares
Common per Share
Dividend Rate
Equivalent?
Preferred Dividend Income ______

Convertible bonds
Bonds at Face Value ______
Proceeds ______
Number of Bonds ______
Shares per Bond ______
Proceeds ______
Total shares ______
Interest Rate ______
Yield ______
Equivalent? (Y, N) ______
After Tax Interest Expense ______

Figure 3-12—*Continued*

Using the Worksheet to Complete the Computations

	Primary		Fully Diluted	
	Shares	Income	Shares	Income
Per Statement	157,500	225,000	157,500	225,000
Less: Preferred Dividend		(50,000)		(50,000)
Net to Common	157,500	175,000	157,500	175,000
EPS		1.11		1.11
Options	10,000		10,000	
	167,500	175,000	167,500	175,000
EPS		1.04	1.04	
Convertible Securities				
Bonds			30,000	21,000
Total	167,500	175,000	197,500	196,000
EPS		1.04		0.99

Figure 3-13—*Earnings per Share Worksheet*

CHAPTER 4

How to Recognize, Measure and Report Balance Sheet Elements

Introduction

What follows is a guide to help you solve those difficult problems of recognizing, measuring, and reporting assets, liabilities, and equity. The chapter contains a formatted balance sheet keyed to each major component. The material on each component includes the following:

- Official pronouncements
- The underlying GAAP
- Practical computation suggestions
- Account management hints
- Disclosure requirements and examples

Balance Sheet Finding Chart

ABC CORPORATION
BALANCE SHEET
Date

Assets

	Reference
Current Assets	
Cash	A
Marketable securities	B
(market value $)	
Accounts Receivable	C

(*Continued on next page*)

Figure 4-1—***Balance Sheet Finding Guide***

Less: Allowance for doubtful accounts	
Inventories (at)	D
Prepaid expenses	E
Total Current Assets	
Long Term Investments	F
Investment in Stocks	
Investment in Bonds	
Property and Equipment	
Cost	G
Accumulated Depreciation	H
Net Book Value	
Intangible Assets	I
Trademarks (net)	
Patents (net)	
Goodwill (net)	J
Total Assets	
Liabilities and Stockholders' Equity	
Current Liabilities	K
Accounts payable	
Accrued expenses	
Income taxes payable	L
Advances from customers	
Current portion of long-term debt	
Current portion of obligations under capital leases	
Total current liabilities	
Other Liabilities	
Long-term debt	M
Deferred income taxes	L
Obligations under capital leases	N
Total long-term debt	
Total Liabilities	
Commitments and Contingent Liabilities	O
Stockholders' Equity	P
Contributed Capital	
Common Stock, $ par (shares authorized, shares issued and outstanding)	
Addition paid in capital on common stock	
Preferred stock	
Premium on preferred stock	
Retained earnings	
Less: Treasury stock	
Total Stockholders' Equity	
Total Liabilities and Stockholders' Equity	

Figure 4-1—*Continued*

A. Cash

Cash in an asset which must be available, *now* to pay current obligations, and, as such, is held in

— checking accounts
— savings accounts
— certificates of deposit
— petty cash funds

How to Use a Petty Cash Fund to Pay Small Bills

When a company uses cash to pay its smaller bills, an *imprest* petty cash fund is very handy.

1. Determine how much should be set aside. That amount should be large enough to cover most minor purchases for about a week.

Caution: Do not tempt fate by putting too much into the cash fund.

2. Designate a petty cash custodian and write the reimbursement checks payable to that person.
3. Reimburse the fund for the exact amount of cash payout.

Example of an Imprest Fund

Specified Fund Balance			200.00
Cash in fund		113.56	
Cash payout slips			
Office supplies	12.87		
Postage paid	32.32		
Coffee	2.75		
Flowers for secretary	38.50		
Total Cash payout in fund		86.44	
Total		200.00	

A reimbursement check in the amount of $86.44 is now made payable to the petty cash custodian. The payout slips will serve as the backup to those expenses recorded in the general ledger.

How to Use a Four Column Proof of Cash Analysis to Easily Find Checking Account Reconciliation Errors

The form looks this:

PROOF OF CASH FORM

	Beginning	Receipts	Checks	Ending
Bank Statement				
Deposit in transit				
Beginning				
Ending				
Outstanding Checks				
Beginning				
Ending				
Per Bank Statement				
Per General Ledger				
Difference				

Figure 4-2—*Proof of Cash Form*

Example: Assume you have attempted to reconcile the checking account and discover the following:

Cash Balance per Bank Statement	17,543.23
Deposits in transit	3,456.50
	20,999.73
Less: Outstanding checks	8,642.08
Reconciled balance	12,357.65
Per books	13,426.54
Books (Over) Bank Reconciliation	(1,068.89)

Use the proof of cash form to spotlight the difference relatively easily:

PROOF OF CASH FORM

	Beginning	Receipts	Checks	Ending
Bank Statement	20,542.45	86,543.22	(89,542.44)	17,543.23
Deposit in transit				
Beginning	5,433.45	(5,433.45)		
Ending		3,456.50		3,456.50
Outstanding checks				
Beginning	(12,543.33)		12,543.33	
Ending			(8,642.08)	(8,642.08)
	13,432.57	84,566.27	(85,641.19)	12,357.65
Per General Ledger	13,432.57	84,566.27	(84,572.30)	13,426.54
Difference	0.00	0.00	(1,068.89)	(1,068.89)

Figure 4-3—***Proof of Cash Example***

It is apparent that the problem lies in the cash disbursements.

When Checks Written but Not Released May Be a Problem

Often, many companies will write all the checks they need to cover all their unpaid bills at one time, and then release each check as additional cash is received. This creates the following problems:

- An understatement of cash
- An understatement of accounts payable

Since these two counteract, working capital is not affected. However, an uninformed reader will misinterpret the results because

1. The Statement of Cash Flows will be misstated, and
2. Financial ratios will be misleading.

For example, assume that a company has written $12,000 in checks but has not, as yet, released them.

	After release	Before release
Current Assets		
Cash	1,234.56	13,234.56
Other	5,554.32	5,554.32
Total	6,788.88	18,788.88
Current Liabilities		
Accounts Payable	897.54	12,897.54
Other	2,457.98	2,457.98
Total	3,355.52	15,355.52
Current Ratio	2.0:1	1.2:1

Beware of Old Outstanding Checks

The existence of an old outstanding check may be quite benign. On other hand, its presence may indicate bills in dispute and other problems that might need investigation.

When Savings Accounts Should Be Handled Differently

Savings accounts are accounted for the same way as checking accounts if their liquidity is generally unimpaired. However, in certain instances savings account cash should be treated differently.

1. Certificates of Deposit may have maturity dates that may extend beyond the current operating cycle, or have other restrictions placed on their liquidity.
2. The accounts may have been set up as *sinking funds* to finance a future purchase.

These accounts may not only have to be segregated from other cash balances, but, may also need to be reported in the non-current asset section of the balance sheet.

How to Report Compensating Balances

Many bank loans contain provisions that require a company to maintain minimum cash balances. If those balances drop below a certain amount, the company may be in default.

The absence of sufficient compensating balances may force a long-term loan into default. When this occurs, the loan itself may have to be reclassified into the current liability section of the balance sheet.

Information regarding compensating balances should be disclosed in the notes to the financial statements and referenced to both the cash and notes payable accounts.

Caution: It is important to review and abstract the various bank note provisions in order to be able to warn management about potential dangers.

How to Earn Interest by Using Zero Balance Checking Accounts

It is foolish to keep money in a checking account. It's a better idea to deposit directly into saving, and then when it is time to pay bills, transfer only what is needed. Furthermore, unless the firm is able to use the early payment discounts, it's advisable to limit check writing to once or twice per month.

B. Marketable Securities

Official Pronouncement

FASB #12 Accounting for Certain Marketable Securities—December, 1975

When Are They Current Assets?

Inasmuch as corporations invest for many reasons, you should try to figure out management's *intent* in order to make classifications between current marketable securities or long-term investments.

Requirements for Classification as Current

1. Temporary
2. Readily convertible into cash
3. Expected be converted into cash within the current operating cycle

Valuation

Marketable securities should be carried at the lower of cost or market.

Cost: the basic price of the security plus any commissions and taxes required to affect the purchase.

Market: the amount that can be realized if the security were sold at balance sheet date.

How to Calculate the Lower of Cost or Market (LCM)

The valuation of marketable securities cannot exceed the market value of the portfolio.

Example:

Investment Portfolio	Cost	Market	Difference
Able Company	$ 3,550	$ 4,250	$ 700
Baker Company	1,200	800	(400)
Charley Company	15,400	13,000	(2,400)
	$20,150	$18,050	$(2,100)

There is an unrealized loss of $2,100 which is charged to income.

Balance sheet and income statement presentation follow:

Balance Sheet

Marketable Securities	$20,150
Less allowance for decline in value of marketable securities	2,100
Marketable Securities at Lower of Cost or Market	$18,050
Income Statement	
Unrealized Loss	$ 2,100

Figure 4-4—***Marketable Securities Presentation***

If the securities now increase in value: The gain is added back to income. This is limited to the amount of the original write down.

If, by the next year end, the market value of the portfolio is now $22,000, it has increased in value by $3,950. Nevertheless, the adjustment to income is limited to the amount ($2,100) that will bring its balance back up to the original cost.

Recording Sales of Marketable Securities

A sale of a security in this category should be recorded in the usual way. In addition, the remaining portfolio must be revalued.

Example: Assume that Baker Corporation was sold for $1,000.

Cash	$1,000	
Marketable Securities		$1,200
Loss on Sale	200	

The following portfolio remains

	Cost	Market	Difference
Able Company	$ 3,550	$ 4,250	$ 700
Charley Company	15,440	13,000	(2,400)
	$18,950	$17,250	$(1,700)

Inasmuch as the original valuation reserve was $2,100 it must be reduced by $400 to $1,700.

Valuation Reserve	$400	
Unrealized Loss or Recovery		$400

Disclosure *guidelines*

1. Carrying value (cost, lower of cost or market) of marketable securities.
2. Securities pledged as collateral.

C. Accounts Receivable

Accounts receivable are claims against customers arising through the normal course of business.

Note: In order to be classified as current, collection of these accounts should be reasonably expected to occur within the current operating cycle (one year).

Valuation

Accounts receivable are carried at their net realizable value which is computed as follows:

Net Realizable value = Gross amount due − Allowance for bad debts

Four Ways to Record Bad Debt Losses

1. Direct write-off method
2. Percentage of sales

3. Percentage of accounts receivable
4. Accounts receivable aging

Warning: The direct write-off method does not conform to GAAP because it fails to match losses against sales.

Ways to Make the "Best" Estimate of Potential Uncollectible Accounts

1. Data from trade reports
2. Information from other customers
3. Sales persons' reports
4. General economic situation. ("Are we expecting a downturn?")
5. Prior payment history
6. Length of time the account been outstanding.

How to Improve Predictability by Preparing an Enhanced Aging Schedule

We can infer that a bad debt loss is a function of:

- The age of account
- Specific information related to that account.

The enhanced aging schedule further divides the accounts receivable aging into general and specific categories. Fortunately, there are certain computer programs that make the job easier.

Example: The Maine Line Company has analyzed its accounts receivable and has determined that $5,433 are problem accounts of which 75% will probably be lost. Then, the allowance for bad debts will be figured on the other receivables based on previous trends.

MODIFIED AGING REPORT

Total Accounts Receivable	145,679
Potential Problem Accounts	5,433
Unclassified Receivables	140,246

(Continued on next page)

Figure 4-5—*Accounts Receivable Aging*

	Total	Special	Unclassified	Bad Debt %	Est Bad Debts
Current	89,295	271	89,024	3.50%	3,116
30 days	28,756	815	27,941	15.00%	4,191
60 days	16,452	1,087	15,365	20.00%	3,073
90 days	6,954	1,358	5,596	35.00%	1,959
over 90	4,222	1,902	2,320	45.00%	1,044
Total	145,679	5,433	140,246		13,383
Special Accounts			5,433	75.00%	4,075
Total Allowance for Bad Debts					17,458

Figure 4-5—*Continued*

How to Accumulate Data to Manage Accounts Receivable

A company's accounts receivable management efficiency is dependent upon its:

1. Credit policy,
2. Collection ability

Analysis of the following trends will help gauge management efficiency in this area:

1. Sales on account
2. Accounts receivable turnover
3. Accounts receivable (year end)
4. Allowance for bad debts (beginning)
5. Provision for doubtful accounts
6. Accounts written off
7. Allowance for doubtful accounts (ending)
9. Average days to collect on account
10. Percentage aging analysis
11. Bad debt allowance as percentage of
    a. Sales on account
    b. Accounts receivable

This information can be accumulated in the ensuing schedule format:

ACCOUNTS RECEIVABLE ANALYSIS SCHEDULE

Year	1986	1987	1988	1989
Sales on Account	675,432	776,747	784,514	825,444
Receivables	118,432	125,444	136,555	145,679
Allowance				
Beginning	4,044	6,500	7,904	11,592
Provision	2,456	2,647	5,333	6,115
Write-Offs		(1,243)	(1,645)	(249)
Ending	6,500	7,904	11,592	17,458
Turnover		6.37	5.99	5.85
Average Days		57	60	62
Aging Analysis				
Current	64.84%	62.71%	63.05%	61.30%
30 days	17.42%	18.44%	19.22%	19.74%
60 days	13.04%	12.15%	13.33%	11.29%
90 days	3.20%	4.40%	1.80%	4.77%
over 90	1.50%	2.30%	2.60%	2.90%
	100.00%	100.00%	100.00%	100.00%
Allowance as % of				
Sales	0.96%	1.02%	1.48%	2.11%
Receivables	5.49%	6.30%	8.49%	11.98%
Provision as % of				
Sales	0.36%	0.34%	0.68%	0.74%
Receivables	2.07%	2.11%	3.91%	4.20%

Figure 4-6—*Accounts Receivable Analysis Schedule*

How to Record Accounts Receivable Financing

Generally, there are two ways that a company can borrow money on its accounts receivable:

1. Assignment
2. Factoring

Assignment: When accounts receivable are assigned they become collateral for loans. The accounting treatment is equivalent to many other forms of borrowing.

a. The lender agrees to make a loan against a specified percentage of the applicable receivables.

Note: Accounts that are seriously past due will usually *not* be accepted as collateral for the loan.

b. As the money is collected, a portion equal to the amount advanced will be remitted to the lender.

Scheduling Techniques

Loan Percentage	X
Accounts Receivable	
Beginning	A
Less: Unacceptable Accounts	B
Net Collateral Balance	C = A − B

Accounts Receivable

Beginning	C
Sales	D
Collections	E
Ending	F = C + D − E

Loan Availability

Total	G = X*F
Net Owed	L
Available	M = G − L

Borrowing

Beginning	H
Loans	I
Payments from Collections	J = (E*X)
Other Payments	K
Net Owed	L = H + I − J − K

Figure 4-7—***Accounts Receivable Financing Worksheet***

Example of above

% Financing	80.00%			
Accounts Receivable				
Beginning			$145,679	
Less: Unacceptable Accounts			(4,222)	
Total Collateral Balance			$141,457	

		Jan 15	Jan 25	Jan 31
Accounts Receivable (collateral)				
Beginning		$141,457	$153,518	$161,640
Sales		34,394	26,455	28,990
Collections		(22,333)	(18,333)	(19,996)
Ending		$153,518	$161,640	$170,634
Total	@ 80.00%	$122,814	$129,311	$136,506
Net Owed		42,134	17,467	41,470
Available		$ 80,680	$111,844	$ 95,036
Borrowing				
Beginning		$ 60,000	$ 42,134	$ 17,467
Loans				40,000
Payments from Collections		(17,866)	(14,667)	(15,997)
Other Payments			(10,000)	
Net Owed		$ 42,134	$ 17,467	$ 41,470

Figure 4-8—*Accounts Receivable Financing Analysis*

Presentation

Balance Sheet

Current Assets		
Accounts receivable		$ 4,222
Accounts receivable assigned	$170,634	
Less: Note payable	(41,470)	
Equity in assigned accounts receivable		129,164
Total accounts receivable		133,386
Less: Allowance for doubtful accounts		17,458
Net collectible equity		115,928

Figure 4-9—*Accounts Receivable Financing Presentation*

Footnote: Accounts receivable in the amount of $170,634 are assigned to the bank as collateral for its loan. Annual interest on that loan is X% per annum.

Factoring: In these arrangements the actual title to the accounts receivable is transferred. When this conveyance takes place, the buyer (factor) assumes all risks of collection. Therefore, the sale is non-recourse.

Example: Assume that the Maine Line Company sells its accounts receivable to a factoring company. The factor agrees to buy $141,457 of these accounts, charges a commission of 12%, and advances 90% of the balance.

Accounts receivable sold	$141,457
Commission	(16,975)
Net to be received	124,482
Amount advanced	112,034
Receivable from factor	$ 12,448

The following entry will be recorded

Cash	112,034	
Receivable from factor	12,448	
Factoring expense	16,975	
Accounts receivable		141,457

Figure 4-10—***Accounts Receivable Factored Analysis***

Footnote Disclosure: Certain accounts are factored without recourse as to credit risk. An allowance for loss is provided for accounts not factored based on a periodic review of the accounts.

What Special Accounting Predicaments Are Caused by Other Receivables?

Loans and advances that do not arise from sales of goods and services in the ordinary course of the business should be separated from the accounts receivable classification and disclosed as necessary.

Types:

- Loans to employees
- Notes receivable that should be classified as investments
- Loans and advances to officers and shareholders

Two Reasons to Be Cautious About Loans and Advances to Officers and Shareholders

1. There are potential income tax problems. The IRS's dim view of officers' loans outstanding could lead to some very unpleasant tax consequences.
2. These loans may *not* be actually collectible. Managers of a closed or controlled corporation often tend to treat the business's cash as their private checking account.

To satisfy yourself, you must look for evidence that a loan was actually intended.

- Are there signed notes?
- Do they provide for timely payments of principal and interest?
- Have those payments been made?

If you cannot satisfy yourself on these points, a strong case exists for reclassification to salaries or dividends.

When Is an Officer's or Shareholder's Loan a Current Asset?

If the borrower can exercise significant control over the affairs and finances of the corporation, he or she is not compelled to repay the advances within a proscribed period.

Disclosure Guidelines

The following should be disclosed on the face of the financial statements or by separate footnotes.

1. What is included in accounts receivable.
2. The amount and description of non-trade receivables.
3. Accounts receivable financing and factoring agreement:
   terms of the agreement,
   interest rates,
   amount,
   description of collateral,
   any restrictive covenants.
4. Excessive amounts due from any one customer or industry, especially if economic signs point to trouble in that sector.

5. Estimated uncollectible amounts. Describe any potential problems that may not be able to be quantified in the allowance.
6. Any unbilled amounts.

D. Inventories

Definition: Goods held by the enterprise for sale or for further production in the ordinary course of business.

The Three Components of a Good Inventory Control System

In a merchandising or manufacturing company, control and accounting of inventories is critical to its health as well as its future well being.

a. *Keep the inventories at the right levels:* If the inventory is too high, money will be wasted for extra storage space, interest, insurance, and various inventory control expenses. On the other hand, inventory shortages may lose customers or stop the production line.

Note: Economic Order Quantity (EOQ) equations attempt to optimize inventory levels by balancing ordering and holding costs. These computations and applications will be discussed in Chapter 00.

b. *Control inventory acquisitions:* The best purchase quantity should be derived only after marketing, production, and cash flow forecasts are prepared. The following procedure may be used:

Step 1: Forecast Sales

Step 2: Allocate to Major Product Lines

Step 3: Estimate quantities by dividing by average sales price

Step 4: Estimate Purchase requirements by using following equation:

$$\text{Purchasing requirement} = \text{Projected sales} + \text{Ending inventory} - \text{Beginning inventory}$$

c. *Watch out for inventory obsolescence.* Because of today's rapid changes in technology and styles, obsolescence losses can sneak up very rapidly.

Suggestion: Prepare an inventory obsolescence reporting Schedule

You will notice that the following framework is similar to the accounts receivable aging schedule.

Big Brad Stores, Inc.
Inventory Obsolescence Schedule
December 31, 1988

Production Number	15444	23098	24332	45444
Classification	couch	chair	chair	table
Description	antique	modern	abstract	metal
Late date acquired	9/25	8/15	1/12	4/12
Quantity on Hand	23	6	44	19
Valuation	$4,600	$210	$1,540	$1,425
Recent Sales (Quantity)				
December	3			1
November	5	4		1
October	7	4		3
September	1	6		5
August				6
Earlier			3	7

Figure 4-11—*Inventory Aging Schedule*

As the above indicates, the last abstract chair sales were made prior to August (6 months ago), and the metal table sales might be tapering off. This schedule helps the user to either:

1. Decide to aggressively market these slow-moving items through a combination of advertising and price reduction techniques.
2. Write down these units.

Beware of Inventory "Cushions"

In order to manipulate profits, some companies try to keep their ending inventories down. They establish a cushion, or unreported inventory, by a variety of undercounting or underpricing techniques.

As the following example shows, a manipulated reduction of inventories and profits in one year overstates the income in the following period:

	Correct Inventories		Cushion	
	YEAR 1	YEAR 2	YEAR 1	YEAR 2
Sales	$100,000	$150,000	$100,000	$150,000
Cost of Goods Sold				
Beginning Inventory	20,000	30,000	20,000	20,000
Purchases	75,000	97,000	75,000	97,000
Merchandise Available	95,000	127,000	95,000	117,000
Ending Inventory	(30,000)	(45,000)	(20,000)	(45,000)
Total	65,000	82,000	75,000	72,000
Gross Profit	$ 35,000	$ 68,000	$ 25,000	$ 78,000

Figure 4-12—*Inventory Distortions*

As Alternative B shows, the $10,000 ending inventory cushion in year one leads to an overstatement of profit in the following year. Once used, the cushion quite often becomes an addiction. And, the manipulator has to continue to understate inventories.

Two Ways to Record Inventory Acquisitions

a. *The periodic method*

When used: For lower value and higher volume products.

How used: Cost of goods sold is calculated by subtracting what is left over from the input (purchases + beginning inventory).

(1) As goods are acquired, purchases are debited.

(2) At the end of the accounting period, the inventory is calculated by physical count priced at per unit prices. The books are adjusted to the new value.

b. *The perpetual method*

When used: This method is favored for higher-valued goods.

How used:

(1) Each acquisition is debited to the balance sheet inventory account.

(2) The inventory account is credited as the applicable units are sold.

How to Value Inventories

Official Pronouncement

Accounting Research Bulletin #43; Restatement and Revision of Accounting Research Bulletins—June, 1953.

Chapter 4; Inventory Pricing

Inventories are initially valued at cost, the price paid or consideration given. Cost includes the following:

—invoice price

—expenditures (direct and indirect) to manufacture

—freight and duty

—direct labor and overhead if a manufacturing concern

Applying Cost Flows

Inasmuch, as purchases take place at different times and varying costs, their prices are scrambled as they find their way into the production/sales process. To obtain consistency, the inventory's valuation methods must be based on a patterned flow of costs.

The three most common forms are:

—*FIFO;* First in First out

—*LIFO;* Last in First Out

—*Weighted Average*

Each produces the following:

FIFO

Inventory Valuation: At most recent prices
Cost of Goods Sold: Earliest purchases

LIFO

Inventory Valuation: At earliest acquisitions
Cost of Goods Sold: At most recent acquisitions

Weighted Average: Valuation and cost of goods sold at weighted-average prices.

The method chosen significantly effects inventory valuation as well as product costs.

Example:

Purchases	Units	@	Total
January 1	100	100	$ 10,000
March 1	150	200	30,000
September 1	250	300	75,000
Total	500		$115,000
Sold	350	400	$140,000

Alternative inventory valuation:

	Units	@	Total
FIFO	150	$300	$45,000
LIFO	50	$200	$10,000
	100	$100	$10,000
			$20,000
WEIGHTED AVERAGE	150	230	$34,500

Resulting gross profits:

	FIFO	LIFO	WEIGHTED AVERAGE
SALES	$140,000	$140,000	$140,000
COST OF GOODS SOLD			
Purchases	115,000	115,000	115,000
Ending Inventory	(45,000)	(20,000)	(34,500)
Net	70,000	95,000	80,500
GROSS PROFIT	$ 70,000	$ 45,000	$ 59,500

What You Should Know Before You Choose a Cost Flow Alternative

FIFO
Advantages:

1. Approximates the physical flow of goods and the costs to gather information are minimized.
2. The inventory's valuation is closest to replacement costs.

Disadvantages: It is not a satisfactory measure of income in periods of rising prices.

LIFO
Advantages:

1. Produces the lowest taxable income in periods of rising prices.
2. Charges to income are closest to current market value.

Disadvantages:

1. Increased information costs, especially when LIFO layers have to be reduced or liquidated.
2. The balance sheet reflects the oldest acquisition costs.
3. A company can increase profits by delaying purchases.

For example:

Sales price	$100	
Sale to be filled		300

Inventory on hand

Date Acquired	Units	@	
Anticipated	400	$40	$16,000
11/88	500	$20	$10,000
10/88	600	$15	$9,000
9/88	400	$10	$4,000

Gross Profit Analysis

	Purchase Made	Purchase Delayed
Sales	30,000	30,000
Purchases	12,000	6,000
Gross Profit	18,000	24,000

Note: Dollar Value LIFO has been found useful in eliminating many of the bookkeeping costs of the conventional LIFO method. This method uses price indices to convert prior LIFO costs to a common base.

Weighted Average

The weighted-average mehod is a good common ground between FIFO and LIFO.

Retail Inventory Method

This method is used to cost inventories when there is a consistent pattern between cost and retail values. The technique, which is appropriate for retail stores, converts inventories taken at retail values to cost.

How to Use Lower of Cost or Market to Price Inventories

Inventories must be carried at the lower of cost or market.

Official Pronouncement: Accounting Research Bulletin 43

What is market value? Market is equivalent to replacement value. It should be used when less than cost. However, it is subject to the following constraints:

Upper and Lower Ranges:

Highest Market Value / Net Realizable Value (NRV) <= selling prices − costs of completion and dispo

Lowest Market Value / Minimum = Maximum (NRV) − allowance for normal profit margin

Once determined, the lower of cost or market computations may be applied as follows:

- To individual items
- To inventory classes
- The inventory taken as a whole.

Example:

Examples	A	B	C	D	E
Replacement Cost	$11.00	$ 6.50	$ 7.50	$ 5.50	$ 9.00
Sales Price	15.00	8.00	8.00	8.00	13.00
Disposal Costs	12.00	1.00	1.00	1.00	1.85
Net Realizable Value (Ceiling)	3.00	7.00	7.00	7.00	11.15
Normal profit margin	1.00	1.00	1.00	1.00	0.65
Floor	2.00	6.00	6.00	6.00	10.50
Constraint by Ceiling & Floor	11.00	6.50	7.50	6.00	10.50
Cost	10.00	10.00	10.00	10.00	10.00
Lower of Cost or Market	$10.00	$ 6.50	$ 7.50	$ 6.00	$10.00

Disclosure Guidelines

1. Method of valuation: Cost or Market whichever is lower
2. Cost flow assumptions: FIFO, LIFO, Weighted Average, other
3. Major classes of inventory:

   Raw material
   Work in process
   Finished goods

4. Liens or pledges on inventory

Example: Inventories are stated at the lower of cost or market. Cost is determined by the first-in, first-out method.

E. Prepaid Expenses

The assets that are classified as prepaid expenses come about because of the matching concept of expense recognition. Expenditures that will benefit future periods are capitalized and then apportioned to the future periods expected to be served.

For example, a company purchases a 3-year insurance policy on January 1, 1988. The total premium is $3,600. For 1988, the insurance expense will be $1,200 and the prepaid expense at December 31, will be $2,400 of which $1,200 is classified as current.

What to Put in a Prepaid Expense Schedule

In general

—date of acquisition

—term or expiration date

—payee

—description of benefits received

—amount of benefits received

—prepaid at balance sheet date

Specifics
1. *Insurance*

Insurance policies

Amount of coverage

Expiration date

Essential information: The amount of insurance coverage should be periodically compared to fair market values of the respective assets to determine if the protection is sufficient.

2. *Rent*

Property covered

Expiration date

Essential information:

a. Amount of capital leases
b. Expiration date

3. *Interest*

In most cases, prepaid interest should not be carried as an asset. Instead, the imputed interest rate should be computed and an amortization schedule be prepared. However, any prepaid interest carried on the books should be netted against the applicable loan balance for financial statement presentation purposes.

Example: An asset is purchased for $3,000, with no money down. The contract provides for 36 monthly payments of $110. Therefore, the following could be improperly surmised:

Term months	36.00
Monthly payment	110.00
Total Contract	3,960.00
Cost of Asset	3,000.00
Interest add on (prepaid)	960.00

The actual interest rate is calculated by using present value equations.

Calculated Interest Rate	
Present Value	$3,000
Payment (per month)	110
Term (months)	36
Interest rate calculated	19%

The liabilities and the interest expense after one year's payments are shown below:

Calculated Interest Rate

	Prepaid	@ 19% Interest
Prepaid interest	640.00	NA
Note balance	1,680.00	2,181.11
Interest expense	960.00	501.11

F. Long Term Investments

Official Pronouncements

APB #18—The Equity Method of Accounting for Investments in Common Stock—March, 1971

APB #21—Interest on Receivables and Payables—August, 1971

APB 29—Accounting for Nonmonetary Transactions—May, 1973

Topics Covered

- Stock investments
- Investments in corporate bonds
- Long-term notes receivable

When Are Investments Classified as Long Term

Acquisitions of long-term investments are intended

1. To earn income
2. To gain control

Stock Investments

The method of reporting and accounting for long-term stock investments is dictated, to a very large degree, by the percentage of ownership.

This is shown on the following chart:

Percentage Owned 0	20%	>50%
LCM		Consolidated statements

a. *Lower of Cost or Market (LCM) (0– <20%)*

It is assumed here that control has *not* been achieved. Therefore, the investment is treated the same way as a marketable security, but with one significant difference:

When long term investments are evaluated downward to market value, the adjustment is charged to an equity account, "Unrealized loss on securities."

For example, refer to the illustration portrayed in Marketable Securities. When the investment is *long term*, the loss is not charged to income. Instead, the following presentation results:

Stockholders' Equity	
Unrealized Loss on Stock Investments	$2,100

b. *Equity Method (=>20%)*

Although there are cases when control is effected when ownership is less than 20%, GAAP assumes that control exists at the minimum percentage. Therefore, the investment balance and income is computed as follows:

Investment Balance

Initial cost + Share of income − Share of dividends

Investment Income

Investee's net income * Ownership Percentage

Note: This will be discussed in greater detail in the Chapter 5 under the heading Consolidated Statements.

How to Solve the Dilemma of Accounting for Investments in Closed Corporations in Which Control Is Not Held

In these situations, since market quotations are not available, alternative procedures have to be applied:

1. *By output valuation:*

a. Select a publicly held corporation that is in the same industry and has the same general characteristics.

b. Try to establish relationships between the market value of that firm and its earnings, sales or equity.

For example, the Buyer Corporation acquired 10% of the Seller Company (a closed corporation) for a total cost of $30,000. The following fair market value information about Big Sales, Inc., a comparable publicly held corporation, has been obtained:

Earnings per share	$ 4
Price per share	$60
RE ratio	15
Privately Held Corporation	
Earnings	$32,000
X PE ratio	$480,000
Percentage owned	10.00%
Gross investment value	$48,000

The amount derived will probably have to be discounted because of a lack of marketability.

Discount Factor	40.00%
Investment value	$48,000
Less discount (40%)	(19,200)
Net investment value	$28,800

Question: How much to discount? There is, of course, a great deal of subjectivity here. One can only try to back up guesses by looking at valuations of the underlying assets, and the quality of earnings.

2. *Input value:* The process uses the fair market value of underlying assets and adds goodwill. The goodwill calculation procedures will be discussed in the "Other Assets" section of this chapter.

Small Business Corporations—A Word to the Wise

Closely held small business corporations often do not prepare GAAP statements. Instead, they are more concerned with Internal Revenue Code regulations. In these cases, many income recognition and asset valuation adjustments have to be made.

Investment in Bonds

While FASB #12 does not mention bond investments, it is generally recognized that the provisions are applicable.

Methods of Amortizing Premium or Discount

a. *Straight Line Method*

b. *Compound Interest Method*

Interest Expense = Carrying Value of Bond * Effective Interest Rate

Amortization = Interest Expense − Interest Received

Amortization Examples:

Face Value of bonds purchased	$100,000.00
Interest rate	10.00%
Maturity Date	December 31, 1995
Date Acquired	January 1, 1990
Amount Paid	$94,000.00
Discount	$6,000.00
Straight Line	
Term Remaining	6 years
Annual Amortization	$1,000.00
Entry	
Investment in Bonds	$1,000.00
Interest Revenue	$1,000.00

The Investment in Bonds should be reported on the balance sheet at the end of each year as follows:

January 1, 1990	94,000.00
December 31, 1990	95,000.00
December 31, 1991	96,000.00
December 31, 1992	97,000.00
December 31, 1993	98,000.00
December 31, 1994	99,000.00
December 31, 1995	100,000.00

Interest income from this investment is calculated as follows:

Interest Income	
Amount received	10,000.00
Amortization of discount	1,000.00
Total interest income	11,000.00

Shortcomings of Straight Line Method of Amortization

Because the straight line method reports the same amount of interest revenue each year, and because the carrying value of the bond increases (or decreases in the case of bonds acquired at a premium), the interest *rate* changes as the investment is amortized.

Example from above:

Year	Carrying Value	Interest Expense	%
1994	94,000	11,000	11.70%
1995	95,000	11,000	11.58%
1996	96,000	11,000	11.46%
1997	97,000	11,000	11.34%
1998	98,000	11,000	11.22%
1999	99,000	11,000	11.11%
2000	100,000	11,000	11.00%

How to Calculate the Effective Rate of Interest on a Bond Investment

This method calculates the rate *actually* earned by an investor over the term of a bond by taking into consideration the following:

- The price paid
- Interest receipts
- The term remaining
- Maturity value

Example: Amortization by the effective interest method is computed as follows:

Present Value (Amount paid)	$94,000
Semi annual interest payments	5,000
Term to maturity	6 years
Maturity value	$100,000

Computing the Effective Interest Rate

This rate, which is known as *Yield to Maturity* is computed by the Internal Rate of Return (IRR) equations which require the following components:

Amount invested

Interest receipts scheduled by year

Maturity value scheduled by maturity date

The IRR is easily calculated on most financial calculators or spreadsheet programs.

Computation Example:

Purchase price	94,000
Maturity value	100,000
Annual interest	10,000
Interest rate guess	10%

Schedule of Cash Flows

Year	
	(94,000)
1	10,000
2	10,000
3	10,000
4	10,000
5	10,000
6	10,000
	100,000
Computed IRR	11.41%

Applied to Amortization Schedule

Note: Interest is received semiannually. Therefore, 50% of 11.41% or 5.7% will be used.

Year	Interest Expense	Interest Received	Amort	Carrying Value
				94,000
1	5,358	5,000	358	94,358
	5,378	5,000	378	94,736
2	5,400	5,000	400	95,136
	5,423	5,000	423	95,559
3	5,447	5,000	447	96,006
	5,472	5,000	472	96,478
4	5,499	5,000	499	96,977
	5,528	5,000	528	97,505
5	5,558	5,000	558	98,063
	5,590	5,000	590	98,653
6	5,623	5,000	623	99,276
	5,724	5,000	724	100,000

Long Term Notes Receivable Received in Exchange for Property, Goods, or Services

If the fair market value is known, as follows:

Dr.	Note Receivable	XXX	
Cr.	Sale		XXX

If the fair market value is not known: Interest must be imputed on the contract, or discounted at an applicable rate.

Guidelines to Determining the Applicable Discount Rate

According to APB 21, the Borrower's incremental rate is calculated by considering the following:

1. The borrower's credit rating
2. Prevailing market rates
3. Collateral and covenants
4. Rate at which borrow could obtain funds

Hint: The easiest way to determine the borrower's incremental rate is to obtain the debtor's financial statements and/or credit reports and apply that data to your situation.

How to Calculate the Present Value of a Note Receivable

The carrying value of the note is a function of the interest rate and the number of payments.

Example: A company sold some merchandise and received a non-interest bearing note as consideration. The fair market value of the property transferred is not readily available. The note provides for 36 payments at $425 per month. The borrower/buyer's incremental interest rate is 12%.

Therefore, the note is calculated and reported as follows:

Equipment sold (Net book value)	$11,500	
Interest rate	12.00%	
Payment	$425	
Number of payments	36	
Present value	12,796	
Total amount of payments	$15,300	
Present value	12,796	
Discount on note receivable	$ 2,504	
Note receivable	$15,300	
Discount on note receivable		2,504
Equipment sold		11,500
Gain on sale		1,296

Interest income is calculated by amortizing the discount on the straight line or effective interest methods of amortization.

Disclosure Guidelines

1. Basis of valuation
2. Investments pledged

Disclosure example:

Investments: At December 31, 1988, aggregate cost and market value, and gross unrealized gains and losses for marketable securities are as follows:

Current	
Aggregate cost	$534,666
Aggregate market value	555,466
Gross unrealized gains	22,777
Gross unrealized losses	1,977

(Continued on next page)

Noncurrent	
Aggregate cost	755,667
Aggregate market value	723,444
Gross unrealized gains	12,956
Gross unrealized losses	45,179

At December 31, 1988, in order to reduce the value of long-term investments to carrying value, the valuation allowance account was adjusted to $2,223. Net realized gains of $12,345 and unrealized losses of $4,445 were included in the determination of net income. The cost of the securities sold was determined on a first-in, first-out basis.

G. Property and Equipment

Official Pronouncements

APB #12 Omnibus Opinion. Paragraph 12—1967

APB #29 Accounting for Nonmonetary Transactions, 1973

FASB #34 Capitalization of Interest Costs—October, 1979

Definition: Tangible assets used in the normal operations of a business which have lives of over one year.

What Should Be Included in the Cost of Property and Equipment

1. Purchase price
2. Freight, duty, and delivery charges
3. Installation costs
4. Construction costs

How to Account for the Cost of Self-Constructed Assets

Assets built in-house should be recorded just like manufactured inventory. These costs include:

a. Direct materials in construction
b. Direct labor for design, tooling, and building
c. Overhead should be allocated in the same way that you would use for cost accounting purposes.

How to Use Job Order Costing for Self-Constructed Assets

Set up a form that will accumulate the following information:

1. Description
2. Total units required
3. Job #
4. Estimated materials, labor, and overhead
5. Materials

    Description
    date required
    quantity
    price
    extension

6. Subcontracting costs
7. Direct labor

    design
    tooling
    construction

Note: Watch out for intercompany profits—Any construction performed by one department or division for another may include intra- or intercompany profits. These profits must be eliminated.

When and How Should Interest Costs Be Capitalized?

Interest costs incurred during the time it takes to get the asset made ready for business use should be capitalized. The time frame begins with the first expenditure and ends when the asset is available for service.

For example, assume an office building is under construction. All interest, from the time work starts to the date the notice of completion is filed, should be capitalized.

Interest is generally capitalized in two circumstances:

1. When it is a direct charge of the construction financing.
2. When it is a segment of general interest expense that has to be allocated to the construction. In that case, the applicable interest is calculated as follows:

$$\text{Total interest} * \frac{\text{Weighted average of construction expenditures}}{\text{Weighted average of all expenditures}}$$

Limitation: The amount that can be capitalized should not be greater than all interest costs incurred in any one period.

Note: Capitalized interest may include a prorata share of loan fees and points.

A Partial Listing of Land vs. Construction Costs

Land

- Recorded cost
- The cost of closing the transaction and obtaining title (e.g. escrow fees, title costs, legal fees for the land purchase)
- Past due taxes
- Land survey costs
- Cost of preparing the land for its particular use clearing, grading, demolishing old buildings

Construction

- Contracted cost
- Excavation for the particular building
- Architectural costs
- Building permits
- Capitalized interest costs
- Real estate taxes during construction
- Insurance costs during construction

Three Ways to Allocate Costs in Mixed Purchases

When improved real property is acquired, a portion of the purchase price should be apportioned to the land and the remainder to the structure. There are three good ways to do this:

1. Appraisal of the land.
2. Appraisal of costs to construct the building adjusted to the particular age and condition.
3. Allocation on the basis of property tax bills. The tax bill for any particular property will display assessed valuations for

land and improvements. While these amounts may have little relationship to the actual price, it is the proportions that are useful.

Example:

Cost of property			
Price		$875,000	
Escrow fees and title costs		1,300	
Legal fees		2,500	
Total cost		$878,800	
Property tax bill assessed values		%	Allocation
Land	12,500	25.00%	219,700
Structure	37,500	75.00%	659,100
	50,000	100.00%	878,800

When Should Improvements and Replacements Be Capitalized?

Any costs incurred that increase an asset's future economic benefits over what was originally estimated should be capitalized. To qualify these outlays should:

1. Extend the life of the asset
2. Improve productivity

Recording alternatives:

1. *Reduce accumulated depreciation* If the improvements increase the service lives of the respective assets, it is reasoned that some of the life previously written off has been restored.
2. *Increase the asset account* This is justifiable because the potential use of the asset has increased beyond its original estimated life.

Note: The account, repairs and maintenance is used for normal upkeep and maintenance of the assets and should be expensed.

Suggestion: To save time, a minimum capitalization policy should be established.

For example, the JMR company has instituted a policy to expense any costs related to property and equipment that are less than $500.00.

How to Account for Assets Acquired in Non-Monetary Exchanges

There are two types of swaps:

1. Exchange of dissimilar assets
2. Exchange of similar assets

Dissimilar Assets: Gain or loss is recognized on the difference between what is given up and received.

Example: Jack trades a cow for some beans. The cow has a net book value of $300. The beans are worth $5,000. The transaction is recorded as follows:

Property & Equipment—Beans	$5,000	
Property & Equipment—Cow		$ 300
Gain on Exchange		2,700

According to APB #29: The cost of a non-monetary asset received through an exchange is the fair value of the asset given up.

Which Value Should Be Used? The item that gives the most credible information should be used: For example:

- *Land for common stock in a listed corporation.* If the shares issued are not dilutive, the price per share will probably be more definitive.
- *Land for common stock in a non-public corporation.* Unless, a value of the shares can be conclusively established, the fair market value of the land will probably be a better gauge. In that case, comparable sales in the area should be consulted.

Similar Assets or Like Kind Exchanges

Example: An auto is traded for another.

In general, loss is recognized. However, gain is only recorded to the extent of boot received.

What is boot? Anything received or given up in addition.

Example: A company traded a used car for another auto. In addition, it received $1,000 cash. The $1,000 is boot.

Recording considerations on like kind exchanges: These have to calculate:

- Any gain or loss on the transaction
- The basis of assets received

Let:

NBV = Net Book Value of Asset surrendered

FMV = Fair Market Value of asset surrendered

B = Boot

No Boot Given or Received

$FMV > NBV$

Gain Recognized = 0

Basis = NBV

$FMV < NBV$

Loss Recognized = $FMV - NBV$

Basis = FMV

Facts Used:

Company	A	B
Net Book Value on Books	\$45,000	\$15,000
Fair Market Value of \$ Asset	\$35,000	\$35,000
Entries		
Old Asset	(\$45,000)	(\$15,000)
New Asset	\$35,000	\$15,000
Loss	\$10,000	

Boot Given:

$FMV < NBV$

Loss = $NBV - FMV$

Basis = $NBV + B$

$FMV > NBV$

Gain = 0

Basis = $NBV - B$

Boot Received:

$FMV < NBV$

Loss = $FMV - NBV$

Basis = $FMV - B$

(Continued on next page)

$FMV + B > NBV$

Gain Realized $= FMV - NBV$

Gain Recognized $= (B/(B + FMV) * (FMV - NBV)$

Basis $= NBV - B +$ Gain Recognized

Examples

	Loss Boot Given		Gain Boot Received
Net book value old asset	45,000		15,000
Fair market value of asset	25,000		35,000
Boot received (given)	(10,000)		10,000
Basis of Equipment			
Fair Market value	25,000		
Net book value of old asset			15,000
Boot given (received)	10,000		(10,000)
Recognized gain			4,444
Total	35,000		9,444
Gain (Loss)			
Fair market value	25,000		35,000
Net book value old asset	45,000		15,000
Gain (Loss)	(20,000)		20,000
Gain Recognized			
Consideration			
Boot		10,000	22.22%
Fair market value of asset acquired		35,000	77.78%
		45,000	100.00%
Entries			
New Asset	35,000		9,444
Loss	20,000		
Old Asset	(45,000)		(15,000)
Boot	(10,000)		10,000
Gain			(4,444)

Note: In these cases income tax and GAAP timing of income and expense recognition may be different because GAAP may be contrary to tax law. The effect of this timing difference will be reversed by different charges to depreciation over the life of the new asset(s).

H. Accumulated Depreciation

Definition of depreciation: The systematic and rational allocation of the cost of tangible assets to future years which are expected to be benefitted by the acquisition of these assets.

What Should Be Considered When an Asset's Life Is Estimated?

1. Type of asset
2. Condition of asset
3. Estimated future technological changes
4. History of prior equipment acquisitions
5. Industry guidelines
6. Internal Revenue Service guidelines

How to Apportion an Asset's Cost over Its Useful Life

Key

C = Cost
A = Accumulated depreciation
S = Salvage value
Y = Life in years
X = Times straight line. For example, if 200% *DB* were to be used, X would equal 2.

1. *By the straight line method:* The asset's benefits are expected to be constant over the asset's life.

   Calculation $(C - S)/Y$

2. *Declining balance.* Produces a decreasing depreciation charge by applying a constant rate to the book value of the asset at the beginning of each period.

   Calculation: $((C - A) * X)/Y$

How to Calculate Declining Balance Depreciation to Arrive at a Pre-Specified Residual Value

The residual value, or salvage value, is an estimate of the amount the owner expects to receive at the end of an asset's estimated life. When declining balance depreciation is used the remaining salvage value at the end of that life will, by the very nature of the computation, be some other amount. The following equation will get you the balance you want.

$$\text{Depreciation Rate} = 1 - \sqrt[y]{\frac{S}{C}}$$

Example:

Cost of asset	16,000
Life (Y)	5 years
Depreciation rate	0.4257
Year	
1	6,810
2	3,912
3	2,247
4	1,290
5	741
	15,000
Residual Value	1,000

3. *Sum of the years digits:* Yields a declining charge by applying a decreasing fraction each year to the depreciation base.
   N = Numerator = Year
   D = Denominator $(N * (N + 1))/2$
   $(C - S) * (N/D)$

Example

Cost		$15,000
(a) Life	5	
(b) First Year	1	
(c) Last Year	5	
(d) (b + c)	6	
(e) (d * a) Times Life	30	
(f) (e/2)	15	
Depreciation	Numerator	Depreciation
	5	$5,000
	4	4,000
	3	3,000
	2	2,000
	1	1,000
	$15,000	

(*Continued on next page*)

The sum of the year digits depreciation method is not commonly used because two depreciation rates are required when acquisitions are made at interim dates.

Example:

Assume the above asset was acquired on October 1, 1989.

	Numerator	%	Amount
Year 1	5	25%	1,250
Year 2	5	75%	3,750
	4	25%	1,000
			4,750

What About Leasehold Improvements?

Leasehold improvements are expenditures made on premises owned by others, and, whose useful life ends when the premises are vacated or the lease expires. Accordingly, they are amortized over the lease term or its renewal period, whichever is longer. If the premises are abandoned while there is still an undepreciated balance, whatever is left over should be written off.

How to Keep Good Property and Equipment Records

The following information should be retained for each item:

1. Description of asset
    a. name
    b. serial number
    c. how used (or by whom)
    d. vendor
    e. date acquired
2. Depreciation
    a. life
    b. method
    c. how life estimated
    d. method used for income tax purposes

This data should be summarized into a master schedule that reports the following:

Cost
- Asset classification
- Balance at beginning of period
- Additions
- Sales and disposals
- Balance at ending of period

Accumulated depreciation
- Asset classification
- Balance at beginning of period
- Additions
- Sales and disposals
- Balance at ending of period

The Mechanics: This record keeping task has become easier with the increased used of electronic data processing. There are many off-the-shelf programs, or you can utilize a spreadsheet analysis.

Disclosure Guidelines

Cost by classification: Land and improvements, Building and building improvements, Machinery and equipment, Leasehold improvements, Furniture and fixtures, Computers, Automotive equipment

Depreciation method and life

Capitalized leases

Assets pledged as collateral

I. Intangible Assets

Official Pronouncements:

APB #17—Intangible Assets, August, 1970

FASB #2, Disclosure of Research and Development Costs, October, 1974

FASB #86—Accounting for the Costs of Computer Software to be Sold, Leased and Otherwise Marketed, August, 1985

Definition: Intangible assets do not have physical substance and result from legal or contractual obligations.

Valuation of Intangible Assets

Intangible assets are recorded at their purchase price plus any other costs required to transfer title. If the asset is developed internally, any unidentifiable costs are normally expensed as incurred.

Intangible Asset Classification Chart

Classification

Name	Accounting treatment	Life
Research & Development	Expensed immediately	
Patents	Capitalize	17 years
Copyrights	Capitalize	Economic life renewable up to 40 years
Trademarks and Trade-names	Capitalize	Economic life up to 40 years
Franchises	Capitalize	Economic life up to 40 years
Organization costs		Economic life up to 40 years

How to Depict Computer-Software Costs

Until technological feasibility is attained, computer software costs are treated the same way as research and development costs—they are expensed immediately unless technological feasibility is attained. Technological feasibility is accomplished when the program is complete and available for general release. No costs can be capitalized after release.

Costs of computer software developed for internal purposes, including selling and general and administrative systems, may be capitalized.

Disclosure Guidelines

1. Segregation by types
2. Carrying values
3. Amortization method and period

J. Goodwill

Definition

The difference between the purchase price of a company, as a whole, and the fair market value of its assets. It is therefore gauged as the ability of the acquisition to earn a more than normal rate of return on the market value of its identified net assets.

Valuing Goodwill in Four Steps

1. Ascertain the fair market value of the identifiable net assets.
2. Project future average earnings.
3. Estimate the desired rate of return on identifiable net assets.
4. Calculate the estimated excess annual earnings.

Step 1. Ascertain the fair market value of the identifiable net assets.

Financial statements are prepared by using historical cost accounting principles. Therefore, it is necessary to reevaluate the assets and liabilities contained in these statements to their current value at the date of analysis. The aim here is not to portray *conservative* amounts, but rather, the best valuation possible. When you do this, consider the following for possible adjustments:

a. *Accounts receivable:* net realizable value.

b. *Inventories:* net realizable value.

Note: When inventories are carried at LIFO, the valuation, at prior period costs, may be considerably lower than present current value.

c. *Prepaid expenses, and deferred charges* should probably be written off to zero.

d. *Property and equipment:* current value adjusted for the condition of the particular assets and the applicable state of technology.

e. *Goodwill on books:* write off to zero.

f. *Other intangible assets:* adjusted to present value of future estimated earnings.

g. *Notes payable* should be adjusted to the present value of scheduled payments at the current market interest rate.

For example, a $100,000 note payable bears an interest rate of 10% and is payable over five remaining years by monthly payments of $2,103.66. The current market rate for a note of this type is 12%. The present value of the note is $95,516.

The following trial balance will illustrate this first step:

Janice Company
Trial Balance

	Per Books	FMV
Cash	23,500	23,500
Accounts receivable	172,450	150,000
Less: allow for bad debts	(17,245)	
Inventories (LIFO)	45,500	85,000
Property equipment	125,000	250,000
Accumulated depreciation	(35,000)	
Goodwill	125,000	0
Accounts payable	(50,000)	(50,000)
Note payable	(100,000)	(95,516)
Stockholders' equity	289,205	362,984

Step 2. *Project future average earnings.*

Start by examining the investee company's prior period earnings to determine its track record, and, a basis to project into the future.

Caveat: If it is a small, closely run business, these prior earnings might need some cleaning up.

- Auto, travel and entertainment expense accounts, officers' salaries, and other personal expenses, should be removed before proceeding further.
- Interest expenses should be adjusted or removed if the acquirer plans to liquidate these debts or use alternate financing.
- Other adjustments may also be required if the assets are revalued to their fair market value.

Example:

Average annual revenues			$650,000
Average annual expenses			
Cost of goods sold	$390,000		
Inventory adjustments	(20,000)	$370,000	
Expenses	200,000		

(Continued on next page)

Goodwill amortization	(3,125)		
Depreciation adjustment	12,500		
Interest on note	(10,000)		
Average excess salaries	(30,000)		
Expense accounts	(5,000)	164,375	
Total Adjusted Expenses			534,375
Pre-tax income			115,625
Income taxes (@ 40%)			46,250
Adjusted net income			$ 69,375

Step 3. *Estimate the desired rate of return on identifiable net assets.* There are two parts to this calculation.

a. Estimate a reasonable rate of return on the fair market value of the assets. Average ROIs can be derived by reviewing the reports of publicly held companies in the same industry.

Tip: The conventional ROI calculation uses the net book value of assets rather than their fair market value for the denominator of the equation. If current value accounting is included as supplementary data, it should be utilized instead.

Tip: Industry trade associations may be able to provide information on average ROIs or multiples.

b. Build in risk factors. If the potential investee is not a publicly held company, the lack of marketability alone increases the risk of the investment. This should be reflected by using a higher desired rate of return.

Example:

Researched average return on FMV	12.00%
Risk premium	120.00%
Return required	14.40%

Step 4. *Calculate the estimated excess annual earnings.*
Example:

Adjusted net income		69,375
Fair market value of assets	362,984	
Return required	14.40%	52,270
Estimated excess annual earnings		17,105

Alternate method: There are many influences that may change the excess annual earnings used in these calculations, (e.g. economic, competitive, social, and so on) which forecasted statements should consider.

Step 5. *Compute Goodwill*

Goodwill is calculated by determining the present value of estimated excess annual earnings over a forecasted period of time using a carefully considered discount rate.

Example: This example assumes that these earnings will continue for 10 years into the future. The discount rate used is 14.4%.

Estimated years of excess earnings	10
Present value of estimated excess earnings	$100,496

The present value of the estimated excess earnings is the calculated goodwill.

Disclosure Guidelines

—Method of Amortization, Life Used

—Carrying basis.

—Explanation of treatment of pre November 1, 1970 items.

K. Current Liabilties

Definition: Contractual obligation for goods and services that have been received or incurred and are payablewithin the current operating cycle.

Types

1. *Accounts payable:* Liabilities that are incurred by purchasing goods and services on open acount.
2. *Accrued expenses:* Liabilities tha accumulate systematically over time. These are incurred as a function of the matching process.
3. *Notes payable:* Written promises to pay over a certain time.

Qualification: A note payable usually requires the payment of interest. If the interest rate is non-existent or below the current market rate, the provisions of APB 21 (Interest on Receivables and Payables) apply. See Section F of this chapter under the heading Investment in Notes.

Regarding Amortizing Notes Payable: Refer to Chapter 2 for explanation of method of calculating current portion of long-term debts.

4. *Taxes payable:* This category includes various (non-income) federal, state, and local taxes; payroll taxes; sales taxes; and property taxes.

OCBOA Moderation: Small companies, although they use modified cash basis accounting, may still accrue the employer's portion of payroll taxes payable.

L. Income Taxes Payable

Official Pronouncement:

FASB 96—Accounting for Income Taxes, December, 1987

Refer to Chapter 3 for detailed calculation procedures.

Where to Show Estimated Tax Payments

1. Payments on current tax liability for income earned to date should be deducted from the computed income tax liability.
2. Payments in advance should be reported as a prepayment and classified as a current asset.

M. Long-Term Debt

Official Pronouncements:

APB #14—Accounting for Convertible Debt and Debt Issued with Stock Purchase Warrants— March, 1969

APB #21—Interest on Receivables and Payables—1971

FASB #15—Accounting for Debtors and Creditors for Troubled Debt Restructuring—June, 1977

FASB 76—Extinguishment of Debt—-November, 1983

How to Account for Bonds Payable

Bonds payable are treated much like any other note payable, *subject to two complications:*

Bond issue costs are incurred when bonds are sold. They include the following:

- Printing,
- Legal fees, and
- Registration expenditures.

These expenditures are recorded separately as Deferred Bond Issue Costs, and are amortized over the term of the bond by the straight line method.

Premiums and discounts arise if the proceeds on the sale of a bond are different than its face or maturity value:

Proceeds > Issue Value = Premium
Proceeds < Issue Value = Discount
Example:

Face value \$100,000
Issue Costs \$8,000

A. Premium on bonds payable	\$ 15,000
B. Discount on bonds payable	\$ 20,000

Journal Entry

Bonds issued at a premium

Cash	107,000	
Deferred bond issue costs	8,000	
Premium on bonds payable		15,000
Bonds payable		100,000

Bonds issued at a discount

Cash	72,000	
Deferred bond issue costs	8,000	
Discount on bonds payable	20,000	
Bonds payable		100,000

Financial Statement Presentation
Assets

Deferred Bond Issue Costs	8,000	
	A	B
Bonds payable	\$100,000	\$100,000
Unamortized premium	15,000	
Unamortized discount		(8,000)
Carrying Value of Bonds Payable	\$115,000	\$ 92,000

How to Account for Convertible Bonds

According to APB 14, convertible bonds should be treated solely as debt. However, if the bonds contain stock warrants (rights) which can be detached and converted into stock, the issuee should be allocated between debt and equity as follows:

$$\text{Amount assigned to bonds} = \frac{\text{Market value of bonds without rights}}{\text{Market value Bonds without rights} + \text{Market value of rights}}$$

Amount assigned to rights = 1 − amount assigned to bonds

Example: The Rhoda Corporation issued $900,000 of 10% bonds. The following information is pertinent:

Total issue	900,000	
Amount of each bond	1,000	
Number of bonds	900	
Warrants per bond	10	
Market value		
Bonds (ex rights)	908	
Right	5	
Total market value		%
Bonds	882,000	95.15%
Rights	45,000	4.84%
Total market value	927,000	100.00%
Allocation of issue		
Bonds	856,311	
Rights	43,689	
Total issue	900,000	

Troubled Debt Restructuring and Early Debt Extinguishment

The resulting gain or loss is to be classified an extraordinary item in the statement income. Refer to Chapter 3.

N. Obligations under Capital Leases

Official Pronouncements:

FASB #13—Accounting for Leases—November, 1976

FASB #13 has established criteria for distinguishing between the following types of leases:

Operating lease: The lessor retains substantially all of the risks and benefits of ownership of the property that is leased.

Capital lease: A lease that transfers substantially all of the risks and benefits of ownership and becomes, in substance, a purchase.

When Is a Lease Not a Lease?

When you can answer Yes to *any* of the criteria listed below.

1. Does the lease transfer ownership of the property to the lessee at the end of the lease term?
2. Does the lease contain a bargain purchase option?
3. Is the lease term equal to at 75% or more of the estimated useful life of the property?
4. Is the present value of the minimum lease payments equal to 90% or more of the fair value of the leased property?

If none of the above were answered in the affirmative, then the lease is an *operating lease* and should be treated like an everyday rental.

What Additional Qualifications Apply to the Lessor?

The lessor will account for the transaction as either a finance lease or a sales type lease. However, the following two conditions must also exist:

1. The collectibility of the lease is relatively assured.
2. No important uncertainties exist.

Does the lease transfer title? The following table describes the alternative treatments for positive and negative answers:

	Yes	*No*
Asset classification:	Property and Equipment	Right in leased property
Liability	Note payable	Amount due on capitalized leases
Allocation of costs:	Depreciation	Amortization
Term:	Estimated life	Lease term

How Much Should Be Capitalized?

The lower of the following:

1. The sum of the present value at the beginning of the lease term.
2. The fair value of the leased property at the inception of the lease.

How to Determine the Discount Rate

This should be the smaller of the following:

1. The lessee's incremental borrowing rate: i.e., the rate the lessee would have to pay a similar purpose.
2. The lessor's implicit interest rate, if known by the lessee. The implicit rate is the rate if used to calculate the present value of the payments on the lease plus the residual amount, will equal the fair value of the property in the hands of the lessor.

Example of Capital Lease Recording by Lessee

Bargain purchase option	1,000
Estimated economic life	5
Lease term (months)	60
Fair market value of property	22,997
Lessee's incremental borrowing rate	10.00%
Interest rate implicit in lease	11.00%
Monthly lease payments	500
Present value	
Monthly lease payments	23,533
Bargain purchase option	621
Calculated present value of lease	24,154
Amount capitalized	22,997

Inasmuch as the fair market value is less than the present value of the payments plus residential value, it will be the amount used. A note payable in the amount of $22,997 will be recorded. The interest rate used will be the amount that most closely approximates the fair market value.

Because the terms of the lease (bargain purchase option) assume a transfer, the property will be depreciated over 5 years.

Sale Leaseback Transactions

When this occurs, the owner sells the property to another party and immediately leases it back from the buyer. The gain on sale is recorded as unearned income and amortized to profit over the term of the lease. The accounting for the lease elements of the transaction is the same as explained above.

Leveraged Leases

When a lease is leveraged, the property owner (A) leases it to a lessee (B). The property is used to collateralize a mortgage made by a long-term creditor (C). The debt is nonrecourse.

Lessee's books—Same accounting treatment.

Lessor's books—Considered a direct financing lease.

Investment in leveraged leases are recorded net of nonrecourse debt.

Disclosure Guidelines

Description of leases

Terms of leases

Classification—operating versus capital

Minimum annual rents if operating lease

O. Contingent Liabilities

Official Pronouncement:

FASB #5—Accounting for Contingencies—March, 1975

Definition: A loss contingency is an obligation that may arise because of the occurrence or non occurrence of one or more specific events.

Two Ways That Loss Contingencies Can Be Accounted For

1. *By a charge to income.* An entry to record the loss contingency should be made under the following conditions:

a. if it is *probable* that, as of the date of the financial statements, a loss has occurred, and the information has been discovered prior to the date of issuing the statements.

b. if the amount of loss can be reasonably estimated.

2. *By footnote disclosure* if it is *possible* that a loss *will* occur.

Disclosure Guidelines

a. explanation of the circumstances
b. estimated amount of loss that may occur
c. management's opinion of the probability that the loss will be sustained

Example:

The company is a defendant in a lawsuit claiming damages in the amount of $25,000. Management believes that this claim is without foundation.

Note: The materiality of the potential loss may change the auditor's opinion from an unqualified opinion, to a subject to opinion, to an outright disclaimer.

P. Stockholders' Equity

The equity section of the balance sheet portrays the residual interest of the stockholders in the net assets of the corporation.

Components

- Contributed
- Unrealized
- Earned

Definitions

Legal Capital: computed by multiplying the preferred and common shares outstanding by their respective par or stated values. It is the minimum amount a corporation can receive for its securities.
Contributed Capital: the net proceeds received by the corporation by issuing preferred and common stock. It consists of the following:

Preferred stock, at par
Common stock, at par or stated value
Premium on preferred stock
Excess paid in capital from the issuance of common stock

Unrealized Capital: Includes the following:

- Unrealized losses on write down of investments to market value
- Foreign currency translation adjustments

Earned Capital or Retained Earnings is a historical accumulation of the following:

Net income − dividends + or − prior period adjustments

Two Ways to Account for Treasury Stock

Treasury stock is a corporation's own previously issued and paid for capital stock that has been reacquired by the corporation and is being held for future reissuance. There are two alternative accounting techniques—the cost and the par value methods.

	Cost	*Par Value*
dr Treasury Stock	cost	Par value
dr Excess paid in	n/a	Original excess per share
dr Retained earnings	n/a	Excess paid—original issue price
cr Cash		Cash

Financial Statement Presentation

Cost = Retained earnings—treasury stock at cost
Par Value =
 common stock—treasury stock at par
 excess paid in—treasury stock at original excess
 Retained earnings, adjusted for difference

Four Features of Preferred Stock

Preferred stock is a senior equity security that usually gives dividend and liquidation preference to the holders.

1. *Cumulative versus non-cumulative features*

Cumulative preferred shareholders will receive their dividends before anything is paid to common shareholders. Any dividends unremitted at the end of the year, are in arrears, and carryforward to the next year.

Non-cumulative: unpaid dividend rights lapse at the end of each year.

2. *Call features*

Preferred stock may be retired at the *option of the corporation*. The call price is the amount that will be paid for each share, and usually sets a ceiling on the market price.

3. *Conversion features*

Preferred stock may be converted at the *option of the stockholders*. There is no special accounting treatment required.

4. *Participation features*

Preferred stockholders are entitled to receive either a fixed amount or a specified rate of dividends per share. If the stock is participating, it will share dividends with the common shareholders in a specified ratio.

Note: The dividend rate, expressed as a percentage or dollar amount per share is usually stated before the description.

For example, the Brad Corporation has issued 500,000 shares of $5 preferred stock. The par value is $100. It is fully participating. The company has earned $6,000,000.

Number of shares of preferred		500,000
Number of shares of common		400,000
Earnings		$6,000,000
Dividends to preferred (500,000 @ $5)		(2,500,000)
		3,500,000
Dividends to common		
Number of shares	400,000	
Dividends per share	$5	(2,000,000)
Remainder distributed equally		$1,500,000

	Preferred	Common
First preference	$2,500,000	
Common dividends		$2,000,000
Remainder	750,000	750,000
Total	$3,250,000	$2,750,000

When to Record Dividends Payable

The following dates are important:

- *Declaration date:* The date the board of directors formally declares that dividends will be paid to stockholders of record. *This is the date when the dividends become a liability.*

- *Ex-dividend date:* The date the stock stops selling with dividends attached.
- *Date of record:* The cut-off date. Only stockholders of record as of this date can participate in dividends.
- *Payment date.*

How to Account for a Small and a Large Stock Dividend

The key question here is whether the issuance of additional shares will dilute the market price of the stock.

Small stock dividend: A small stock dividend is less than 20% to 25% of the previously outstanding shares. It is therefore reasoned that the value of the stock will not be diluted. Thus, the dividend will be calculated as:

$$\text{Shares issued} * \text{Market price per share}$$

Large stock dividend: A large stock dividend is assumed to be dilutive. Therefore, it is treated the same way as a stock split, there is no accounting entry required.

What Is a Compensatory Stock Option Plan and How Should It Be Accounted For

Official Pronouncement:

APB #25—Accounting for Stock Issued to Employees—October, 1972

A compensatory stock option is considered a portion of a selected employees earnings package.

Total Compensation at the Measurement Date

$$(\text{market price} - \text{option price}) * \text{number of shares}$$

When Is the Measurement Date?

First date on which both the following are known:

1. The number of shares any individual employee is entitled to receive.

2. The option or purchase price, if any.

Entries:

dr. Deferred compensation	xxx	
cr. Common stock option warrants		xxx

to record the total compensation at the measurement date.

Note: Deferred compensation is a negative stockholders' equity account and is subtracted from the common stock option account. It is amortized to compensation expense over the expected service period.

Example: An employee is granted a stock option to acquire 1,500 shares of ABC Corporation's common stock at $50 per share. The market value of the stock at the measurement date, January 1, 1989, is $85. The expected service period is 2 years.

Number of shares	1,500
Market value	85
Option price	50
Differential	35

Total compensation = 1,500 shares * $35 per share

	1/1/89	12/31/89	12/31/90
Deferred compensation	52,500		
Common stock options	(52,500)		
Compensation expense		26,250	26,250
Deferred compensation		(26,250)	(26,250)
Cash (1,500 shares * $50 per share)			75,000
Common stock options			52,500
Common stock ($10 par)			(15,000)
Excess paid in capital			(112,500)
Presentation in contributed capital			
Common stock options	52,500	52,500	0
Less: deferred compensation	(52,500)	(26,250)	0
	0	26,250	0

Figure 4-13—***Stock Options***

Disclosure Guidelines for Stockholders' Equity

1. Title of each stock issue
2. Par or stated value
3. Number of shares authorized
4. Number issued
5. Preferred stock
    a. call price
    b. dividend rate
    c. conversion features, if any
    d. cumulative features
    e. dividend arrearage
6. Treasury stock
    a. carrying basis; cost or par value
    b. number of shares
7. Stock options
    a. number of shares reserved
    b. option price
    c. dates of grants
    d. expiration periods
    e. number of shares exercised during period
8. Retained earnings appropriations
9. Stock dividends
10. Dividend restrictions

Overall Disclosure Guidelines

1. Assets and liabilities should be segregated into current and noncurrent amounts.
2. Assets expected not to be realized and liabilities expected not to be paid within one year should be classified as noncurrent.
3. Asset valuation accounts should be deducted from their related assets.
4. Describe and show the amount of assets pledged to secure notes and other liens.
5. Contingent liabilities should be disclosed if material.
6. The stockholders' equity section should be classified into contributed, unrealized and earned capital.

CHAPTER 5

Special Reporting Situations

Introduction

While most accounting problems can be solved by analyses of the structural framework and FASB pronouncements, due to their unusual nature certain subjects need to be separately considered. The following will be discussed in this chapter:

- Partnerships
- Financial statement combinations
- Oil and gas industry accounting
- International accounting
- Governmental accounting
- Accounting for not for profit organizations
- Accounting for rate regulated enterprises
- Insolvencies and bankruptcy
- Defeasance agreements

Organization of Each Section

1. A listing of the applicable official pronouncements
2. Some theoretical background
3. Computational examples
4. Disclosure guidelines

How to Solve Those Difficult Partnership Accounting Problems

Official Pronouncement:

The Uniform Partnership Act (1914): This act has been adopted throughout the country except by Georgia and Louisiana.

Definition: A partnership is an association of two or more persons to carry on as co-owners a business for profit.

How to Help the Attorney Use "Good Accounting" to Prepare the Partnership Agreement

The attorney has the primary responsibility to prepare the articles of co-partnership. However, the accountant is the person who has a long-term relationship with the client and is more aware of that client's financial as well as emotional state.

We are in an excellent position to help to guide the attorney by asking your client the following questions:

1. *Why do you want to form your business as a partnership?*

As you are well aware, if things do not turn out as expected, your client could be personally responsible for all liabilities of the partnership, regardless of his or her capital contribution. There are better ways to go into business with another, while, at the same time, avoiding the inherent hazards in partnerships.

For example:

Corporations

Limited partnerships

2. *Will each partner receive fair value for assets contributed to the partnership?*

If the partners contribute non-cash assets, these assets should be carefully valued. If a partners are credited for less than their investments are really worth, somewhere down the line someone will suffer.

For example, Jones and Smith form a partnership. Jones contributes $50,000 cash. Smith invests a parcel of land that cost $50,000, but is now worth $80,000. Smith is given credit for $50,000. The partners agree to divide profits equally. If the partnership sells the land immediately, the following will result:

		Jones	Smith
Capital Accounts		$50,000	$50,000
Sale of Land			
Sales price	80,000		
Partnership Basis	50,000		
Gain	30,000		
Distributed		15,000	15,000
Total Capital Accounts		$65,000	65,000
Value of Smith investment			80,000
Inequity to Smith			$(15,000)

3. *How will profits be divided?*

If all partners' investments are equal and each agrees to work as hard and make as many intangible (creative) contributions as the others, then the profits should probably be divided equally. However, when conditions are not identical, then the following should affect the profit distribution formulas:

a. Capital contributions
b. Time devoted to partnership business
c. Talent brought into partnership

Note: While everything might be amicable at the beginning, things do change. And, all too often, differences, real or perceived, may lead to future unhappiness and lawsuits. Although, we are not licensed as psychologists, we must be aware of our clients' feelings and desires. Most important, we should always urge them to openly communicate.

4. *How are the partners compensated if the association dissolves?*

According to the Uniform Partnership Act, a partnership will dissolve when one or more of the following events occur:

a. the partnership is liquidated
b. a partner withdraws from the partnership
c. a new partner is admitted
d. a partner dies
e. a partner becomes bankrupt

If any of these incidents take place, the remaining partners should be compensated fairly for their interest. Your task is to see that a good evaluation is made. It is therefore important to append a buy-and-sell agreement to the partnership contract. That agreement should contain provisions for periodical revaluations. Furthermore, the partnership agreement should contain stipulations for insurance funding in the event of a partner's death.

Four Ways to Divide Partnership Profits

Partners can agree to divide profits in any way they desire. Just as long as they describe the method(s) in their agreement, and, in the absence of any conflicting income tax regulations or other laws, anything goes. The distribution can be made by one or more of the following computations:

1. *Agreed-upon percentages:* The negotiated profit sharing percentages are a major segment of the articles of co-partnership. They could

be influenced by capital balances, respective talents, or a host of other things.

Caveat: Under common law, if the percentages are not spelled out, then all profits and losses will be divided equally.

2. *Partners' salaries:* The situation may call for different profit distributions because one or more of the partners devotes more time and effort than the others.

For example, there are three partners: Able, Baker, and Charlie. The profit sharing ratio is 40:40:20. Baker is entitled to salary of $50,000. The profit before salary allowance is $45,000. The division is calculated as follows:

	TOTAL	A	B	C
Profit	45,000			
Salary to Baker	(50,000)		50,000	
Loss	(5,000)	(2,000)	(2,000)	(1,000)
Total Distribution	45,000	(2,000)	48,000	(1,000)

Remember: Under most of these agreements, salaries to partners are not considered expenses, but, instead, divisions of profits.

3. *Partner bonuses:* A bonus, computed as a certain percentage of income, is one way to compensate a partner who is instrumental in the business's success. There are generally two way to compute bonuses:

a. As a percentage of profit. However, as Alternative A shows, this may provide excess profits to that partner.
b. As a percentage of profit, after deducting the salary and the bonus.

Example: Smith is entitled to a bonus of 10% of profits after deducting his salary and his bonus.

The equation is:

$$\text{Bonus} = (\text{Profit} - \text{Salary} - \text{Bonus}) * \text{Bonus Percentage}$$

Profit before salary and bonus	100,000
Salary to Smith	20,000
Bonus to Smith	10.00%

Alternatives	A	B
Profit	$100,000	$100,000
Salary to Smith	(20,000)	(20,000)
Bonus to Smith	(10,000)	(7,273)
Net	$ 70,000	$ 72,727

Payments to Smith		
Salary	$ 20,000	$ 20,000
Bonus	10,000	7,273
Total payments	$ 30,000	$ 27,273
Bonus percentage	14.29%	10.00%

Let P = profit
S = salary
B = bonus

$$B = .10\ (P - S - B)$$
$$= .10\ (10{,}000 - 20{,}000 - B)$$
$$B = 8000 - .1B$$
$$1.1B = 8.00$$
$$B = 7.273$$

4. *Interest on partners' capital*

If the partners' capital contributions are uneven, then a provision for interest on this disparity may be necessary.

There are three alternative ways to calculate interest on capital.

a. on beginning balances
b. on ending balances
c. on weighted-average balances

Example: Refer back to the Jones and Smith partnership. The articles of co-partnership state that each partners shall receive 12% interest on their capital accounts.

	Jones	Smith
Capital Balance		
December 31, 1988	60,000	40,000
Investment April 1, 1989	20,000	
Investment, July 1, 1989	10,000	10,000
Balance, Ending	$90,000	$50,000
Interest		
On beginning	7,200	4,800
On ending	10,800	6,000
On weighted average	9,600	5,400

Weighted Average Calculation

	Jones		Smith	
	total %	of year	total %	of year
12/31/88	60,000	25.00%	40,000	50.00%
4/1/89	80,000	25.00%		
7/1/89	90,000	50.00%	50,000	50.00%

Weighted Average Capital

Jones	80,000
Smith	45,000

SUGGESTION: In addition, there are other problems that may result when the net partners' investments are not synchronized. Assume that Jones and Smith divide the profits equally. Look at the following:

Capital Balances	12/31/89	%
Jones	90,000	64.29%
Smith	50,000	35.71%
Total	140,000	100.00%

Jones has over 64% of the capital, but he is only entitled to 50% of the profits. While this is somewhat resolved by allowing interest on capital balances, other problems (admission of new partners or liquidation) might surface. The following are better alternatives:

a. Bring the capital accounts down to $50,000 each and classify Jones's extra $40,000 balance to a loan payable account.
b. Bring the capital accounts up to $90,000 each and classify Smith's shortage to a loan receivable account.

How to Record the Admission of a Partner

When a new partner is admitted, there are a number of options. These are shown in the matrix below.

I. Interest purchased from individual partner
II. Interest purchased from all partners
III. Interest purchased from partnership

I. *Interest purchased from individual partner*

The new partner merely steps into the shoes of the original partner. Thus, no partnership accounting is required.

II. *Interest purchased from all partners*

In this case, none of the investment funds are received by the partnership itself.

There are two alternative ways to handle the transaction:

A. *Do not Revalue the Partnership Accounts:* Any differences will be treated as bonuses which affect the existing partners' accounts.

B. *Revalue the Partnership Accounts:* Any difference will require the following:

1. Adjustment of the tangible assets and liabilities to their fair market value.
2. The recording of goodwill.

The solution approach is shown in the following array:

Let P = new partner
PI = new partner investment
OB = old partnership balance
NB = new partnership balance = $OB + PI$
$\%$ = P ownership percentage

Form of Purchase	*Revalue*	
From partners	yes	$PI = (OB/\%) * \%$
	no	$PI = OB * \%$
From partnership	yes	$PI = (NB/\%) * \%$
	no	$PI = NB * \%$

Example: Assume that Doe invests $60,000 for a 50% interest. The original capital accounts total $100,000.

- *From Partners—Revaluation:* Inasmuch as Doe has contributed $60,000 for a 50% interest, the total capital accounts will be revalued to double his interest to equal $120,000.
- *From Partners—No revaluation:* The capital accounts will remain at a $100,000.
- *From Partnership—Revaluation:* After Doe's admission, the original partners' capital accounts of $100,000 will now total 50% of the net worth which will become $200,000. Doe will receive a credit of $100,000 and goodwill will be created for the difference.
- *From Partnership—No Revaluation:* Doe will be given credit for 50% of the now $160,000 total capital accounts.

In each of the above cases, the original partners' capital accounts will be debited to bring their capital accounts to the proper proportions.

Entries:

	From Partners		From Partnership	
Revalue?	y	n	y	n
Cash			60,000	60,000
Goodwill	20,000		40,000	
Jones	20,000	25,000		10,000
Smith	20,000	25,000		10,000
Doe	(60,000)	(50,000)	(100,000)	(80,000)

Capital Accounts	Jones	Smith	Doe
From partners revalue			
Original balance	$50,000	$50,000	
Doe investment	(20,000)	(20,000)	$ 60,000
Total	$30,000	$30,000	$ 60,000
%	25.00%	25.00%	50.00%
Do not revalue			
Original balance	$50,000	$50,000	
Doe investment	(25,000)	(25,000)	$ 50,000
Total	$25,000	$25,000	$ 50,000
%	25.00%	25.00%	50.00%
From Partnership Revalue			
Original balance	$50,000	$50,000	
Doe investment			$100,000
Total	$50,000	$50,000	$100,000
%	25.00%	25.00%	50.00%
Do not revalue			
Original balance	$50,000	$50,000	
Doe investment	(10,000)	(10,000)	$ 80,000
Total	$40,000	$40,000	$ 80,000
%	25.00%	25.00%	50.00%

Partnership Liquidation Procedures

1. Liquidate all non-cash assets.
2. Recognize and record gains and losses which should be allocated to each partner in his or her respective profit and loss sharing ratio.
3. Pay expenses of liquidation.
4. Pay all liabilities in the following priority:
    a. amounts owed to creditors other than partners
    b. loans from partners

Note: If the above process forces any individual partners' capital accounts into deficits, the partnership, by right, should be compensated by those partners. However, if any are personally insolvent, then their deficits will have to be absorbed by the remaining partners according to their respective profit and loss ratios.

How to Prepare an Installment Liquidation Plan

An installment plan is used when a liquidating partnership has non-cash assets (e.g., real estate) which will take time to sell, liabilities that will not be paid off immediately, and partners who desire to begin to cash out their interests *before* all assets are sold. The plan should be constructed in a way to guarantee that partners do not get their money before all creditors and liquidation expenses are paid.

Using Loss Absorption Calculations

Loss absorption calculations determine the maximum partnership loss that any partner can absorb, and is used to prioritize payments to those partners that can absorb the greatest damage.

For example, assume that Able, Baker, and Charlie have decided to liquidate their partnership. Profits and losses are allocated in a 40:40:20 ratio. Assume the following capital and loan balances:

	Able	Baker	Charlie
Capital accounts	80,000	30,000	30,000
Loan receivable	(10,000)		
New capital	70,000	30,000	30,000

The partners' net capital accounts are divided by their respective profit and loss percentages, to determine the maximum amount of loss each can absorb.

	Able	Baker	Charlie
P & L ratios	40.00%	40.00%	20.00%
Maximum loss ability	175,000	75,000	150,000

This indicates the partnership would have to lose $175,000 in order to wipe out Able's capital. Since his ability to absorb is the highest, distributions should be made to Able until his and Charlie's ability to absorb losses are the same.

	I. Able		II. Charlie	
Distribution Plan	Capital	Ability	Capital	Ability
Balance	70,000	175,000		
Distribution	(10,000)	(25,000)		
	60,000	150,000	30,000	150,000
Distribution	(30,000)	(75,000)	(15,000)	(75,000)
Balance	30,000	75,000	15,000	75,000

Balance after distributions

	Capital	Ability
Able	30,000	75,000
Baker	30,000	75,000
Charlie	15,000	75,000

From this point on, all distributions can be made in the profit and loss ratios.

How to Understand Financial Statement Combinations and Prepare Consolidated Financial Statements

Official Pronouncements:

APB #16—Accounting for Business Combinations—August, 1970

APB 18—The Equity Method of Accounting for Investments in Common Stock—March, 1971

FASB 10—Extension of "Grandfather" Provisions for Business Combinations (Amendment of APB #16)—October, 1975

FASB 38—Accounting for Preacquisition Contingencies of Purchased Subsidiaries—September, 1980

FASB 79—Elimination of Certain Disclosures for Business Combinations (Amendment of APB #16)—February, 1984

FASB 94—Consolidation of All Majority Owned Subsidiaries—October, 1987

A Checklist for Your Clients Involved in Mergers and Acquisition (M&A) Activities

Review the following:

I. *The financial statements of the potential acquiree*

A. Analyze the balance sheet

1. Are the assets fairly valued?

a. Are the net carrying value of the accounts receivable collectible?
b. Inventories

(1) Are there inventory cushions or other misstatements that must be considered?
(2) Have all obsolete and slow moving items been accounted for?

c. Have all non-recoverable prepaid expenses been removed?
d. What is the fair value of property and equipment?

(1) Have changes in technology either enhanced or reduced their worth?
(2) Is there deferred maintenance that should be considered?

e. Investments

(1) Are they fairly valued?
(2) If they are not readily marketable have they been discounted?
(3) If these assets are disposed, what will be the impact on income?

f. Have goodwill and other intangibles been written off or devalued?

2. Are there substantial unreported liabilities?

a. Are all accounts payable recorded?
b. Are there any potential liabilities that should be recorded? e.g. guarantees, warranties, lawsuits, income tax audits

3. Hidden reserves. Are there any unrecorded assets that may have significant effects on the balance sheet?

    (1) usable plant and equipment
    (2) research and development projects
    (3) license agreements
    (4) long-term leases at advantageous terms
    (5) oil and gas properties and reserves.

4. Are there any balances with officers or stockholders that should be eliminated?

B. Review the Statements of Income

1. Are there unusual items that are not expected to continue?
2. Are there inventory distortions that affect income reporting?
3. Are there tax reduction transactions that should be adjusted?

    a. auto allowances
    b. entertainment and travel
    c. other expense accounts
    d. group medical, disability, and life insurance
    e. officer salaries

4. Analyze environmental forces that may positively or negatively impact earnings.

II. Are there any outstanding agreements that may influence valuation or future income?

A. Bank covenants and restrictions
B. Employee stock options
C. Pension and/or medical insurance commitments
D. Employment contracts

III. Can all the rights and operations of the company be acquired?

A. Lease agreements?
B. Employment contracts?
C. Purchase contracts and agreements?

IV. The price

A. What is the price?

1. How was it negotiated?
2. Is it reasonable after considering the previous questions?

B. What are the terms? If not cash,

1. Can the future payments be made with reasonable certainty?
2. What is the collateral on the notes?
3. Are personal guaranties required?

C. Is stock to be used?

1. Is there sufficient evidence that the future prospects of the acquiring company support the payment?
2. Will the stock have to registered?

V. What is to be acquired?

A. The entire company?

1. If yes, are there audited statements?
2. Are there "hold harmless" agreements for potential unrecorded liabilities?

B. Assets only?

1. Have they been adequately appraised?
2. Are there "hold harmless" agreements on potential liabilities?

Understanding M & A Terminology

This section will explain the various terms and how they should be used:

- *Merger:* The assets or stock of one company (B) is acquired by another company (A), then B is liquidated and merged into A.
- *Consolidation:* Two companies exist, A & B. A new company C is formed. A & B are liquidated and consolidated into C.
- *Acquisition:* The stock of one company, (S) is acquired by another company, (P). Company S becomes a subsidiary of P.

  Note: This is the form of M & A that is commonly accounted for in consolidation accounting.

Forms of Acquisitions

Most consolidation accounting is designated in one of two ways:

a. Pooling of interests
b. Purchase

Pooling of Interests

The pooling of interest method assumes that the ownership interests of the combined companies are united and all assets and liabilities are brought together at the same carrying value as shown on their separate records.

Requirements

1. The parties must have been independent companies for at least two years prior to the combination.
2. The exchange must be effected with common stock only. Furthermore, substantially all of the acquired company's stock must be obtained by the acquiror. The term, "substantially all" means at least 90% of that stock.
3. In addition, the transaction must be a *fait accompli*, with no outstanding repurchase, exchange, or rights limitation agreements.

Purchase

When this method is used, one entity acquires the net assets of the other(s). Consideration can include cash, bonds, notes, and stock of the acquiring corporation.

Reporting Differences

1. *Net Income*

Pooling: The consolidated statements will portray *all* income of both the parent and subsidiary for the current statement and prior period comparative statements, if included.

Purchase: The consolidated statement for any fiscal period will report all of the parent's income plus its share of the subsidiaries net profit or loss *subsequent* to the purchase date.

For example, the fiscal year of Parent and Subsidiary are both December 31, 1989. Parent acquires 100% of Subsidiary stock at October 1, 1989. Income is assumed to be earned equally throughout the year. The income is reported as follows:

Parent Income		100,000
Subsidiary Income		24,000
Reporting	Pooling	Purchase
Parent	100,000	100,000
Subsidiary	24,000	6,000
Total	124,000	106,000

2. *Assets and Liabilities*

Pooling: Net assets and liabilities are reported at their respective net book values. There is no new basis of accounting under the pooling method.

Purchase: Net assets and liabilities of the subsidiary are reported at the parent company's cost at the date of acquisition. The cost of purchase is allocated as follows:

1. Subsidiary's assets and liabilities—at fair market value.
2. Excess of purchase price over fair market value of subsidiaries assets and liabilities—to goodwill.

How to Account for a Purchase Acquisition on the Books of the Investor

Official Pronouncement:

APB #18—The Equity Method of Accounting for Investments in Common Stock—March, 1971

Note: Refer to Chapter 4 for various other investment valuation alternatives.

Is Investment Made for Control?

No: The investment account is valued at the lower of cost or market.

Yes: The Equity Method is used to keep track of the cost. According to APB #18, the equity method is to be employed when the investor achieves *control* of the investee corporation, which, as defined in that opinion, is attained when 20% or control of the voting stock is acquired. At that point, the stockholder can now exercise significant influence over the investee's operations and policies.

Note: Although 20% or more is considered the cutoff point, there are times under that situation when control is not achieved. For example, if the subsidiary is a foreign company and unable to remit to the parent, control has *not* been realized.

Accounting for the Investment Under the Equity Method

Investment = Cost or opening balance + share of income − share of divid

Example: Assume the following:

Subsidiary's net income		100,000
Dividends paid		50,000
Ownership interest	10%	20%
Share of income earned		20,000
Share of dividend income	5,000	
Income from investment	5,000	20,000
Investment cost	50,000	100,000
Share of income		20,000
Dividend income		(10,000)
Investment balance	50,000	110,000

Preparing Consolidated Statements

When one company (P) owns 50% or more of another company (S), although each remains an independent entity, consolidated statements are usually required. The objective of the consolidation process is to favor substance over form and present financial information for a single, integrated unit or entity. That entity will only report balances and transactions as they connect to the outside world. Therefore, there

1. Should be no intercompany profits and losses.
2. Should be no intercompany loans.
3. Should be no intercompany transactions.
4. Will be no investment in subsidiary account.
5. Will be no subsidiary stockholders' equity.

Consolidation Steps

1. Make sure all necessary adjustments for all companies have been made and entered on their individual ledgers.
2. Eliminate reciprocal accounts. i.e. intercompany loans receivable and payable, and intercompany sales and purchases.
3. Record the fair market value of the subsidiary's assets and liabilities and the resulting goodwill at acquisition date.
4. Amortize and depreciate the accounts resulting from Step 3.

5. Eliminate the following:
    a. Investment in subsidiary
    b. Equity of subsidiary
6. Record minority interests. Minority interests are defined as the percentage of securities owned by outsiders.

For example, if P acquires 80% of S, the minority interest is 20%.

When the above process is completed, the following should be reflected:

a. net consolidated income = parent's separate income + share of subsidiary income
b. consolidated retained earnings = parent's retained earnings

Note: These eliminations will be made to the worksheets. No book entries are recorded. Therefore, they will need to be repeated every time consolidated statements are prepared.

Example: The above consolidation procedures will reflect transactions at the following times:

January 1, 1989, the acquisition date

December 31, one year later

Company P acquired 80% of the stock of Company S for a total consideration of $252,000. S's balance sheet at cost and fair market value at January 1, 1989 is shown below:

Worksheet
January 1, 1989

		Subsidiary	
	Parent	Cost	FMV
Cash	8,000	12,500	12,500
Accounts receivable		52,750	52,750
Investment in S	252,000		
Land		170,000	215,000
Investment in S			
Accounts payable		(15,250)	(15,250)
Common stock	(60,000)	(10,000)	(10,000)
Excess paid in	(200,000)	(90,000)	(90,000)
Retained earnings		(120,000)	(165,000)
	0	0	0

S's net worth at fair market value totaled $265,000. First, allocate the purchase price to 80% of that FMV. Then record the remainder as goodwill. This will lead to consolidated worksheets at the acquisition date.

P Acquired 80% of S		
Total Consideration		252,000
Fair Market Value of S	265,000	
Allocated to Net Assets (80%)		212,000
Goodwill		40,000

The eliminating and consolidating entries are then made. Schedules for fair market value adjustments and minority interests are shown below:

Fair Market Value Adjustments

	Cost	FMV	Diff	@80%
Land	170,000	215,000	45,000	36,000

Minority Interest Calculation

Common Stock	10,000
Excess Paid in	90,000
Retained Earnings	120,000
Total S Equity	220,000
Minority Interest @ 20%	44,000

The following consolidated working papers at acquisition date are now prepared:

P Company and Subsidiary
Consolidating Workpapers
January 1, 1989

	P	S	Elims.	Cons.
Cash	8,000	12,500		20,500
Accounts receivable		52,750		52,750
Investment in S	252,000	0	(252,000)	0
Land		170,000	36,000	206,000
Goodwill			40,000	40,000
Accounts payable		(15,250)		(15,250)
Minority interest			(44,000)	(44,000)
Common stock	(60,000)	(10,000)	10,000	(60,000)
Excess paid in	(200,000)	(90,000)	90,000	(200,000)
Retained earnings		(120,000)	120,000	0
	0	0	0	0

A consolidated balance sheet is derived from the above workpapers.

P & Subsidiary
Consolidated Balance Sheet
January 1, 1989

Assets		
Cash		$ 20,500
Accounts receivable		52,750
Land		206,000
Goodwill		40,000
Total Assets		$319,250
Liabilities & Stockholders Equity		
Liabilities		
Accounts Payable		$15,250
Minority Interest		44,000
Stockholders' Equity		
Common Stock	$60,000	
Excess Paid in	200,000	
Retained Earnings	0	
Total Stockholders' Equity		260,000
		$319,250

How to Prepare Subsequent Consolidated Statements

The same procedures should be used whenever consolidated statements are prepared. If there are intercompany transfers of assets or liabilities, the carrying amount should be reduced by any profit charged to the affiliate but which has not been realized on sale to the ultimate buyer. The accounts that may be affected by these transfers are:

1. *Inventories:* Any profits in either the beginning or ending inventories should be eliminated as follows:

   Beginning inventory

   Dr: Retained earnings
   Cr: Cost of Goods sold

   Ending inventory

   Dr: Cost of goods sold
   Cr: Inventory

2. *Property and Equipment:* The following will have to be eliminated:

    a. unrealized profit on intercompany equipment sale
    b. depreciation on unrealized profit

3. *Bonds payable:* All intercompany bonds payable must be eliminated. This elimination is treated as a retirement. The difference between the carrying value of the liability (Face value − unamortized discount or Face value + unamortized discount) and the investment basis will be recorded as a profit or loss on the consolidated statements. Furthermore, any intercompany interest expense and income, should also be eliminated.

Example: Company S sold merchandise to P at a profit. P's December 31 worksheet reports inventory at P's cost. Therefore, that profit must be eliminated.

Sales to P	$250,000	100.00%
Cost to S	100,000	40,00%
Gross Profit	$150,000	60.00%

Unrealized Profit	
Inventory, P's cost	$50,000
Cost to S (40%)	20,000
Unrealized Profit	$30,000

Downstream Versus Upstream Intercompany Transactions

The net consolidated income will be affected by which company initiates the intercompany transaction.

Downstream: If the sale is made, and profit earned by the parent company, the entire profit from that sale is eliminated and there is no impact on the minority interests.

Upstream: If, on the other hand, the transaction is initiated by the subsidiary, the unrealized profits on assets remaining on the parents books are eliminated. This affects the parent's share of the subsidiary's net income, and the minority interest.

Example:

Income from S	
S Income	$135,000
Inventory profit	(30,000)
Total	105,000
P's Share (80%)	$84,000

How to Compute Consolidated Income: The consolidated income will be the same as the income reported by the parent.

Net Consolidated Income		
P Separate Income		$160,000
Income from S		
S Income	$135,000	
Inventory profit	(30,000)	
Total	105,000	
P Share	84,000	
Goodwill Amort	(1,000)	83,000
Consolidated Income		$243,000

Treatment of Goodwill According to APB #17: Goodwill is to be amortized over a period not exceeding 40 years. Furthermore, since consolidated entries are only made to the workpapers, the net unamortized balance of the goodwill must be reflected on the consolidated trial balance each year.

Above Example: The maximum life has been used.

Goodwill	
Goodwill, January 1, 1989	$40,000
Amortization	(1,000)
Goodwill, December 31, 1989	$39,000

Investment in Subsidiary on the Parent's Books: A parent company, required to use the equity method, must record amortization on fair market valuations and goodwill on its own set of books.

Investment in S	
Balance, January 1, 1989	$252,000
Share of S Income (per above)	83,000
Dividends (80%)	(40,000)
December 31, 1989	$295,000

Minority Interest in Income: This is 20% of the net subsidiary income

S Income	$105,000
Minority Interest	$21,000

Minority Interest: This is 20% of the beginning of the year equity plus earnings minus dividends declared.

S Equity	
Common Stock	$ 10,000
Excess Paid in	90,000
Retained Earnings	120,000
Dividends Paid	(50,000)
S Income	105,000
Total S Equity	275,000
Minority Interest	$ 55,000

The following worksheet and financial statements result:

P Company and Subsidiary
Consolidated Workpapers
December 31, 1989

	P	S	elims	cons
Cash	258,000	35,000		293,000
Accounts receivable		35,000		35,000
Due from parent		100,000	(100,000)	0
Inventory	50,000		(30,000)	20,000
Investment in S	295,000		(295,000)	0
Land		170,000	36,000	206,000
Goodwill			39,000	39,000
Due to subsidiary	(100,000)		100,000	0
Accounts payable		(35,000)		(35,000)
Minority interest			(55,000)	(55,000)
Common stock	(60,000)	(10,000)	10,000	(60,000)
Excess paid in capital	(200,000)	(90,000)	90,000	(200,000)
Retained earnings	0	(120,000)	120,000	0
Dividends paid		50,000	(50,000)	0
	243,000	135,000	(135,000)	243,000
Sales	(400,000)	(250,000)	250,000	(400,000)
Purchases	250,000	100,000	(250,000)	100,000
Ending Inventory	(50,000)		30,000	(20,000)
Income from S	(83,000)		83,000	0
Expenses	40,000	15,000		55,000
Goodwill Amortization			1,000	1,000
Minority Income			21,000	21,000
	(243,000)	(135,000)	135,000	(243,000)

P & Subsidiary
Consolidated Balance Sheet
December 31, 1989

Cash		$293,000
Accounts receivable		35,000
Inventory		20,000
Land		206,000
Goodwill		39,000
Total Assets		$593,000
Liabilities		
Accounts Payable		$ 35,000
Minority Interest		55,000
Stockholder's Equity		
Common Stock	$ 60,000	
Excess Paid in	200,000	
Retained Earnings	243,000	
Total Stockholders' Equity		503,000
		$593,000

P Company & Subsidiary
Statement of Income
For Year Ended December 31, 1989

Sales	$400,000
Cost of Goods Sold	80,000
Gross Profit	320,000
Expenses	
Operating Expenses	55,000
Goodwill Amortization	1,000
Total Operating Expenses	56,000
Operating Income	264,000
Less: Minority interest in income	21,000
Net Income	243,000
Retained Earnings, Beginning	0
Retained Earnings, Ending	$243,000

Footnote: Principles of Consolidation—The consolidated financial statements include the accounts of P and its subsidiary S. The transaction is being accounted for as a purchase. All significant intercompany accounts and transactions have been eliminated.

How to Account for Oil and Gas Activities

Official Pronouncements:

FASB #19 Financial Accounting and Reporting by Oil and Gas Producing Companies—December, 1977

FASB #25 Suspension of Certain Accounting Requirements for Oil and Gas Companies (Amendment of FASB #19)—February, 1979

FASB #69—Disclosures about Oil and Gas Producing Activities—November, 1982

Knowing the Key Ingredients

- *Properties:* Ownership interests in rights to extract oil and gas. Also includes nonoperating interests, e.g. royalty or production interest.
- *Reservoir:* Separate confined underground formation
- *Fields:* Groups of reservoirs

Determining the Quantities in the Ground

Generally, the amount of *proved reserves* define the estimated quantities of crude oil, and various forms of natural gas which have been determined to exist with reasonable certainty by geological and engineering data. These reserves are considered *proved* if there is supported economic productibility. Depending upon the facts, they are treated as either developed or undeveloped.

- *developed*—expected to be recovered through existing wells with existing equipment.
- *undeveloped*—expected to be recovered from new wells.

Cost Flows

Oil and gas activities generally follow the ensuing cost flow:

Acquisition **Exploration** **Development** **Production**

Acquisition—Costs to acquire the property

Exploration—Costs incurred to explore property

Development—Costs to Prepare proved reserves for completion

Production—Includes all costs lifting the oil and the gas to the surface

Which Costs Should Be Capitalized?

Under GAAP, as it has evolved, there are two main alternatives:

Full Costing (FC): FC capitalizes all costs (including those used in unsuccessful efforts) and allocates them to revenue producing properties.

For example, dry hole costs are capitalized under the FC method.

Successful Efforts (SE): The SE method expenses costs where there are no identifiable benefits.

For example, dry hole costs are *not* capitalized under the SE method.

How to Account for Oil and Gas Activities Under the SE Method

The following "Successful Efforts Overview" chart (Exhibit 5-1) has been reprinted from:

Gallium, Rebecca A

Stevenson, John W

Fundamentals of Oil & Gas Accounting

Second Edition

Penn Wells Books—1986

How to Amortize Successful Efforts Costs

Amortization or depletion is computed on the units of production method.

The unit rate is computed as follows:

$$\frac{\text{Cost} - \text{Residual Value}}{\text{Units}}$$

The residual value includes the salvage value of drilling rigs and any recovery value in property interests.

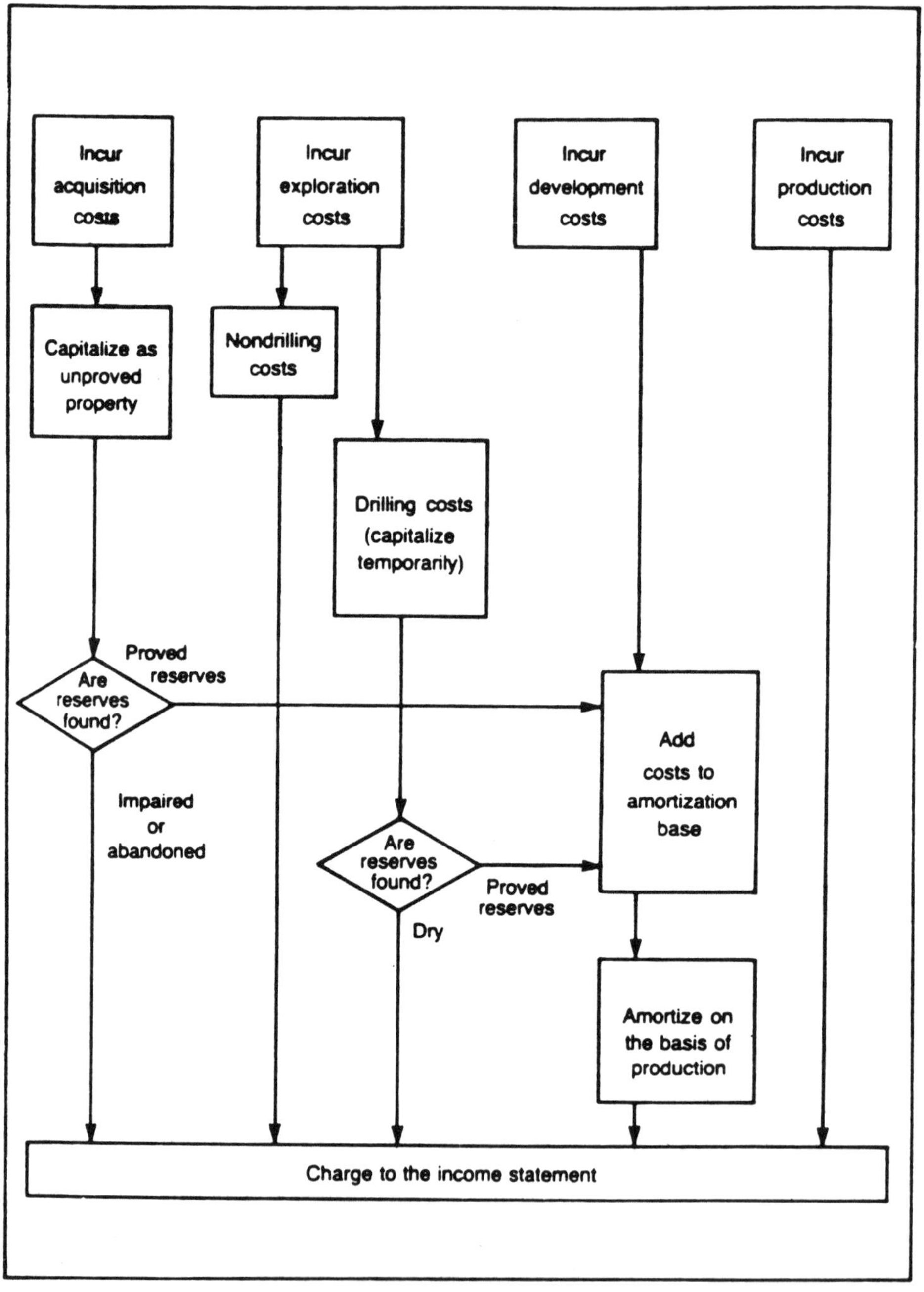
Incur acquisition costs
Incur exploration costs
Incur development costs
Incur production costs
Capitalize as unproved property
Nondrilling costs
Drilling costs (capitalize temporarily)
Proved reserves
Are reserves found?
Impaired or abandoned
Add costs to amortization base
Are reserves found?
Proved reserves
Dry
Amortize on the basis of production
Charge to the income statement

Exhibit 5-1

Accounting Example

The Big Hole Oil Company incurred the following costs:

Acquisition Costs	$75,000
Exploration Costs	
Dry holes	$1,750,000
Successful	$600,000
Development Costs	$150,000
Production Costs	25,000

Proven Reserves	3,200,000 bbls.
Sales price per bbl	$20
Sales in period (bbl)	120,000

Calculation of Amortization		per unit
Acquisition Costs	$75,000	$0.023
Successful exploration costs	600,000	0.188
Development costs	150,000	0.047
Total Amortization base	$825,000	$0.258

Big Hole Company
Statement of Income

Revenues		$2,400,000
Expenses		
Dry holes	$1,750,000	
Production costs	25,000	
Amortization	30,938	
Total expenses		1,805,938
Net Income		$594,062

Partial Balance sheets	
Oil Properties	$825,000
Less: Accumulated Amortization	30,938
	$794,062

The Effect of Temporary Differences on Income Tax Accounting

Intangible drilling costs on successful efforts include acquisition exploration and development expenditures which are capitalized for GAAP purposes, but, expensed on the company's income tax return. The resulting differences must be use tax effect accounting (See Chapter 3.)

Disclosure Guidelines

The following information should be disclosed:

1. Proved oil and gas reserve quantities
2. Capitalized costs
3. Costs incurred for property acquisition, exploration, and development activities
4. Results of operations
5. A standardized reserve valuation using discounted cash flows

How to Account for International Operations

Official Pronouncements:

FASB #52—Foreign Currency Translation—November, 1981

What Is a Foreign Transaction?

A foreign transaction is one that is denominated in a currency other than that of the reporting entity.

Example 1: An American company buys goods from a British firm. The transaction is denominated in British pounds. That transaction *is* a foreign exchange.

Example 2: An American company buys goods from a British firm. The transaction is priced and will be settled in dollars. That transaction is *not* foreign exchange.

How to Convert Currencies

Let:

	\$	= U.S. Currency Unit
	FC	= Foreign Currency Unit
	n	= Number of Units
If	1\$	= nFC
then	1*FC*	= \$/n

Example: The following is an extract from the business pages in the section: Exchange Rates

One dollar buys

Japan (Yen)	139.30
Britain (Pound)	0.6129

Therefore

Yen = 1/$139.30 = $.007178
Pound = 1/$0.6129 = $1.6315

How to Figure the U.S. Cost of a Foreign Exchange Transaction

Assume the following purchases:

	Foreign Currency	Rate	U.S. $
Purchases			
Yen	1,000,000	$ .007178	7,178
Pounds	100,000	$1.6315	163,150

How to Figure Gains and Losses from Changes in Exchange Rates

An exchange rate gain or loss will occur if the dollar increases or drops relevant to the involved foreign currency. Consider the following chart regarding the movement of the dollar relevant to foreign currency units:

Dollar Movement	Purchase	Sale
Up	Gain	Loss
Down	Loss	Gain

For example, after some time, the following exchange rates prevail:

Yen	0.007500	133.33
Pounds	1.600000	0.6250

Purchase

	Yen	Pound
Original Cost $'s	$7,178	$163,150
Settled Cost	7,500	160,000
Gain (Loss) on settlement	$ (322)	$ 3,150

Sale

	Yen	Pound
Original Cost $'s	$7,178	$163,150
Settled Sales Price	7,500	160,000
Gain (Loss) on settlement	$ 322	$ (3,150)

Exchange Rate Terminology

The following terms are used in foreign exchange transactions:

Spot rate: The exchange rate used for immediate delivery of respective currencies.

Current rate: The rate at which one unit of currency can be exchanged for another at the balance sheet date.

Historical rate: The rate in effect at the date a specific transaction or event occurred.

How to Account for Forward Exchange Transactions

A forward exchange contract is a device to avoid the risks of foreign currency transactions:

For example, you can see that the U.S. company lost money when it bought goods denominated in yen and the dollar dropped. If, instead, you utilized a forward exchange contract to acquire yen at a future delivery date, you locked in the price.

Four Reasons to Use Forward Exchange Contracts and Their Applicable Accounting Rules

a. *To speculate in foreign currency price movements*
Included in income in the period(s) in which the foreign exchange rates changed.

b. *Hedge against exposed net asset or liability position*
Serves as protection against risks arising from excess of assets or liabilities denominated in a foreign currency.

 (1) Gain or loss recognized at statement date on currency price movements.

 (2) Cost of forward exchange contract amortized.

c. *Hedging an Identifiable Foreign Currency Commitment*
Arises from a contract for purchase or sale of goods and services which are denominated in foreign currency.

(1) Exchange gain or loss deferred and offset by conversion of contract at maturity date.

(2) Premium paid adjusts sales proceeds or purchase price.

d. *Hedge of net investment in foreign entity*

(1) Exchange gains or losses recognized as equity adjustments.

(2) Premiums and discounts amortized to income or included in equity adjustments

How to Consolidate Foreign Subsidiaries

A consolidated financial statement attempts to present one unified picture of a parent and its subsidiaries. If any of these subsidiaries are foreign entities, their results have to be translated to U.S. dollars in order to complete the consolidation process.

How to Translate Foreign Entity Financial Statements

Translation means the conversion of the functional currency used on the books of the foreign entity to that of the reporting company. The FASB pronouncements set forth different conversion rates for various classes of accounts. Therefore, a net debit or credit balance will remain after the translations have been made. This difference is considered a result of the consolidation process not an actual transaction or exchange. Thus, the outcome is reported as an equity adjustment. See the chart below which provides the translation rates.

What Is Functional Currency?

An organization's functional currency is the currency of its primary environment. If that organization's legal tender is *not* its functional currency then the parent's must be used.

Why Is the "Functional Currency" Concept Important

If the currency is functional the foreign currency statements are translated to the reporting currency. But, if the currency is *not* functional then the numbers have to be remeasured first *before* they can be translated.

How to Determine if the Currency Is Functional

All of the following questions have to be answered to determine whether the subsidiary's currency is functional:

Question re: foreign entity	*Functional Currency?*
Sales prices determined by local competition	Y
Sales prices determined by short range exchange rate changes or worldwide markets	N
Sales market in parent country or in parent currency	N
Expenses are primarily local costs	Y
Financing in local currency	Y
High volume of intercompany transactions	N
High inflation rate in local currency*	N

A note about inflation: FAS #52 defines a highly inflationary economy as one with a cumulative three year inflation rate of approximately 100% or more.

What Is Remeasurement?

The remeasurement process converts the entity's financial statements to the functional currency before translation. Gains and losses from remeasurement are reported on the income statement.

Rates Used in Translation and Remeasurement

Current Rate: Rate in effect at financial statement date.

Historical Rate: Rate in effect when transaction took place.

Recording of Adjustments Under Conditions of Translation and Remeasurement

Translation: Adjustment to stockholders' equity

Remeasurement: Adjustment to statement of income

Remeasurement/Translation Chart

	Remeasurement	*Translation*
Assets		
Cash, demand deposits, and time deposits	Current	Current
Marketable securities carried at cost:		
Equity Securities	Historical	Current
Debt Securities	Historical	Current
Accounts and notes receivable and related unearned discounts	Current	Current
Allowance for doubtful accounts	Current	Current
Inventories		
Carried at Cost	Historical	Current
Prepaid expenses	Historical	Current
Refundable deposits	Current	Current
Property, plant, and equipment	Historical	Current
Accumulated depreciation	Historical	Current
Cash surrender value of life insurance	Current	Current
Deferred income tax charges	Current	Current
Patents, trademarks, licenses, and formulas	Historical	Current
Goodwill	Historical	Current
Liabilities		
Accounts, notes payable, overdrafts	Current	Current
Accrued expenses	Current	Current
Deferred income tax credits	Current	Current
Deferred income	Historical	Current
Other deferred credits	Historical	Current
Bonds payable and other long term debts	Current	Current
Equity		
Common Stock	Historical	Historical
Preferred Stock at par	Historical	Historical
Other paid in capital	Historical	Historical
Retained earnings	Not remeasured	Not translated

(continued on next page)

	Remeasurement	*Translation*
Income Statement Items Related to Non Monetary Items		
Cost of goods sold	Historical	Current
Depreciation and amortization	Historical	Current
Amortization of deferred income taxes	Current	Current
Amortization of deferred charges and credits	Historical	Current

How to Prepare Financial Statements for Governmental Units

Official Pronouncement:

Governmental Accounting Standard Board, Codification of Governmental Accounting and Financial Reporting Standards as of June 15, 1987, 2nd ed.—1987

The Major Reasons for Governmental Accounting

Governmental accounting's reason for being is to report financial information in accordance with the various finance related legal and contractual provisions of the governing jurisdiction.

What Is Funds Accounting?

A fund is a self-balancing set of accounts used to record a series of activities which have been provided by legal and/or fiscal authority.

For example, the City of Buzzard's Breath borrowed $1,000,000 to finance the construction of a library. The library cost $800,000. The accounting transactions flowed through the following funds:

General Fund:	
Revenue	$1,000,000
Expenditures	800,000
General Long-Term Debt Group	
Bonds payable	$1,000,000
General Fixed Asset Group	
Library	800,000

How Funds Are Grouped

There are three major data collection points:

1. Governmental funds
2. Proprietary funds
3. Trust and agency funds

The characteristics of each of these categories is detailed below:

Fund Grouping: Governmental

Purpose: To account for the normal business of government

Funds included: General Fund
Special Revenue Funds
Capital Projects Funds
Debt Service Funds

Accounting Basis: Modified accrual
Budgetary accounting required? Yes
Depreciation recorded? No

Fund Grouping: Proprietary

Purpose: Account for operations that are financed and operated in a manner similar to private business

Funds included: Enterprise funds
Internal Service funds
Accounting Basis: Accrual
Budgetary accounting required? No
Depreciation recorded? Yes

Fund Grouping: Trust and Agency

Purpose: Account for assets held by a governmental unit in a trustee capacity

Sinking Funds:

To accumulate funds set aside to payoff long term debt.

Groups of Accounts:

These are established to maintain accountability for certain assets and liabilities:

General fixed assets:
To keep track of buildings, land, equipment and other fixed assets.
General long term debt:
To account for all long term debt liabilities.

How Budgetary Accounting Is Maintained on Governmental Funds

A governmental fund starts each fiscal year by preparing a budget and entering that budget on the accounts.

For example, the City's budget has estimated revenues of $1,000,000 and expenditures of $800,000. The budget is recorded as follows:

Estimated revenues	$1,000,000	
Appropriations		800,000
Fund balance		200,000

A governmental unit also records purchase orders as they are granted. This is done through an *encumbrance account*.

For example, the city grants a purchase order of $75,000 for outside training services. The actual cost is $60,000. The entries are made as follows:

1. When the contract is made		
Encumbrances	$75,000	
Reserve for encumbrances		75,000
2. When the services are performed		
Expenditure	$60,000	
Vouchers payable		60,000
3. The reserve for encumbrances is reversed		
Reserve for encumbrance	$75,000	
Encumbrances		75,000

How to Determine the Maximum Additional Spending Authority for a Governmental Unit

A governmental unit is entitled to spend only what its budget authorizes. If encumbrances are outstanding, the authority will be further reduced. The worksheet to determine this amount follows:

Appropriations (authorized expenditures)	$
Less: expenditures to date	________
Unexpended appropriations	
Less: Encumbrances	________
Unencumbered appropriations	________

The City of Thousand Oaks Governmental Accounting in Action

The City of Thousand Oaks financial statements (reprinted with permission of the City), which are presented in the ensuing pages, are a guide to ease your job of putting together governmental financial statements. Please note the following:

1. The balance sheet groups the funds by governmental, proprietary, fiduciary fund types, and account groups.
2. The totals in the far right columns are for memo only.
3. The combined statements of revenues, expenditures, and changes in fund balances do not include the proprietary funds. These are presented in separate exhibits.

How to Account for Non Profit Organizations

Official Pronouncements:

SOP 78-10 Accounting Principles and Reporting Practices for Certain Non Profit Organizations

FASB #32—Specialized Accounting and Reporting Principles and Practices in AICPA Statements of Position and Guides

Accounting and Auditing Matters.—September, 1979

Comparison of Accounting for Various Non-Profit Entities

Many of the principles and procedures used are similar to governmental accounting, because non profit organizations are also regulated by certain legal and fiscal restrictions. The following chart lists accounting requirements for the following types of non profit organizations:

A. Voluntary health and welfare
B. Colleges and universities
C. Hospitals
D. Other

	A	*B*	*C*	*D*
Accrual basis required	y	y	y	y
Fund raising revenues and costs separately identified	y	n	n	y*
Fixed assets capitalized	y	y	y	y
Pledges recorded as assets	y	o	y	y
Depreciation recorded	y	y	y	y**

* = yes, if it receives substantial public support
o = optional

** = No, if for house of worship

CITY OF THOUSAND OAKS

Combined Balance Sheet - All Fund Types and Account Groups

June 30, 1988
with comparative totals for June 30, 1987

	Governmental Fund Types				Proprietary Fund Type	Fiduciary Fund Type	Account Groups		Total (memorandum only)	
Assets	General	Special Revenue	Debt Service	Capital Projects	Enterprise	Trust and Agency	General Fixed Assets	General Long-Term Debt	1988	1987
Cash and investments (note 2)	$ 4,593,030	14,612,947	-	46,007,158	18,066,007	6,935,038	-	-	90,214,180	74,557,357
Accounts receivable	226,728	-	-	1,274,882	809,023	64	-	-	2,310,697	1,037,126
Notes receivable	500,000	-	-	1,290,150	12,740	-	-	-	1,802,890	1,731,411
Loans receivable (note 11)	475,000	-	-	-	-	-	-	-	475,000	475,000
Advance to other governments	-	-	-	1,650,000	-	-	-	-	1,650,000	-
Accrued interest receivable	317,928	-	-	82,777	71,366	-	-	-	472,071	677,470
Due from other governments	2,180	575,686	-	1,316	12,171	-	-	-	591,353	509,926
Due from other funds (note 5)	1,564,751	205,589	-	175,475	4,810	-	-	-	1,950,625	3,636,206
Inventories - supplies	153,621	-	-	-	251,360	-	-	-	404,981	273,258
Prepaid expenses and other assets	750	-	-	19,700	-	-	-	-	20,450	830,985
Restricted cash and investments	-	-	7,959,079	-	1,617,340	-	-	-	9,576,419	1,417,605
Property, plant and equipment, net (note 3)	-	-	-	-	58,765,099	-	49,368,606	-	108,133,705	78,262,798
Amount available in Debt Service Fund	-	-	-	-	-	-	-	7,944,187	7,944,187	721,445
Amount to be provided for the payment of long-term debt	-	-	-	-	-	-	-	56,268,850	56,268,850	15,889,628
	$ 7,833,988	15,394,222	7,959,079	50,501,458	79,609,916	6,935,102	49,368,606	64,213,037	281,815,408	180,020,215

(Continued)

Exhibit 5-2

CITY OF THOUSAND OAKS

Combined Balance Sheet - All Fund Types and Account Groups, Continued

June 30, 1988
with comparative totals for June 30, 1987

Liabilities and Fund Equity	Governmental Fund Types				Proprietary Fund Type	Fiduciary Fund Type	Account Groups		Total (memorandum only)	
	General	Special Revenue	Debt Service	Capital Projects	Enterprise	Trust and Agency	General Fixed Assets	General Long-Term Debt	1988	1987
Liabilities:										
Accounts payable	$ 2,016,014	1,629,000	-	650,812	1,864,076	427,742	-	-	6,587,644	7,537,726
Accrued liabilities, including current portion of compensated absences	785,703	35,712	14,892	130,516	152,973	-	-	-	1,119,796	833,068
Due to other funds (note 5)	17,918	50,507	-	674,948	1,207,252	-	-	-	1,950,625	3,636,206
Due to other governments	-	-	-	104,306	-	44,001	-	-	148,307	386,561
Deferred compensation payable (note 8)	-	-	-	-	-	2,270,976	-	-	2,270,976	1,804,370
Deferred revenue	825,130	2,815,607	-	5,134,073	1,389,816	-	-	-	10,164,626	8,267,605
Other	-	-	-	-	-	1,992,383	-	1,070,203	3,062,586	2,507,009
Notes and loans payable (note 4)	-	-	-	-	-	-	-	2,089,835	2,089,835	10,303,070
Bonds payable (note 4)	-	-	-	-	8,016,909	-	-	44,275,000	52,291,909	13,418,397
Certificates of participation (note 4)	-	-	-	-	-	-	-	16,470,000	16,470,000	530,000
Facilities reimbursement agreements	-	-	-	-	357,230	-	-	-	357,230	572,040
Compensated absences payable - long-term portion (note 4)	-	-	-	-	-	-	-	307,999	307,999	284,889
Total liabilities	3,644,765	4,530,826	14,892	6,694,655	12,988,256	4,735,102	-	64,213,037	96,821,533	50,080,941
Fund equity:										
Contributed capital	-	-	-	-	6,797,443	-	-	-	6,797,443	6,432,365
Investment in general fixed assets	-	-	-	-	-	-	49,368,606	-	49,368,606	26,780,917
Retained earnings:										
Reserved (note 10)	-	-	-	-	13,744,220	-	-	-	13,744,220	17,691,203
Unreserved	-	-	-	-	46,079,997	-	-	-	46,079,997	36,876,195
Fund balances:										
Reserved for debt service	-	-	7,944,187	-	-	-	-	-	7,944,187	-
Other reserved (note 10)	4,189,223	10,473,624	-	37,517,169	-	-	-	-	52,180,016	35,173,200
Unreserved - designated (note 10)	-	389,772	-	6,289,634	-	2,200,000	-	-	8,879,406	6,985,394
Total fund equity	4,189,223	10,863,396	7,944,187	43,806,803	66,621,660	2,200,000	49,368,606	-	184,993,875	129,939,274
	$ 7,833,988	15,394,222	7,959,079	50,501,458	79,609,916	6,935,102	49,368,606	64,213,037	281,815,408	180,020,215

See accompanying notes to general purpose financial statements.

Exhibit 5-2 *(Cont'd.)*

(continued on next page)

Year ended June 30, 1988
with comparative totals for the year ended June 30, 1987

	Governmental Fund Types				Fiduciary Fund Type	Total (memorandum only)	
	General	Special Revenue	Debt Service	Capital Projects	Expendable Trust	1988	1987
Revenues:							
Taxes	$ 13,635,013	3,608,735	-	5,276,661	-	22,520,409	20,706,178
Licenses and permits	1,938,250	-	-	-	-	1,938,250	1,914,803
Fines and forfeitures	208,127	761,506	-	-	-	969,633	892,579
Use of money and property	1,405,207	936,635	290,981	1,772,105	-	4,404,928	3,402,285
Charges for current services	1,962,582	973,149	-	877,523	-	3,813,254	3,624,884
Intergovernmental	3,449,024	2,116,370	-	-	-	5,565,394	6,736,019
Other	50,128	311,682	-	1,449,146	-	1,810,956	2,733,114
Total revenues	22,648,331	8,708,077	290,981	9,375,435	-	41,022,824	40,009,862
Expenditures:							
Current:							
General government	4,788,796	-	-	-	-	4,788,796	4,453,215
Public safety	5,994,027	641,253	-	-	-	6,635,280	6,056,173
Transportation	4,392,430	4,129,053	-	-	-	8,521,483	6,099,911
Community development	5,650,884	357,076	-	3,845,589	-	9,853,549	10,439,735
Health	-	-	-	-	-	-	23,195
Culture and leisure	119,050	2,978,888	-	9,194	-	3,107,132	2,827,632
Debt service:							
Principal	-	-	8,378,235	-	-	8,378,235	550,192
Interest	-	-	2,809,415	-	-	2,809,415	894,860
Lease payment	-	-	-	-	-	-	44,075
Issuance cost	-	-	266,434	-	-	266,434	-
Capital outlay	10,294,002	635,308	-	12,804,519	-	23,733,829	7,368,523
Total expenditures	31,239,189	8,741,578	11,454,084	16,659,392	-	68,094,153	38,757,511
Excess of revenues over (under) expenditures	(8,590,858)	(33,501)	(11,163,103)	(7,283,867)	-	(27,071,329)	1,252,351
Other financing sources (uses):							
Operating transfers in	2,781,031	3,655,714	9,383,645	2,105,740	-	17,926,130	5,935,320
Operating transfers out	(2,498,479)	(3,982,593)	(5,492,452)	(6,449,506)	-	(18,423,030)	(6,406,903)
Proceeds from (repayment of) bonds/notes (note 4)	-	-	14,472,765	39,940,479	-	54,413,244	(159,960)
Total other financing sources (uses)	282,552	(326,879)	18,363,958	35,596,713	-	53,916,344	(631,543)
Excess of revenues and other sources over (under) expenditures and other uses	(8,308,306)	(360,380)	7,200,855	28,312,846	-	26,845,015	620,808
Fund balances, beginning of year	12,847,529	11,223,776	721,445	15,515,844	1,850,000	42,158,594	41,537,786
Residual equity transfers (note 14)	(350,000)	-	21,887	(21,887)	350,000	-	-
Fund balances, end of year	$ 4,189,223	10,863,396	7,944,187	43,806,803	2,200,000	69,003,609	42,158,594

See accompanying notes to general purpose financial statements.

Exhibit 5-2 *(Cont'd.)*

CITY OF THOUSAND OAKS

Combined Statement of Revenues, Expenditures and Changes in Fund Balances - Budget and Actual - General and Certain Special Revenue Fund Types

Year ended June 30, 1988

	General Fund			Special Revenue Funds		
	Budget	Actual	Variance - favorable (unfavorable)	Budget (Note 12)	Actual (Note 12)	Variance - favorable (unfavorable)
Revenues:						
Taxes	$ 13,605,000	13,635,013	30,013	3,763,400	3,608,735	(154,665)
Licenses and permits	1,927,000	1,938,250	11,250	-	-	-
Fines and forfeitures	140,000	208,127	68,127	750,000	761,506	11,506
Revenue from use of money and property	1,396,000	1,405,207	9,207	32,500	936,635	904,135
Charges for current services	2,391,000	1,962,582	(428,418)	671,300	973,149	301,849
Intergovernmental	3,553,000	3,449,024	(103,976)	2,016,000	1,974,866	(41,134)
Other	50,000	50,128	128	10,000	311,682	301,682
Total revenues	23,062,000	22,648,331	(413,669)	7,243,200	8,566,573	1,323,373
Expenditures:						
Current:						
General government	7,973,668	4,788,796	3,184,872	-	-	-
Public safety	6,046,940	5,994,027	52,913	786,410	641,253	145,157
Transportation	3,522,761	4,392,430	(869,669)	9,607,309	4,129,053	5,478,256
Community development	4,496,912	5,650,884	(1,153,972)	125,750	215,572	(89,822)
Culture and leisure	112,962	119,050	(6,088)	3,032,158	2,978,888	53,270
Capital outlay	21,617,725	10,294,002	11,323,723	2,591,700	635,308	1,956,392
Total expenditures	43,770,968	31,239,189	12,531,779	16,143,327	8,600,074	7,543,253
Excess of revenues over (under) expenditures	(20,708,968)	(8,590,858)	12,118,110	(8,900,127)	(33,501)	8,866,626
Other financing sources (uses):						
Operating transfers in	2,623,000	2,781,031	158,031	2,513,850	3,655,714	1,141,864
Operating transfers out	(2,662,230)	(2,498,479)	163,751	(2,436,050)	(3,982,593)	(1,546,543)
Total other financing sources (uses)	(39,230)	282,552	321,782	77,800	(326,879)	(404,679)
Excess of revenues and other sources over (under) expenditures and other uses	(20,748,198)	(8,308,306)	12,439,892	(8,822,327)	(360,380)	8,461,947
Fund balances, beginning of year	12,847,529	12,847,529	-	11,223,776	11,223,776	-
Residual equity transfer	(350,000)	(350,000)	-	-	-	-
Fund balances, end of year	$ (8,250,669)	4,189,223	12,439,892	2,401,449	10,863,396	8,461,947

continued on next page

Exhibit 5-2 *(Cont'd.)*

Combined Statement of Revenues, Expenses and Changes in Retained Earnings - Enterprise Fund Type

Year ended June 30, 1988
with comparative totals for the year ended June 30, 1987

	Total 1988	Total 1987
Revenues:		
Sales of water and wastewater services	$ 9,649,179	8,554,444
Bus fares	48,968	44,895
Green fees, cart rentals and course memberships	1,227,553	1,184,059
Other	360,728	327,641
	11,286,428	10,111,039
Operating expenses:		
Operations	8,572,576	8,932,805
Depreciation	1,354,440	1,327,852
Administration	1,309,481	1,244,374
	11,236,497	11,505,031
Income (loss) from operations	49,931	(1,393,992)
Nonoperating revenues (expenses):		
Interest income	1,543,151	1,530,166
Interest expense	(473,239)	(517,277)
Connection fees	2,977,799	4,559,220
Rental of facilities	30,391	86,417
Federal and state grants	-	24
Property taxes	520,703	464,984
State tax subventions	24,945	26,662
Other, net	(124,896)	(372,449)
	4,498,854	5,777,747
Income before operating transfers	4,548,785	4,383,755
Operating transfers in	2,021,810	2,292,140
Operating transfers out	(1,524,910)	(1,820,557)
Net operating transfers	496,900	471,583
Net income	5,045,685	4,855,338
Retained earnings, beginning of year before prior period adjustment	54,567,398	49,712,060
Prior period adjustment (note 13)	211,134	-
Retained earnings, beginning of year after prior period adjustment	54,778,532	49,712,060
Retained earnings, end of year after prior period adjustment	$ 59,824,217	54,567,398

See accompanying notes to general purpose financial statements.

Exhibit 5-2 *(Cont'd.)*

CITY OF THOUSAND OAKS

Combined Statement of Changes in Financial Position - Enterprise Fund Type

Year ended June 30, 1988
with comparative totals for the year ended June 30, 1987

	Total 1988	Total 1987
Financial resources were provided by:		
Operations:		
Net income	$ 5,045,685	4,855,338
Items not requiring working capital:		
Depreciation	1,354,440	1,327,852
Amortization of bond discount	8,511	8,511
Prior period adjustment	-	(211,134)
Working capital provided by operations	6,408,636	5,980,567
Increase in deferred revenue	145,654	238,058
Retirement of property, plant and equipment	119,836	51,292
Increase in contributed capital	365,078	1,302,975
Total sources of working capital	7,039,204	7,572,892
Financial resources were used for:		
Acquisition of property, plant and equipment	8,546,359	4,574,971
Increase in restricted cash and investments	199,735	326,605
Reduction of long-term bonds payable	1,021,488	961,489
Reduction in facilities reimbursement agreement	214,810	331,067
Total uses of working capital	9,982,392	6,194,132
Increase (decrease) in working capital	$(2,943,188)	1,378,760
Increase (decrease) in working capital components:		
Cash and investments	$(3,061,551)	2,206,690
Receivables	172,625	(128,758)
Due from other funds	2,718	1,854
Due from other governments	2,167	(6,579)
Inventory - supplies	94,566	(7,430)
Prepaid expenses	(76,419)	24,968
Current maturities of long-term debt	(60,000)	(75,000)
Accounts payable	49,664	(727,381)
Accrued liabilities	22,010	(17,764)
Due to other funds/agencies	(88,968)	108,160
Increase (decrease) in working capital	$(2,943,188)	1,378,760

See accompanying notes to general purpose financial statements.

Exhibit 5-2 *(Cont'd.)*

When Can the Cash Basis Be Used

The accrual basis is generally required for non-profit organizations. However, small associations are permitted to use the cash basis method if the accounts are not materially distorted.

How to Account for Contributions and Grants

There are a number of ways to account for contributions and grants which are dependent upon the:

1. Nature of the contribution or grant:
   i.e., What was the donor's intentions?
2. Charter of the organization
3. Specific AICPA industry guides

Classifications:

1. *Unrestricted contributions* can be used as the board designates and are normally accounted for in an unrestricted fund.
2. *Restricted donations* cannot be shown as revenues until the restrictions are removed.
3. *Grants* require detailed accounting to the grantor concerning the use of the applicable funds. Grant accounting requires income to be recognized only as expenditures are made against the grant. The remaining funds are recorded as deferred grant revenue.
4. *Pledges* are promises to make contributions at a later date. If they are legally enforceable, they may be recorded as income. The related receivables are recorded as assets with a contra allowance for doubtful accounts.

How to Use Functional Reporting

Many NPOs are organized to emphasize service programs.

For example, a charitable fund may service orphan agencies, boys clubs, and homeless shelters. Both revenues and expenses may be allocated to each of these service activities.

Allocating Expenses to Service Activities

The following is an example of an allocation of indirect expenses to service activities:

1. *Salaries:* by time spent for each employee on each program
2. *Payroll taxes and employee benefits:* based on allocation of salaries
3. *Telephone:* number of phone extensions in each department
4. *Postage:* postage-use log
5. *Supplies:* invoices or vouchers used by each department
6. *Depreciation:* percentage of floor space

How to Account for Rate Regulated Industries

Official Pronouncements:

FASB #71—Accounting for the Effects of Certain Types of Regulation—December, 1982

FASB #90—Regulated Enterprises—Accounting for Abandonments and Disallowances of Plant Costs (an amendment of FASB #71)—December, 1986

FASB #92—Regulated Enterprises—Accounting for Phase in Plans—August, 1987

What Are the Criteria for Regulated Operations?

In order to be classified as a regulated operation, the following criteria must be met:

1. An independent third party regulator has been empowered to establish or approve rates the enterprise can charge its customers.
2. The rates set are intended to recover the specific costs of the regulated services or products.
3. The rates set are reasonable and likely to be collected.

Rate Setting

Rates are based on specific incurred costs of the enterprise.

Financial Reporting

As the following financial statements show, utility industry reporting emphasizes property and equipment by placing it first on the balance sheet. Also, stockholders' equity is placed before the current liabilities' section.

On the income statement, operations and maintenance costs include all the items that are controllable at the department level.

Rude Noises Power Company
Balance Sheet
December 31, 1991

Assets		
Property, plant & equipment		$4,500,000
Less: depreciation & amortization		3,000,000
Net property, plant & equipment		1,500,000
Current assets		
Cash & equivalents	$62,000	
Accounts receivable	350,000	
Fuel stored	125,000	
Materials & supplies	45,000	
Other current assets	125,000	
Total current assets		707,000
Other assets		160,000
Total Assets		$2,367,000
Liabilities		
Common stock	$240,000	
Additional paid in capital	325,000	
Retained earnings	57,000	
Common stockholders' equity		$622,000
Long term debt		1,200,000
Current liabilities		
Debt due	14,000	
Accounts payable	216,000	
Accrued taxes	90,000	
Other accruals	150,000	
Total current liabilities		470,000
Other liabilities		75,000
Total liabilities		$2,367,000

What Are the Usual Allowable Costs?

The allowable costs that an entity may recover include the following:

- All actual costs and/or estimated costs that are required to provide services to the public.
- A return on investment to cover costs of long term debt and equity capital.

Rude Noises Power Company
Statement of Earnings
For the Year Ended December 31, 1991

Operating Revenues		$450,000
Operating Expenses		
Purchased fuel	$140,000	
Operations	132,000	
Maintenance	17,000	
Depreciation & amortization	65,000	
Taxes other than income	11,000	
Income taxes	5,000	
Total operating expenses		370,000
Income before debt charges		80,000
Long term debt interest		2,500
Net income		$77,500

Accounting for Specific Costs

1. *Abandonments:* When plants are abandoned, their net book values are allowed to be used in the rate setting structure. Under FASB 90, the future revenue expected to result from inclusion in that process must be reported at its present value when the abandonment becomes probable.
2. *Disallowance of plant costs:* Any plant costs that are disallowed in the rate setting process are required to be charged to income.
3. *Phase in plans:* Because of the high costs of constructuring new plants, especially nuclear facilities, these costs can result in

rate spikes, or an unusually high one-time increase in rates. To solve this problem, regulating commissions have developed phase in plans. FASB 92 sets certain criteria that must be met before any of the costs allowed for future recovery may be deferred.

4. *Capitalized interest:* The regulations may require that an enterprise capitalize a portion of the interest incurred during construction as part of an asset's cost. However, according to FASB #90, these costs may be capitalized only if it is probable that they will be included as an allowable cost of the related asset in the rate setting process.

How to Account for Insolvencies and Bankruptcies

Generally, an insolvent entity is unable to pay its bills. The Federal Bankruptcy Act, which is organized into three chapters, has established conditions for relief from creditors:

- *Chapter 7* is the prevalent form of personal bankruptcy. The debtor's assets are liquidated by the trustee and the proceeds distributed to the creditors.
- *Chapter 11* is reserved for corporations. A creditors' committee is formed which supervises the operation of the entity. The corporation continues in operations and tries to make prespecified payments.
- *Chapter 13* is another form of personal bankruptcy which is usually reserved for individual wage earners. The debtor remains in possession of assets and agrees to make pre specified payments to creditors.

Who Gets Paid First?

The Act establishes the following priorities:

1. *Secured claims* interests supported by valid liens

   For example, a lien on an automobile would be satisfied by the property.

2. *Unsecured priority claims*

   a. Administrative expenses involved in preserving and liquidating the estate. Includes the following
      i. trustee's fees
      ii. legal
      iii. accounting

   b. Claims incurred between the date of filing an involuntary petition and the date a trustee is appointed.

   c. Claims for wages, salaries, and commissions earned within 90 days of filing the petition.
      Note: The limit is $2,000 per individual

   d. Claims for contributions to employee benefit plans arising from services rendered within 180 days of filing the petition and limited to $2,000 per employee.

   e. Claims of individuals (not to exceed $900) arising from the purchase, lease, or rental of property that was not delivered or the purchase of services that were not provided by debtor.

   f. Claims of governmental units for taxes and duties.

3. *Unsecured non-priority claims*

   a. Allowed claims that were timely filed.

   b. Allowed claims where proofs of claims were filed late.

   c. Allowed claims for any fine, penalty, or forfeiture or for multiple, exemplary or punitive charges arising prior to the order for relief or appointment of trustee.

   d. Claims for interest on the unsecured priority claims or the unsecured non-priority claims above.

4. *Stockholders' claims*

How Trustee Accounting in Bankruptcy Is Handled

A trustee in bankruptcy takes over the assets of the debtor and is accountable for those assets until released by the bankruptcy court. The following accounting reports result:

1. A statement of affairs, which reports the net realizable values of the assets liabilities in the order of priority, is prepared in the following sequence:

Note: A sample statement follows this discussion.

a. Start with the assets, liabilities, and equity per the books.
b. List the fully and partially pledged assets at their estimated liquidation values.
c. Offset fully secured notes payable and related interest against pledged assets. The excess is available for unsecured creditors and priority claims.
d. Offset partially secured liabilities against pledged assets. Any shortage will become an unsecured non-priority liability as shown in item i.
e. Record and total the estimated liquidation values of other assets.
f. Subtract the priority liabilities from item "e".
g. The remainder is the amount available for unsecured creditors.
h. List the secured and priority creditors.
i. All other liabilities are listed as unsecured non priority claims.
j. Finally, calculate the estimated deficiency.

2. Start the asset liquidation process. All gains and losses are recorded in the equity accounts.
3. Record the cash receipts and disbursements.
4. Close each period by preparing a statement of changes in equity. This statement is constructed as follows:

Estate equity, beginning (net book value)		
Add: Net gain on asset liquidation		______
Less:		
Net loss on asset liquidation	______	
Liability for utilities discovered	______	
Administrative expenses	______	
Trustee fees	______	
Net increase (decrease for period)		______
Estate equity, (deficit) ending		======

Example:

CarBrad Corporation
Statement of Affairs
July 1, 1991

Assets

(a) Book Value			(b) Realizable Values Liability offsets for secured creditors	(e) Realizable Values Available for unsecured creditors
(c)	*Pledged for fully secured creditors*			
$17,500	Automobiles		$15,000	
	Less: Contract payable	$8,000		
	Interest due	1,000	9,000	$6,000
(d)	*Pledged for partially secured creditors*			
13,000	*Accounts receivable*		11,000	
	Less: Note payable		20,000	0
(e)	*Available for priority and secured creditors*			
4,500	Cash			4,500
62,500	Inventories			55,000
1,250	Prepaid expenses			0
44,550	Equipment—net			47,500
8,750	Intangible assets			0
	Total available			113,000
	Less: Priority liabilities			12,500
(g)	Total available for unsecured creditors			100,500
(j)	Estimated deficiency			54,150
$152,050				$154,650

Liabilities & Stockholders' Equity

Book Value		(h) Secured & Priority Claims	(i) Unsecured Nonpriority claims
(g)	*Priority liabilities*		
$5,000	Wages payable	$5,000	
7,500	Property taxes payable	7,500	
		$12,500	
	Fully secured creditors		
8,000	Contract payable	$8,000	
1,000	Interest due	1,000	
		9,000	
	Partially secured creditors		
20,000	Note payable	20,000	
	Less: Accounts receivable pledged	11,000	9,000
	Unsecured creditors		
145,650	Accounts payable		145,650
	Stockholders' equity		
10,000	Capital stock		
(45,100)	Retained earnings (deficit)		
$152,050			$154,650

How to Use Defeasance Arrangements to Improve the Financial Statements

Official Pronouncements:

FASB #76—Extinguishment of Debt—November, 1983

Defeasance arrangements are an in-substance extinguishment of debt. According to FASB #76, debt is extinguished when, the debtor:

1. Pays the debt to the creditor or buys back its own debt obligations.

2. Is legally released as the primary obligor under the debt, and it is probable that the debtor will not be required to make future payments.
3. Places cash or certain other assets in a irrevocable trust for the sole purpose of servicing the interest and principal payments of the debt, and there is only a remote possibility that the debtor will have to make any other payments on the debt.

How Defeasance Works—An Example

Consider the following balance sheets:

Noushk Corporation
Balance Sheet
December 31, 1988

		Before	Adjustment	After
Assets				
Current Assets		$500,000	$(36,785)	$463,215
Long Term Investments	12%	980,000	(831,545)	$148,455
Other Assets		200,000		$200,000
Total Assets		$1,680,000	$(868,330)	$811,669
Liabilities & Stockholders' Equity				
Liabilities				
Current Liabilities		$381,780	$9,502	$391,282
Long Term Debt	7%	900,000	(900,000)	0
Total Liabilities		1,281,780	(890,498)	391,282
Stockholders' Equity				
Common Stock (100,000 shares)		100,000		100,000
Retained Earnings		298,220	22,168	320,388
Total Stockholders' Equity		398,220	22,168	420,388
Total Liabilities & Equity		$1,680,000	$(868,330)	$811,670

Noushk Corporation
Statement of Income
For the Year Ended December 31, 1988

Revenues	$800,000		800,000
Operating Expenses	500,000		500,000
Income from Operations	300,000	0	300,000
Other Revenues and Expenses			
Interest Revenue	117,600	(99,785)	17,815
Interest Expense	(63,000)	63,000	0
Income before Taxes	354,600	(36,785)	317,815
Taxes (30%)	106,380	(11,036)	95,344
Net Income	248,220	(25,750)	222,470
Extraordinary Items (Net of Tax)		47,918	47,918
Net Income	$248,220	$22,168	270,388

To enact the defeasance program, the investments are used to payoff the long-term debt. A trust is established and sufficient funds are deposited to cover the following:

1. The ultimate payment of the trust principal
2. The interest payments as they become due
3. A trust fee

We assume, here that the principal is due in fifteen years and any funds placed in trust will earn interest at the rate of 10%. Furthermore, there will be a trust fee of 2%. The present value is calculated as follows:

			PV
Calculation of Trust Principal			
Interest Rate	10.00%		
Term Remaining	15		
Long-Term Debt		900,000	215,453
Annual interest payments		63,000	479,183
Trust Fee (2%)		18,000	136,909
Total			831,545
Note balance			900,000
Gain on extinguishment			68,455

By placing $831,545 into trust, the long-term debt is removed from the balance sheet and an extraordinary gain on extinguishment of debt of $68,455 is reported on the income statement in column B.

In addition to improving this year's as well as future years' income statements, the financial ratios are enhanced.

	Before	After
Ratios		
Debt Equity Ratio	3.22	1.69
Return on Ending Assets	14.78%	31.15%
Return on Ending Equity	62.33%	83.76%
Earnings per Share	$2.48	$2.70

Restrictions on Defeasance

1. The funds must be placed in an irrevocable trust.
2. These funds are necessarily risk free monetary assets that are denominated in U.S. currency and limited to the following:
   a. direct obligations of the U.S. government
   b. obligations that are guaranteed by the U.S. government
   c. securities that are backed by the U.S. government obligations under a collateral arrangement which provides that in the event of a default, interest, and principal on the collateral flow immediately through to the holder of the security.

CHAPTER 6

Generally Accepted Auditing Standards

The Auditing Standards Committee has issued Statements on Auditing Standards (SAS). The major categories are listed below:

Responsibility and function of the independent auditor
Pre-engagement planning
Generally accepted accounting principles
Generally accepted auditing standards
Planning the engagement
Study and evaluation of internal control
Evidence
Related party transactions
Auditor's reports
Auditor's special reports

Coverage of Auditing

General Standards

Chapter 6

Standards of Field Work

Chapter 7—Planning, performing and completing an audit
Chapter 8—Statistical sampling
Chapter 9—How to audit financial statement elements

Standards of Reporting

Chapter 10—Reporting on audited financial statements
Chapter 11—Special reporting situations
Chapter 12—SEC procedures and regulations
Chapter 13—The controller and the internal audit function

Overview of the Generally Accepted Auditing Standards

General Standards

1. *Training* The examination is to be performed by a person or persons having adequate technical training and proficiency as an auditor.
2. *Independence* In all matters relating to the assignment, an independence in mental attitude is to be maintained by the auditor or auditors.
3. *Care* Due professional care is to be exercised in the performance of the examination and the preparation of the report.

Standards of Field Work

1. *Planning* The work is to be adequately planned and assistants, if any, are to be property supervised.
2. *Internal Control* There is to be a proper study and evaluation of the existing internal control as a basis for reliance thereon and for the determination of the resultant extent of the tests to which auditing procedures are to be restricted.
3. *Evidence* Sufficient, competent evidential matter is to be obtained through inspection, observation, inquiries, and confirmations to afford a reasonable basis for an opinion regarding the financial statements under examination.

Standards of Reporting

1. *Principles of accounting* The report shall state whether the financial statements are presented in accordance with generally accepted accounting principles.
2. *Consistency* The report shall identify those circumstances in which such principles have not been consistently observed in the current period in relation to the preceding period.
3. *Disclosures* Informative disclosures in the financial statements are to be regarded as reasonably adequate unless otherwise stated in the report.
4. *Opinion expression* The report shall contain either an expression of opinion regarding the financial statements taken as a whole, or an assertion to the effect that an opinion cannot be expressed. When an overall opinion cannot be expressed, the

reasons therefor should be stated. In all cases where an auditor's name is associated with financial statements, the report should contain a clear-cut indication of the auditor's exception if any, and the degree of responsibility he or she is taking.

Official Pronouncements

SAS #1—Codification of Auditing Standards and Procedures

SAS #2—Reports on Audited Financial Statements

SAS #25—The Relationship of Generally Accepted Auditing Standards to Quality Control Standards

What Are the Responsibilities and Functions of the Independent Auditor?

As you know, when you audit financial statements, you are responsible for determining whether the financial statements are prepared in accordance with GAAP.

Remember: That engagement must, of course, be conducted according to your professional judgment.

To Whom Are You Responsible?

1. Your client
2. Outsiders including investors, creditors, governmental agencies, and other users
3. The accounting profession itself

Responsibility Guidelines

Both your responsibility and the work you do to fulfill that obligation are guided by the three general auditing standards:

1. Adequate training of staff and partners
2. Real and perceived independence
3. Sufficient care in the planning, conduct, and completion of the audit engagement

Note: The scope and degree of auditing procedures is dependent on the company's internal control systems.

How to Conduct a Continuing Training Program

If there was no general auditing standard mandating adequate training, it would be necessary to create one. We are in a era of rapid environmental changes that affect the economy, our clients, accounting and auditing principles, and our firms. Therefore, it is only logical that a quality firm adapt to these changes. The process of adaption begins with training.

What Should Be Taught?

Information about the firm, its clients, and the profession should be communicated to members of your firm.

Understanding the Firm

An accounting firm, like any entity, is an organism that has its own culture, strengths, weaknesses, and peculiarities. These components should be continually studied and communicated to the staff and partners alike.

Note: When you explain your firm's culture, procedures, and philosophies, try to encourage a dialogue between different levels of management.

The Firm's Characteristics

1. Firm's history and culture
2. Firm's strength and weaknesses
3. Responsibilities and authorities (who does what?)
    a. partners
    b. professional staff
    c. support staff
4. The firm's facilities and resources
    a. EDP equipment
    b. outside data processing
    c. other offices
    d. outside consultants
5. Compensation policy
    a. overtime
    b. vacations and holidays
    c. health insurance and other perks
6. How to get ahead in the firm

Understanding the Accounting Environment

Try to keep yourself, your partners, and your staff aware and up to date about the accounting environment including the following:

1. Organization of the accounting profession
2. How FASBs and SASs are prepared
3. Environmental influences on technical matters
4. Changes in specific areas of
    a. accounting
    b. auditing
    c. management services
    d. electronic data processing
    e. taxes

How to Use a Top Down Approach to Help Partners and Staff Understand Your Clients

It isn't good enough to pick up a supply of workpapers, gather your juniors and seniors, walk into a client's offices, and say, "Hi, We're here to audit." In today's highly paced milieu, that will not work. It is much better to obtain an understanding of your client and how his or her business works, and fits into the environment. To do this, we recommend a top-down analysis to be performed as follows:

Phase I: Analyze environmental factors

Phase II: Analyze your client's industry

Phase III: Analyze your client

Note: The analytical techniques portrayed here will be discussed in greater detail in Chapter 16.

Phase I: Analyze the following environmental factors:

a. demographic
b. social
c. economic
d. political
e. technological

Phase II: Analyze the following industry factors:

a. industry trends (e.g. growing versus declining)
b. industry strengths and weaknesses
c. competition

Phase III: Analyze the following client factors:

a. how the environmental and industry studies affect the client
b. its markets, including its product, pricing, promotional policies and distribution methods
c. its facilities
d. its financial strengths and weaknesses
e. its people
f. its accounting policies and procedures

Teach Through Memo Writing

Accounting is a social art which emphasizes written as well as oral communications. Therefore, it is very important that staff accountants know how to write. A top down analysis memorandum should be prepared by any member assigned to an audit engagement, at least, for the first time.

How Should Training Be Delivered?

There are a number of methods to present training from the highly structured lecture to various forms of staff participation. Each has its pros and cons. However, the most effective training approach involves a variety of the following different forms:

Formal Lectures are the conventional way of delivering information. They are direct and relatively inexpensive. However, the instructor's teaching ability is critical. It is very easy to lose students.

Independent study courses are relatively low cost and furthermore, do not create scheduling problems. However, it is difficult to monitor participants' performance and assess results.

Correspondence courses offer a broad array of choices, which, again do not create scheduling problems. Inasmuch as these programs require completion of written examinations, the results are easier to assess than independent study courses. However, it is difficult to monitor the results.

Conventions and conferences deliver several educational experiences in a short time. However, many of these programs may not be job related.

Case studies are usually written descriptions of problem situations which work well by artificially simulating reality or experience. However, they require a great deal of time to be effective, and can be difficult to write, depending upon their complexity.

Role playing is a dramatized situation in which learners are asked to play the parts of other people and is also appropriate for artificially simulating experience. However, role playing is not useful if learners do not actively try to act out their parts.

Computer simulations are a dramatic representation of reality. They often combine case study and role playing. These simulations are a good way to transfer information because they can be focused on the particular circumstances. However, they are very time consuming and expensive.

Note: The number of off-the-shelf computer programs is increasing dramatically.

How to Write an Instructional Package

Of course, what goes into the package depends upon the information to be covered and the methods used to deliver that information. Its content is also dependent upon the teaching ability of the instructor and the detail that you believe is necessary to present. The following should be put into the package.

1. A set of how-to-use instructions
2. A brief description of the instructor's role
3. Sequence of activities
4. A description of the attendees
5. The means by which their training needs were assessed
6. Program handouts and visual aids
7. Means to assess student performance
8. Text or script
9. Questionnaires to be used by participants to assess instructor.

Should Your Firm Have a Training Department?

Preparation of instructional material is a common task of a training department. In addition, training professionals

- Perform needs assessments within the firm
- Prepare instructor
- Evaluate and retain outside training programs.

But a training department requires additional payroll, facilities, and special equipment. To decide whether you can or should afford the costs, consider the following:

1. What is the status of your present training program? Is it sufficient to deliver valuable information and keep your staff up to speed?
2. How much does it cost in terms of lost billing time for members of our firm to prepare and deliver the program?

Options to a Training Department

1. There are outside training specialists that will customize programs for your partners and employees. These courses can be conducted on site at your own convenience.
2. The American Society for Training and Development (ASTD) provides a wealth of information on course design and procedures. You may contact them at

   American Society for Training and Development
   1630 Duke Street
   Box 1443
   Alexandria, Va 22313-9833

The CPA's Code of Professional Conduct

The following rules have been established by the AICPA and govern all members. These have been incorporated into the statutes of many states.

Rule 101—Independence
A member in public practice shall be independent in the performance of professional services as required by standards promulgated by bodies designated by Council.

Rule 102—Integrity and Objectivity
In the performance of any professional service, a member shall maintain objectivity and integrity, shall be free of conflicts of interest, and shall not knowingly misrepresent facts or subordinate his or her judgement to others.

Rule 201—General Standards
A member shall comply with the following standards and with any interpretations thereof by bodies designated by council.

A. *Professional Competence.* Undertake only those professional services that the member or the member's firm can reasonably expect to be completed with professional competence.

B. *Due Professional Care.* Exercise due professional care in the performance of professional services.

C. *Training and Supervision.* Adequately plan and supervise the performance of professional services.

D. *Sufficient Relevant Data.* Obtain sufficient relevant data to afford a reasonable basis for conclusions of recommendations in relation to any professional services performed.

Rule 202—Compliance with Standards
A member who performs auditing, review, compilation, management advisory, tax, or other professional services shall comply with standards promulgated by bodies designated by Council.

Rule 203—Accounting Principles
A member shall not (1) express an opinion or state affirmation that the financial statements or other financial data of any entity are presented in conformity with generally accepted accounting principles, or (2) state that he or she is not aware of any materials modifications that should be made to such statements or data in order for them to be in conformity with generally accepted accounting principles, if such statements or data contain any departure from an accounting principle promulgated by bodies designed by Council to establish such principles that has material effect on the statements or data taken as a whole. If, however, the statements or data contain such a departure and the members can demonstrate that due to unusual circumstances the financial statements or data would otherwise have been misleading, the member can comply with the rule by describing the departure, its approximate effects, if practicable, and the reasons why compliance with the principle would result in a misleading statement.

Rule 301—Confidential Client Information
A member in public practice shall not disclose any confidential client information without the specific consent of the client.

This rule shall not be construed (1) to relieve a member of his or her professional obligations under Rules 202 and 203, (2) to affect in any way, the member's obligation to comply with a validly issued and enforceable subpoena or summons (3) to prohibit review of a member's professional practice under AICPA or state CPA society authorization, or (4) to preclude a member from initiating a complaint with or responding to any inquiry made by a recognized investigative or disciplinary body.

Members of a recognized investigative or disciplinary body and professional practice reviewers shall not use to their own advantage or disclose any member's confidential client information that comes to their attention in carrying out their official responsibilities. However, this prohibition shall not restrict the exchange of information with a recognized investigative or disciplinary body or affect, in any way, compliance with a validly issued and enforceable subpoena or summons.

Rule 302—Contingent Fees
Professional services shall not be offered or rendered under an arrangement whereby no fee will be charged unless a specified finding or result is attained, or where the fee is otherwise contingent upon the findings or results of such services. However, a member's fees may vary depending, for example, on the complexity of services rendered.

Fees are not regarded as being contingent if fixed by courts or other public authorities or, in tax matters, if determined based on the results of judicial proceedings or the findings of governmental agencies.

Rule 501—Acts Discreditable
A member shall not commit an act discreditable to the profession.

Rule 502—Advertising and Other Forms of Solicitation
A member in public practice shall not seek to obtain clients by advertising or other forms of solicitation in a manner that is false, misleading, or deceptive. Solicitation by the use of coercion, overreaching, or harassing conduct is prohibited.

Rule 503—Commissions
The acceptance by a member in public practice of a payment for the referral of products or services of others to a client is prohibited. Such action is considered to create a conflict of interest that results in a loss of objectivity and independence.

A member shall not make a payment to obtain a client. This rule shall not prohibit payments for the purchase of an accounting practice or retirement payments to individuals for formerly engaged in the practice of public accounting or payments to their heirs or estates.

Rule 505—Form of Practice and Name
A member may practice public accounting only in the form of a proprietorship, a partnership, or a professional corporation whose characteristics conform to resolutions of Council.

A member shall not practice public accounting under a firm name that is misleading. Names of one or more past partners or shareholders may be included in the firm name of a successor partnership or corporation. Also, a partner or shareholder surviving the death or withdrawal of all other partners or shareholders may continue to practice under such name which includes the names of part partners or shareholders for up to two years after becoming a sole practitioner.

A firm may not designate itself as "Members of the American Institute of Certified Public Accountants" unless all of its partners or shareholders are members of the institute.

Other Rules

The Council of the AICPA has also established rules regarding income tax practice and management advisory services.

Are You Independent?

The second general auditing standard states:

In all matters relating to the assignment, an independence in mental attitude is to be maintained by the auditor or auditors.

Auditing standards subdivide this requirement into

- actual independence: the lack of an direct or indirect interest in the client, and
- perceived independence: the absence of control by others.

The following questionnaire will help you gauge your independence with respect to a particular client:

A Questionnaire to Determine if You Are Independent

Client ____
Date ____
Fee percentage to total firm revenues ____________________

Actual Independence

Any "yes" answer indicates a lack of independence.

Does any member of the firm

1. Own or have a commitment to acquire any direct or material indirect financial enterprise in the client?

2. Act as a trustee or executor or administrator of any estate if such trust has or was committed to acquire any direct or material indirect financial interest in the client?
3. Have any joint, closely held business investment with the client or any of its officers, directors, or principal shareholders that was material in relation to the member's net worth or the net worth of your firm?
4. Have any loan to or from the client or any officer, director or principal shareholder of the client.

Note: These loans will not impair independence: if they are not material in relation to the net worth of the borrower, home mortgages, other secured loans.

5. Connected with the client as a promoter, underwriter, or voting trustee, as a director or officer, in any capacity equivalent to that of a member of management or of an employee.

Perceived independence

A "yes" answer to the following questions does not definitely state that you're firm is not independent. However, each affirmative answer should be judged as to how you would appear to others.

1. Does the firm perform write-up work for the client?
2. Does the firm perform management and advisory services for the client?

Example: A CPA firm reviews a proposed acquisition and advises a client to proceed. Subsequently, on audit, it is discovered that significant irregularities have existed. Will this knowledge, that the faulty data, upon which the go ahead decision was based, impair the CPAs independence?

3. Does your firm render tax advise to the client?
4. Will the loss of the client seriously hurt the firm?
5. Are the collections of your accounts receivable from that particular client large, past due and dependent upon successful completion of the audit?

How to Decide When to Accept and Keep a Client

While we all enjoy the practice of accounting, we have grown accustomed to our lifestyle and would like the fees we earn to continue to grow. Therefore, we find it very difficult to turn down a potential new client.

However, we have all heard the horror stories about what can happen when a client goes bad. You know, there are lawsuits, problems with regulatory agencies, and (to add salt to the wounds) you don't collect the money you're owed. Therefore, we must be especially careful.

The following checklist will help you decide whether to accept or reject a new or continuing client:

Client Name ______________________________
Industry ______________________________
Date ______________________________
If accepted, next review date ______________________________

1. How was contact established?
2. Have they left other accountants?
3. Why?
4. What do the prior accountants say?
5. What is the nature of the services requested?
6. How much are they willing to pay for those services?
7. Does that amount fall within your fee schedule?
8. Will the work requested disrupt your normal activities?
9. Do they want the work yesterday?
10. Are the services requested within your firm's expertise?
11. Do the company's financial statements reveal any hazards?
12. Have all tax returns been timely filed?
13. Do you see any potential tax problems that could create a risk for your firm?
14. Are they in a business that might make you uncomfortable?
15. Could the retention of this client have a negative affect on your other clients, referral sources, or lenders?
16. What do you know about the background of the key personnel?
17. Have you made the following independent checks?
    a. articles about the potential client
    b. ratings from independent credit agencies
    c. inquiries from your bankers
    d. discussions with your firm's attorneys

Remember: Professional ethics mandate that you maintain a confidential relationship with clients.

Peer Reviews

Recently, the AICPA and many State Boards of Accountancy have required all member firms to submit to a peer review which will be conducted by an independent firm of CPAs. If a firm does not have this review, not only will the firm be barred form AICPA membership, but so will any members of that firm.

How to Prepare for Peer Reviews

Refer to Statement of Quality Control Standards No. 1.

The firm should document its compliance to the following standards:

1. *Independence:* Reasonably assure that all members of the firm are independent. The forementioned checklist should be attached to a client list and circulated among all members of the firm.
2. *Assignment of personnel:* Staff should be assigned to engagements according to their ability and training. The firm should maintain detailed personnel and training records for each employee. In addition, the work done by each staff member on any engagement should be documented.
3. *Consultation:* There should be an atmosphere of open communication within the firm which will encourage any staff member to seek advice when needed. Furthermore, consultations, whenever possible, should be documented.
4. *Supervision:* The firm should have adequate workpapers that establish the level of supervision and review.
5. *Hiring:* Policies should be established to hire the most qualified staff available. These policies should be documented in the firm's personnel files.
6. *Professional development:* As previously discussed, the firm should devote careful thought and effort to its training programs. Course outlines, and attendance logs should be maintained.
7. *Advancement:* Each staff should be properly and impartially evaluated before advancement. These procedures should be documented.

Note: We have found it useful, in this process, to ask the staff member do a self evaluation. These ratings can then be compared to the supervisor's judgment and the differences discussed.

8. *Acceptance and continuance of clients:* This subject has been previously discussed.
9. *Inspection:* Procedures should be established to determine whether the other quality control procedures are being followed.

Note: In the next section, we will discuss the workings of an internal audit function in the CPA firm.

How Your Firm Should Be Organized to Effectively Perform the Attest Function

The following organization chart can work for most small- and medium-size firms. It should ensure quality of work, as well as effectiveness and time efficiency.

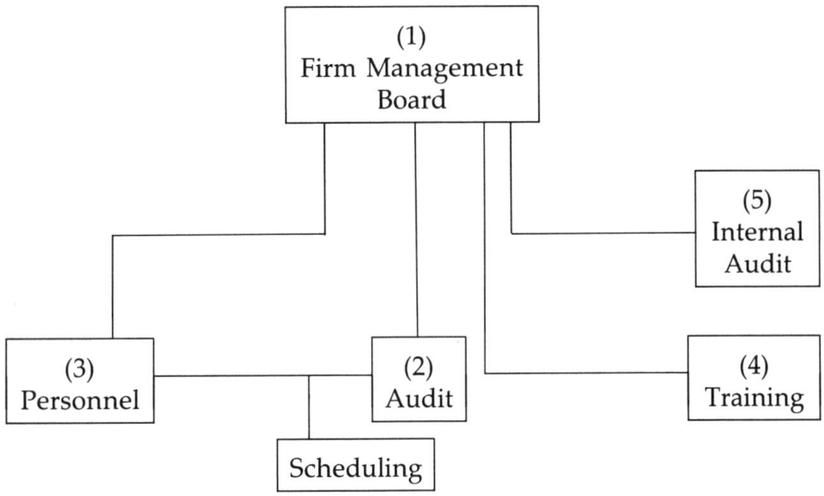

Keys to Organization Chart

1. *Management board:* Each small- to medium-size CPA firm should have a management board, staffed by all partners, which is responsible for the following:
    a. firm's growth and continuance
    b. decisions regarding acceptance and retention of clients
    c. problems regarding fees and collections
    d. policies regarding new FAS, SAS and other regulations

Note: The acceptance rejection decision of all new clients should be made at this level.

The management board should hold regular meetings, use an agenda, and keep written notes of its proceedings.

2. *Audit:* Responsible for the planning, performance, supervision, and review of all audit engagements.
3. *Personnel:* Responsible for hiring, evaluation, promotion, and termination procedures. The personnel department will work closely with the audit department on staff scheduling.

Note: The use of the program evaluation review technique (PERT) for audit scheduling will be discussed in Chapter 7.

4. *Training:* Depending upon the firm's size, responsibility should be assigned either to specified partner(s) or a separate training staff.
5. *Internal Audit:* A separate organizational group, reportable to the firm's management board, should be responsible for quality control. This function should be concerned with the following:

    a. the quality control activities previously discussed under "Peer Review"

    b. final reviews of all independent audit and other jobs as required

    Whether your firm is large or small, this organizational structure can improve your effectiveness and ability to compete. Often staff members who are "fast track" candidates may serve in some of these functions.

A Finding Chart for GAAS Coverage

		SAS Number
Accounting Estimates	Evidence	57
Adequacy of Disclosure	Auditor's Reports	32
Analytical Procedures	Evidence	56
Application of GAAP	Special Reports	50
Audit Committees	Internal Control	61
Audit Risk		47
Audit Sampling	Evidence	39
	Evidence	43
Audited Financial Statements		1

A Finding Chart for GAAS Coverage

		SAS Number
Auditor's Reports		58
		64
		26
	Accompanying Information	29
	Adequacy of Disclosure	32
	Consistency	43
Client Representations	Evidence	19
Communication	Internal Control	60
Computer Processing	Internal Control	48
Condensed Statements	Special Reports	42
Consistency	Auditor's Reports	43
		43
Errors & Irregularities		53
Evidence		8
	Accounting Estimates	57
	Analytical Procedures	56
	Audit Sampling	39
	Audit Sampling	43
	Client Representations	19
	Evidential Matter	31
	Going Concern	59
	Lawyer Letters	12
	Oil & Gas Reserves	45
	Ommitted Procedures	46
	Public Warehouse Inventories	43
	Segment Information	21

(continued on next page)

A Finding Chart for GAAS Coverage

		SAS Number
Evidence (Cont'd.)	Substantive Tests	45
	Supplementary Information	52
	Using Specialist	11
	Working Papers	41
Evidential Matter	Evidence	31
Federal Securities Statutes	Special Reports	37
GAAP	Present Fairly	52
		2
GAAS		1
		43
	Quality Control Standards	25
Going Concern	Evidence	59
Governmental Units		63
Illegal Acts		54
Independent Auditor	Responsibility	1
Interim Financial Information		
Internal Audit Function	Internal Control	65
Internal Control	Audit Committees	61
	Communication	60
	Computer Processing	48
	Internal Audit Function	65
	Working Papers	41

A Finding Chart for GAAS Coverage

		SAS Number
Internal Control Reports	Special Reports	30
Internal Control Structure		55
Lawyer Letters	Evidence	12
Oil & Gas Reserves	Evidence	45
		45
Ommitted Procedures	Evidence	46
Other Countries	Special Reports	51
Planning		22
Pre-Engagement Planning		7
Public Warehouse Inventories	Evidence	43
Quality Control Standards	GAAS	25
Related Parties		45
Review	Interim Financial Information	36
Sampling		39
Segment Information	Evidence	21
Special Purpose Reports	Internal Control Structure	44

(continued on next page)

A Finding Chart for GAAS Coverage

		SAS Number
Special Reports		62
	Application of GAAP	50
	Condensed Statements	42
	Federal Securities Statutes	37
	Internal Control Reports	30
	Other Countries	51
	Unaudited Public Companies	35
	Underwriters Letters	49
Substantive Tests	Evidence	45
Supplementary Information	Evidence	52
Unaudited Public Companies	Special Reports	35
Underwriters Letters	Special Reports	49
		43
Using Specialist	Evidence	11
Working Papers	Internal Control	41
	Evidence	41

CHAPTER 7

How to Plan, Perform and Complete an Opinion Audit

Introduction

Chapter 7 covers the Standards of Field Work as set forth in SAS #1:

1. *Planning:* The work is to be adequately planned and assistants, if any, are to be properly supervised.
2. *Internal control:* There is to be a proper study and evaluation of the existing internal control as a basis for reliance thereon and for the determination of the resultant extent of the tests to which auditing procedures are to be restricted.
3. *Evidence:* Sufficient competent evidential matter is to be obtained through inspection, observation, inquiries, and confirmations to afford a reasonable basis for an opinion regarding the financial statements under examination.

Official Pronouncements

SAS-1 Standards of Fieldwork

SAS-7 Communications between predecessor and successor auditors

SAS-11 Using the work of a specialist

SAS-12 Inquiry of a client's lawyer

SAS-22 Planning and Supervision

SAS-31 Evidential Matter

SASs 43 & 45—Omnibus Statement on Auditing Standards

SAS-47 Audit Risks and materiality in Conducting an Audit

SAS-48 The effects of computer processing on the examination of financial statements

SAS-55 Considerations of the internal control structure in a financial statement audit

SAS-56 Analytical Procedures

Rule 201 and Rule 301—Code of Professional Conduct

The Financial Audit

The following procedure will take you through most financial audits:

I. Preliminary conference
II. Communication with prior accountant
III. Decision to accept
IV. Engagement letter
V. Analysis of dynamics
VI. Initial review of internal control
VII. Analyze audit risks
VIII. Write audit program
IX. Estimate time and schedule personnel
X. Perform interim work
XI. Confirmations and observations
XII. Year end audit procedures
XIII. Workpaper review
XIV. Prepare preliminary report
XV. Discuss with client
XVI. Final review
XVII. Issue audit report and management letter

What to Do Before You Start the Job Steps I—IV

I. Hold Initial Conference

It is the first conference that is critical. You will try to discover the following:

- Is the chemistry right?
- Will you be able to work with these people in a professional manner within your firm's fee structure?

It is important to obtain an understanding of the following to set the proper pattern:

1. What specific services are to be rendered?
2. How much will the client's staff do?
3. When will they be ready for you to start?
4. When do they want the completed audit?
5. Are there any significant limitations that are being placed on you?
6. Why did they leave their prior accountant?
7. Can you agree on a fair fee for your services?

II. Talk to Former Accountants

If SAS-7, the requirement that you communicate with your prior accountant, did not exist, it would still make good business sense to do so.

Note: The SEC requires a company changing auditors to file Form 8-K which is used to explain the reason for the change. The prior auditors are also required to provide a letter which states their agreements and disagreements with the client.

In any event, as the succeeding auditor you should ask the following:

1. Did you have any significant agreements about the application of accounting principles?
2. Did your former client attempt to restrict the scope of your work?
3. Were there any instances where management tried to circumvent the internal controls?
4. Did management encourage its employees to cooperate with you?
5. Were there any problems regarding your fee?
6. Have you been paid for all of your work?

Remember: The confidentiality requirement may prevent the former accountants from answering your questions. Therefore, make sure that you have your potential client request their cooperation.

III. Decide Whether or Not to Accept the Client

Refer to Chapter 6 for a questionnaire on this topic.

IV. Obtain a Signed Engagement Letter

An engagement letter will set forth, in writing, the agreements reached at the initial conference.

Example: Jay Ruben Accountancy Corporation has agreed to perform an audit of The Devenport Corporation for the year ended December 31, 19XX. The following engagement letter has been prepared:

Mrs. Constance Siegel, President
Devenport Corporation
123 Tired Hollow
Buzzards Breath, Il.

Dear Mrs. Siegel:

In accordance with the agreement reached in our conference on September 12, 19XX, we are to perform an examination of the balance sheet of Devenport Corporation as of December 31, 19XX, and of the related statements of income, retained earnings, and statements of cash flow for the fiscal year then ended. The audit report will be worded as follows:

"To the Board of Directors and Stockholders
Devenport Corporation

We have audited the accompanying balance sheet of The Devenport Agency at December 31, 19XX, and the related statements of income, retained earnings, and cash flows for the year then ended. These financial statements are the responsibility of The Company's management. Our responsibility is to express an opinion on these financial statements based on our audit.

We conducted our audit in accordance with generally accepted auditing standards. Those standards require that we plan and perform the audit to obtain reasonable assurance about whether the financial statements are free of material misstatement. An audit includes examining, on a test basis, evidence supporting the amounts and disclosures on the financial statements. An audit also includes assessing the accounting principles used and significant estimates made by management, as well as evaluating the overall financial statement presentation. We believe that our audit provides a reasonable basis for our opinion.

In our opinion, the financial statements referred to above present fairly, in all material respects, the financial position of Devenport

Corporation at December 31, 19XX, and the results of its operations and its cash flows for the year then ended in conformity with generally accepted accounting principles."

Our audit will be performed in accordance with generally accepted auditing standards and, accordingly, will include such tests of the accounting records and such other auditing procedures as we consider necessary to enable us to express an opinion regarding your financial statements. It should be noted that the financial statements are the primary responsibility of management and such an audit is not primarily designed, and cannot be relied on, to disclose all errors, defalcations, and other similar irregularities, although they may be discovered as a result of the audit.

Our audit will include an evaluation of your company's internal control structure. The purpose of this evaluation is to determine the scope of our audit engagement and is not performed to detect all errors in the processing of information. On the basis of our evaluation of that structure, we will make suggestions, where appropriate, for improving the system. If we should discover reportable conditions in the design or the execution of the system, we will disclose these to you in writing before the conclusion of our audit.

Based on our discussions with your personnel and the prior auditor, and a preliminary review of the accounting records, we estimate the cost of the audit engagement will be approximately $85,000. It should be recognized that the estimated fee could be affected by unusual circumstances we cannot foresee at this time. However, if we should encounter such problems, we will immediately contact you to discuss the implications of the new development.

We appreciate the opportunity to work with you. Please, do not hesitate to contact us if you have any questions about the engagement or desire other professional services.

If the terms set forth in this letter are satisfactory, please sign in the space provided below and return the duplicate copy of the letter to us.

Sincerely

Jay Ruben Accountancy Corporation

Accepted by: ______________________________

Title: ______________________________

Date: ______________________________

V. Understand the Client

Before we begin an audit, we have to understand the client and the dynamics of the business. As previously considered we use a form of top down analysis in the following order:

1. Environmental analysis
2. Industry analysis
3. Company analysis

How to Keep Abreast of the Environment

As auditors, we are more than technicians. Instead, each of us is a professional who must keep aware of the trends in the environment in order to do a good job. There are a number of environmental factors that affect the audit:

a. demographics
b. social
c. political
d. economic
e. technological

What follows below is a quick way to bring yourself up to speed on he pertinent environmental factors.

1. *Look at the business publications*
   Business newspapers: *Wall Street Journal*
   Weekly and monthly business journals: *Business Week, Forbes, Fortune.*
2. *Read the daily newspapers* particularly the news, metropolitan, opinion, and view sections.
3. *Study weekly and monthly news magazines*
   For example, *Time* and *Newsweek.*
4. *Become familiar with magazines that cover cultural trends* such as *Harpers, Atlantic Monthly.*

None of these have to be read, cover to cover. An awareness is sufficient.

Hint: As you browse through these publications, look for articles that may pertain to your existing clients. A clipping with a short note is a great public relations device.

How to Understand the Client's Industry

Your client is a player in his or her industry and is, of course, affected by changes that take place in that trade. It is important, as you design your audit, to be aware:

1. growth trends
2. state of market development
3. the competition

How to Get Industry Data

- trade journals
- trade associations
- investor services, e.g. Value Line

Note: Any good college library will have most of this information.

How to Understand Your Client

Your client is more than a set of journals and ledgers. It is the product, people, finances, and facilities that make up its corporate whole. Your knowledge gathering process should include the following:

1. *Find out about its marketing:* The company's marketing effort can be described by its product, price, promotion, and distribution methods.
   - Talk to personnel in the marketing department.
   - Look at its advertising and catalogs.
   - If pertinent, get a demonstration of the company's major products.
   - Find out how the products are priced and the type of discount policies in effect.
   - Discuss the methods of distribution and salesperson compensation.
2. *Obtain some comprehension of the product*
   - Find out how the product is acquired and/or manufactured
   - Get an understanding of the raw materials and their cost, scarcity, and lead times
   - Understand the role of skilled, semi-skilled, and unskilled labor required to manufacture the product.

3. *Describe the people*
   - Read the payroll policy manual if it exists
   - Find out How the company train its personnel
   - Understand its compensation and promotion policies
4. *Tour the facilities.* Ask questions about the following:
   - What is their condition?
   - Is the technology up to date?
   - What about capacity? Is the company short or does it have excess capacity?
   - Do they own or lease the facilities?

VI. How to Use the Cradle to the Grave Method to Review, Test and Evaluate Internal Controls

The Second Standard of Field Work

"There is to be a proper study and evaluation of the existing internal control as a basis for reliance thereon and for the determination of the resultant extent of the tests to which auditing procedures are to be restricted."

Internal Control Defined

The overall plan of organization and the methods employed by a company to:

(1) safeguard its assets
(2) ensure the reliability of its accounting data
(3) ensure compliance with established company policies

Tracing the Life Cycle of a Transaction

The *cradle to grave method* is advocated as the most efficient and effective way to review, test, and evaluate the internal control. It is based on the premise that every accounting transaction has a beginning and an end. And, the best way to understand the effectiveness of the controls is to follow the transactional flow through its entire existence.

For example, the sales collection cycle would have a life line as follows:

Receive Order	—	Prepare Shipper	—	Invoice & Shipment	—	Accounts Receivable	—	Collection	—	Deposit

A Four-Step Procedure to Understand Internal Control Strengths and Weaknesses

1. Flowchart the Cycle
2. Do a cradle to grave test of *THREE* transactions
3. Answer an internal control questionnaire
4. Perform heavy testing where weaknesses are discovered

Why only three transactions? To give us a feel of the entire process. By itself, the three transaction test, does not evaluate internal control. However, it acts as a starting point to perform the bulk of the work in this area.

What Are Compliance, Substantive and Analytical Tests? And, How Are They Used to Test and Evaluate Internal Control?

Compliance tests are used to determine how well the system of internal control is performing.

Example: The company's accounting policy manual requires all purchase orders to be supported by a purchase requisition which has been properly authorized. A compliance test would match a sample of purchase orders to properly approved purchase requisitions.

Substantive tests are employed to provide evidence to the auditor that the representations made by management are properly reflected in the financial statements.

Example: Vouching invoices which support property and equipment purchases.

Analytical tests study and compare relationships.

The Testing Process Illustrated

The next pages present:

1. Flowchart symbols
2. A simple flowchart
3. Internal control questionnaire

Sample flowchart As you prepare flowcharts, remember the cradle to grave concept. Every transaction has to have a beginning and an end. And, that is just as true with regard to the documents that support a system.

For example, assume you are charting the flow of sales order, which has five copies. Make sure that you account for every copy.

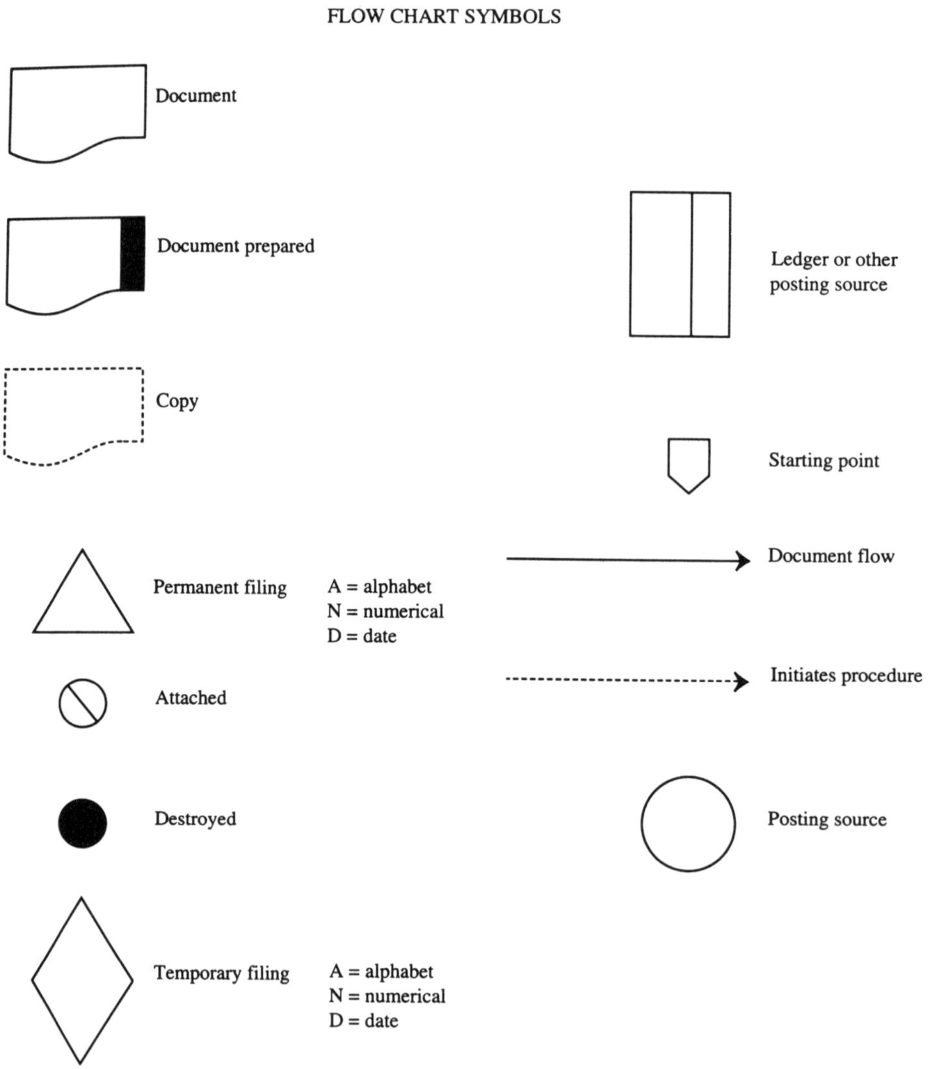

Exhibit 7-1

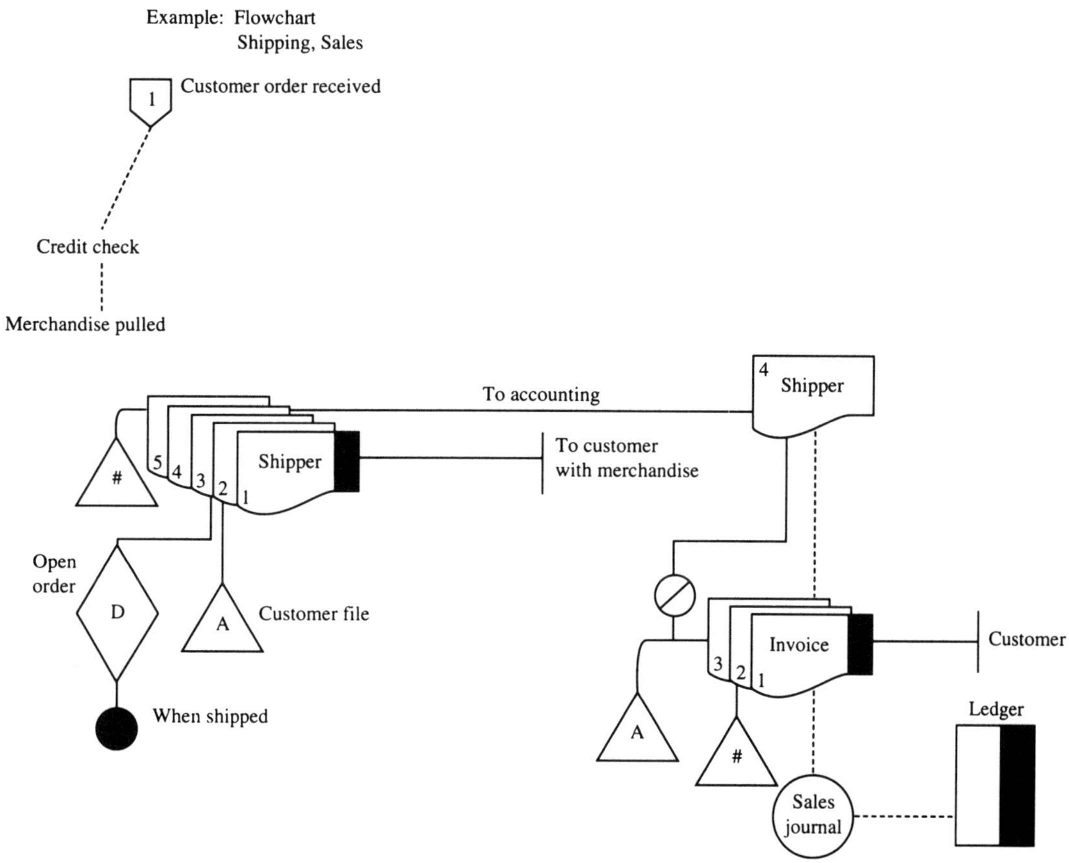

Exhibit 7-1 ***(Continued)***

Internal Control Wrap Up

As you prepare flowcharts and answer the questions posed in the various lead sheets, note the unsatisfactory answers. These will require substantive and compliance testing, which will be dictated by your concept of materiality and audit risk.

Effect of EDP

The following knowledge is recommended:

1. Basic concepts and EDP controls
2. Transactions and file processing
3. Working understanding of the computer languages used

Note: As the chapters on EDP will show, at present there are four levels of computer programming languages. Generally, most auditors need only to be aware of the highest level, or the Fourth generation programs.

4. Ability to use a generalized audit package. These programs ease your work by performing mathematical functions, identifying exceptions, and helping to make selections.

Caution: Many of these systems are very sophisticated and beyond your basic knowledge as an accountant and auditor. We strongly recommend that you consult an expert.

INTERNAL CONTROL QUESTIONNAIRE

Sales, Receivables, Receipts Cycle

	Yes	No
1. Are all shipped goods invoiced?	☐	☐
2. Credit approval prior to shipment?	☐	☐
3. Are all invoices recorded in the accounts?		
4. Are receivables properly credited?	☐	☐
5. Do controls exist against lapping?	☐	☐
6. Are all receipts deposited?	☐	☐
7. Are overdue accounts attended to?	☐	☐
9. Are invoices correctly prepared?	☐	☐
10. Are miscellaneous receipts controlled?	☐	☐

1. Are all shipped goods invoiced?
   Factors
   - Follow up of shipping or sales order numbers
   - Identify non routine sales
   - Segregated shipping, billing, cash receipts
   - Shipping area access control
2. Credit approval prior to shipment?
3. Are all invoices recorded in the accounts?
   Factors
   - Billing segregated from receivables
   - Follow up of invoice numbers
   - Matching of shipping or sales order documents to posting
4. Are receivables properly credited?
   Factors
   - Independent credit approval
   - Prenumbered credit memos
   - Proper support
5. Do controls exist against lapping?
   Factors
   - Independent delinquency follow up
   - Independent receivable posting, balancing and aging
   - Queries followed up independently
6. Are all receipts deposited?
   Factors
   - Cashier runs control tape
   - For deposit only stamp
   - Receipts deposited promptly
   - Receipts direct to cashier
   - Separation of cashier and receivable functions
7. Are overdue accounts attended to?
   Factors
   - Aged trial balance
   - Independent follow up

9. Are invoices correctly prepared?
   Factors
   - Approval of pricing, quantities and extensions
   - Standard price list

10. Are miscellaneous receipts controlled?

Exhibit 7-1 *(Continued)*

Purchases, payables, payments cycle

1. Are all purchases authorized?
    - Factors
        - Purchase approval
        - Requisition approval
        - Segregation of purchasing, receiving, payables

2. Does payable set up requiring receiving documentation?
    - Factors
        - All invoices to payables not purchasing
        - Investigation of unmatched documents
        - Prenumbered receiving slip
        - Receiving inspection
        - Segregation of receiving from payables

3. Are all payments properly supported?
    - Factors
        - Checks mailed out directly
        - Control of bank transfers
        - Discounts taken
        - Independent bank reconciliations
        - Independent check signers
        - Invoice checking
        - Invoices marked "paid"

4. Are non routine payment controlled?

5. Are suppliers statements reconciled to invoices and payments?

6. Are codings checked?

7. Is petty cash controlled?
    - Factors
        - Imprest funds
        - Periodic counts
        - Vouchers canceled

8. Are controls over property and equipment purchases adequate?
    - Factors
        - Adequate insurance coverage
        - Periodic inspection
        - Scrap and disposal reports
        - Self constructed asset work orders

Exhibit 7-1 *(Continued)*

Personnel, payroll cycle

1. Is payroll controlled against overpayments? | | |
   - Factors
     - Budgetary control
     - Distribution by non supervisor
     - Identification of employee
     - Rotation of duties
     - Segregation of check signing from distribution
     - Segregation of check signing from preparation
     - Segregation of payroll from personnel
     - Unclaimed pay controlled

2. Are payments limited to work done? | | |
   - Factors
     - Salesperson commissions compared to sales
     - Time clocks

3. Are payroll errors avoided? | | |
   - Factors
     - Approvals, distribution reviewed
     - Changes authorized
     - Rates and changes in personnel records

Inventory and Cost Accounting

1. Are there safeguards against loss or pilferage? | | |
   - Factors
     - Inventory records separated from stock
     - Responsible storekeepers
     - Up to date cost system
     - Use of stock requisitions

General Ledger and Journals

1. Are entries coded correctly? | | |
   - Factor
     - Budgetary control
     - Monthly trial balance

2. Are journal entries adequately supported and checked? | | |

3. Are there sufficient Administrative controls? | | |
   - Factor
     - Accounting manuals
     - Adequate fidelity insurance
     - Books kept up to date
     - Branch operation controls
     - Internal audit department
     - Rotation of duties
     - Timely internal reporting

4. Are adequate procedures in place for peak, slack and and vacation periods | | |

Exhibit 7-1 *(Continued)*

The Impact of Risk on Audit Procedures

As the following matrix shows, there is an overall hazard in every audit:

Conclusion	*Actual*
The financial statements are fairly presented.	They are *not* fairly presented.
The financial statements are *not* fairly presented.	They *are* fairly presented.

Generally, audit risks are divided into the ensuing categories:

1. *Risk of error occurring* This risk is subject to two conditions:
    a. *The inherent risk:* How easy is it for an account to be misstated. Certain items are more subject to error:
        - non-monetary arrangements
        - mergers and acquisitions
        - items requiring considerable accounting judgment
        - accounts subject to theft (e.g. cash)
        - accounting estimates

    b. *The internal control risk:* No system is foolproof. Errors can and do occur.
2. *Audit detection risk* An audit cannot be expected to eliminate all risks. However, within certain limitations, the more analytical and substantive tests that are conducted, the better the chance to find errors.

How to Customize Your Audit Programs

The audit plan is a function of the following:

1. Your agreement with your client
2. Information disclosed by obtaining an understanding of your client.
3. Your review, tests, and evaluations of internal control
4. Perceived risks
5. Audit objectives

Audit procedures for specific accounts are covered in Chapter 9.

How to Use PERT to Budget and Schedule Audits

What Is PERT?

Many managers use the Program Evaluation and Review Technique (PERT) and Critical Path Method (CPM) to plan, schedule and control projects that consist of numerous tasks performed at a variety of times by a variety of individuals. An audit is that kind of a project. The PERT technique has been found to be useful to help an auditor schedule and complete an audit on time with the best mix of resources.

What Audit Questions Will PERT Answer?

1. When the audit is expected to be started and completed?
2. When should each specific task be expected to be started and completed?
3. Which tasks (activities) are critical and must be completed exactly on time to keep the project on schedule?
4. How long can non-critical jobs be delayed before they set back the entire audit?

The Procedures

We will use the Devenport Corporation as an example.

1. Make a clear statement of the objectives of the audit, specifically identifying what has to be accomplished.

   Devenport audit objective: To render an opinion on the financial statements.

2. Make a list of all activities and their immediate predecessors.

Activity		*Predecessors*
A	Internal control	
B	Plan audit	A
C	Transaction tests	B
D	Preliminary work	B
E	Observe inventory	B
F	Confirmations	B

(*Continued on next page*)

Activity		*Predecessors*
G	Client ready	B
H	Final work	C, E, G
I	Accounts receivable	F
J	Accounts payable	G
K	Statements	D, H, I, J
L	Review	K

3. Estimate the time required to complete each audit activity. When planning an audit, you must, of course, estimate your time. A typical PERT network uses three approximations for each job:

   Optimistic or least time (a): How long each task will take if everything proceeds in an ideal manner.
   Most probable time (m): The most likely time under normal conditions
   Pessimistic (most) b: The time required if we encounter delays

   These three estimates are components of the following equation:

$$t = \frac{a + 4m + b}{6}$$

   Devenport time estimates: The following is a budget of time, in days, for Devenport:

   Jay Ruben Accountancy Corporation
   Audit Schedule and Time Budget
   Client: Devenport Corporation
   Fiscal Year End: December 31, 19XX
   Date: September 1, 19XX

Time (days)	Least	Most likely	Most	Computed
Partner/Manager				
Internal Control	1.00	2.00	4.00	2.17
Plan Audit	2.00	3.00	5.00	3.17
Supervision	4.75	8.35	13.00	8.53
Review	2.00	3.50	5.00	3.50
Conferences	0.50	1.00	3.00	1.24
Total	10.25	17.85	30.00	18.61

Time (days)	Least	Most likely	Most	Computed
Staff				
Preliminary				
Internal Control	3.00	5.00	6.00	4.83
Cash	0.50	1.00	1.50	1.00
Accounts Receivable	2.00	4.00	7.00	4.17
Inventories	3.00	5.00	9.00	5.33
Prepaid expenses	1.50	2.00	3.50	2.17
Investments	2.00	3.00	5.00	3.17
Property/Equipment	4.00	6.00	9.00	6.17
Intangibles	1.00	2.00	4.00	2.17
Income taxes	0.50	1.00	1.50	1.00
Notes payable	3.00	4.00	6.00	4.17
Equity	1.00	2.00	3.00	2.00
Income/Expenses	2.00	5.00	7.00	4.82
	23.50	40.00	62.50	41.00
Year End				
Confirmations	1.00	2.00	3.00	2.00
Cash	0.50	1.00	1.50	1.00
Accts Receivable	2.00	5.00	9.00	5.17
Inventories				
Observation	3.00	5.00	8.00	5.17
Pricing	2.00	4.00	6.00	4.00
Prepaid expenses	1.00	1.50	2.00	1.50
Investments	1.00	1.50	2.50	1.58
Property/Equipment	2.00	4.00	5.00	3.83
Intangibles	0.50	1.00	1.50	1.00
Accounts Payable	2.00	3.00	4.00	3.00
Income taxes	1.00	2.00	3.00	2.00
Notes payable	1.00	2.00	4.00	2.17
Equity	2.00	3.00	5.00	3.17
Income/Expenses	2.00	4.00	6.00	4.00
Statements	2.00	3.50	5.00	3.50
Conference	2.00	3.00	5.00	3.16
Total	25.00	45.50	70.50	46.25
Staff Total	48.50	85.50	133.00	87.25

4. Compute the audit fee. As you see, the estimated times have been segregated between partner and staff days which allows us to estimate our fee:

Time Estimate	Days	Hours	Rate	Total
Partner/Manager	18.61	148.88	150.00	22,332
Staff	87.25	698.00	75.00	52,350
Total				74,682
Contingency (10%)				7,468
Total Fee Estimate				82,150

5. Develop the network.

   Devenport network: See below.
   You will note, it is constructed in two forms:

   - Flowchart (below)
   - Barchart (page 269)

6. Perform the PERT/CPM calculations to develop a schedule for the project and identify the critical path activities. There are two ways to do this work:

   - By hand (a good management sciences text will show you how)
   - By computer program. The following computations were performed by STORM which is published by Holden-Day, Inc. What follows are two exhibits produced by the program:

     Activities in order of latest allowed start date

     Schedule of critical path

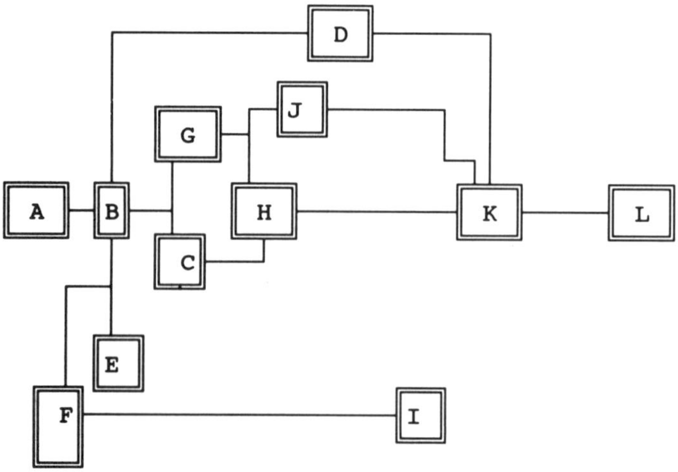

The Devenport Agency - PERT Analysis : Bar chart

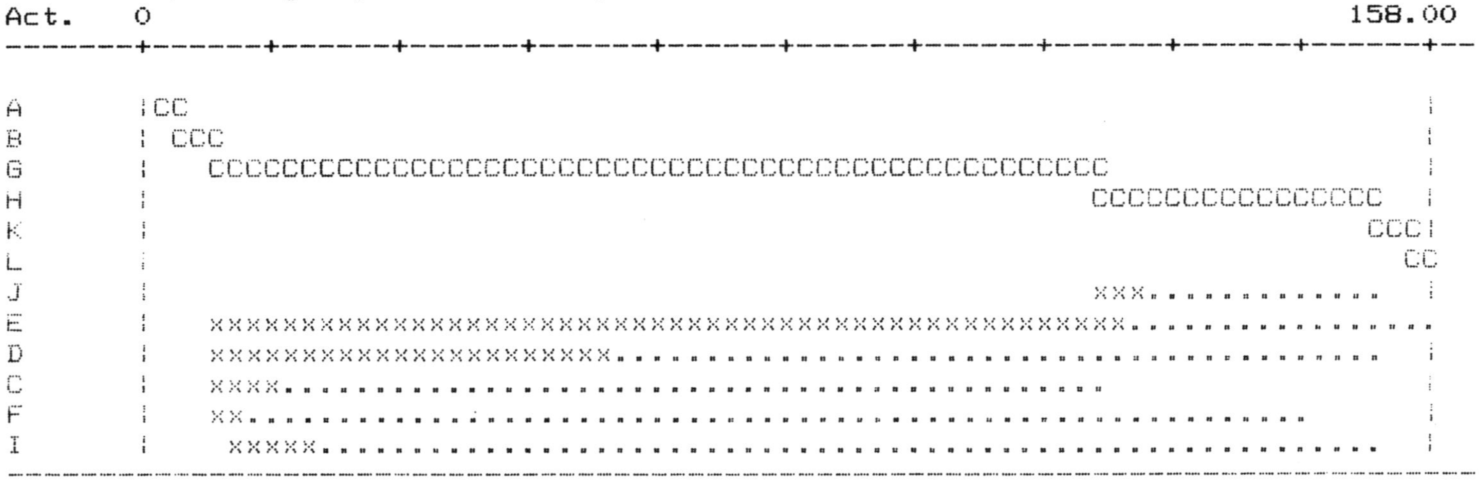

The data to run the program made the following assumptions:

1. A factor was added for weekends.
2. The inventory could not be observed before December 31, and the client's closing would not be completed before January 2.

Devonport Corporation
PERT audit schedule

Critical Path	Days	Adjusted for Weekend	Last Start Date	Completion Date
A Internal Control	2.17	3.04	25-Dec-88	28-Dec-88
B Planning	3.17	4.44	28-Dec-88	02-Jan-89
C Wait for Client		0.00		02-Jan-89
H Final (see below)	34.42	48.19	02-Jan-89	19-Feb-89
K Statements	3.50	4.90	19-Feb-89	24-Feb-89
L Review	3.50	4.90	24-Feb-89	28-Feb-89

Final Work

Confirmations	2.00	2.00
Cash	1.00	1.40
Accounts Receivable	5.17	7.24
Inventories	4.00	5.60
Prepaid Expenses	1.50	2.10
Investments	1.58	2.21
Property/Equipment	3.83	5.36
Intangibles	1.00	1.40
Accounts Payable	3.00	4.20
Income Taxes	2.00	2.80
Notes Payable	2.17	3.04
Equity	3.17	4.44
Income/Expenses	4.00	6.40
	34.42	48.19

Critical Path

A. Preliminary internal control review
B. Plan audit
C. Wait for client to finish closing
H. Final audit work
K. Prepare statements
L. Review

The data shows that The Devonport Corporation audit should be finished by February 28, 1989. The program will also portray the following information:

- Activities sorted by slack and earliest start
- Non-critical activities by slack
- Non-critical activities by earliest start

How to Reduce Audit Time Span by Performing Interim Work

If possible, the following procedures should be started as soon as the audit plan is completed:

1. Complete internal control tests
2. Vouch all asset additions to date
3. Check computations of allocations and estimates

   For example: Depreciation computations

4. Bring permanent file up to date for:

   a. property and equipment
   b. patents, copyrights, and trademarks
   c. investments
   d. long-term leases
   e. loan contracts
   f. articles of incorporation
   g. corporation minutes and by laws
   h. stock certificate books
   i. stock option plans

5. Begin to write management letter.

Note: Confirmation, observation and year-end audit procedures are discussed in Chapter 9.

How to Design Your Audit Review in Order to Conform to GAAS

If it can be shown that an audit was conducted in accordance with Generally Accepted Auditing Standards, you will usually be in a good position to defend your work.

General Standards

1. *Training*
   - A. Did each person assigned to the engagement write memos of work done and conclusions?
   - B. Do these memos show good application of auditing and accounting knowledge and composition?
   - C. Was their performance evaluated by the supervisor?
2. *Independence*
   - A. Did anything come to your attention which could impair your firm's independence? If yes,
     1. Was it resolved?
     2. Was the independence questionnaire completed? (See Chapter 6)
3. *Due Professional Care*
   - A. If necessary, were consultants services used?
   - B. Does the audit conform to the standards of field work?
   - C. Has the tax department examined the workpapers?
   - D. Was the audit reviewed by another partner?
   - E. Do you think this audit would pass a peer review?

Standards of Field Work

1. *Planning*
   - A. Was the audit plan written in accordance with internal control conditions as disclosed?
   - B. Were risk and materiality appropriately considered?
   - C. Was it efficiently scheduled?
   - D. How were excess time problems resolved?
2. *Internal Control*
   - A. Were Cradle to Grave analyses done for the major cycles?
   - B. Were the tests of transactions procedures designed to cover any internal control deficiencies disclosed?
   - C. Were the internal control conclusions valid?
   - D. Are problems noted in the management letter?

3. *Evidence*

   Note: The functions and forms of evidence will be discussed in Chapter 9.

   A. Was sufficient evidentiary material obtained to support our audit conclusions and the fairness of the financial statements?

   B. Were all confirmation or observation problems disclosed?

Standards of Reporting

4. *Accordance with GAAP*

   A. Does our report state that the financial statements were stated in accordance with GAAP?

   B. Do the conclusions reached by our audit support an unqualified opinion?

   C. If not, describe the circumstances.

      1. Has this been discussed with the client?
      2. Has it been fully documented?
      3. Have we obtained an opinion of our counsel as to possible damages to the firm?

5. *Consistency*

   A. Were consistent GAAP applied to the financial statements?

   B. Have we made analytical reviews (e.g. inventory turnover, gross profit analyses) to support consistency?

6. *Disclosures*

   A. Are all significant matters sufficiently disclosed in the financial statements?

   B. Are the footnotes adequate?

   C. Have all contingencies been disclosed?

   D. Has our report been dated?

   E. Are there any subsequent events that should be disclosed or reported?

7. *Opinion Expression*

   A. Have we drafted our opinion?

   B. Has it been approved by the client?

   C. Does it clearly state the degree of responsibility we have taken?

CHAPTER 8
Statistical Sampling

Introduction

The main task of financial auditing is to gather evidence to support the amounts carried on the financial statements. Statistical sampling is a valuable tool to not only quantify the extent of our tests, but also to assess the inherent risks that arise from examining only a portion of this data.

Chapter 8 will provide a handy guide to show you why and when statistical sampling should be used in substantive and compliance testing. The following subjects will be covered:

- Terminology
- Attribute versus Variable Sampling
- The right sample size
- Selecting the samples
- Attribute sampling
- Sampling for variables
- Avoiding the dangers

Official Pronouncement

SAS 39: Audit Sampling. Effective June 25, 1982

Why Use Statistical Sampling?

When we conduct a financial audit, we only examine a portion of the data. In order to decide what and how much to observe, we must rely upon our professional judgment. The techniques of statistical sampling help us avoid some inherent subjectivity by converting our judgment into quantifiable items. This includes:

1. A mathematical inference about the sufficiency of evidentiary material

2. A way to evaluate sample results
3. Some quantification of risks

We need to take this information and come to a conclusion about the results of our work.

The Terminology of Statistical Sampling

Statistical sampling, like so many disciplines, has its own meta language of buzz words and terms. Since many of them will be used throughout the chapter, a quick working glossary is presented.

N = *Population:* The set of all possible units for which meaningful information can be obtained relative to a characteristic of interest.

Example: All sales invoices

n = *Sample:* A subset, or a collection of elements taken from a population.

Example: a selection of sales invoices

$\overline{X}$ = *Mean:* The average value. The sum of the particular data divided by the number of items.

Median: The value in the middle position of the array of data observed.

Mode: The value in an array of distributions that occurs most frequently.

Standard deviation: The degree of variance of data from the average value. The greater the standard deviation, the more the variance. The standard deviation equation follows:

$$\sigma = \sqrt{\frac{\Sigma X^2 - \frac{(\Sigma X)^2}{N}}{N}}$$

Confidence level: The measure of assurance the auditor desires. *Example:* The sample indicates a 10% error rate. How confident does the auditor want to be that the sample rate reflects the state of the population.

Using the Definitions—An Example

The sales invoice distribution for The Noushkel Company is presented below:

Note: f = frequency

At Least	Less Than	Mid point	X^2	f	fx	fx^2
100	150	125	15,625	2	250	31,250
200	250	225	50,625	6	1,350	303,750
300	350	325	105,625	6	1,950	633,750
400	450	425	180,625	12	5,100	2,167,500
500	550	525	275,625	16	8,400	4,410,000
600	650	625	390,625	6	3,750	2,343,750
700	750	725	525,625	2	1,450	1,051,250
				50	22,250	10,941,250

The above information reveals the following:

Mean	445
Variance	20,800
Standard deviation	144

The distribution of this data is presented graphically on the following page:

How Confidence Levels Work

If Normal Probability Distribution Tables are consulted, the following confidence levels are found:

Confidence Level	Standard Deviation
80%	1.28
90%	1.65
95%	1.96
99%	2.55

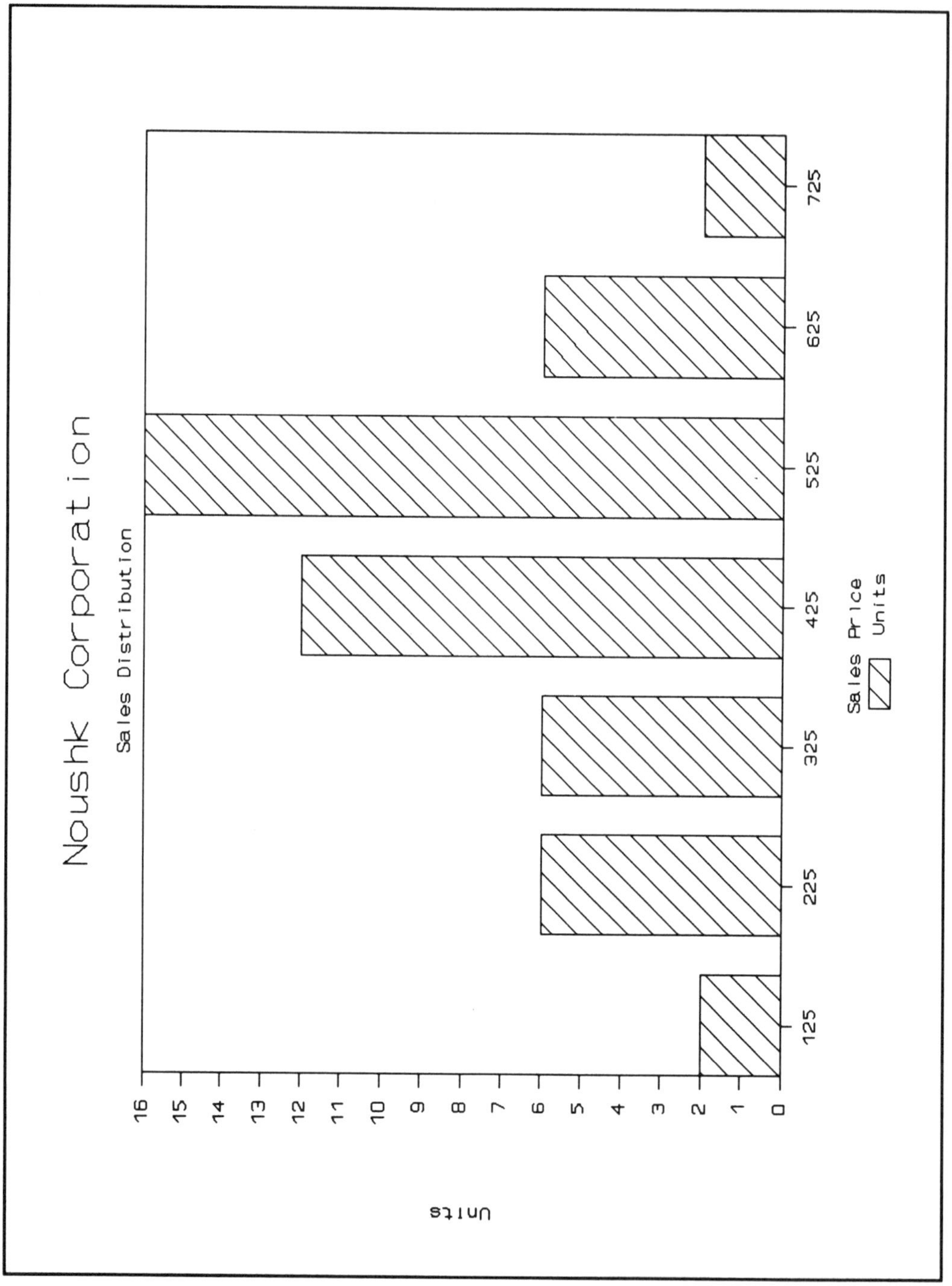
Noushk Corporation
Sales Distribution
Units
0
1
2
3
4
5
6
7
8
9
10
11
12
13
14
15
16
125
225
325
425
525
625
725
Sales Price
Units

By using these tables, we derive the following:

Confidence Desired	# Strd Dev	Amount*	Range Lower	Range Upper	Spread
80.00%	1.28	$185	$260	$630	$370
90.00%	1.65	238	207	683	476
95.00%	1.96	283	162	728	566
99.00%	2.55	368	77	813	736

144 * 1.28 144 * 1.96
144 * 1.65 144 * 2.55

Therefore, we can be 80% confident that the average invoice will fall in a range between $260 and $630 and 99% confident that the average invoice will fall in a range between $77 and $813.

In other words, our confidence increases as the area of possible events widens.

How to Tell When You Should Use Attribute or Variable Sampling

Attribute Sampling

Attribute sampling measures the frequency of a specific occurrence and is used for compliance testing.

Example: How many payments lacked attached purchase authorization?

Variable Sampling

Variable sampling is a form of substantive testing, and is used to estimate the dollar value of a specified population.

Example: Inventory valuation

The following chart lists the characteristics and uses of attribute and variable sampling:

	Attribute	Variable
Type of Test	Determine internal control effectiveness	Verify dollar value
Determine deviation conditions	Departure from proscribed condition	
Define the Population	Period covered Sampling unit Consider completeness	Define the sampling unit. Consider population completeness. Identify individually significant items.
Method of sample selection	Random number	Unrestricted random Stratified
Calculate the sample size	Consider acceptable risk Consider tolerable error rate	Consider the population expected rate. Consider population size, variations within the population, acceptable risk level, tolerable error.
Perform the sampling plan		
Evaluate the results	Calculate the deviation rate Consider the sampling risk Consider qualitative aspects	Reach an overall conclusion. Project error to population. Consider qualitative aspects.

How to Determine the Right Sample Size

A change in any of the following factors will affect the required audit sample size:

Factor	Sample Size
Auditor's Judgment:	
Risk	
As the perceived risk increases	Increases
Confidence level (Reliability)	
As the auditor's need to feel assured that the sample results are a good representation of the population characteristics increases	Increases
Tolerance for errors (Precision)	
As the auditor's tolerance for errors increases	Decreases
Population Characteristics:	
Variability of items in population standard deviation	
As the standard deviation of a population increases	Increases
Expected occurrence rate	
As the expected number of occurrences increase	Increases
Population	
As the population increases	Increases

Note: Mathematically, the population size is the *least* important factor.

How to Select the Samples

A major requirement of statistical sampling is to see that every item in the population has an equal chance of being selected. This is important for two reasons:

1. Bias is eliminated
2. The items sampled are a fair representation of the population.

Techniques

Systematic sampling examines every *n*th item.

For example, assume the population contains 1,000 items, and you have decided to sample 10%, you would start with number 100, then look at 200, and so forth.

This form of sampling is easy and lacks bias. However, if events occur in any form of regular pattern, the results will not be representative.

Cluster sampling views a group of items and examines each cluster in detail. It could be a month, a letter of the alphabet, or a file drawer. Cluster sampling is easy and inexpensive, but may not be very representative.

Random selection plans allow every population unit to have an equal chance of being included in the sample. The results derived should be the close representation of the universe.

Suggestion: There are random number tables and computer programs that can be utilized. In addition, various forms of auditing software are designed to make the entire selection.

Note: It is important to establish correspondence between the chosen items and the tables. If the units are renumbered, the task is easy. However, you will have to be creative at times.

For example, if you are selecting alpha items, assign the first two columns of the table or the program to the letter of the alphabet. e.g. A = 01, L = 12.

How to Construct and Evaluate an Attribute Sampling Plan

The following checklist should guide you through the intricacies of an attribute sampling plan:

1. *State the objectives of the test.* You will be looking for characteristics in the population (attributes) that could signify an unacceptable rate of errors.
2. *Define the population.* This should include whatever data you require.

   Example: If you are concerned about support of expenses, the population could be all items in the purchase journal.
3. *Define the sampling unit.* This will include the item of interest which you want to view.

Example: A purchase invoice.

4. *Define the attributes of interest.* You want to decide the specifics you need to examine.

   Example: Do the prices agree with the purchase orders?

5. *Specify the desired upper precision limit.* The error rate that your professional judgment allows you to permit and still rely on the internal controls.
6. *Choose your confidence level.* The statistical way of expressing the probability that the population error rate does not exceed the stated upper precision limit.

   Question: How much reliability do you need? Once again, it is a question for your professional judgment.

7. *Estimate the population error rate.* Derived by using the results of prior adults as a gauge.
8. *Determine the initial sample size.* You will do this by using the tables found in the appendix to this chapter.
9. *Select a random sample.* This will be discussed later in this chapter.
10. *Perform the normal audit procedures to the sample selected.*
11. *Apply the sample results to the population.* The effect on the population of the error discovered from the sampling can be derived.
12. *Perform error anlaysis.* Answer the following questions:
    - What were the nature of the errors discovered?
    - What types of internal control breakdowns may have caused them?
    - How will your other audit work be affected?
    - What will the impact be on the financial statements?
13. *Decide if the population is acceptable.* If the error rate discovered, applied to the population as a whole, exceeds the tolerable limits you had previously set, then you may have to choose among the following options:

    A. Do you revise the upper precision limit?

    B. Do you change your desired confidence level?

    C. Should you expand the size of the sample?

D. Should you perform additional and/or different substantive procedures?

E. Or, do you decide that the internal control system is *not* reliable? You may have to consider resigning from the audit.

An Example of Attribute Sampling

Suppose you are reviewing the internal controls of Devenport Corporation and want to know how many invoices do not have shipping documentation attached. The test parameters are defined below:

Type of test: Compliance

Objectives: Determine internal control effectiveness

Deviation conditions: Invoices without shipping documentation

Population definitions:

Period covered: The year, 19XX

Sampling unit: Copy of sales invoice

Completeness: All invoices

Sample selection method: Random selection

Acceptable risk: We want a 95% confidence level. Therefore, we will accept a risk of 5%.

Consider the tolerable rate: ≤ 5%

Expected population error rate: ≤ 2.%

Sample size: 181

Using the Tables

The tables in the appendix to this chapter have been prepared by the AICPA. They are calibrated for a 5% risk of overreliance. This equals a confidence level of 95%.

Effect of population: While the population is the *least* important factor, it should be considered. The following equation will adjust for population size:

$$n = \frac{n'}{1 - \dfrac{n'}{N}}$$

n = revised sample size
n' = sample size without considering the effect of population
N = population size

Example: Assume the following poulations and their effect on the sample size:

N	n
500	143
1,000	167
3,000	188
5,000	192
10,000	196

It is obvious, the impact of population is minor.

Evaluating the Effect of Observed Errors

Refer to the second table in the appendix. Assume four errors were observed.

Actual Errors Observed

1. Find the *number observed rate* at the top of the evaluation table.
2. Read down to where the sample size is close to that selected. It should be somewhere between 150 and 200. The sample indicates the following:

There is a 95% probability that the rate of observed error in the population does not exceed 6%.

At this point, decisions have to be made about the need for

- further testing,
- changing the precision and reliability rates, or
- rejecting the system of internal controls.

How to Construct and Evaluate a Variable Sampling Plan

Variable sampling is used to derive an estimation of a particular population. To use variable sampling, take the following steps:

1. *State the objectives of the audit test.*
2. *Define the population.*

3. *Define the sampling unit.*
4. *Take a random sample.*

   Note: We recommend you select 30 items. This is enough to estimate some parameters of the population, but not so large as to be burdensome.

5. *Compute the sample standard deviation.* See the standard deviation equation.
6. *Define the confidence level.* Again, this is a statistical way of expressing the probability that the population error rate does not exceed the stated upper precision limit.

   Question: How much reliability do you need? Once again, it is a reflection of your professional judgment.

7. *Determine the sampling precision.* The sampling precision is the tolerable error rate.
8. *Calculate sample size.* The sample size is computed by using the following equation:

$$n = \left(\frac{Z * s}{e}\right)^2$$

   where

   n = sample size
   Z = number of standard deviations
   s = standard deviation of sample
   e = tolerable error

9. *Select the sar:ple.*
10. *Evaluate sample results.*

Example

We want to use statistical sampling to estimate the value of the inventory.

Type of test: Substantive

Objectives: Estimate value of inventory

Population definition:

Sampling unit: inventory item
Population completeness: All inventory items

Submitted Inventory Amount	$5,390,000
Number of Items	1,100,000

Take a Preliminary Sample

The following inventory items were selected:

Item	Value
1	6
2	7
3	7
4	5
5	3
6	5
7	6
8	7
9	5
10	5
11	3
12	7
13	3
14	3
15	5
16	6
17	4
18	5
19	5
20	8
21	6
22	5

(Continued on next page)

Item	Value
23	4
24	3
25	5
26	5
27	4
28	3
29	3
30	7
Average	5.00
Standard Deviation	1.46
Calculated	5,500,000
Percentage Difference	2.04%

Estimated sample sizes under various confidence levels are:

Acceptable error	$0.50
Confidence level	
80%	14
90%	23
95%	33
99%	57

How to Reduce Sample Size by Using Stratified Sampling

Assume the following sample selection:

Item	Value
1	6
2	7
3	150
4	5

Item	Value
5	3
6	5
7	535
8	7
9	5
10	5
11	464
12	7
13	3
14	297
15	5
16	344
17	4
18	5
19	446
20	8
21	6
22	546
23	4
24	3
25	612
26	5
27	4
28	3
29	3
30	713
Average	140.33
Standard Deviation	225.11
Calculated	154,366,667
Percentage Difference	2763.95%

This problem has been caused by a mixture of many high and low priced items. Under these conditions, the required sample sizes would have to climb beyond reason: This is shown below:

Acceptable Error	$0.50
Confidence Level	
80%	332,105
90%	545,185
95%	778,696
99%	1,100,000

When we stratify a population, we divide the populations into segments where the values of the items selected are more homogeneous. We'll apply this process to the above data:

		Group 1	Group 2
Item	**Value**	**Value**	**Value**
1	6	6	
2	7	7	
3	150		150
4	3	3	
5	3	3	
6	5	5	
7	535		535
8	7	7	
9	5	5	
10	5	5	
11	464		464
12	7	7	
13	3	3	
14	297		297
15	5	5	0
16	344		344
17	4	4	

		Group 1	Group 2
Item	**Value**	**Value**	**Value**
18	5	5	
19	446		446
20	8	8	
21	6	6	
22	546		546
23	4	4	
24	3	3	
25	612		612
26	5	5	
27	4	4	
28	3	3	
29	3	3	
30	713		713
Average	140.27	3.37	410.70
Standard Deviation	225.15	2.55	205.86

As you see, the standard deviations are now a smaller proportion of the average of the items selected. The sample sizes are now calculated in two strata:

Stratified Group 1

Sample Size

Acceptable Error $0.25

Confidence Level

80%	170
90%	279
95%	399
99%	692

Stratified Group 2

Sample Size

Acceptable Error	$25.00
Confidence Level	
80%	111
90%	182
95%	260
99%	451

How to Avoid the Dangers of Statistical Sampling

Even though you conduct your statistical work to the letter of the rules and procedures, there are still dangers. These are:

1. The risk of accepting an unacceptable population.
2. The risk of rejecting an acceptable population.
3. The risk of misinterpreting or improperly conducting your audit tests.

For example, if your test is designed to find a certain type of error, and you overlook it, statistical sampling would be negated.

Table 8-1
Attribute Sampling Chart
Upper Limit = 5% risk of occurrence

Expected Error Rate	2%	3%	4%	5%	6%	7%	8%	9%	10%	15%
0.00%	149 0	99 0	74 0	59 0	49 0	42 0	26 0	32 0	29 0	19 0
0.25%	236 1	157 1	117 1	93 1	78 1	66 1	58 1	51 1	46 1	30 1
0.50%	*	157 1	117 1	93 1	78 1	66 1	58 1	51 1	46 1	30 1
0.75%	*	208 2	117 1	93 1	78 1	66 1	58 1	51 1	46 1	30 1
1.00%	*	* *	156 2	93 1	78 1	66 1	58 1	51 1	46 1	30 1
1.25%	*	* *	156 2	124 2	78 1	66 1	58 1	51 1	46 1	30 1
1.50%	*	* *	192 3	124 2	103 2	66 2	58 1	51 1	46 1	30 1
1.75%	*	* *	227 4	153 3	103 2	88 2	77 2	51 1	46 1	30 1
2.00%	*	* *	* *	181 4	127 3	88 2	77 2	68 2	46 1	30 1
2.25%	*	* *	* *	208 5	127 3	88 2	77 2	68 2	61 2	30 1

Expected Error Rate	2%	3%		4%		5%		6%		7%		8%		9%		10%		15%	
2.50%	*	*	*	*	*	*	*	150	4	109	3	77	2	68	2	61	2	30	1
2.75%	*	*	*	*	*	*	*	173	5	109	3	95	3	68	2	61	2	30	1
3.00%	*	*	*	*	*	*	*	195	6	129	4	95	3	84	3	61	2	30	1
3.25%	*	*	*	*	*	*	*	*	*	148	5	112	4	84	3	61	2	30	1
3.50%	*	*	*	*	*	*	*	*	*	167	6	112	4	84	3	76	3	40	2
3.75%	*	*	*	*	*	*	*	*	*	185	7	129	5	100	4	76	3	40	2
4.00%	*	*	*	*	*	*	*	*	*	*	*	146	6	100	4	89	4	40	2
5.00%	*	*	*	*	*	*	*	*	*	*	*	*	*	158	8	116	6	40	2
6.00%	*	*	*	*	*	*	*	*	*	*	*	*	*	*	*	179	11	50	3
7.00%	*	*	*	*	*	*	*	*	*	*	*	*	*	*	*	*	*	68	5

*Sample size too large to be cost effective
Numbers after sample size are expected errors

Table 8-2
Attribute Sampling Results Evaluation
Upper Limits = 5% Risk of Occurrence

Sample Size	0	1	2	3	4	5	6	7	8	9	10
25	11.3	17.6	*	*	*	*	*	*	*	*	*
30	9.5	14.9	19.6	*	*	*	*	*	*	*	*
35	8.3	12.9	17.0	*	*	*	*	*	*	*	*
40	7.3	11.4	15.0	18.3	*	*	*	*	*	*	*
45	6.5	10.2	13.4	16.4	19.2	*	*	*	*	*	*
50	5.9	9.2	12.1	14.8	17.4	*	*	*	*	*	*
55	5.4	8.4	11.1	13.5	15.9	18.2	*	*	*	*	*
60	4.9	7.7	10.2	12.5	14.7	16.8	18.8	*	*	*	*
65	4.6	7.1	9.4	11.5	13.6	15.5	17.4	19.3	*	*	*
70	4.2	6.6	8.8	10.8	12.6	14.5	16.3	18.0	19.7	*	*
75	4.0	6.2	8.2	10.1	11.8	13.6	15.2	16.9	18.5	20.0	*
80	3.7	5.8	7.7	9.5	11.1	12.7	14.3	15.9	17.4	18.9	*
90	3.3	5.2	6.9	8.4	9.9	11.4	12.8	14.2	15.5	16.8	18.2
100	3.0	4.7	6.2	7.6	9.0	10.3	11.5	12.8	14.0	15.2	16.4
125	2.4	3.8	5.0	6.1	7.2	8.3	9.3	10.3	11.3	12.3	13.2
150	2.0	3.2	4.2	5.1	6.0	6.9	7.8	8.6	9.5	10.3	11.1
200	1.5	2.4	3.2	3.9	4.6	5.2	5.9	6.5	7.2	7.8	8.4

* = over 20%

CHAPTER 9

How to Audit the Financial Statement Elements

Introduction

The third standard of field work states:

> Sufficient competent evidential matter is to be obtained through inspection, observation, inquiries, and confirmations to afford a reasonable basis for an opinion regarding the financial statements under examination.

This chapter will focus on evidence:

- What are the types?
- How should it be gathered?
- How should it be evaluated?

A Guide to Auditing Specific Accounts

The audit procedures are dependent upon:

- Audit objectives
- Results of substantive and compliance testing
- External and internal evidence

What Is Evidence?

The following flowchart will show relationships between the various forms of evidence and how each contributes to specific audit objectives.

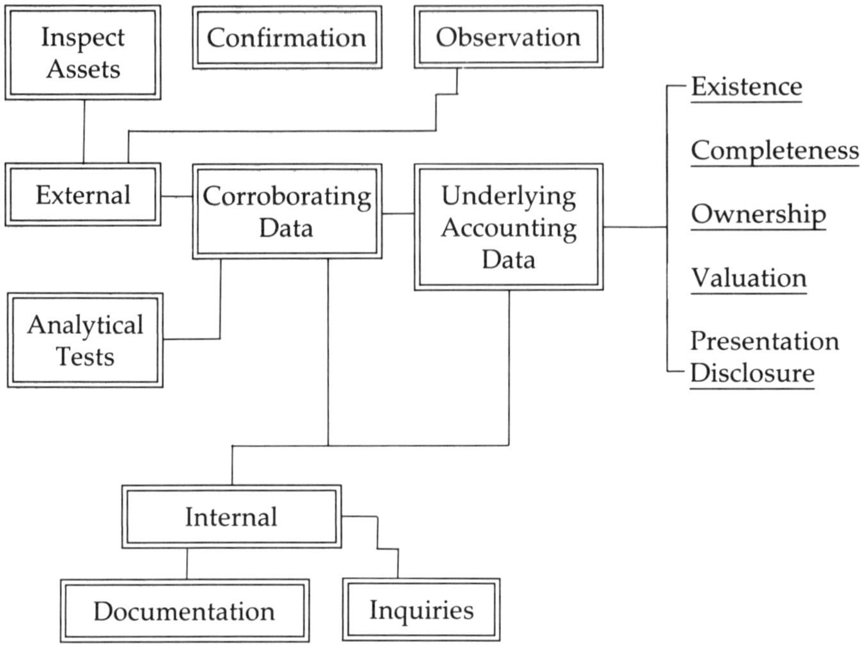

As the chart indicates, there are two forms of evidence:

1. Underlying accounting records
2. Corroborating data

Corroborating Data

Corroborating data supports the fairness of the information presented on the financial statements. It consists of external and internal support and analytical tests.

External Data: Derived from outside sources and provides a stronger degree of support. External data is gathered as follows:

1. *Inspect assets:* Cash and security counts, and inspection of inventories, property, and equipment.
2. *Confirmations:* Obtaining direct verification from debtors or holders.
   For example: Receivables and cash confirmations.
3. *Observation:* Because of the flack resulting from the McKesson Robbins case, GAAS now requires inventories, when they are material, be counted while observed by an independent auditor.

Internal Data: Internal data is gathered from sources within the company. This includes:

Documentation: Data generated by the company or received from others in the company's possession:

For example, a purchase of equipment is documented by the vendor's invoice.

Inquiries: Information is obtained by going to the horse's mouth; management, staff, and the various line employees.

How Is Evidence Rated

The following diagram rates evidence by its degree of competence.

High ↑

External evidence

- Independence of source
- Qualification of source

Internal evidence

- Documentation
- Inquiries

Low ↓

Using the Five Objectives to Design your Audit

1. *Existence/occurrence.* Do the assets and liabilities exist and have the recorded transactions occurred?
2. *Completeness.* Are all material assets and liabilities recorded?
3. *Ownership/obligation.* Can we verify that the company owns and has clear title to all material assets?
4. *Valuation.* Are the assets valued in accordance with GAAP?
5. *Presentation and disclosure.* Are all sections of the financial statement properly presented, described and disclosed?

Never Overlook Internal Control

Remember: Always **review, test, and evaluate internal control** before you perform any other audit functions. See Chapter 7.

How to Find Out About Liens and Contracts by Contacting Your State Offices

If a lien has been recorded, that information will be on file. You just have to know where to look.

- *Real property:* The offices of the County in which the property is located.
- *Personal property:* Most States subscribe to the Uniform Commercial Code (UCC). The creditor has the right to file a UCC notification with the applicable State covering any pledged personal assets.

How to Prepare Workpapers to Document Your Evidence

Everything you do in an audit should be documented by your workpapers. As the following example illustrates, the workpapers should be constructed to show the following:

1. The evidence gathered
2. Tests performed
3. Support of audit objectives
4. Conclusions

How to Index Your Workpapers

Good workpapers should not only document the account balances, but also, the work done and your conclusions. However, they should also be easy to locate. The ensuing index form, which is an integral part of every audit file, tabs an audit into these sections.

Audit Lead Sheet

Client ______________________________
Year end ______________________________
Partner in charge ______________________________
Staff assigned ______________________________
____
____
Date completed ______________________________
Date reviewed ______________________________
Date delivered ______________________________

Audit Sections

I.	Audit program
II.	Time budget and schedule
III.	Engagement letter and other client correspondence
IV.	Trial balance and financial statements
V.	Review memos and conclusions
VI.	Notes and queries
VII.	Confirmation checklist
VIII.	Internal control memos and conclusions
IX.	Specific audit workpapers

Index to Accounts and Their Audit Procedures

Cash	A
Investments	B
Accounts receivable	C
Inventories	D
Prepaid expenses	E
Property and equipment	F
Intangible assets	G
Accounts payable	H
Accrued expenses	I
Taxes payable	J
Notes payable	K
Commitments and contingent liabilities	L
Stockholders' equity	M

Account Subsections

With regard to specific audit workpapers, we recommend you index each one in outline format.
For example:

IXA: Cash lead schedule
IXA-1-n: Specific schedules
IXA-1C: Bank confirmations
IXA-IC: Internal control memos
IXA-M: Memos and conclusions

How to Audit Specific Accounts

The next section will provide the following:

1. Guides to audit specific accounts designed around questions concerning their audit objectives.
2. Recommended substantive tests.
3. Audit confirmation forms.

A. Cash

Objectives

1. Do cash balances exist as reported?
2. Have all transactions been recorded?
3. Are there liens or other encumbrances outstanding?
4. Is all cash liquid and realizable?
   Consider foreign currency and certificates of deposit.
5. Are there any restrictions on the use of cash?

Substantive Tests

1. Confirm bank balances
2. Check bank reconciliations
3. Test cash transfers
4. Count petty cash
5. Verify and explain old outstanding checks

Confirmations

Note: As our society becomes more complicated, so does the banking industry. There are many departments within a bank and it is very important that your confirmation be delivered to the right person in the right section. Otherwise, it might turn up lost.

Bank balances: The standard AICPA Bank Confirmation form is used to not only confirm the bank balances, but notes and guaranties as well.

Outstanding checks and deposits in transit: Use the following cutoff bank confirmation:

To: Bank

Will you kindly furnish directly to our auditors, Jay Ruben Accountancy Corporation, 123 Anystreet, Nowhere, USA, the following information relevant to their examination of our accounts as of the close of business December 31, 19XX.

1. The information requested in the enclosed standard bank confirmation form.
2. Statement of all securities or other items you hold for our account as of December 31, 19XX, for collection or safekeeping or as agent or trustee, and
3. Statement of our account and the related paid checks for the period from January 1 to January 15, 19XX, inclusive

Very truly yours

Devonport Corporation

by

B. Investments

Audit Objectives

1. Do securities reported on the balance sheet exist. Are they owned by the client?
2. Are all securities owned by the client reported on the books?
3. Are these securities fairly valued, at lower of cost or market, in accordance with GAAP?
4. Is all material income from securities fairly reported?
5. Are they properly classified between current versus noncurrent?
6. Are the securities margined or pledged as collateral?

Substantive Tests

1. Count and inspect all securities owned by corporation at financial statement date.

   Note: Make sure you control all securities at this time.

2. Determine that the investments are fairly valued in accordance with GAAP. If any of these securities are publicly held, stock quotations should be sufficient. If not, financial statements should be secured and audited, if substantial.
3. Check the following forms of investment income: dividends, interest, gains, and losses. Cross check against assets reported.

Confirmations:

To: Stockbroker

Will you kindly furnish directly to our auditors, Jay Ruben Accountancy Corporation, 123 Anystreet, Nowhere, USA, the following information relevant to their examination of our accounts as of the close of business December 31, 19XX:

1. A Statement of all securities or other items you hold for our account as of December 31, 19XX, for safekeeping or as agent or trustee, and
2. Amount owed by us to you at December 31, 19XX.

Very truly yours

Devonport Corporation

by

C. Accounts Receivable

Audit Objectives

1. Are recorded accounts receivable valid?
2. Are the accounts collectible?
3. Is the allowance for doubtful accounts reasonable?
4. Are non-trade receivables segregated?
5. Have the accounts receivable been pledged or factored?

Substantive Tests

1. Agree accounts receivable list to general ledger.
2. Check aging.

3. Verify adequacy of allowance by scheduling subsequent collections.

Confirmations

The procedures discussed in Chapter 8 (statistical sampling) may be useful to help you quantify the number of accounts to be tested. After considering internal control, the size and the age of the individual accounts, you may decide to stratify the process into:

1. Positive confirmations for large and critical accounts.
2. Negative confirmations for smaller and less critical items.

Positive Confirmation

Devonport Corporation
Address

Dear:

In accordance with the request of our auditors, Jay Ruben Accountancy Corporation, address, we ask that you kindly confirm to them your indebtedness to us at December 31, 19XX, which, according to our records, amount to $xxxx.xx.

If the amount shown is in agreement with your records, please so indicate by signing in the space provided below and return this letter directly to our auditors in the enclosed envelope. Your prompt compliance will facilitate the examination of our accounts.

If the amount is *not* in agreement with your records, please inform our auditors directly of the amount shown by your records, with full detail or differences.

Remittances should not be sent to the auditors:

Very truly yours,

Devonport Corporation

The above stated amount is correct as of December 31, 19XX.

____
Debtor of Client

____
Title or Position

Negative Confirmation

Devonport Corporation
Address

Dear:

According to our records, we show your indebtedness to us at December 31, 19XX amounted to $xxxx.xx.

If this amount is not correct, please write promptly, using the enclosed envelope and provide details of all differences to our auditor,

Jay Ruben Accountancy Corporation
Address

who is now making his periodic examination of our accounts.

Unless you promptly report a difference to our auditors, they will assume that you consider the balance to be correct.

Remittances should not be sent to our auditors.

Very truly yours

The Devonport Corporation

D. Inventories

Audit Objectives

1. Do the inventories exist as reported on the financial statements?
2. Are they in salable condition?
3. Are all material inventories owned by the company?
4. Are inventories fairly valued at the lower of cost or market?
5. Have the inventories been valued in accordance with the applicable cost flows specified?
6. If the inventories are manufactured, does the cost system fairly account for applicable costs?
7. Are the inventories subject to liens?

Inventory Observation

According to SAS #1, if inventories are material:

> It is ordinarily necessary for the independent auditor to be present at the time of count, and, by suitable observation, tests and inquiries, satisfy himself respecting the effectiveness of inventory taking and the measure of reliance which may be placed upon the client's representations about the quantities and physical condition of the inventories.

INVENTORY OBSERVATION CHECKLIST

Client's Procedures:

1. A written inventory program is prepared.
2. the plant is closed or restricted in order to minimize inventory movement.
3. Pre-numbered tags or another methods to establish audit trails, are used.
4. Overall responsibility for inventory taking is assigned to one employee.
5. The inventory is taken by two person teams; one person counts, the other fills out forms.
6. Recounting is done by appropriate management.
7. Damaged, obsolete, overstocked, and discontinued goods are segregated.

Observation Procedures

1. Arrange to staff all locations at same time.
2. Review client inventory procedures.
3. Use a specialist, if necessary.
4. Use statistical sampling to pre-determine test counts for later checking.
5. Make test counts.
6. Note and resolve discrepancies.
7. Release areas when you are satisfied of counts.
8. Confirm or observe inventory held off premises.

9. Perform cutoff procedures:
   a. last receiving document
   b. last shipping document/sales invoice
   c. last cash deposit
   d. last checks written
10. Compare test counts to perpetual inventories, if applicable.

Substantive Tests

1. Trace test counts to final inventories.
2. Vouch invoices to determine if inventory is owned by client.
3. Analyze cost system and verify costs.
4. Perform net realizable value tests. (See Chapter 4).

E. Prepaid Expenses and Deposits

Objectives

1. Are all balances correctly recorded?
2. Are these amounts supported by verifiable transactions?
3. Will the amounts capitalized benefit future periods?
4. Is the amortization method reasonable and correctly calculated?

Substantive Tests

1. Vouch additions.
2. Verify that these amounts will benefit future periods.

For example, if it is 1989, a three-year unexpired insurance policy will benefit future periods.

3. Check the amortization method and computations.
4. Determine if insurance coverage is adequate.

Note: We are not experts on replacement costs and other valuation methods. Therefore, we might have to rely on the services of an expert.

Confirmations

Insurance

Devonport Corporation
Address

Our auditor, Jay Ruben Accountancy Corporation is examining our financial statements as of December 31, 1988.

In connection with this, please furnish him the following regarding our insurance coverage:

Policy #(s)
Carrier
Coverage (Description)
Coverage (Amount)
Premium
Term

Amount of unpaid insurance premiums:

Please sign, date, and return this information to our auditor at your earliest convenience.

Devonport Corporation

Deposit:

Devonport Corporation
Address

Our auditor, Jay Ruben Accountancy Corporation is examining our financial statements as of December 31, 19XX.

According to our records, we ask that you verify the following:

Deposit with you:
Amount $
Refundable/Non Refundable
Refund date

If the information shown is in agreement with your records, please so indicate by signing in the space provided below and return this letter directly to our auditors in the enclosed envelope. Your prompt compliance will facilitate the examination of our accounts.

If the amount is *not* in agreement with your records, please inform our auditor directly of the amount shown by your records, with full detail or differences.

Very truly yours,

Devonport Corporation

The above is correct as of December 31, 1988.

____

Debtor of Client

____

Title or Position

F. Property and Equipment

Audit Objectives

1. Do the assets exist?
2. Are they owned by the client?
3. Are additions and/or disposals properly recorded?
4. Are they properly valued?
5. Will they benefit future periods?
6. Is the amount provided for depreciation reasonable and correctly computed?
7. Are the assets pledged as collateral?

Substantive Tests

1. Physically insepct major assets
2. Vouch additions
3. Examine ownership documentation
4. Examine repairs and maintenance and related expense accounts to determine if:
   a. any items need to be capitalized
   b. "excess" repairs and maintenance indicates an impairment in value or life.

5. Check depreciation policy by comparing methods and life to prevalent methods for applicable items in the industry.
6. Check depreciation computations.

G. Intangible Assets

Audit Objectives

1. Do the assets exist?
2. Does the client have satisfactory title to these assets?
3. Are these costs appropriately deferred to future periods which will be benefitted?
4. Are the methods of amortization supportable and reasonable?

Substantive Tests

1. Vouch additions
2. Examine legal documentation
3. Check expiration dates to determine that rights have not expired.
4. Determine future value by examining related income accounts.

H. Accounts Payable

Audit Objectives

1. Are all material obligations recorded?
2. Have material expenses of period under review been recorded?

Substantive Tests

1. Trace cutoff tests performed at year end to accounts payable recording.
2. Perform a search for unrecorded liabilities. This search may include the following:
   a. bills unpaid as of year end.
   b. payments made subsequent to year end.
   c. old outstanding checks that may indicate potential liabilities.
   d. amounts disclosed in other confirmations.

Confirmation

The object of the accounts payable confirmation procedure is to determine if any liabilities exist that are *not* carried on the books. Therefore, merely sending out letters to creditors displayed on your client listing will not do the complete job. It is much better to develop your own list by scanning the journals and ledgers to build a sample of vendors with whom the company has done business and then mail the following confirmation to each one:

Devonport Corporation
Address

Our auditor, Jay Ruben Accountancy Corporation, address is conducting an examination of our records as of December 31, 19XX.

In connection with this examination, please furnish him with the following information as of December 31, 19XX:

1. Itemized statement of our unpaid account
2. Itemized statement due you on notes or trade acceptances
3. Itemized statement of merchandise held on consignment or memorandum for your account
4. Statement of any contingent liability to you
5. Itemized statement of purchase commitments
6. Statement of any collateral you hold as security

Please sign, date, and return this information to our auditor at your earliest convenience.

Thank your for your cooperation.

Very truly yours,

I. Accrued Expenses

Audit Objectives

1. Are all material-accrued expenses recorded?
2. Have liabilities for the following expenses been recorded?
    a. Insurance
    b. Salaries
    c. Commissions
    d. Wararnties
    e. Interest (See Notes Payable)

Substantive Tests

1. Review expenses to determine if all material amounts are:
   a. Recorded in the proper fiscal period
   b. Matched to applicable revenues
2. Examine the following:
   a. Personnel manual and records
   b. Commission payment policies
   c. Product warranty agreements
   d. Other pertinent contracts

J. Taxes Payable

Audit Objectives

1. Are the following tax liabilities sufficiently recorded in all material respects?
   a. Income taxes payable
   b. Sales taxes payable
   c. Payroll taxes payable
   d. Property taxes payable
   e. Business licenses
2. Are deferred income taxes calculated in accordance with FAS #96—Accounting for Income Taxes?

Substantive Tests

1. Vouch payments for taxes
2. Compare tax expense accounts to liabilities
3. Have tax department review
   a. tax computations
   b. income statements and balance sheets for potential tax problems
   c. correspondence from various tax bureaus

K. Notes Payable

Audit Objectives

1. Are all material notes payable recorded?
2. Are liabilities properly classified:
   a. current versus non-current
   b. collateral
3. Does the company comply with all note requirements?
4. Has collateral been fully disclosed?

Substantive Tests

1. Examine note contracts for:
   a. amount
   b. payment terms
   c. interest
   d. collateral
   e. restrictions
2. Vouch note payments
3. Examine paid notes when applicable
4. Schedule interest expense and tie it into note activity
5. Determine that the company is not in violation of any note covenants.
6. Check computation of current portion.
   Note: See Chapter 2.

Confirmation

Devonport Corporation
Date

Our auditor, Jay Ruben Accountancy Corporation, address, is conducting an audit of our records as of December 31, 19XX.

In connection with this examination, please confirm directly to him the following information as of December 31, 19XX:

Note payable due you at December 31, 19XX
Interest rate

Unpaid interest due at December 31, 19XX
Due date
Date of Note
Collateral

Please compare this information with your records, and, if correct, please indicate below. If the data shown is not correct, please indicate the differences on the reverse side of this letter.

Please sign, date and return your reply directly to our auditor at your earliest convenience.

A self-addressed, stamped envelope is enclosed for your convenience.

Very truly yours

_______ The details above are correct
_______ The details above are not correct. Details on reverse side.

____
Signature Date

L. Commitments and Contingent Liabilities

Audit Objectives

Are all material contingent liabilities disclosed or recorded on the financial statements?

Substantive Tests

1. Review corporate minutes
2. Read news releases

Note: If your client is publicly held, pertinent information might be found in the *Wall Street Journal* Index.

3. Talk to company personnel and mangement
4. Read correspondence files
5. Read various sales contracts
6. Vouch legal expenses

Note: Always keep your eyes and ears open.

Confirmations

Attorneys

Our auditor, Jay Ruben Accountancy Corporation is making an examination as of December 31, 19XX of our financial statements. Please furnish to him the information requested below involving matters as to which you have been engaged and to which you have devoted substantial attention on behalf of the Company in the form of legal consultation or representation.

Pending or Threatened Litigation Excluding Unasserted Claims and Assessments

Please prepare a description of all material litigation claims and assessments (excluding unasserted claims and assessments. The description of each case should include:

a. The nature of the litigation
b. The progress of the case to date
c. How management is responding or intends to respond to the litigation. e.g. to contest the case vigorously or to seek an out of court settlement, and
d. An evaluation of the likelihood of an unfavorable outcome and an estimate, if one can be made, of the amount or range of the potential loss.

Unasserted Claims and Assessments

We have represented to our auditor that there are no unasserted possible claims or assessments that you have advised us are probable and must be disclosed in accordance with Statement of Financial Accounting Standards No. 5.

We understand that, whenever, in the course of performing legal services for us with respect to a matter recognized to involve an unasserted possible claim or assessment that may call for financial statement disclosure, you have formed a professional conclusion that we should disclose or consider disclosure concerning such possible claim or assessment as a matter of professional responsibility to us, you will so advise us and will consult with us concerning the question of such disclosure and the applicable requirements of the Statement of Financial Accounting Standards No. 5. please specifically confirm to our auditors that are understanding is correct.

Response

Your response should include matters that existed as of December 31, 19XX and during the period from that date to the effective date of your response.

Please specifically identify the nature of, and reasons for, any limitations on your response.

Other Matters

Please indicate the amount we were indebted to you for services and expenses on December 31, 19XX.

Very truly yours,

Note: In order to preserve the confidential relationship with their client, the attorneys may not furnish the information as requested. In that case, you may have to specifically list all asserted and unasserted claims.

Client Representation Letter The financial statements are the primary responsibility of the management of the company being audited. Therefore, the representation letter is designed to obtain your client's response about matters pertinent to the audit.

Client Letterhead

Audit Date

Jay Ruben Accountancy Corporation

Gentlemen:

The following representations are made to you incident to your examination of the balance sheet of Devonport Corporation as of the close of business December 31, 19XX, and of its related Statements of Income and Retained Earnings and Cash Flows for the year then ended, such representations as to the matters referred to being true, or fair estimates, to the best of our knowledge and belief:

ACCOUNTS RECEIVABLE

All accounts receivable exist as reported. The allowance for doubtful accounts is sufficient to cover all bad debt losses.

INVENTORIES

All inventories reported have been determined by physical count. The inventories are carried at the lower of cost or market and are accounted for under the (cost flow: FIFO, LIFO, etc.) method. Provision has been made for damaged, obsolete, discontinued, or overstocked items.

PROPERTY AND EQUIPMENT

Property and equipment charges during the year, stated at cost, were actual additions to property. Property disposed of or abandoned was removed from the accounts. Balances at year end represent all the property and equipment owned by the company, and the company holds satisfactory title thereto. It is our opinion that the amount of accumulated depreciation and obsolescence at December 31, 19XX is reasonably adequate.

PURCHASE AND SALE COMMITMENTS

The Company at December 31, 19XX had no important unfilled contracts for purchases of materials, merchandise, or services in excess of normal requirements or at prices substantially in excess of market at that date or for sales or products at prices that are expected to result in loss.

DIRECT LIABILITIES

With the possible exception of a few minor accounts, all direct liabilities of the company were recorded on the books at December 31, 19XX.

MINUTES

Minutes of stockholders' and directors' meetings as exhibited to you are complete and authentic records of such meetings.

GENERAL

No events have occurred and no facts have been discovered since December 31, 19XX which would make the balance sheet as of that date or the Statements of Income and Retained Earnings and Cash Flows for the year then ended materially inaccurate or misleading. No shortages or irregularities have been discovered, either already closed or in abeyance, that have not been disclosed to you, and to our knowledge, there is nothing reflecting upon the honesty of members of our organization.

No charges are pending against the company for alleged violations of federal, state, or local laws which would have any material effect on the company's financial statements.

We understand that you have examined or tested accounting records of the company and other supporting evidence or method, and, to the extent you deemed appropriate for the purpose of expressing an opinion on the financial statements, and that such tests would not necessarily disclose all irregularities should any exist.

Very truly yours,

Client Name

____

Authorized signature

M. Stockholders' Equity

Audit Objectives

1. Are all stockholders' interests fully reported?
2. Do they reflect the consideration received by the corporation?
3. Are the components of stockholders' equity properly classified?
4. Are all stock options reflected?
5. Is the retained earnings stated in accordance with GAAP?

Substantive Tests

1. Review the articles of incorporation to determine authorized capital.
2. Examine the minutes for approvals to issue stock.
3. Schedule stock issued from stock certificate book, if privately held.
4. If publicly held:
   a. excerpt SEC registration documents
   b. schedule and confirm stock held by transfer agents

5. Review stock option agreements.
6. Schedule retained earnings changes.

The Recognition, Disclosure, and Auditing of Subsequent Events

What is a Subsequent Event?

A subsequent event is an incident that occurs after the financial statement date that should either be disclosed or recorded. There are two broad classifications:

Type I: Require Adjustment

These events provide additional evidence regarding conditions that existed at the balance sheet date and affect estimates made in the process of preparing financial statements.

Example: A major account receivable is subsequently found to be uncollectible.

Type II: Require Disclosure

These events do not affect conditions that existed at the balance sheet date, but, if material must be disclosed.

Example: A plant of the company's is destroyed by fire after the financial statement date.

What Is the Auditor's Responsibility?

The auditor is responsible to report on subsequent events up to the date of his or her opinion. That date has been generally considered to be the completion of field work. However, it is more likely to be the date when an agreement was reached with the client about the acceptability of the reports.

Note: Although you only have responsibility for events occurring up to the audit conclusion, if you later learn of a subsequent event, you are still required to disclose its effect. The dating would then read as follows:

> February 15, 1989, except for the subsequent event disclosed in Note A, which is date February 28, 1989.

How to Look for Subsequent Events

1. Read all available information including interim financial statements, corporate minutes, correspondence, and news releases.
2. Make inquiries about subsequent financing and unusual transactions.
3. Obtain opinion of legal counsel.
4. Refer to subsequent events in the representation letter.

CHAPTER 10

How to Report on Audited Financial Statements

Introduction

This chapter will first present the general unqualified opinion format, and then present instances and methods of reporting when there are deviations from GAAS or GAAP.

The formats used are based upon the Standards of Reporting reproduced below:

Reporting Standard No. 1

The report shall state whether the financial statements are presented in accordance with generally accepted accounting principles.

Reporting Standard No. 2

The report shall identify those circumstances in which such principles have not been consistently observed in the current period in relation to the preceding period.

Reporting Standard No. 3

Informative disclosures in the financial statements are to be regarded as reasonably adequate unless otherwise stated in the report.

Reporting Standard No. 4

The report shall contain an expression of opinion regarding the financial statements taken as a whole, or an assertion to the effect that an opinion cannot be expressed. The reason therefor should be stated. In all cases where an auditor's name is associated with financial statements, the report should contain a clear-cut indication of the auditor's examination, if any, and the degree of responsibility he/she has taken.

The Unqualified Opinion

Unqualified Opinion with Annotations

To the Board of Directors and Stockholders
Devonport Corporation

1. We have examined the accompanying balance sheet of Devonport Corporation as of December 31, 19XX, and the related statements of income, retained earnings, and cash flows for the year then ended. These financial statements are the responsibility of the Company's management. Our responsibility is to express an opinion on these financial statements based on our audit.
2. We conducted our audit on these financial statements in accordance with generally accepted auditing standards. Those standards require that we plan and perform the audit to obtain reasonable assurance about whether the financial statements are free of material misstatement. An audit includes examining, on a test basis, evidence supporting the amounts and disclosures in the financial statements. An audit also includes assessing the accounting principles used and significant statement presentation. We believe that our audit provides a reasonable basis for our opinion.
3. Explanatory paragraph, if required.
4. In our opinion, the financial statements referred to above present fairly, in all material respects, the financial position of Devonport Corporation as of December 31, 19XX and the results of its operations and its cash flows for the year then ended in conformity with generally accepted accounting principles.

February 15, 19XX

Jay Ruben Accountancy Corporation

Exhibit 10-1—***Unqualified Opinion***

Index to Keyed Items

1. Introductory paragraph
2. Scope paragraph
   Describes how the audit was conducted, and the division of responsibility.

3. Explanatory paragraph
   Additional disclosures, or reasons for variance from GAAS or GAAP.
4. Opinion paragraph
   Refers to GAAP

How to Describe Reporting Variances

The following flowchart illustrates how variances form GAAS or GAAP should be reported:

Extent of Variance

0 ——————————————————— High

Description

GAAP	Departure Disclosure Consistency	— Except for —	Adverse
GAAS	Scope Uncertainty	— Subject to —	Disclaimer

Exhibit 10-2—*Variance Examples*

Variances from GAAS

Assume a net income of $1,000,000. Accounts receivable were not confirmed or verified by other means.

A. Accounts receivable total $5,000. Considering all else equal (e.g. absence of problem accounts which could cause problems to other segments of the statements), the amount is insignificant and scope variations need not be diclosed.
B. Total accounts receivable, $500,000. This amount is material. Therefore, we are unable to state that the audit was conducted in accordance with GAAS. A disclaimer is required.
C. Accounts receivable total $75,000. By itself, the scope reduction, probably is not significant enough to negate the GAAS

requirement. However, it will probably require a qualified opinion.

Variance from GAAP

Assume a net income of $1,000,000. The audit discloses that the inventories are not recorded in accordance with GAAP. The financial statements are *not* adjusted:

A. The misstatement is $10. This amount is obviously immaterial and nothing need be disclosed.

B. The misstatement is $500,000. This amount is so significant that the financial statements are misleading and are not prepared in accordance with GAAP. An adverse opinion would have to be issued.

C. The misstatement is $50,000. This is not large enough to cause the statements to be materially misleading. However, it should be disclosed. The result will be a qualified opinion.

Remember: When all else is said and done, the answer to the question, "What's material?" is in the eyes of the beholder, or the independent auditor.

How to Report Variances

The remainder of the chapter presents report writing formats when either the audit was not conducted in accordance with GAAS or the financial statements was not prepared in accordance with GAAP.

Procedure: In each case discussed below, refer to the applicable paragraph which may have to be changed. You may be able to assume that the other paragraphs will remain untouched. When a portion of a paragraph needs to be modified, the sections revised will be underlined.

When to Use the Explanatory Paragraph

Paragraph 3 should be used to explain modifications to the scope or opinion paragraphs. It should also be employed to provide additional information, when informative disclosures are not adequate on the financial statements. Such disclosures include the following:

- An industry practice is used that is contrary to GAAP.
- Change from an unacceptable to an acceptable GAAP.

- Change in reporting equity.
- Significant related party transactions.

Scope Variances

Scope variances will change paragraph 2 and require an explanation in Paragraph 3.

Forms of Scope Variances

1. Insufficient evidential material
2. Other scope limitations
3. Part of engagement conducted by other auditors

Disclaimer of Opinion

1. We were engaged to audit the accompanying Balance Sheet of Devonport Corporation as of December 31, 1988, and the related Statements of Income, Retained Earnings and Cash Flows for the year then ended. *These financial statements are the responsibility of management.*
2. We were unable to confirm the accounts receivable of Devonport Corporation as of December 31, 19XX which are stated at $500,000. We were unable to apply sufficient alternative procedures to the Company's accounts receivable.
3. Since we are unable to confirm the accounts receivable and were not able to apply alternative auditing procedures to satisfy ourselves as to inventory quantities, *the scope of our work was not sufficient to enable us to express, and we do not express, an opinion on the financial statements referred to above.*

Qualified Opinion

1. No change.
2. *Except as discussed in the following paragraph,* we conducted our audit in accordance with generally accepted auditing standards.
3. We were not above to confirm accounts receivable of as of December 31, 19XX stated at $75,000. In addition, we were unable to determine the validity of accounts receivable through alternative procedures.

4. In our opinion, subject to the validity of accounts receivable, the financial statements present fairly. . . . . . .

Accounting Principle Variances

Accounting principle variances will change paragraph 4 and require explanations in paragraph 3.

Forms of Principle Variances

1. Departure from GAAP
2. Lack of consistency
3. Uncertainty
4. Subsequent events that require adjustment

Remember: The financial statements are the responsibility of management. Your report must be modified if management does not comply with GAAP.

Departures from GAAP

Adverse Opinion

1. No change
2. No change
3. *As disclosed in Note* C to the financial statements, the Company reports its inventories at fair market value for financial accounting purposes and on its tax return. *In our opinion, generally accepted accounting principles require* that inventories be valued at the lower of cost or market. *As a result of these departures from generally accepted accounting principles,* inventories and gross profits are overstated by $500,000, and income tax expense is overstated by $200,000. The total effect of these departures on retained earnings is $300,000, which results in an increase in earnings per share of $3.00.
4. *In our opinion, because of the effects of* the matter discussed in the preceding paragraph, the financial statements referred to above *do not present fairly,* in conformity with generally accepted accounting principles, the financial position of Devonport Corpo-

ration as of December 31, 19XX or the results of its operations or its cash flows for the year then ended.

Qualified Opinion

1. No change.
2. No change
3. *As disclosed in Note* C to the financial statements, the Company reports its inventories at fair market value for financial accounting purposes and on its tax return. *In our opinion, generally accepted accounting principles require* that inventories be valued at the lower of cost or market. *As a result of these departures from generally accepted accounting principles,* inventories and gross profits are overstated by $50,000, and income tax expense is overstated by $20,000. The total effect of these departures on retained earnings is $30,000, which results in an increase in earnings per share of $.30.
4. In our opinion, *except for the effect of the matter discussed in the preceding paragraph on the balance sheet and the statement of income,* the financial statements referred to above *present fairly,* in all material respects, the financial position of Devonport Corporation as of December 31, 19XX or the results of its operations or its cash flows for the year then ended in conformity with generally accepted accounting principles.

Lack of Consistency

When, for whatever reason, GAAP is not consistently applied, disclosure should be written as follows:

Paragraph 3: Explain the change and its impact on the financial statements.

Paragraph 4: The wording is dependent upon the type of change and its materiality:

Type of Change	*Effect on Opinion*
Accounting principle	
Non acceptable to acceptable	None
Acceptable to non acceptable	Adverse or "Except for"
Accounting estimate	None
Correction of error	None
Change in reporting entity	None

Uncertainty

In General

1. No change
2. No change
3. As stated in Note F to the financial statements, the company is a defendant in a lawsuit claiming breach of contract. The amount of damages, if any, that could result from this litigation cannot be reasonably determined at this time. Accordingly, no provision for any actual liability that may arise as a result of this litigation has been made.

Disclaimer

1. Due to the materiality of the litigation described above, we do not render an opinion on the financial position at December 31, 19XX or the results of its operations and cash flows for the year then ended.

Qualification

1. In our opinion, *subject to the effect on the financial statements of the previously described litigation*, the financial statements referred to above present fairly, in all material respects, the financial position of Devonport Corporation as of December 31, 19XX and the results of its operations and its cash flows for the year then ended in conformity with generally accepted accounting principles.

Uncertainties About Continuing as a Going Concern

1. No change
2. No change
3. The accompanying financial statements have been prepared assuming that the Company will continue as a going concern. As discused in Note S. to the financial statements, the Company has experienced substantial losses over the past five years, which have resulted in a deficit equity position. The company's financial position and operating results raise substantial doubts about its ability to continue as a going concern. The financial statements do not include any adjustments that might result from the outcome of this uncertainty.
4. No change

Subsequent Events

This subject has been discussed in detail in Chapter 9. The following chart suggests reporting alternatives:

Type of Event	*Explanation Paragraph*	*Effect on Opinion*
Class I—No adjustment required		
Does Client disclose?		
Yes	None	None
No	Explain	None
Class II—Adjustment required		
Does Client Adjust?		
Yes	None	None
No	Explain	"Except for" or Adverse

How to Report Lack of Independence

An auditor may lack independence for many reasons:

- Ownership of company, or
- Position in management.

The reason for the independence should *not* be disclosed.

Why? If the reason were stated, the readers would be inclined to evaluate it and make their own decisions about its significance. According to GAAS, this evalution must be left completely up to the auditor.

Independence Disclaimer Example

We are not independent with respect to Client Company, and the accompanying balance sheet as of December 31, 19XX, and the related statements of income, retained earnings and cash flows were not audited by us, and, accordingly, we do not express an opinion on them.

Reporting Modifications Summarized

Condition	*Effect on Scope*	*Effect on Opinion*
Scope		
Insufficient Evidence	Explain	Subject to or Disclaimer
Limitations	Explain	Subject to or Disclaimer
Accounting Principles		
Lack of adherence to GAAP	None	Except for or Adverse
Consistency		
Inconsistent Treatment	None	Except for or Adverse
Changes		
Changes in Accounting Principles		
Acceptable to unacceptable	None	Except for or Adverse
Unacceptable to acceptable	None	None
Estimate	None	None
Uncertainty	None	Subject to or Disclaimer
Ability to Continue as Going Concern	None	None
Subsequent events		
Type I	None	None
Type II	None	Except for or Adverse

CHAPTER 11

Review and Compilation Engagements

Introduction

This chapter presents methods to improve the reporting formats most utilized by small and medium size practitioners; reviews and compilations and will be dedicated to the following:

- Review and compilation procedures
- Sample engagement letters
- Sample accountant's reports

Review Engagements

Overview

A review provides a level of assurance between audited reports and compilations.

Its essence: A review says that, "The accountant is unaware of any material misstatements."

Procedures Required

In General:

1. Describe the procedures for recognizing, classifying, and recording transactions.
2. Determine if accounting principles have been consistently followed and applied.

Cash:

1. Check bank reconciliations and tie into general ledger balances.
2. Count petty cash funds.

3. Investigate old outstanding checks and other in-transit situations.
4. Check cash cutoff.
5. Determine if any significant cash restrictions exist.

Accounts Receivable:

1. Perform analytical tests to determine if the allowance for doubtful accounts is adequate and that uncollectible accounts have been written off.
2. Check sales cutoff and tie into accounts receivable recording.
3. Segregate any non-trade receivables.
4. Schedule pledging, discounting, or factoring of receivables.
5. Determine that receivables are properly classified between current and non-current.
6. Compute accounts receivable turnover and compare to prior periods.

Inventories:

1. Describe methods used to determine inventory quantities.
2. If inventories were taken at dates other than balance sheet date, show how these counts were reconciled to the statement date.
3. Check valuation methods. Determine that materials, labor and overhead are properly included if applicable.
4. Discuss provision for write-off of obsolete, overstocked, or discontinued inventories.
5. Tie into purchase cutoff work.
6. Schedule and describe inventory pledge agreements, if applicable.
7. Compute the gross profit percentage and compare to prior periods.
8. Calculate inventory turnover and compare to prior periods.

Prepaid Expenses:

Describe the nature of prepaid expenses, how they will benefit future periods, and check amortization.

Investments:

1. Schedule investments and classify them between marketable securities, long-term acquisitions, and various security forms.

2. Match investment income to applicable assets.
3. Determine that assets are valued in accordance with GAAP.
4. If "controlling" interests are carried, ascertain that the equity method has been used and proper consolidation procedures are followed.
5. Schedule encumbrances.

Property and Equipment:

1. Schedule property and equipment and related depreciation.
2. Describe the policy followed by the company to capitalize acquisitions.
3. Review repairs and maintenance account to determine that only expense items are included.
4. Describe depreciation policy and check calculations.
5. Describe and schedule capital leases.
6. Schedule encumbrances.

Other Assets:

1. Schedule and describe
2. Explain how these assets will benefit future periods
3. Schedule encumbrances

Accounts Payable and Accrued Liabilities:

1. Obtain schedules and agree to the general ledger.
2. Perform search for unrecorded accounts payable and accrued expenses.
3. Segregate payables to employees and related parties.

Notes Payable:

1. Schedule notes payable and describe the following: balances due, current portion, collateral, interest rate, repayment terms, and restricting covenants.
2. Schedule interest expense and reconcile to notes payable.

Taxes Payable:

1. Schedule all tax liabilities.
2. Review income tax provision, noting whether the liability complies with the tax code.
3. Record deferred income taxes in accordance with the provisions of FASB 96.

4. Discuss outstanding income tax audits with management.
5. Schedule other tax liabilities and check to see that company has complied with filing and payment requirements.

Other Liabilities, Contingencies and Commitments:

1. Schedule and describe other liabilities.
2. Discuss the nature of any contingencies, including lawsuits, guaranties, income tax audits, discounted notes, and other unsettled claims.
3. Schedule and describe lease, pension, outstanding purchase orders, and other commitments.

Equity:

1. Schedule and describe contributed and earned equity.
2. Review articles of incorporation, minutes, and other records to obtain necessary information about authorized capital, par value of shares, classes of stock and amounts received when issued.
3. Describe stock performances and dividend arreages, if any.
4. Schedule and describe stock options outstanding.
5. Schedule any acquisitions of the company's own stock.
6. Disclose any retained earnings' restrictions.

Revenues and Expenses:

1. Describe the company's policy of recording revenues and expenses.
2. Check sales and expense cutoffs.
3. See that discontinued operations are appropriately scheduled and segregated.

Other:

1. Discuss the following with management and others:
   a. Material subsequent events.
   b. Significant financial uncertainties.
2. Obtain a representation letter.

Note: A review does not require understanding and testing internal control procedures or confirming or observing accounts.

Review Engagement Letter

To the Board of Directors
Devonport Corporation

This letter is to confirm our understanding of the terms and objectives of our engagement and the nature and limitations of the services we will provide.

We will review the balance sheet of Devonport Corporation as of December 31, 19XX and the related Statements of Income and Retained Earnings, and Cash Flows for the year then ended in accordance with standards established by the American Institute of Certified Public Accountants. We will not perform an audit of such financial statements, the objective of which is an expression of an opinion regarding the financial statements taken as a whole and, accordingly, we will not express an opinion on them. Our report on the financial statements is expected to be stated as follows:

We have reviewed the accompanying Balance Sheet of Devonport Corporation as of December 31, 19XX and the related Statements of Income, Retained Earnings and Cash Flows for the Year then Ended in accordance with standards established by the American Institute of Certified Public Accountants. All information included in these financial statements is the representation of the management of Devonport Corporation.

A review consists principally of inquiries of Company personnel and analytical procedures applied to financial data. It is substantially less in scope than an audit in accordance with generally accepted auditing standards, the objective of which is the expression of an opinion regarding the financial statements taken as a whole. Accordingly, we do not express such an opinion.

Based on our review, we are not aware of any material modifications that should be made to the accompanying financial statements in order for them to be in conformity with generally accepted accounting principles.

Our engagement cannot be relied upon to disclose errors, irregularities, or illegal acts, including fraud or defalcations, that may exist. However, we will inform you of any such matters that come to our attention.

Our fees for these services are $7,500. We will progress bill you each month. Our fees are payable upon receipt of invoice. If anything occurs that will require more work, we will inform you before proceeding.

If the foregoing is in accordance with your understanding, please sign the copy of this letter in the space provided and return it to us.

Sincerely,

JAY RUBEN ACCOUNTANCY CORPORATION

Approved

Devonport Corporation

Representation letter for Review Engagement

February 15, 19XX

To: Jay Ruben Accountancy Corporation

In connection with your review of our Balance Sheet as of December 31, 19XX, the Statement of Income and Retained Earnings and the Statement of Cash Flows for the Year then Ended for the purpose of expressing limited assurance that there are no material modifications that should be made to the statements in order for them to be in conformity with generally accepted accounting principles, we specifically confirm

a. The Company's accounting principles, practices, and methods followed in applying them, agree with disclosures made in the financial statements.
b. There have been no changes during the year ended December 31, 19XX in the Company's accounting practices and procedures.
c. We have no plans or intentions that may materially affect the carrying value or classifications of assets or liabilities.
d. There are no material transactions that have not been reflected on the financial statements.
e. There are no material losses (such as from uncollectible accounts, obsolete inventory or commitments) that have not been properly accrued or disclosed in the financial statements.
f. In addition to items disclosed and reported, there are no violations or possible violations of laws or regulations or loss contingencies that would affect the financial statements and should be disclosed in the financial statements that are required to be recorded or disclosed.

g. The Company has satisfactory title to all owned assets, there or no liens, pledges, or encumbrances on such assets that have not been disclosed.
h. There are no related party transactions or related amounts receivable that have not been properly disclosed in the financial statements.
i. We have complied with all aspects of contractual agreements that would have a material effect on the financial statements in the event of noncompliance.
j No events have occurred subsequent to the balance sheet date that would require adjustment to, or disclosure in the financial statements.
k. We have advised you of all actions taken at meetings of stockholders, board of directors, management, and other committees that may affect the financial statements.
l. We have responded fully to all inquiries made to us by you during your review.

Signature and titles

Review Report

We have reviewed the accompanying Balance Sheet of Devonport Corporation as of December 31, 19XX and the related Statements of Income, Retained Earnings and Cash Flows for the Year then Ended in accordance with standards established by the American Institute of Certified Public Accountants. All information included in these financial statements is the representation of the management of Devonport Corporation.

A review consists principally of inquiries of Company personnel and analytical procedures applied to financial data. It is substantially less in scope than an audit in accordance with generally accepted auditing standards, the objective of which is the expression of an opinion regarding the financial statements taken as a whole. Accordingly, we do not express such an opinion.

Based on our review, we are not aware of any material modifications that should be made to the accompanying financial statements in order for them to be in conformity with generally accepted accounting principles.

Jay Ruben Accountancy Corporation

February 15, 19XX

Compilation Engagements

A compilation is an accounting service, in which the accountants' services are limited to preparing or assisting the client to prepare financial statements. No assurance is expressed that the statements are either in conformity with GAAP, or accurate, or complete.

Compilation Procedures

1. Obtain a knowledge of the client and its industry.
2. Describe, in general, the accounting principles used to prepare the ledgers and financial statements.
3. Determine that the financial statements agree to the general ledgers and subsidiary records.
4. Obtain and agree schedules to pertinent accounts.
5. Compile and read the financial statements to judge whether they are:
   a. free from material errors.
   b. arithmetically and clerically correct.
   c. appropriate for the client and its industry.

Note: Inasmuch as the scope of compilation work is much less than that performed on audits and reviews, your responsibility to find and report irregularities is considerably diminished. If, however, in the course of your work, you discover any abnormalities, your duty is to alter your report for any significant effects.

Compilation Engagement Letter

To the Board of Directors
Devonport Corporation

This letter is to confirm our understanding of the terms and objectives of our engagement and the nature and limitations of the services we will provide.

We will perform the following services:

1. We will compile, from information provided by you, required balance sheets, statements of income, retained earnings and cash flows for Devonport Corporation. We will not audit or review such financial statements. Our report on the financial statements of Devonport Corporation is expected to be presented as follows:

We have compiled the accompanying balance sheet of Devonport Corporation as of December 31, 19XX and the related statements of income, retained earnings, and cash flows for the year then ended, in accordance with standards established by the American Institute of Certified Public Accountants.

A compilation is limited to presenting in the form of financial statements, information that is the representation of management. We have not audited or reviewed the accompanying financial statements, and, accordingly, do not express an opinion or any other form of assurance on them.

If, for any reason, we are unable to complete the compilation of your financial statements, we will not issue a report on such statements as a result of this engagement.

2. We will assist your staff in adjusting the books of accounts and prepare the appropriate worksheets to use to prepare the compiled financial statemets.
3. We will prepare all required federal and state income tax returns for the year ended December 31, 19XX and thereafter.
4. We will consult with you and advise you on any financial and tax matters that we believe should be considered.

Our engagement cannot be relied upon to disclose errors, irregularities, or illegal acts, including fraud or defalcations. However, we will inform you of any such matters that come to our attention.

Our fee will be computed on our standard per diem rates of the staff persons assigned. You will be billed monthly for our services. Our invoices are payable upon presentation.

If the foregoing is in accordance with your understanding, please sign the copy of this letter in the space provided and return it to us.

Sincerely,

Jay Ruben Accountancy Corporation

Approved

Devonport Corporation

by

Compilation Reports

The following report should be attached to compiled financial statements when all required disclosures and reports are included:

> We have compiled the accompanying balance sheet of Devonport Corporation as of December 31, 19XX and the related statements of income, retained earnings, and cash flows for the year then ended, in accordance with standards established by the American Institute of Certified Fublic Accountants.
>
> A compilation is limited to presenting in the form of financial statements, information that is the representation of management. We have not audited or reviewed the accompanying financial statements, and, accordingly, do not express an opinion or any other form of assurance on them.

Note: The above report form assumes that the statements were prepared on the accrual basis. If OCBOA statements are drafted, the compilation reports would be different. These will be discussed in Chapter 12.

Compilations Without Full Disclosure

Although, the degree of assurance is somewhat less for a compiled financial statement, all items that could materially affect the financial reports (cash flows, long-term leases, collateral agreements) must nevertheless, be disclosed. If management elects to omit them, the following paragraph should be added to the compilation.

> Management has elected to omit substantially all of the disclosures required by generally accepted accounting principles. If the omitted disclosures were included in the financial statements, they might influence the user's conclusions about the Company's financial position, results of operations, and cash flows. Accordingly, these financial statements are not designed for those who are not informed about such matters.

CHAPTER 12

Other Accounting and Reporting Engagements

Introduction

This chapter presents guidelines to help you do work on other kinds of financial statements. The material will focus on the special problems they present, various procedures, engagement letters, and sample reports for the following:

- Statements prepared in accordance with Other Consistent Bases of Accounting
- Comparative statements
- Personal financial statements
- Financial forecasts and projections

OCBOA Reports

Overview

The accounting procedures for these statements have been described in Chapter 2. Generally, there are three formats:

A. Cash Basis

Balance Sheet

Statement of Assets, Liabilities and Equity Resulting from Cash Transactions

Income Statement

Statement of Cash Receipts and Disbursements

B. Modified Cash Basis

Balance Sheet

Balance Sheet on a Modified Cash Basis

Income Statement

Statement of Income on a Modified Cash Basis

C. *Income Tax Basis*

Balance Sheet

Statement of Assets and Liabilities—Income Tax Basis

Income Statement

Statement of Revenues and Expenses—Income Tax Basis

Engagement Letter for OCBOA Work

To: Client

This letter is to confirm our understanding of the terms and objectives of our engagement and the nature and limitations of the services we will provide.

1. We will (review, compile, audit) the (*) of Client Company at (date) and the related Statements of (**) for the period then ended in accordance with standards established by the American Institute of Certified Public Accountants.
2. We will not perform an audit of such financial statements, the objective of which is an expression of an opinion regarding the financial statements taken as a whole and, accordingly, we will not express an opinion on them. Our report on the financial statements is expected to be stated as follows:
3. (Compilation report wording inserted here)

Our engagement cannot be relied upon to disclose errors, irregularities, or illegal acts, including fraud or defalcations, that may exist. However, we will inform you of any such matters that come to our attention.

Our fees for these services are $XXXXXX. We will progress bill you each month. Our fees are payable upon receipt of invoice. If anything occurs that will require more work, we will inform you before proceeding.

If the foregoing is in accordance with your understanding, please sign the copy of this letter in the space provided and return it to us.

Sincerely,

Description of Keyed Items

1. The title of the statements included in the report. See OCBOA overview for

   * Balance Sheet

   ** Statement of Income

2. This paragraph will be eliminated if the engagement calls for an opinion audit.
3. Paragraph 3 will present your expected report. See the next section.

Report Format

The report should contain up to four paragraphs:

1. Explanation
2. Scope
3. Additional Description
4. Opinion

Whether you prepare an opinion, review or compilation, your letter should, to the extent possible, follow the ensuing format. As you describe the included statements, you'll can insert the titles listed above.

Cash Receipts and Disbursements Method

To: Client

1. We have audited the accompanying Statement of Assets, Liabilities and Equity Resulting from Cash Transactions at December 31, 19XX and the related Statement of Cash Receipts & Disbursements for the year then ended. These financial statements are the responsibility of the Company's management. Our responsibility is to express an opinion on these financial statements based on our audit.

2. Same.

3. As described in Note A, the Company's policy is to prepare its financial statements on the basis of cash receipts and disbursements; consequently, certain revenues and related assets are recognized when received rather than when earned, and certain expenses are recognized when paid rather than when the obligation is incurred.

Accordingly, the accompanying financial statements are not intended to present financial position and results of operations in accordance with generally accepted accounting principles.

4. In our opinion, the financial statements referred to above present fairly, in all material respects, the assets, liabilities and equity of resulting from cash transactions of CashCo at December 31, 19XX, and its cash receipts and disbursements for the year then ended in conformity with generally accepted accounting principles.

Modified Cash Basis

1. * Balance Sheet on a Modified Cash Basis
   ** Statement of Income on a Modified Cash Basis

2. Same.

3. As described in Note A, the Company's policy is to prepare its financial statements on the basis of cash receipts and disbursements; consequently, certain revenues and related assets are recognized when received rather than when earned, and certain expenses are recognized when paid rather than when the obligation is incurred. However, depreciation is recorded in the accounts. *Accordingly, the accompanying financial statements are not intended to present financial position and results of operations in accordance with generally accepted accounting principles.*

4. In our opinion, the financial statements referred to above present fairly, in all material respects, the Balance Sheet on a Modified Cash Basis at December 31, 19XX and the Statement of Income on a Modified Cash Basis for the year then ended in conformity with generally accepted accounting principles.

Income Tax Basis

1. * Statement of Assets and Liabilities—Income Tax Basis
   ** Statement of Revenues and Expenses—Income tax basis

2. Same.

3. As described in Note A, the Company's policy is to prepare its financial statements on the accounting basis used for income tax purposes; consequently, certain revenues and related assets are recognized when received rather than when earned, and certain expenses are recognized when paid rather than when the obligation is incurred. *Accordingly, the accompanying financial statements are not intended to present financial position and results of operations in accordance with generally accepted accounting principles.*

4. In our opinion, the financial statements referred to above present fairly, in all material respects, The Statement of Assets and Liabilities—Income Tax Basis at December 31, 19XX and the Statement of Revenues and Expenses—Income tax basis for the year then ended in conformity with generally accepted accounting principles.

Comparative Statements

Comparative financial statements portray information for one or more periods and are usually presented side by side. The degree of responsibility (audit, review, compilation) may differ from one time to another.

Reporting Interperiod Variances

Present your opinion for the current year in the usual fashion and, add a paragraph to separately describe your work for prior years as follows:

Prior Compilation

The accompanying (prior year(s)') financial statements were compiled by us. A compilation is limited to presenting in the form of financial statements information that is the representation of management. We have not audited or reviewed the (prior year(s)') financial statements and, accordingly, do not express an opinion or any other form of assurance on them.

Prior Review

The accompanying (prior year(s)') financial statements were previously reviewed by us, and my report dated Month, Day, Year stated that we were not aware of any material modifications that should be made to these statements in order to be in conformity with generally accepted accounting principles. We have not performed any procedures in connection with that review engagement after the date of my report on the (prior year(s)') financial statements.

Prior Audit

The financial statements for the year(s) ended (prior) were examined by us and we expressed an unqualified opinion on them in our report dated Month, Day, Year, but we have not performed any auditing procedures since that date.

Note: If the prior financial statements were audited by other accountants, simply substitute the term *other accountants* in place of *us*.

Personal Financial Statements

Official Pronouncements

AICPA—Personal Financial Statement Guide

AICPA Statement of Position 82-1; Accounting and Financial Reporting for Personal Financial Statements.

The relevant GAAP for personal financial statements is found in Chapter 2 of this book.

This section deals with various reporting forms. Remember, the rules of GAAS must be followed.

Engagement Letter

The following letter can be used for each of the three reporting forms:

> This letter is to confirm our understanding of the terms and objectives of our engagement and the nature and limitations of the services we provide.
>
> We will (audit, review, or compile) personal financial statements for (name).
>
> *Present Your Proposed Report*
>
> If, for any reason, we are unable to complete our (compilation, review, audit) of your financial statements, we will not issue a report on such statements as a result of this engagement.
>
> We will also provide such additional accounting services as are necessary to obtain necessary information from which to (compile, review, audit) the statements. The performance of these additional accounting services does not alter the fact that you are responsible for the content of the financial statements, including the estimated current values of assets and the estimated current amounts of liabilities.
>
> Our engagement cannot be relied upon to disclose errors, irregularities, or illegal acts, including fraud or defalcations that may exist. However, we will inform you of any such matters that come to our attention.
>
> Our fees for these services will be based on our standard per diem rates for the staff persons assigned to this engagement. Our bills and rendered monthly and payable upon demand.

If the foregoing is in accordance with your understanding, please sign the copy of this letter in the space provided and return it to us.

Client Representations

The following client representations should be obtained regardless of whether the engagement was compilation, review or audit:

To the Accountant:

1. We are responsible for the fair presentation in the statements of financial condition and changes in net worth in conformity with generally accepted accounting principles.

2. Assets are presented at their estimated current values which have been determined in accordance with guidelines set forth by the American Institute of Certified Public Accountants.

3. All financial records and supporting documents have been made available to you.

4. There are no material gain or loss contingencies that should be accrued or disclosed in the financial statements.

5. All related party transactions and related receivables and payables have been properly segregated and disclosed in the financial statements.

6. There are no legal matters or violations of any laws that should be accrued or disclosed.

7. We have no plans or intentions that may materially affect the financial statements.

8. All material transactions have been properly reflected.

9. All sales of assets are final and no repurchase agreements exist.

10. There are no income tax audits in process that have not been disclosed in the financial statements.

11. All material subsequent events, if any, have been disclosed.

12. We have satisfactory title to all owned assets and all encumbrances or liens have been disclosed.

13. There are no litigation matters outstanding that have not been disclosed in the financial statements.

14. We are not in violation of any agreements or contracts.

Reports on Personal Financial Statements

Compilation Report

Engagement letter:

We will compile from information you provide, the statement of financial condition of Willett and Eleanor Ryder as of December 31, 19XX, and the related statement of changes in net worth for the year then ended, in accordance with standards established by the American Institute of Certified Public Accountants. We will not audit or review such financial statements. Our report on the financial statements is expected to read as follows:

Report:

We have compiled the accompanying statement of financial condition of Willett and Eleanor Ryder as of December 31, 19XX, and the related statement of changes in net worth for the year then ended, in accordance with standards established by the American Institute of Certified Public Accountants.

A compilation is limited to presenting, in the form of financial statements, information that is the representation of the individuals whose financial statements are presented. We have not audited or reviewed the accompanying financial statements, and, accordingly, do not express an opinion or any other form of assurance on them.

Review Report

Engagement letter:

We will review the statement of financial condition of Beth Ruben as of December 31, 19XX, and the related statement of changes in net worth for the year then ended, in accordance with standards established by the American Institute of Certified Public Accountants. We will not perform an audit on such financial statements, the objective of which is the expression of an opinion, regarding the financial statements taken as a whole, and, accordingly, we will not express an opinion on them. Our report on the financial statements is expected to read as follows:

Report:

We have reviewed the accompanying statement of financial condition of Beth Ruben as of December 31, 19XX, and the related statement of changes in net worth for the year then ended in accordance with standards established by the American Institute of Certified

Public Accountants. All information included in these financial statements is the representation of Mrs. Ruben.

A review of personal financial statements consists principally of inquiries of the individuals whose financial statements are presented and analytical procedures applied to financial data. It is substantially less in scope than an examination in accordance with generally accepted auditing standards, the objective of which is the expression of an opinion regarding the financial statements taken as a whole. Accordingly, we do not express such an opinion.

Based upon our review, we are not aware of any material modifications that should be made to the accompanying financial statements for them to be in conformity to with generally accepted accounting principles.

Audited Personal Financial Statements

The major audit differences lies in gathering evidence about fair market valuations of assets. There are many alternative methods. But, whatever is chosen, it is important to support and document your work. Furthermore, the bases of carrying amounts should be disclosed.

Engagement letter:

We will audit the statement of financial condition of Lucy Roxanne as of December 31, 19XX, and the related statement of changes in net worth for the year then ended. Our report on the financial statements is expected to read as follows:

Report:

We have audited the accompanying statement of financial condition of Lucy Roxanne as of December 31, 19XX and the related statement of changes in net worth for the year then ended. These financial statements are the responsibility of Mr. and Mrs. Roxanne. Our responsibility is to express an opinion on these financial statements based on our audit.

We conducted our audit in accordance with generally accepted auditing standards. Those standards require that we plan and perform the audit to obtain reasonable assurance about whether the financial statements are free of material misstatement. An audit includes examining, on a test basis, evidence supporting the amounts and disclosures in the financial statements. An audit also includes assessing the accounting principles used and significant estimates made in the preparation of the financial statements, as well as evaluating the overall financial statement presentation. We believe that our audit provides a reasonable basis for our opinion.

In our opinion, the financial statements referred to above present fairly, in all material respects, the financial condition of Lucy Roxanne as of December 31, 19XX, and the changes in net worth for the year then ended in conformity with generally accepted accounting principles.

Financial Forecasts and Projections

Official Pronouncement

AICPA—Financial Forecasts and Projections, September 1986

Definitions

Both forecasts and projections portray an organization's estimated future financial position, income and cash flow. The difference between the two is in the way the assumptions are derived:

Forecast: Prepared on assumptions made on conditions that are expected to occur during future periods and expected actions if the anticipated events take place.

For example, changes in the inflation rate.

Projection: Predicts what should happen if one or more hypothetical assumptions do occur and what would be done if these assumptions materialize.

For example, what would happen if we increase our selling price?

Assumptions

The relevance of these statements depends on the assumptions made. The following should be considered and disclosed:

1. The nature and condition of the market:
    a. trends
    b. prices
    c. technological factors
2. The availability and cost of resources needed to service sales and to operate.

3. General economic trends
   a. inflation
   b. leading indicators
   c. government intervention
4. The probability of obtaining reasonable financing:
   a. amount
   b. terms
   c. interest rate

Engagement Letter

This letter is to confirm our understanding of the terms and objectives of our engagement and the nature and limitations of the services we will provide.

We will (compile, audit), in accordance with standards established by the American Institute of Certified Public Accountants, from information management provides, the forecasted (projected) balance sheet and related statements of income and retained earnings and cash flows and summaries of significant assumptions and accounting policies of Devonport Corporation for the years ending December 31, 1990–1994. We will not express any form of assurance on the achievability of the forecast.

For compilation add: or on the reasonableness of the underlying assumptions.

Description of compilation and audit

If, for any reason, we are unable to complete our (compilation, audit) of your forecast, we will not issue a report on it as a result of this engagement.

Description of forecast or projection

Management is responsible for representations about its plans and expectations and for disclosure of significant information that might affect the ultimate realization of the forecasted results.

There will usually be differences between the forecasted and actual results because events and circumstances frequently do not occur as expected, and those differences may be material. Our report will contain a statement to that effect.

We have no responsibility to update our report for events and circumstances occurring after the date of our report.

At the conclusion of our engagement, management agrees to supply us with a representation letter which, among other things, will confirm management's responsibility for the underlying assumptions and the appropriateness of the financial (forecast, projection) and its presentation.

In order for us to complete this engagement, management must provide assumptions that are appropriate for the (forecast, projection). If the assumptions provided are inappropriate and are not revised to our satisfaction, we will be unable to complete the engagement and, accordingly, we will not issue a report on the forecast.

Our fees for these services are based on our standard per diem rates of the staff persons assigned to this engagement. You will be billed monthly. Invoices are payable upon presentation.

If management intends to reproduce and publish the (forecast, projection) and our report thereon, they must be reproduced in their entirety, and all drafts of the document containing the (forecast, projection) must be submitted to us for our approval.

If you approve the terms and conditions of this letter, please sign where indicated.

Description of Services

Compilation:

A compilation of a financial (forecast, projection) is based on management's assumptions and the performance of limited other procedures without evaluating the support for, or expressing a conclusion, or any other form of assurance, on the assumptions underlying the statements.

Review

Forecasts and projections are not reviewed. The standard review letter states the following: "*We are not aware of any material modifications that should be made to these statements in order to be in conformity with generally accepted accounting principles.*" By their very nature, forecasts and projections are dependent upon assumptions that may or may not occur. Therefore, there could certainly be "major modifications."

Audit

An audit of a financial (forecast, projection) is based on management's assumptions and our examination made in accordance with standards for the examination of a (forecast, projection) established by the American Institute of Certified Public Accountants and accordingly includes such procedures as we considered necessary to evaluate both the assumptions used by management and the preparation and presentation of the (forecast, projection).

Description of Forecast and Projection

Forecast:

A financial forecast presents, to the best of management's knowledge and belief, the Company's expected financial position, results of operations, and cash flows for the forecast period. It is based on management's assumptions reflecting conditions it expects to exist and the course of action it expects to take during the forecast period.

Projection:

A financial projection presents, to the best of management's knowledge and belief, the Company's expected financial position, results of operations, and cash flows for the projections period assuming that management takes a certain action. It is based on management's assumptions, reflecting conditions it expects would exist and courses of action it expects would be taken during the projection period assuming management takes a certain action.

How to Write Your Report on Forecasts and Projections

Compilation:

We have compiled the accompanying (forecasted, projected) balance sheet, statement of income, retained earnings and cash flows for Devonport Corporation for the Years 1990–1994, in accordance with standards established by the American Institute of Certified Public Accountants.

A compilation is limited to presenting, in the form of a (forecast, projection), information that is the representation of management and does not include evaluation of the support for the assumptions underlying the (forecast, projection). We have not examined the forecast and, accordingly, do not express an opinion or any other form of assurance on the accompanying financial statements or assumptions. Furthermore, there will usually be differences between the forecasted and actual results, because events and circumstances frequently do not occur as expected, and those differences may be material. We have no responsibility to update this report for events and circumstances occurring after the date of the report.

Audit:

We have examined the accompanying (forecasted, projected) balance sheet, statement of income, retained earnings and cash flows of Devonport Corporation for the Years 1990–1994. Our examination was made in accordance with standards of examination of a forecast established by the American Institute of Certified Public Accountants and, accordingly, included such procedures as we considered necessary to evaluate both the assumptions used by management and their preparation of the forecast.

In our opinion, the accompanying forecast is presented in conformity with guidelines for presentation of a forecast established by the American Institute of Certified Public Accountants, and the underlying assumptions provide a reasonable basis for management's forecast. However, there will usually be differences between the forecasted and actual results, because events and circumstances frequently do not occur as expected, and those differences may be material. We have no responsibility to update this report for events occurring after the date of this report.

CHAPTER 13

Special Auditing Responsibilities

Introduction

This chapter deals presents a review of the responsibilities that any accountant faces and the body of common and statutory law that deals with these matters including:

- Legal liabilities to your client
- Responsibility for ordinary and gross negligence, and fraud
- Illegal acts by your clients
- The Foreign Corrupt Practices Act
- Auditing foreign financial statements
- Reports on internal control

To help you protect yourself, to the extent possible, from many of these dangers, we conclude the chapter with a Liability Reduction Checklist.

Liabilities to Your Clients

Generally, you have two obligations to your client:

- Contractual obligations
- Duty to express care

Contractual Obligations

Every engagement is a contract.

- The client expects certain work.
- You expect to be paid.

A breach of that agreement by either party may be grounds for a lawsuit.

Should You Sue to Get Paid?

My usual answer to that question is no. Why? Because, as you know, the quality of any professional services is in the eye of the beholder. Therefore, any legal action you institute may be met by a your client's cross complaint. And, then, you're off to the legal races.

Further danger: The malpractice insurance carriers are loath to issue coverage for accountants involved in legal matters even as plaintiffs.

Therefore, a good healthy awareness is the best way to avoid collection problems.

1. Make sure your fee and billing arrangements are spelled out clearly in the engagement letter.
2. Progress bill your client at least once a month.
3. If time problems arise, discuss them with your client immediately.
4. If you think there will be collection problems, ask for an advance retainer.

Duty to Exercise Care

You have an obligation to your client to perform your work under the highest standards of professional care. In order to hold you liable, your client needs to prove the following:

1. That care was required
2. That there was a breach of care
3. That he or she suffered damages
4. That there was a causal connection between the damages suffered and your breach of care

What Is Sufficient Care?

That definition depends upon the following:

1. The type of engagement
2. The ability and skill of the provider
3. Whether or not GAAS was followed

If, under these conditions, sufficient care is found to be lacking, the court may rule that *ordinary negligence* has occurred, and hold in favor of the client.

What Is Ordinary Negligence?

You may be found guilty of ordinary negligence if you fail to exercise reasonable care in the performance of your engagement. This standard is judged by a comparison of your work with that of other practitioners who are, generally, in the same circumstances.

Liability to Whom

The Ultramares case (Ultramares v. Touche, Niven & Co, New York, 1931) held that a CPA was *not* liable for ordinary negligence to third parties. Since then, other cases have tended to erode that doctrine. In Rusch Factors, Inc. v. Levin the court held that a CPA can be liable for ordinary negligence to *foreseen* classes of persons.

For example, a bank that makes a loan, which is dependent upon the audited report, is a foreseen class of persons.

Over the years, the courts have held the accountant to be liable in the following situations:

1. Embezzlement by employees was not discovered.
2. The client was not warned of a serious financial condition.
3. Computational errors were made by the accountant.
4. Erroneous tax advice was given.
5. The accountant breached his or her fiduciary duties.

Liability to Third Parties

Note: The issues discussed here exclude securities law violations which will be covered in Chapter 14.

Accountants are liable to third parties for *gross negligence.*

Gross Negligence and Fraud. Gross negligence is loosely defined as a failure to act with reasonable care.

For example, if a CPA disregards GAAS by failing to observe inventories when they are material and does not verify them by any other means, he or she might be found guilty of gross negligence.

When Is the CPA Responsible to Find Fraud?

Normally, a CPA is not responsible to find fraud that may exist as long as the audit is conducted in accordance with GAAS. However, you *may* be liable if you discover but do not report misleading information.

And, of course, fraud obviously exists when the CPA *knowingly* issues a false report.

Illegal Acts by Client

Official Pronouncement

SAS #17: Illegal Acts by Client, 1977

According to SAS #17, if we perform an audit under GAAS, we are *not* expected to ensure users that illegal acts by clients will be discovered. However, we have to always be aware of the possibility.

Note: When the waters are dangerous, don't go swimming. In other words, be careful when you accept clients. Refer to Chapter 6, which presents a Client Acceptance Questionnaire.

What Do You Do if You Discover Illegal Acts?

The presence of illegal acts does not only indicate potential financial statement distortion. It also could be a symptom of overall management dishonesty. If you have discovered a client has been acting illegally, be very careful. Consult a lawyer, one who is familiar with these kinds of matters, before you do anything else.

After obtaining legal representation, what should you do next?

1. Calculate the effects on the financial statements. Will adjustments, and/or disclosures be required?
2. Bring the matter to management's attention. It is what *they* do with this information that dictates your next actions.
3. Consider the act's significance, and, if necessary, inform the board of directors and/or the shareholders.
4. If management does not take, what you believe, are the right steps, you may have to withdraw from the engagement.
5. Inform the regulatory authorities.

How to Comply with Provisions of the Foreign Corrupt Practices Act

The Foreign Corrupt Practices Act (FCPA) has been written for publicly held corporations (registrants). However, there are provisions of The Act which are applicable here.

According to the FCPA, which was written in 1977, payments of bribes by any domestic corporation, its officers, or other agents to any foreign official, are prohibited. To assure compliance, the registrant is required to:

1. Keep detailed books.
2. Maintain a system of internal control sufficient to ensure that:
   a. The transactions are executed in accordance with management's authorizations.
   b. The record keeping is sufficient to provide auditable financial statements.
   c. There is limited access to assets.
   d. There is sufficient accountability for the assets.

Auditor Involvement

As an auditor, the FCPA requires you to determine that the internal control is sufficient to prevent illegal payments as defined in the Act. But, this requirement really exists for all financial audits. However, the GAAS requirement to analyze, review and test internal control, as a basis for rendering an opinion on the financial statements may not be enough in this case. Therefore, a specific engagement, to perform a special review of the internal controls, may be necessary.

How to Report on a Company's Internal Controls

Official Pronouncement

SAS #30, Reporting on Internal Accounting Control.

SAS #55, Considerations of the Internal Control Structure in a Financial Statement Audit.

SAS #58, Reports on Audited Financial Statements.

SAS #60, Communications of Internal Control Structure Related Matters in an Audit.

A report on internal accounting control may be written as part of the examination of the financial statements, or as a result of a separate engagement. If it's a special engagement, the scope of your work will be targeted to this one area. Therefore, the procedures you follow, will, of course, have to be more extensive, in scope, than those employed in a financial audit engagement.

Internal Control Opinion Sample—Unqualified Opinion

1. We have made an examination of the internal control structure of Devonport Corporation at December 31, 19XX. Our examination was conducted in accordance with standards established by the American Institute of Certified Public Accountants.

2. The management of Devonport Corporation is responsible for establishing and maintaining an internal control structure. In fulfilling this responsibility, estimates and judgments by management are required to assess the expected benefits and related costs of control procedures. The objectives of the internal control structure are to provide management reasonable assurance that financial data are recorded, processed, summarized, and reported consistent with the assertions embodied in the financial statements. The internal control structure comprises the control environment, the accounting system, and the control procedures.

3. Because of inherent limitations in any internal control structure, errors or irregularities may nevertheless occur and may not be detected. Also, projection of any evaluation of the structure to future periods is subject to the risk that policies or procedures may become inadequate because of changes in conditions or that the degree of compliance with the policies or procedures may deteriorate.

4. In our opinion, the internal control structure of Devonport Corporation in effect at December 31, 19XX, taken as a whole, was sufficient to meet the objectives stated above insofar as those objectives pertain to the prevention or detection of errors or irregularities in amounts that would be material in relation to the financial statements.

Index to Keyed Items

1. Description of the scope of your work
2. States that the internal control structure is the responsibility of management
3. Explanation of the objectives and limitations of the system
4. Explanation of exceptions
5. Opinion

Reporting on Material Weaknesses

If material weaknesses are discovered, any assurance that the structure would detect irregularities or errors is lessened. The following exception report should be drafted:

Paragraph 1–3: No changes

Paragraph 4:

Our examination discloses the following condition in the internal control structure of Devonport Corporation in effect at December 31, 19XX, which, in our opinion, results in more than a relatively low risk that errors or irregularities in amounts that would be material in relation to the financial statements may occur and not be detected within a timely period.

Paragraph 5:

During the evaluation of Devonport Corporation's inventory procedures, it was noticed that access to the stock was not controlled. Under this condition, inventory could be misappropriated. This weakness is due to an inadequate design of the Company's internal control structure. This condition was considered in determining the nature, timing, and extent of audit tests to be applied in our audit of the 19XX financial statements, and this report does not affect our report, dated ______ on those financial statements.

Note: If the client corrects the condition to your satisfaction, the actions taken may be noted in the report.

How to Audit Foreign Financial Statements

While there are risks in auditing financial statements of *domestic* companies, the perils of examining the statements of *foreign* organizations increase exponentially. What are the reasons?

1. Different accounting principles are used
2. Variations in environment (cultural, political, economic) complicate international audits
3. Geographic distances
4. Communication problems
5. Differences in business practice

Three Alternatives to Auditing Foreign Companies

1. Do the audit yourself. However, if you're unfamiliar with the environment, its language, its culture, your level of exposure to risk could be higher than you're willing to accept.
2. Use a local accounting firm. A local firm will not only be most familiar with the environment, but it may have a close rela-

tionship to the business people in that country. However, there are different licensing standards and it's difficult to select to evaluate the firm's qualifications.

3. Use an international accounting firm that has offices locally as well as in the host country.

Checklist—How to Reduce the Risks of Legal Exposure

1. Decide if the client should be accepted.
2. Prepare and have the client sign an engagement letter.
3. Determine that you are qualified.
4. Thoroughly plan all your work.
5. Make sure that you have adequately staffed all engagements.
6. Fully understand each client including its business and systems.
7. Thoroughly review your work.
8. Have adequate insurance coverage.
9. Use legal counsel and other experts whenever necessary.
10. Voluntarily subscribe to peer review.

CHAPTER 14

SEC Engagements

Introduction

Practicing before the SEC can be very exciting and rewarding. However, there are also many opportunities to bloody and permanently hurt yourself. You see, when a company issues securities to the public, you, as the accountant, are immediately responsible to an entirely new group of interested parties; stockholders, underwriters and the SEC (Securities and Exchange Commission).

This chapter will provide an overview of the mechanics of public securities offerings, the governing laws, the role of the SEC, and the various forms, disclosures and representations required of you from the SEC, and the underwriters.

NOTE: *THE SEC FILING PROCESS IS VERY COMPLICATED AND SHOULD NOT BE ATTEMPTED WITHOUT HELP FROM EXPERTS; ACCOUNTANTS, LAWYERS, AND SO FORTH.*

What Are the Necessary Steps to Go Public?

When a company has gone as far as it could on its internal capital and available loan sources, it may be time to prepare an initial stock offering (IPO). The following is an approximate program of activities that occur:

1. The company's meets with its advisors (accountants, lawyers, and bankers) and reviews its capital requirements. If expansion needs are greater than present available funds, an IPO may be the answer.
2. Underwriters are contacted and the following is discussed:
    a. whether the underwriter is interested in the company
    b. how its plans to market the company's securities
    c. how it computes its fees and charges

3. Management and its advisors discuss the economics of the IPO, and, from this discussion, make the "go, no-go" decision.
4. Assuming that the decision is to go, management begins to assemble the package that will contain the legal documents, business descriptions, explanations of how the proceeds will be used, and financial statements and disclosures prepared in accordance with Regulation S-X.
5. The package is printed as specified by regulation and sent to the SEC for approval.

   Note: This preliminary package is called a *red herring* and cannot be used to sell securities.
6. Comments are received from the SEC and changes are made to the exhibits as required.
7. The SECs final approval is secured.
8. A "Due Diligence" meeting, which brings all the participants together, is held. This meeting allows inquiries to be made and resolves any matters that might affect the offering.
9. The offering price and underwriting agreement is approved.
10. The offering document is distributed.
11. The stock is sold to the public.

How to Determine if Going Public Makes Sense

The economics of the offering are dependent upon the following:

1. Amount of capital needed
2. Costs to raise capital:
   a. underwriter's charges
   b. audit fees
   c. legal fees
   d. printing and other costs
3. Amount of dilution, or how much the original stockholders will have to give up. This may lead to loss of control and freedom of action.

Often, as the following example will show, what might be a good idea at the beginning, may turn out sour because of adverse stock market factors or unfavorable earnings trends of the company itself.

Example:

Devonport Corporation is considering going public. As the following schedule indicates, they will need $1,135,000 to expand their operations and pay off some debt.

PROJECTED USE OF FUNDS

Build new plant	$ 600,000
Working capital during start up period	100,000
Pay off bank debt	350,000
Increased research and development	85,000
Net Funds Needed	$1,135,000

Costs to register the securities are expected to total $24,500 (as shown below) and underwriting costs are estimated at 2%.

COSTS

Audit Fees	$ 6,000
Legal Fees	15,000
Printing and other Costs	3,500
Total Costs	$24,500

Therefore Devonport will need to sell securities in the amount of $1,183,163. (($1,135,000 + 24,500)/(1 − .02))

In order for the deal to make sense, excess *dilution* must be avoided. Assume the issued is projected to be sold at 10 X earnings. As the following illustrates, the amount of dilution under Scenarios A and B is quite different. Scenario A will allow the existing shareholders to retain over 60% of the stock, while the smaller earnings projected in Scenario B may force the original owners to turn over 68% to the public and lose control.

SCENARIO	A	B
Earnings	300,000	175,000
Earnings Multiple	10	10
Market Value of Company	3,000,000	1,750,000
Proceeds from Stock Sale	1,183,163	1,183,163
New Stockholders Percentage	39.44%	67.61%
Old Shareholders Percentage	60.56%	32.39%
	100.00%	100.00%

Your Legal Responsibilities when You Engage in Securities Work

Because you're responsible not only to your client, but a large number of users of financial information, including the SEC and various state agencies, your legal exposure increases exponentially.

The Securities Act of 1933

This act establishes disclosure requirements and is primarily concerned with the initial public offering. Under the Act, the accountant is required to render an opinion on the financial statements included. In addition, the law requires the accountants to review the registration statement and other disclosures in order to determine that discrepancies between the registration documents and the financial statements are avoided.

The Securities Exchange Act of 1934

This act regulates securities of companies that have already registered, and the accountants reporting on these companies.

Blue Sky Laws

Most states have regulations that affect *intra* state registration of stocks. Like the above, these laws are varied and complex and require your careful attention.

SEC Regulatory Provisions

The Agency can regulate registrants by using one or more of the following tools:

1. *Injunctions:* The Agency can bring an action in federal district court to prevent a violation from occurring.
2. *Administrative sanctions:* The SEC has been delegated administrative power to disqualify accountants from practicing before the Agency for a variety of reasons.
3. *Criminal sanctions:* The SEC may bring criminal action against accountants.

How to Work with Underwriters

The underwriter or investment banker's function is to market and distribute securities of the registering company.

The Registration Team

A number of people are involved in the process. Some of these are:

1. The underwriter
2. The securities attorney
3. The independent accountant
4. Other experts, as required

Key Going Public Questions

Your input is valuable to help your client determine:

1. The type of securities that should be offered
2. The timing of the registration
3. The number of shares to be offered and their price

Note: You client may also want to ask your advice on the underwriting agreement itself. While this is primarily a legal question, there are certain economic factors that you may be best qualified to resolve.

There are three types of underwriting agreements:

1. Firm Commitment
2. Best efforts
3. All or none

Each of these options has different costs and benefits which should be considered.

What Is a Full Registration? And, What Is Required?

According to SEC regulations, a "full" registration is required when the company does not meet any of the exemptions. Most full registrations are submitted with Form S-1. The following information is required:

PART I:

1. Distribution Spread
2. Plan of Distribution
3. Use of Proceeds to Registrant
4. Sales Otherwise than for Cash
5. Capital Structure
6. Summary of Operations
7. Organization of Registrant
8. Parents of Registrant
9. Description of Business
10. Description of Property
11. Organization within last 5 years
12. Legal Proceedings
13. Capital Stock being Registered
14. Long-Term Debt being Registered
15. Other Securities Being Registered
16. Directors and Executive Officers
17. Renumeration of Directors and Officers
18. Options to Purchase Securities
19. Principal Holders of Securities
20. Interest of Management and Others in Certain Transactions
21. Financial Statements

PART II:

1. Marketing Arrangements
2. Other Expenses of Issuance and Distributions
3. Relationship with Registrant of Experts Named in Registration Statement
4. Sales to Special Parties
5. Recent Sales of Unregistered Securities
6. Subsidiaries of Registrant
7. Franchises and Concessions
8. Indemnification of Directors and Officers
9. Treatment of Proceeds from Stock Being Registered
10. Financial Statements and Exhibits
11. Number of Equity Security Holders

What Financial Statements Are Required in the S-1 Registration?

The following financial statements are required to be submitted:

- Audited balance sheet
- Three years of audited comparative income statements
- Three years of audited comparative statements of cash flows
- Summary of operations
- Management's analysis and discussion
- Disclosure information per Regulation S-X

Hint: If your client is considering going public in the foreseeable future, but does not want to incur the audit expense until the decision is made, it may make sense for you to perform certain audit procedures at each year's end that *can't* be accomplished in future years.

Example:

1. Year end inventory observations.
2. Year end cut-off work.

Unaudited "Stub" Periods

Unaudited interim statements should be included for periods after the audited year end. Where these are presented, comparable data for the most recent preceding year should also be submitted.

Exemptions from Full Registration

The securities act pertains only to issues sold interstate, through the mails, or in foreign commerce. In addition, the following transactions are exempted:

1. A private offering.
2. A Regulation A exemption: "Reg A" applies to issues of securities whose total sales price to the ultimate investor does not exceed $1.5 million.

   Note: Regulation A offerings still have to comply with *certain* registration procedures.
3. Other specifically excluded transacions.

What Is Regulation S-X and How Does It Affect Your Work?

Regulation S-X uses GAAP as its basis and will accept it in most instances. The major areas of difference are caused by S-X's more detailed disclosure requirements. The schedules required are listed below:

Schedule I: Marketable Securities—Other Security Investments

Column A– Name of issuer and title of each issue

Column B – Number of shares or units-principal amounts of bonds or notes

Column C – Cost of each issue

Column D– Market value of each issue at balance sheet date

Column E – Amount at which each portfolio of equity security issues and each other security issue carried in balance sheet

Schedule II: Accounts receivable from underwriters, promoters, directors, officers, employees, and principal holders (other than affiliates) of equity securities of the person and its affiliates

Column A– Name of debtor

Column B – Balance at beginning of period

Column C – Additions

Column D– Deductions

1. Amounts collected
2. Amounts written off

Column E – Balance at end of period

1. Current
2. Not current

Schedule III: Investment in, Equity in Earnings of, and Dividends Received from Affiliates and Persons

Column A– Name of issuer and description of investment

Column B – Balance at Beginning of Period

1. Number of shares or units. Principal amount of bonds and notes
2. Amount in dollars

Column C – Additions

1. Equity taken up in earnings (losses) of affiliates and other persons for the period
2. Other

Column D– Deductions
1. Distribution of earnings by persons in which earnings (losses) were taken up
2. Other

Column E – Balance at end of period
1. Number of shares or units. Principal amount of bonds and notes
2. Amount in dollars

Column F – Dividends received during the period from investments not accounted for by the equity method

Schedule IV: Indebtedness of Affiliates and Other Persons—Not Current

Column A– Name of Person

Column B – Balance at Beginning of Period

Column C– Balance at End of Period

Schedule V: Property, Plans and Equipment

Column A– Classification

Column B – Balance at beginning of period

Column C– Additions at Cost

Column D– Retirements

Column E – Other changes—add (deduct) describe

Column F – Balance at End of Period

Schedule VI: Accumulated Depreciation, Depletion and Amortization of Property Plant and Equipment

Column A– Classification

Column B – Balance at beginning of period

Column C– Additions at Cost

Column D– Retirements

Column E – Other changes—add (deduct) describe

Column F – Balance at End of Period

Schedule VII: Intangible Assets, Pre operating Expenses and Similar Deferrals

Column A– Description

Column B – Balance at Beginning of Period

Column C– Additions at cost—describe

Column D– Deductions
1. Charged to costs and expenses
2. Charged to other accounts—describe

Column E – Other changes—add (deduct)—describe

Column F – Balance at close of period

Schedule VIII: Accumulated Depreciation and Amortization of Intangible Assets

Column A– Description

Column B – Balance at Beginning of Period

Column C– Additions
1. Charged to costs and expenses
2. Charged to other accounts—describe

Column D– Deductions—describe

Column E – Balance at close of period

Schedule IX: Bonds, Mortgages and Similar Debt

Column A– Name of issuer and title of each issue

Column B – Amount authorized by indenture

Column C– Amount issued and not retired or canceled

Column D– Amount included in column C, which is
1. held by or for account of issuer thereof
2. not held by or for account of issuer thereof

Column E – Amount included in sum extended under caption "bonds, mortgages, and similar debt" in related balance sheet

Column F – Amount in sinking fund and other special funds of issuer thereof

Column G– Amount pledged by issuer thereof

Column H– Amount held by affiliates for which statements are filed herewith
1. Persons included in consolidated statements
2. Others

Schedule X: Indebtedness to Affiliates and Other Persons—Non Current

Column A– Name of Person

Column B – Balance at Beginning of Period

Column C– Balance at End of Period

Schedule XI: Guarantees of Securities and Other Issuers

Column A– Name of issuer of securities guaranteed by person for which statement is filed

Column B – Title of issue of each class of securities guaranteed

Column C – Total amount guaranteed and outstanding

Column D– Amount owned by person or persons for which statement is filed

Column E – Amount in treasury of issuer of securities guaranteed

Column F – Nature of guarantee

Column G– Nature of any default by issuer of securities guaranteed in principal, interest, sinking fund or redemption provisions or payments of dividends

Schedule XII: Valuation and Qualifying Accounts and Reserves

Column A– Description

Column B – Balance at beginning of period

Column C – Additions
1. Charged to costs and expenses
2. Charged to other accounts—describe

Column D– Deductions—describe

Column E – Balance at end of period

Schedule XIII: Capital Shares

Column A– Name of issuer and title of issue

Column B – Number of shares issued or authorized by charter

Column C – Number of shares issued and not retired or canceled

Column D– Number of shares included in column C which are
1. Held by or for account of issuer thereof
2. Not held by or for account of issuer thereof

Column E – Shares issued or oustanding as shown on or included in related balance sheet under caption "capital shares"
1. Number
2. Amount at which shown

Column F – Number of shares held by affiliates for which statements are filed herewith

1. Persons included in consolidated statements
2. Others

Column G– Number of shares reserved for options, warrants, conversions, and other rights
1. Directors, officers, and employees
2. Other

Schedule XIV: Warrants or Rights

Column A– Title of issue of securities called for by warrants and rights

Column B – Amount of securities called for by each warrant or right

Column C– Number of warrants or rights outstanding

Column D– Aggregate amount of securities called for by warrants or rights outstanding

Column E – Date from which warrants or rights are exercisable

Column F – Expiration of date of warrants or rights

Column G– Price at which warrant or right exercisable

Schedule XV: Other Securities

No format has been established

Schedule XVI: Supplementary Income Statement Information

1. Maintenance and repairs
2. Depreciation, depletion, and amortization of property, plant, and equipment
3. Depreciation and amortization of intangible asset, pre-operating expenses costs, and similar deferrals
4. Taxes, other than income taxes
5. Rents
6. Royalties
7. Advertising costs

Schedule XVII: Real Estate and Accumulated Depreciation (For Certain Real Estate Companies)

Column A– Description

Column B – Encumbrances

Column C – Initial cost to company
 Land
 Building and improvements

Column D – Cost capitalized subsequent to acquisition
 Improvements
 Carrying costs

Column E – Gross amount at which carried at close of period
 Land
 Building and Improvements
 Total

Column F – Accumulated depreciation

Column G – Date of construction

Column H – Date acquired

Column I – Life on which depreciation in latest income statements is computed

Schedule XVIII: Mortgages Loans on Real Estate (For Certain Real Estate Companies)

Column A – Description

Column B – Interest rate

Column C – Fixed maturity date

Column D – Periodic payment terms

Column E – Prior liens

Column F – Face amount of mortgages

Column G – Carrying amount of mortgages

Column H – Principal amount of loans subject to delinquent principal or interest

Ongoing Reporting

The following reports must be filed by companies that issue their securities to the public:

Form 8-K

Lists certain significant events of the registrant including the following:

1. Changes in control
2. Acquisition or disposal of a significant number of assets not in the ordinary course of business
3. The appointment of a receiver in bankruptcy
4. Changes in the certifying accountant. This form must be filed within 15 days of the action.

Note: The notification of a change in the certifying accountant may indicate significant disagreements. The previous auditor must file his or her response no later than 30 days after the 8-K filling.

Form 10-K

Form 10-K is the annual report to shareholders of registered corporations. It is due 90 days after the end of the fiscal year. However, amendments can be filed up to 120 days after fiscal year end. The following information should be included:

1. Description of the business
2. Summary of operations
3. Property descriptions
4. Listing and explanations of patents and subsidiaries
5. Recitation of any outstanding legal proceedings
6. Changes in outstanding securities and debt
7. Schedule of increases and decreases securities
8. Defaults on senior securities (e.g. bonds payable)
9. Approximate number of equity holders
10. Matters submitted to security votes
11. Listing of executive officers
12. Indemnification of directors and officers
13. Financial statements, exhibits filed, and 8-K filings
14. Security ownership of certain beneficial owners and management
15. Name and data on directors
16. Compensation to directors and officers
17. Security options granted to management
18. Interest of management and other key persons in certain securities

Note Regarding 10-K Financial Statements: The conventional statements (balance sheet, statement of income and statement of cash flows) must be audited and filed with the 10-K. The normal disclosure rules in addition to those mandated by Regulation S-X must be followed.

Form 10-Q

This form must be filed for each of the first three quarters. They are due within 45 days after the end of each quarter.

Note: The subject "Interim Financial Statements" has been covered in detail in Chapter 2.

Information Required

1. Interim financial statements
2. Management's analysis of quarterly income statements
3. Other financial information
4. Review by independent public accountant
5. Exhibits as required
6. Legal proceedings involving the registrant
7. Changes in securities
8. Change in security for registered securities
9. Increase or decrease in outstanding securities or indebtedness
10. Matters submitted for vote by security holders
11. Other material events

What Is a Comfort Letter and How Should It Be Written?

Official Pronouncement

SAS #49—Letters for Underwriters

A comfort letter is not a required part of the registration process. Instead, it is a document that the underwriters request from the accountants to minimize misunderstanding and to improve the due diligence process.

What's in a Comfort Letter?

1. A declaration of your independence
2. An affirmation that the financial statements comply with the Securities Acts and related rules.

3. References to the inclusion of unaudited, interim, and other abbreviated information in the registration documents.
4. Description of financial statement items that have changed since the date of the audited financial statements.
5. Any other necessary financial information.

Reducing Your Liability in Securities Work—A Checklist

1. Use the new client acceptance checklist (see Chapter 6).
2. Establish a working relationship with an attorney that specializes in securities work.
3. Make sure your malpractice insurance policy is amended to cover securities work and high limits are placed on it. Unless, specifically stated, most malpractice insurance excludes securities work.
4. Consider joint venturing with a SEC experienced CPA to render the opinions. You may still be able to do most of the work.

Turning Lemons into Lemonade

You may want be consider taking an equity interest. You will not be able to audit the company. However, your position could bring much more financial reward. Of course, consult with legal counsel before you act.

CHAPTER 15

The Controller and the Internal Audit Function

Introduction

In this chapter, some previous auditing subjects are discussed from an internal perspective. The following topics will be presented:

- The controllership function
- Writing an accounting manual
- Working with outside auditors
- Internal auditing
- Management auditing
- Internal audit reports

How to Get the Most Out of Your Controllership Function

The job of the controller requires much more than bookkeeping and tax preparation. If you want to get the most of this operation, you have to be aware that the job, which encompasses so many tasks, requires a particular kind of talent before it can be effectively utilized.

The following evaluation form will help you decide whether you have the right person for the job:

Controller Evaluation Form

Enter a number where provided, that best describes the characteristic being measured.

5 = Highest, 0 = lowest

1. Technical foundation in accounting, finance, and taxes ______

2. Ability to understand company organization; products, technology, policies, culture	________
3. Understanding of environmental factors: political, social, economic	________
4. Understanding of industry	________
5. Ability to communicate	________
6. Ability to express ideas clearly in writing	________
7. Ability to motivate	________
Total	________

Highest possible score = 35.

How to Organize the Finance and Accounting Departments

In order for your controller to provide maximum value to the company, he or she should be equal in authority to production, marketing, and the other line departments. In many organizations, his/her status is equivalent to a vice president position.

The controller's unit should be adequately staffed to carry out the following tasks:

General Accounting

Responsible for recording transactions.

Financial Planning and Control

Supports and helps to keep the company on track by preparing budgets and forecasts and then performing cost and variance analyses.

Financial Analysis

Counsels management on long term capital budgeting including acquisitions, capacity changes, and make or buy decisions.

Systems Analysis, Design and Maintenance

If the management information systems group (MIS) is within the controller's authority, it should be positioned as a separate sub-department. The department will be responsible to analyze and develop procedures and processes needed to provide better data for management.

Cost Accounting

Establishment and monitoring of product cost gathering and analysis procedures.

Taxes

The tax department of the controller's organization should be responsible for the following:

a. Compliance: To make sure that all tax returns are timely and properly filed.
b. Planning: To help management make tax-wise decisions.

Other

Responsible for insurance, property, and so on.

How to Write an Accounting Manual

What are the reasons for an accounting manual?

- To prevent misinterpretation of accounting policies
- To serve as a training guide
- To help new procedures to be implemented quicker
- To act as a problem resolution source.

Because this manual is so important, its composition should be assigned to people with good written communication skills.

What Should Be Included?

The following topics should be incorporated into the manual:

1. An introductory section describing the manual's purpose and how it should be used.
2. How changes in the accounting practices and procedures are made and approved.
3. A chart and text of accounts.

   For example:

Account #	*Title*
6010	Auto expense

   Description

   Any expenses for the business operation of automobiles. This can include gasoline, oil, lubes and oil changes, repairs, sales person expense reimbursements, and so on.

   The following should *not* be included in this category: Auto lease, auto insurance, auto licenses.

4. Company and department organization charts.
5. Functional descriptions of all accounting units.

   For example, general accounting, financial planning control, and MIS.
6. Description of all finance and accounting policies.

   For example: "All property and equipment purchases under $250 should be expensed."
7. Description of internal and external reports required, including:
   a. responsibility
   b. due dates
   c. distribution
8. Master schedules and examples of required reports.

   For example, format for accounts receivable aging.
9. Procedures to be used to close the books.

   For example, dates, accounts to be closed to, EDP procedures.
10. Any other pertinent information. This can include property controls, form letters, audit procedures, and various product and company descriptions.

Once completed, the manual should be reviewed by a number of users and tried out for a sufficient test period before final approval is secured.

Remember: Conditions change. It is important to update the manual and distribute description of these changes whenever necessary.

How to Work with Outside Accountants and Auditors

The process of choosing an outside accountant is a critical one to the growth of a company. It should not be left to chance. Furthermore, once you have made your decision, the engagement, as well as the assignment of responsibilities should be thoroughly discussed and documented.

Choosing the Accountant

There are a number of factors to be considered here:

1. *Your needs.* If your firm has a strong internal accounting department, your requirements may be different from those of a small organization which would need an accountant to perform more functions, including write-up.
2. *Experience of accountants.* Their time in practice including specialization by either industry, or by function (taxes, auditing, management services)
3. *Size of accounting practice.* When you retain a large firm, you will be able to use their expertise to solve a wide (sometimes esoteric) assortment of problems. A small firm's size may limit the scope of services it can provide. However, if your company is not a large organization, it could get "lost" among other clients of a major CPA firm.
4. *Personality fit.* This may be, by far, the most important consideration. If you and/or your people do not get along with your accountant's philosophy or temperament, the relationship is doomed from the beginning.

The Selection Process

1. Put together a team made up of your company's management, your banker, attorney, and other key advisors.
2. Prepare a list of candidates.
3. Wean the list down to three.
4. Base your selection on personality fit.

Use the Peer Review Process

In the near future, all members of the AICPA will have to undergo peer review. This review consists of an examination of each firm's procedures and practices by another CPA firm. When the examination is completed, a report will be prepared. You can request this as a guide to help you make your selection.

How to Make the Relationship Work

First and foremost, make sure you reach mutual agreement on the following:

1. The work required.
2. Time tables.
3. The fee to be charged.

All of the above should be formalized in a written engagement agreement. The terms of the engagement should be periodically reviewed.

How to Keep Your Accounting Fees Low

When we speak of fee reduction, we are not talking about skipping valuable services to avoid incurring charges. The following steps will help keep your fees at an agreeable level while still obtaining value:

1. *See how much of the work you can do.* If you have engaged an auditor, many of the clerical tasks can be performed by your personnel.

   For example, you can prepare schedules, and obtain the necessary documentation.
2. *Carefully plan reasonable time schedules.*
3. *Discuss procedures before they are begun and try to find "better" ways.*
4. *Ask your accountant before you do something, not after.* It is much cheaper to pay for advice in the beginning than for the subsequent clean up *after* the mess has occurred.
5. *If you agree with the advice, follow it.* If you don't, the relationship probably is not working, and, it could be time for a change.

Note: If you are unhappy and are going to make a change. Do it. Don't let inertia take over.

How to Use Internal Auditors

It's a well defined audit principle; the better the internal control, the more effective and inexpensive the examination. An effective internal audit department will improve these controls.

What Do They Do?

The internal auditors' mandate is to make operational audits to assist management to effectively discharge its responsibilities. By performing objective analyses, these auditors can appraise operations and make educated recommendations.

Their duties include the following:

1. To review, test, and evaluate internal controls.
2. To determine that the members of the organization are complying with established policies, plans, and procedures.
3. To safeguard the assets.
4. To check the capability of the records to produce reliable information.
5. To do performance quality appraisals.

Where Should the Internal Auditors Fit in the Organization?

The internal auditors must, of course, be independent of the various departments and divisions in the organization that they audit. It is our opinion, they should report their findings to the higher levels of the corporation, preferably the CEO and/or the Board of Directors.

A General Operational Audit Questionnaire

1. Are there departmental problems that should be corrected?
2. What are the weaknesses that exist in the records and reporting mechanisms?
3. Are company policy directives properly and promptly followed?
4. Are the internal control procedures effective and are they followed?
5. Are any differences between budget and actual figures explained and followed up?
6. Does the work flow as intended?
7. Is management sufficiently involved in maintaining good procedures?
8. Are there any weaknesses in the organization structure that should be corrected?

The Value of Management Auditing

While operational auditing is interested in determining that the company's policies are being followed, management auditing's task is to look at the overall performance of the officers and directors of the organization. It evaluates their effectiveness as they plan, organize, control, staff, and lead the company.

Who Should Do the Management Auditing?

Management auditing is an in depth process that is supposed to go to the very heart of the organization. It therefore requires the services of many experts;

- Psychologists
- Industrial engineers
- MIS specialists
- Financal analysts
- Economists
- Marketing authorities

and, of course, the operational auditors.

A Sample Management Auditing Questionnaire

1. Is the company organized to fulfill its mission?
2. How effectively is the corporation structured?

   Consider: centralized versus decentralized, functional product type organizations.
3. How healthy are the earnings as compared to prior periods, to other companies in the industry, and to the economy in general?
4. Are the stockholders adequately serviced?

   Consider: dividend payments, appreciation
5. Is the research and development effort viable? Are the long-range benefits sufficient to justify its cost. Will these efforts turn into marketable products?
6. Do the directors provide good overall supervision of management? Do they represent the interests of the shareholders?

   Consider: Their qualifications, and group interaction.
7. Is the debt/equity structure the best combination to utilize leverage while maintaining an acceptable level of risk?

8. Do the production processes in existence contribute to the organization's goals? Do they efficiently and effectively utilize the facilities?
9. Are the marketing policies effective?

   Consider: Pricing, promotion, and distribution
10. How would you evaluate the executives of the company?

    Consider: Their quality, philosophy, and motivational ability.

CHAPTER 16

Financial Statement Analysis by the Top Down Method

Introduction

Financial statement analysis, in order to be meaningful, requires the same attention to detail as required in any accounting task. Because, any educated judgment about a company needs more than mere preparation of financial ratios.

This chapter shows how you should look at the environmental, and industrial factors that affect each organization. The information covered is divided into five sections:

- Top down analysis and how it should be used
- Identifying the six environmental factors
- Analyzing the industry
- Getting the information you need
- Sources of specific information

Chapter 17 covers specific financial analysis methods.

What Is Top Down Analysis and How Should It Be Used?

A company does not exist in a vacuum. Instead, it is a composition of its management, its product, its industry, and its overall environment. Because of this, financial statement analysis, in order to be performed effectively, must be approached from a "top down" progression as follows:

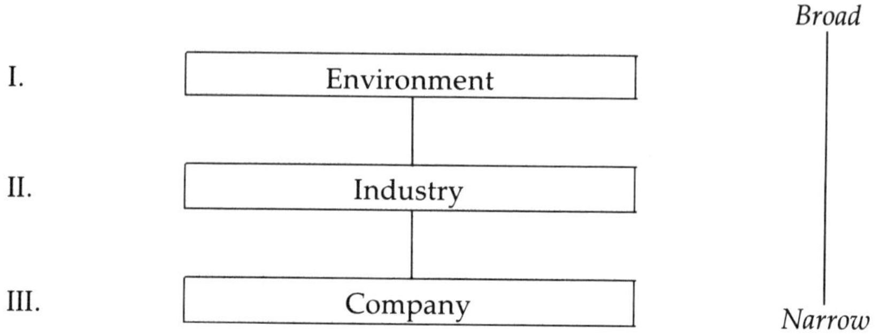

When this form of analysis is performed, start from a very broad environmental perspective, next look at the industry and then study the company itself.

How to Identify the Six Environmental Factors

Any business is a citizen of the world in which it exists. Consequently, there is an interdependence between that organization and its environment. That interdependence is characterized by the following factors:

1. Demographics
2. Economics
3. Political and legal factors
4. Physical components
5. Technology
6. Cultural influences

1. *Demographics*

Demography is defined as the statistical study of human population, and considers many ingredients:

a. Population size
b. Geographical distribution
c. Density
d. Mobility trends
e. Age distribution
f. Marriage rates

g. Birth rates
h. Death rates
i. Ethnic and religious structures

Each of these, in one way or another, could impact a client's business. And, these may be manifested in a number of major and minor trends.

Examples of demographic trends:

a. *There is a worldwide explosive population growth.* What does this portend? Does it mean that there will be a greater gap between the "have not" nations? Will there be more demands on our resources?

b. *At the same time, the U.S. birthrate is slowing down.* A good deal of this decline is being caused by later marriages and fewer children per couple. While this is going on, there is a rise in non-family households. What is the effect on American companies?

For example, there may be less demand for products serving younger children—baby food, toys, and so on.

On the other hand, if couples now spend less on child raising, they may have more to use for themselves.

For example, this could help the automotive, entertainment, and travel industries.

c. *The U.S population is aging.* An aging population will require more health care, smaller living quarters, and abundant and varied retirement facilities and activities.

d. *The divorce rate is increasing.* The single parent family ferments a host of different product and service demands.

e. *There is a greater proportion of working wives.* Many forecasters predict that the white male will soon be a minority in the work force. What does this mean to American industry?

- At work: Day care and expanded health coverage will be required.
- Away from work: Couples will eat out more often, and require more home conveniences.

f. *There are geographical shifts among the population.* Over the past several decades, there have been population movements from the northeast and midwest to the sun belt; Florida, the Southwest, California.

g. *There are changes in ethnic and racial proportions.* America has always been known as a "melting pot" and this tendency certainly shows no sign of changing. In Los Angeles, for instance, demographers predict, that by the year 2000, no racial group will have a majority of the population. Different cultures demand diverse forms of goods.

For example, a number of major food chains are now opening ethnic markets.

h. *There is a shift from mass to micro markets.* No one product fits everyone, at least, not anymore. Consumers now demand more individualized wares and services. This trend indicates companies cannot succeed by turning out "Model T Fords, all black." Instead, they have to tailor their output to a wide variety of tastes and demands. New technology and manufacturing methods are increasingly in demand to support this trend.

2. *Economics*

The one constant in our economy is change. We will see up trends and recessions and, economists will, just like court astrologers, make dire and happy predictions, quite often, at the same time. To get a handle on a specific company's prognosis requires us to understand economic indicators and trends.

Economic indicators should not be studied in a vacuum. Their value lies in our ability to use them to analyze movements and trends. A listing of key economic indicators and where information can be found is at the end of this chapter.

3. *Political and Legal*

Who knows what political changes are in the wind? We all like to guess. But, it's more than a game. It is important to understand what is happening in Washington, the State house, or at city hall. As we all know, government agencies have the power to help or destroy any business.

In a political sense, when we attempt to analyze a particular company we should try to understand the following:

a. What regulatory changes have been made or are anticipated to be made by various government agencies including the IRS, SEC, FTC, and so on?

b. How will new consumer movements, including demands for worker safety, clearer packaging, and so on affect the business climate?

c. How will the company's financial statements be affected by new FASB pronouncements, SEC regulations, and new tax laws?

4. *Physical*

Although our physical environment receives a lot of attention from *social* accountants, it does not get much space in *financial* accounting literature. However, it is too important to be left unmentioned. To paraphrase Buckminster Fuller, "our earth is a spaceship, moving through the universe." Everything we have now or will need is furnished by the confines of that ship.

To attempt to understand a company without comprehending our material world is somewhat akin to performing a heart transplant without knowing the body's circulatory system. Every company takes resources and, often, returns something not entirely pleasant.

Happily, our legal and political systems are beginning to wake up to the situation. Our public servants have been nudged, to some degree, by public opinion. So, we are beginning to see legislation that is attempting to make a try to buy our species more living time on this plant.

As the world's population has grown and its supply of raw materials diminished, we have also in that process, been depleting our ozone layer, destroying our rain forests and fouling our air and water. And, this is all significant to business.

5. *Technological*

There have been more changes in the last half of the twentieth century than throughout the entire previously recorded history. What may be a hot product or service one day may be out of date the next. This pace is accelerated by the increasing research and development investment by business and government alike.

When you analyze a company, be aware of its industry's R&D curve and just where it sits on that curve.

In order to understand the technological forces that affect a company you have to keep your ears and eyes open. Read the trade journals, look at science magazines, watch and attend lectures. Be aware of science and technology.

6. *Cultural changes*

These are changes which have resulted from the American melting pot. People from different racial, ethnic, and national cultures will affect a company as well as employees and customers for the firm's goods.

How to Analyze the Industry

We now narrow the spectrum by movikng from the general environment to the industry in which the company resides.

The following questions should be asked?

a. How would you characterize the industry?
   - Type of product
   - Stage of development

b. What is the industry's overall market size?

c. Is it growing or declining? At what rate?

d. What are typical profit margins for companies in that industry? How do these margins compare to
   - other industries
   - the economy, in general?

e. What is the level of competition?
   - intense?
   - medium?
   - non-existent?

f. How would you describe the ease or difficulty of entering or leaving this field?

g. What are the industry's technological requirements?

h. Is the technology required rapidly changing or relatively stable?

i. How vulnerable is the industry to economic trends?

j. What are its energy and resource requirements?

k. What is the impact of government on the industry?
   - Trade
   - Safety and health

- Packaging
- Ecological

l. What is the state of labor in the industry?

- Supply
- Labor agreements
- Skill/abilities required

How Do You Get the Information You Need?

There is no shortage of information to help you do this analysis. The final section of this chapter will list some of specific sources. This segment is intended to be an overview of information sources and their probable location.

Where to look: The best place to find most of these sources is the local university library.

1. *Business publications*

a. *Investors services.* Investors' services offer a wealth of data about individual companies and their respective industries. The most well known are Standard & Poors, Moodys, and Value Line.

Information provided:

- Earnings trends,
- assets and liabilities,
- stock ratings, and
- editorial data.

Caution: Editorial data, must be read with a grain of salt. While it contains lots of knowledge, it is just one writer's opinion.

Note: If your company isn't freely traded, there probably will not be any direct information. However, these services do contain data by industry which can be used for to obtain ratios and other comparisons.

b. *Wall Street Journal indexes.* The *Wall Street Journal* (published by Dow Jones and Company) provides an index by category or company. Contained in its listings is a brief sentence describing the topic. Then, if you want the complete story, you will be able to find it on microfilm.

c. *Business article abstracts.* Many college libraries have recently installed computer systems which furnish abstracts of practically every article written about a particular subject for the past several years. In addition, you may be able to obtain printouts, or download the data onto computer disk.

d. *Annual reports.* Annual reports and SEC filings contain in-depth information about any publicly held company. These, too, are available at most college libraries. Or, they can be obtained directly from the company.

e. *Business magazines.* There are many magazines devoted to general and specific business topics—*Business Week, Fortune, Forbes, Harvard Business Review,* and *INC.*

f. *Data retrieval services.* You can use your PC to go online to obtain a variety of specific information.

g. *U.S. Government publications.* It often appears that our government has nothing else to do but turn out literature. But, some of it is very good. The next section lists some of the sources.

h. *Trade Journals.* Most occupations publish their own journals. The editorial data and the advertisements, provide interesting data.

2. *General Information*

When you begin to study environmental trends, a good place to start is your local business paper. To get further background, I have found that the following publications to be particularly helpful:

1. *The World Press Review.* Encapsulates how the rest of the world sees itself and us.
2. *Harpers and Atlantic Monthly.* Among other things, focuses on cultural and political trends.
3. *Time and Newsweek.* Provides timely information about a variety of topics.

Sources of Specific Information

This section lists the major indicators and shows you where to find the information you need.

Information	*Source*
Balance of Payments	2, 5, 9, 15
Bonds Yields	2, 5, 15
Building Permits Let	
Business Credit	2, 4, 5, 6, 15
Business Failures	2
Business Loans	2, 4, 5, 6
Commodity Market Indexes	15
Construction—New Housing	4, 6, 8
Construction—Non-residential	4, 6, 8
Consumer Credit	4, 6
Consumer Expenditures	
Corporate Earnings	5, 15
Disposable Income	5, 12
Dividends	15,
Employment	1, 5
Foreign Exchange	2, 15
Gross National Product (GNP)	5, 11, 12, 13
Index of Industrial Population	2, 5
Interest Rates	2, 4, 5, 6, 15
Inventories—Manufacturers	9
Inventories—Retail	9
Inventories—Wholesale	9
Manufacturers Value Added	9
Money Supply	2
National Income	11, 12, 15
Personal Income	11, 12, 15
Population	3, 11
Prices—CPI	12
Prices—Wholesale	1, 2
Production	1, 2, 7
Real Estate Loans	4, 6, 10
Sales—Manufacturers	3, 10
Sales—Retail	2, 3, 10
Sales—Wholesale	3
Stock Market Indexes	2, 15
Unemployment	1, 2

SOURCES

1 Bureau of Labor Statistics
2 *Business Week*
3 Census Bureau
4 Commercial Banks

(*Continued on next page*)

SOURCES

5 Council of Economic Advisors
6 Federal Reserve Banks
7 Federal Reserve Board
8 F.W. Dodge
9 National Industrial Conference Board
10 Predicasts
11 Resources for the Future
12 United States Department of Commerce
13 University Econometric Studies
14 U.S. Department of Agriculture
15 *Wall Street Journal*

CHAPTER 17

How to Analyze a Company

Introduction

This chapter gets into the nitty gritty of financial analysis by looking at the key items that gauge a company's performance and equity. It is divided into six sections:

A. What are the non-financial factors that affect the company's performance?
B. How to start your financial analysis—a broad overview
C. How to use horizontal analysis to spot trends
D. How to use vertical analysis to dissect the financial statements' components.
E. How to use ratios to analyze financial statements
F. Using graphs to enhance your analysis

Chapter Appendixes

1. A list of all financial ratios
2. Complete set of a company's financial statements and analyses

A. What Are the Non-Financial Factors That Affect a Company's Financial Performance?

A business may have good financial statements. It may have poor ones. But, these statements and what they represent are only impressions of all the various non financial activities that make up a firm. The following questionnaire has been designed to help you analyze a company's underlying non financial influences:

Non Financial Analysis Questionnaire

Name of Company ______________________________
Date of Analysis ______________________________
Analysis performed by ______________________________

Refer to the items on this form as you write a description of the company:

The Product Line

1. Describe the strengths and weaknesses of

   A. Its tangible features
   B. Its intangible features
   C. Its pricing policies
   D. The Company's distribution methods.
   E. How well does it meet the competition?
   F. Does it meet the customers' current needs?

Research and Development

1. What is the company doing to the area of basic research?
2. How is it attempting to develop its ideas and exploit unfilled areas of market demand?

Facilities

1. Are they adequate and up-to-date?
2. Does the firm have sufficient capacity to satisfy increased demand?
3. Does the organization have excess capacity?

Management and Employees

1. Is the company adequately staffed?
2. Are there sufficient labor pools available should the firm need to expand?
3. Are the employees adequately trained?
4. In your opinion, are the executives of the company capable of managing the company well under the following circumstances:

   A. Present conditions?
   B. Conditions of growth?
   C. Crisis conditions?

B. How to Start Your Financial Analysis—A Broad Overview

What Do We Want to Know?

1. Does the firm have the *financial flexibility* to adjust to changes in the environment?

   For example, if a profitable opportunity opens, does the company have the "horses" to rush in and exploit this opening?

2. Does the company have enough *liquid assets* to pay its bills and service its debt when due?
3. Does the organization have the *operating capability* to continue to pursue its line of business?

   For example, will it be able to acquire materials, pay employees, and replace equipment and facilities as needed?

4. What is the *quality of the company's earnings?* Quality of earnings is measured by:
   - Its rate of growth
   - How it compares to industry trends
   - Its strength in times of various economic conditions

The Two-Dimensional Approach to Financial Analysis

Horizontal (trends)

Comparative statements
Changes in amounts
Rate of change
Industry patterns
Economic indicators

Vertical (Components)
Dollar amounts
Common size statements
Ratios

C. How to Use Horizontal Analysis to Spot Trends

The purpose of horizontal analysis is to spot trends; trends in sales, earnings, and so on.

1. *Comparative Statements*

These contain the usual information found in annual reports.

Example: The Devonport three-year comparative income statements are portrayed in the appendix. By perusing these statements, you will be able to see when sales and net incomes rose and fell.

The Devonport Agency, Inc.
Comparative Statements of Income

	1984	1985	1986
Sales	1,500,918	1,538,441	1,125,689
Operating income	$42,979	$126,079	$31,634

The comparative balance sheets portray a side by side presentation of their various components:

Devonport Corporation
Comparative Balance Sheets
December 31

	1984	1985	1986
Assets	$631,374	$661,030	$608,752
Liabilities	$537,937	$488,420	$415,285
Equity	93,437	172,610	193,467
	$631,374	$661,030	$608,752

2. *Changes in Amounts*

Instead of portraying the customary accounting statements and forcing the reader to do arithmetic, as separate analyses, the annual fluctuations in selected accounts can highlight significant data.

Devonport Corporation
Changes in Income Statement Components

	1985	1986
Sales	$37,523	($412,752)
Operating Income	$83,100	($94,445)

The Devonport Agency, Inc.
Changes in Balance Sheet Components

	1985	1986
Assets	$29,657	($52,278)
Liabilities	($49,516)	($73,135)
Equity	79,173	20,857
	$29,657	($52,278)

3. *Rates of Change*

By looking at the *rates* of change you can compare the company's performance to various indices including:

- the production index
- the consumer price index
- industry performance indices

Calculation

$$\frac{\text{Current Amount}-\text{Prior Amount}}{\text{Prior Amount}} \times 100$$

Example A: The following is taken from the financial statements of the Devonport Agency:

	Sales	Change	Rate of Change
1984	1,500,918		
1985	1,538,441	37,523	2.50%
1986	1,125,689	(412,752)	−26.83%

Example B: This same process may be applied to various elements of the financial statements:

The Devonport Agency, Inc.
Percentage Change in Income Statement Components

	1985	1986
Sales	2.50%	−26.83%
Operating Income	193.35%	−74.91%

The Devonport Agency, Inc.
Percentage Changes in Balance Sheet Components

	1985	1986
Assets	4.70%	−7.91%
Liabilities	−9.20%	−14.97%
Equity	84.73%	12.08%

4. *Industry and Economic Patterns*

Horizontal analysis is most helpful to judge a company's performance by contrasting it to competing firms and to composite economic patterns. The following industry totals can be used for comparison:

- Sales
- Operating margin percentage
- Depreciation
- Net profit
- Working capital
- Long-term debt
- Net worth
- ROI
- ROE

Note: Refer back to Chapter 16, for a listing of economic indicators which are readily available.

D. How to Use Vertical Analysis to Dissect the Financial Statements' Components

Vertical analysis is used to compute relationships among components of the financial statements.

Common Size Financial Statements

Avoids the inherent problem of comparing competing companies.

For example, suppose we want to get an idea about how well our company (A) is doing when compared to a much larger organization, company (B). The financial statements of each are presented side by side:

	Company A	Company B
Sales	1,875,000	460,000
Cost of Goods Sold	1,312,500	276,000
Gross Profit	562,500	184,000
Operating Expenses	300,000	50,000
Net Income	262,500	134,000
Provision for Income Taxes	91,875	46,900
Net Income	170,625	87,100

However, this mixes apples and oranges because the numbers are not even close.

Common size financial statements, which convert the amounts and are reduced to percentages, display more useful information:

	Company A	Company B
Sales	100.00%	100.00%
Cost of Goods Sold	70.00%	60.00%
Gross Profit	30.00%	40.00%
Operating Expenses	16.00%	10.87%
Net Income	14.00%	29.13%
Provision for Income Taxes	4.90%	10.20%
Net Income	9.10%	18.93%

All else being equal, this provides much better data about which company is operating more efficiently.

What's a Good Ratio?

All too often value judgments are placed on certain financial statement ratios. You'll hear analysts say, "That company has a 2 to 1 current ratio. So, it must be O.K." Unfortunately, this is a rather myopic line of reasoning. A ratio analysis is only meaningful when taken in context with other factors:

- What were the relationships in prior periods?
- What ratios are found in the industry?

There are other problems that should be pondered:

1. Many ratios are calculated at fixed points in time. They may fluctuate greatly during the year.
2. By postponing or accelerating actions, management may easily manipulate the results.

Keeping this in mind, we use Devonport Corporation as an example.

E. How to Use Ratios to Analyze Financial Statements

Liquidity and Solvency

1. *Current Ratio*
Purpose: To test debt paying ability
Equation:

$$\frac{\text{Current Assets}}{\text{Current Liabilities}}$$

2. *Quick Ratio*
Purpose: Tests immediate debt paying ability by comparing highly-liquid current assets (including cash, marketable securities, and accounts receivable) to current liabilities.
Equation:

$$\frac{\text{Quick Assets}}{\text{Current Liabilities}}$$

Example and Analysis of Current and Quick Ratios

	Current Ratio	Quick Ratio
1984	1.25	1.01
1985	1.10	.89
1986	1.01	.84

Evaluation: Devonport's current solvency and quick ratio declined in the years 1985 to 1986. What does this indicate? For one thing, we find that the proportion of current assets tied up in inventory has increased. The inventory turnover ratios will also indicate this occurrence.

3. *Accounts Receivable Turnover*

Purpose: To analyze the quality of accounts receivable

Equation:

$$\frac{\text{Net Sales}}{\text{Average accounts receivable*}}$$

* (Beginning receivables + Ending receivables)/2

$$\text{Days in accounts receivable} = \frac{\text{Number of days in year}}{\text{Accounts receivable turnover}}$$

Example:

	Turnover	Days
1985	8.30	44
1986	5.07	72

Evaluation: This analysis provides some idea of the effectiveness of the company's credit policy. In 1986 it took longer to collect accounts as in 1985.

Caution: It is not always better to reduce average collection time. Most business is conducted on credit, and, customers will choose the supplier that offers the best terms.

4. *Inventory Turnover*

Purpose: To determine if inventory levels are sound for a company's volume.

Equation:

$$\frac{\text{Cost of Goods Sold}}{\text{Average Inventory*}}$$

* (Beginning inventory + ending inventory)/2

$$\text{Days in inventory} = \frac{\text{Number of Days in Year}}{\text{Inventory Turnover}}$$

Example:

	Turnover	Days
1985	6.89	53
1986	3.00	122

Evaluation: Inasmuch as it is expensive to carry inventories, most well-managed companies prefer to keep their stock low. Devonport's had a significant growth in 1986. We have to ask ourselves, "Why?"

Caution: Attempts to hold inventory levels down can be taken too far. Insufficient stocks may lead to lost sales and idle labor.

Equity Position and Solvency

1. *Debt Ratio*

Purpose: To show the proportion of asset acquisitions financed by debt.

Equation:

$$\frac{\text{Debt}}{\text{Assets}}$$

2. *Equity Ratio*

Purpose: To show the proportion of asset acquisitions financed by stockholders.

Equation:

$$\frac{\text{Stockholder's Equity}}{\text{Assets}} \quad \text{or} \quad \frac{1 - \text{Debt}}{\text{Asset}}$$

Example:

	Debt Ratio	Equity Ratio
1984	85.20%	14.80%
1985	73.89%	26.11%
1986	68.22%	31.78%

Evaluation: These ratios show how much of a company's assets are financed by debt and by equity. From the viewpoint of both creditors and stockholders, the greater the leverage the greater the risk. Because, as the debt to equity percentage increases more capital is needed for debt service. But, on the other hand the organization is able to expand more rapidly.

The above analysis indicates that Devonport has been liquidating debt.

Profitability Tests

1. *Gross Profit Ratio*
Purpose: Measures the relationship of gross profit to sales.
Equation:

$$\frac{\text{Gross Profit}}{\text{Sales}} \quad \text{or} \quad \frac{1 - \text{Cost of Goods Sold}}{\text{Sales}}$$

2. *Net Income Ratio*
Purpose: Measures the relationship of net income to sales
Equation:

$$\frac{\text{Net Income}}{\text{Sales}}$$

Example:

	Gross Profit	Net Income
1984	48.00%	1.36%
1985	57.00%	5.15%
1986	75.00%	1.85%

3. *Interest Coverage Ratio*
Purpose: To show the ability to meet the firm's current interest payments.
Equation:

$$\frac{\text{Income Before Interest and Taxes}}{\text{Interest Expense}}$$

Example:

1984	4.78
1985	29.48
1986	8.27

Analysis: The above indicates that Devonport's income has increased relative to its debt and interest requirement. It also signifies that the leverage ratios have decreased.

4. *Return on Investment (ROI)*

Purpose: Measures the percentage a company earns on its total assets.

Note: Total assets, as normally used in this equation, are assets at their net book value.

Equation:

$$\text{Return on Investment (ROI)} = \frac{\text{Net Income}}{\text{Average Assets}}$$

5. *Return on Equity*

Purpose: Measures how much the shareholders earned on their net equity in the business.

Equation:

$$\frac{\text{Net Income}}{\text{Average Shareholders' Equity}}$$

Example:

	ROI	ROE
1985	12.25%	59.52%
1986	3.29%	11.39%

Market Analyses

1. *Price Earnings Ratio*

Purpose: To determine how fairly the firm's common stock is valued compared to other company's in the industry and the market as a whole.

Equation:

$$\frac{\text{Market Price}}{\text{Earnings per Share}}$$

2. *Earnings Yield on Common Stock*
Purpose: To compare the company to other common stock investments.
Equation:

$$\frac{\text{Earnings per Share}}{\text{Market Price per Share}}$$

3. *Dividend Yield on Common Stock*
Purpose: As a comparison with other common stock investments.
Equation:

$$\frac{\text{Dividends per Share}}{\text{Current Market Price}}$$

4. *Dividend Payout Ratio*
Purpose: Indicates whether a company pays out or reinvests a large portion of its earnings.
Equation:

$$\frac{\text{Dividends per Share}}{\text{Earnings per Share}}$$

F. Using Graphs to Enhance Your Anaysis

Graphs are pictures of financial information which provide a more meaningful portrait of a firm's performance.

Graphical analysis can be applied to any form of horizontal or vertical analysis. And, because of the various electronic spreadsheet programs, they are easy to prepare.

Forms

There are many variations you may utilize. Here are three examples:

- Line graphs: Illustrate directional trends
- Bar charts: To compare totals
- Pie charts: For showing relationships

Line Graphs

Assume, a company's sales are listed for the past 20 years. While all pertinent information is there, it is difficult as well as tiresome to interpret the results in this format.

Year	Sales
1	16,343
2	11,881
3	20,188
4	13,510
5	22,607
6	17,689
7	20,655
8	5,148
9	23,764
10	15,286
11	16,500
12	25,260
13	34,015
14	14,924
15	14,370
16	16,975
17	18,118
18	29,884
19	32,973
20	15,528

The graphical presentation is easier to follow:

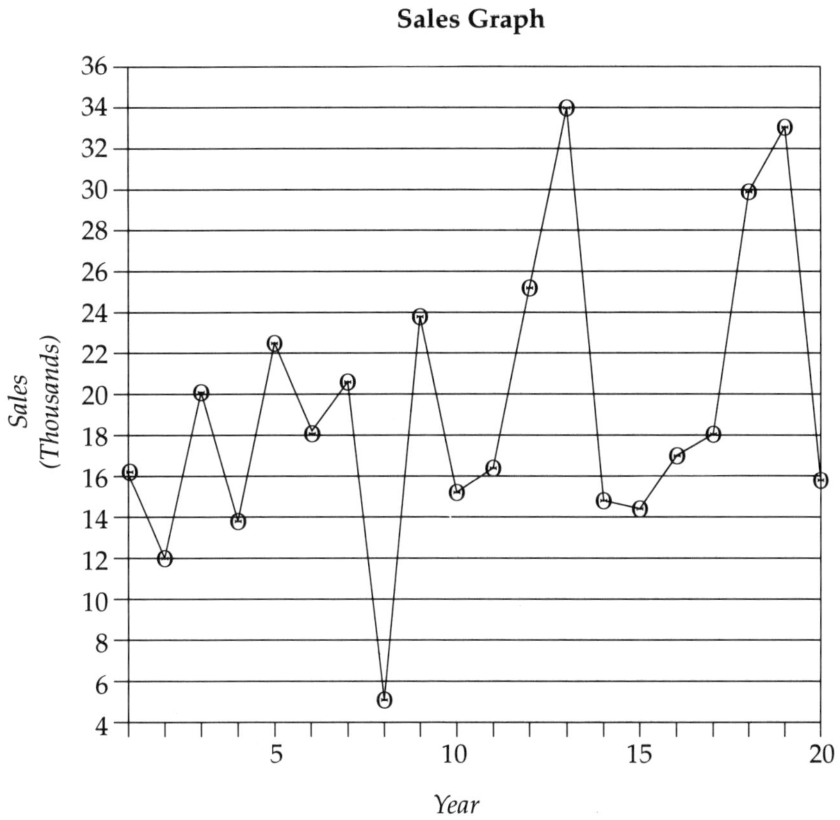

If you study the above graph, you'll quickly see that the sales peaked in 1985, dropped for one year, rose back again and have remained flat.

How to Smooth Out a Graph

While graph A depicts useful information, it could be taken for some poor soul's EKG. It's almost impossible to discern any trend. By using moving averages we are able to derive a more discernible pattern.

Weighted Moving Averages: An accumulation time frame is decided for each data value and then a weighted mean is computed. In this example, we've averaged the sales over six year periods.

Note: Moving average computation hints:

Year 10 = Sum (years 5 − 10)/6
Year 11 = Sum (years 6 − 11)/6

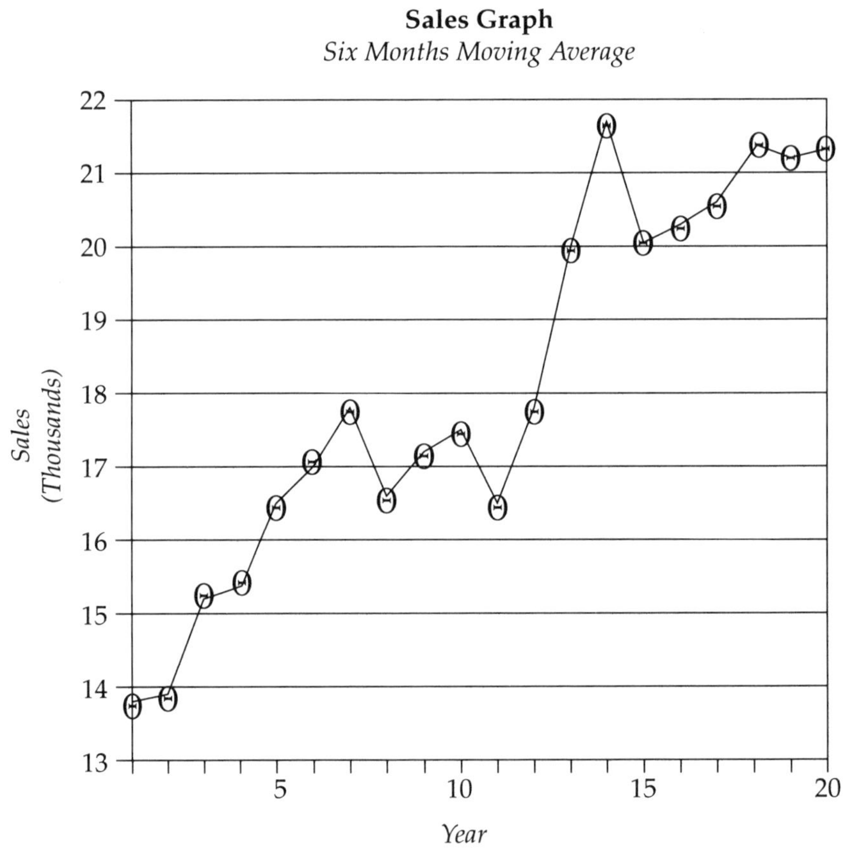

Bar Graphs

These are useful to compare totals. For example, the sales and net operating income of Devonport is displayed below:

The Devonport Company
Sales/Net Income

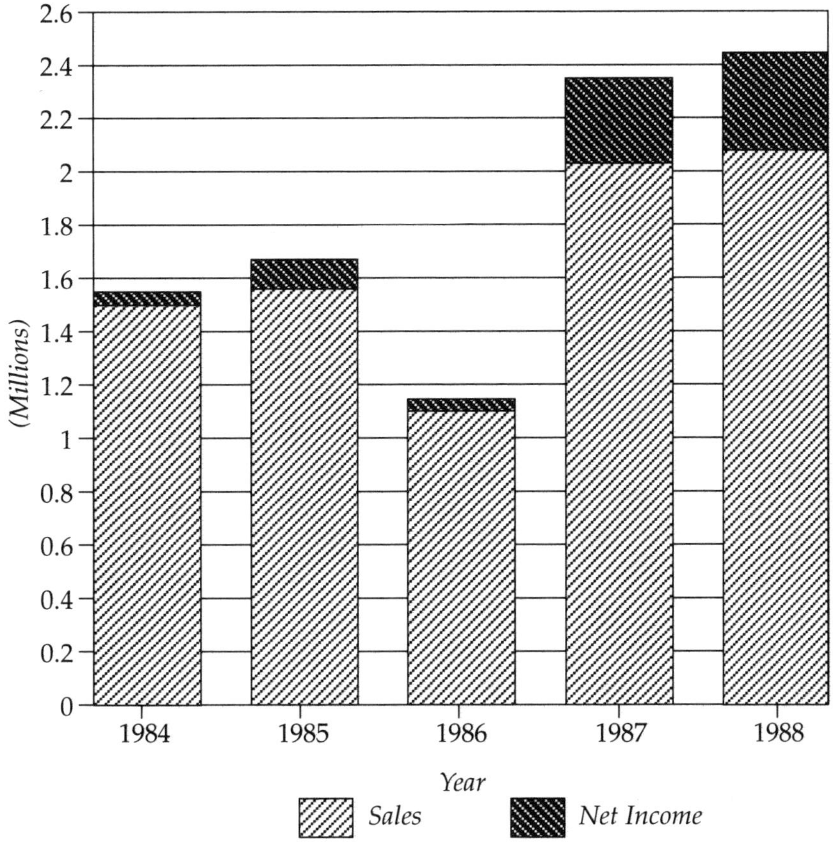

Pie Charts

These are most useful to show percentage relationships. *Example:* Picture the following income statement:

Sales	$125,000
Cost of Sales	87,500
Gross Profit	37,500
Expenses	25,000
Pre Tax Income	12,500
Income Taxes	4,375
Net Income	$ 8,125

As a pie chart, the percentages would be displayed:

Income Statement Percentages
Pie Chart

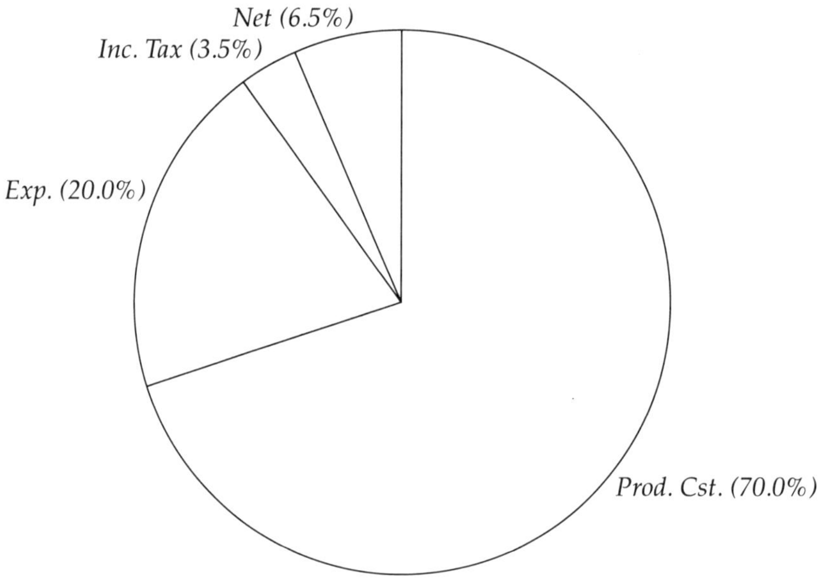

Appendix A
A List of All Financial Ratios

Liquidity and Solvency

1. *Current Ratio*

$$\frac{\text{Current Assets}}{\text{Current Liabilities}}$$

2. *Quick Ratio*

$$\frac{\text{Quick Assets}}{\text{Current Liabilities}}$$

3. *Accounts Receivable Turnover*

$$\frac{\text{Net Sales}}{\text{Average accounts receivable*}}$$

* (Beginning receivables + Ending receivables)/2

$$\text{Days in accounts receivable} = \frac{\text{Number of days in year}}{\text{Accounts receivable turnover}}$$

4. *Inventory Turnover*

$$\frac{\text{Cost of Goods Sold}}{\text{Average Inventory*}}$$

* (Beginning inventory + ending inventory)/2

$$\text{Days in inventory} = \frac{\text{Number of days in year}}{\text{Inventory turnover}}$$

5. *Total Assets Turnover*

$$\frac{\text{Net Sales}}{\text{Average Total Assets}}$$

Equity Position and Solvency

1. *Debt Ratio*

$$\frac{\text{Debt}}{\text{Assets}}$$

2. *Equity Ratio*

$$\frac{\text{Stockholders' Equity}}{\text{Assets}} \quad \text{or} \quad \frac{1 - \text{Debt}}{\text{Assets}}$$

Profitability Tests

1. *Gross Profit Ratio:*

$$\frac{\text{Gross Profit}}{\text{Sales}} \quad \text{or} \quad \frac{1 - \text{Cost of Goods Sold}}{\text{Sales}}$$

2. *Net Income Ratio*

$$\frac{\text{Net Income}}{\text{Sales}}$$

3. *Interest Coverage Ratio*

$$\frac{\text{Income before interest and taxes}}{\text{Interest expense}}$$

4. *Return on Equity*

$$\frac{\text{Net Income}}{\text{Average shareholders' equity}}$$

5. *Return on Investment (ROI)*

$$\frac{\text{Net Income}}{\text{Average Assets}}$$

Market Analyses

1. *Price Earnings Ratio*

$$\frac{\text{Market Price}}{\text{Earnings per share}}$$

2. *Earnings Yield on Common Stock*

$$\frac{\text{Earning per Share}}{\text{Market Price per share}}$$

3. *Dividend Yield on Common Stock*

$$\frac{\text{Dividends per Share}}{\text{Current Market Price}}$$

4. *Dividend Payout Ratio*

$$\frac{\text{Dividends per Share}}{\text{Earnings per Share}}$$

Appendix B

Detailed Financial Statement Analyses and Ratios

Devonport Corporation
Comparative Statements of Income

	1984	1985	1986
Sales	$1,500,918	$1,538,441	$1,125,689
Cost of Goods Sold	780,477	661,530	281,423
Gross Profit	720,441	876,911	844,266
Operating Expenses			
Selling	225,092	295,766	375,069
General & Administrative	452,370	455,066	437,564
Total Operating Expenses	677,462	750,832	812,632
Operating Income	42,979	126,079	31,634
Interest Expense	9,000	4,275	3,825
Pre Tax Income	33,979	121,804	27,809
Provision for Income Taxes	13,592	42,631	6,952
Net Income	$ 20,387	$ 79,173	$ 20,857
Earnings Per Share	4.08	15.83	4.17

Devonport Corporation
Comparative Balance Sheets
December

	1984	1985	1986
Assets			
Current Assets			
Cash	$ 220,505	$ 193,811	$ 60,853
Accounts Receivable	170,578	194,555	249,675
Inventories	95,645	96,081	91,277
Total Current Assets	486,728	484,447	401,805

(Continued on next page)

	1984	1985	1986
Property & Equipment			
Cost	185,444	235,444	285,444
Accumulated Depreciation	40,798	58,861	78,497
Net Book Value	144,646	176,583	206,947
Total Assets	631,374	661,030	608,752
Liabilities & Equity			
Current Liabilities			
Accounts Payable	374,345	395,789	363,333
Income Taxes Payable	13,592	42,631	6,952
Total Current Liabilities	387,937	438,420	370,285
Long-Term Notes Payable	150,000	50,000	45,000
Total Liabilities	537,937	488,420	415,285
Equity			
Common Stock (5,000 shares)	50,000	50,000	50,000
Retained Earnings	43,437	122,610	143,467
Total Equity	93,437	172,610	193,467
	$ 631,374	$ 661,030	$ 608,752

Devonport Corporation
Common Size Statements of Income

	1984	1985	1986
Sales	100.00%	100.00%	100.00%
Cost of Goods Sold	52.00%	43.00%	25.00%
Gross Profit	48.00%	57.00%	75.00%
Operating Expenses			
Selling	15.00%	19.22%	33.32%
General & Administrative	30.14%	29.58%	38.87%
Total Operating Expenses	45.14%	48.80%	72.19%
Operating Income	2.86%	8.20%	2.81%
Interest Expense	0.60%	0.28%	0.34%
Pre-Tax Income	2.26%	7.92%	2.47%
Provision for Income Taxes	0.90%	2.77%	0.62%
Net Income	1.36%	5.15%	1.85%

Devonport Corporation
Common Size Comparative Balance Sheets
December 31

	1984	1985	1986
Assets			
Current Assets			
Cash	34.92%	29.32%	10.00%
Accounts Receivable	27.02%	29.43%	41.01%
Inventories	15.15%	14.54%	14.99%
Total Current Assets	77.09%	73.29%	66.00%
Property & Equipment			
Cost	29.37%	35.61%	46.89%
Accumulated Depreciation	6.46%	8.90%	12.89%
Net Book Value	22.91%	26.71%	34.00%
Total Assets	100.00%	100.00%	100.00%
Liabilities & Equity			
Current Liabilities			
Accounts Payable	59.29%	59.87%	59.68%
Income Taxes Payable	2.15%	6.45%	1.15%
Total Current Liabilities	61.44%	66.32%	60.83%
Long-Term Notes Payable	23.76%	7.57%	7.39%
Total Liabilities	85.20%	73.89%	68.22%
Equity			
Common Stock	7.92%	7.56%	8.21%
Retained Earnings	6.88%	18.55%	23.57%
Total Equity	14.80%	26.11%	31.78%
	100.00%	100.00%	100.00%

Devonport Corporation
Changes in Statements of Income

	1985	1986
Sales	$ 37,523	$(412,752)
Cost of Goods Sold	(118,948)	(380,107)
Gross Profit	156,471	(32,645)

(Continued on next page)

	1985	1986
Operating Expenses		
Selling	70,675	79,303
General & Administrative	2,696	(17,503)
Total Operating Expenses	73,371	61,800
Operating Income	83,100	(94,445)
Interest Expense	(4,725)	(450)
Pre-Tax Income	87,825	(93,995)
Provision for Income Taxes	29,040	(35,679)
Net Income	$ 58,785	$ (58,316)

Devonport Corporation
Changes in Balance Sheets
December 31

	1985	1986
Assets		
Current Assets		
Cash	$ (26,694)	$(132,958)
Accounts Receivable	23,977	55,120
Inventories	437	(4,804)
Total Current Assets	(2,280)	(82,642)
Property & Equipment		
Cost	50,000	50,000
Accumulated Depreciation	18,063	19,636
Net Book Value	31,937	30,364
Total Assets	$ 29,657	$ (52,278)
Liabilities & Equity		
Current Liabilities		
Accounts Payable	$ 21,444	$ (32,456)
Income Taxes Payable	29,040	(35,679)
Total Current Liabilities	50,484	(68,135)
Long-Term Notes Payable	(100,000)	(5,000)
Total Liabilities	(49,516)	(73,135)

	1985	1986
Equity		
Common Stock	0	0
Retained Earnings	79,173	20,857
Total Equity	79,173	20,857
	$ 29,657	$ (52,278)

Devonport Corporation
Percentage Changes in Statements of Income

	1985	1986
Sales	2.50%	−26.83%
Cost of Goods Sold	−15.24%	−57.46%
Gross Profit	21.72%	−3.72%
Operating Expenses		
Selling	31.40%	26.81%
General & Administrative	0.60%	−3.85%
Total Operating Expenses	10.83%	8.23%
Operating Income	193.35%	−74.91%
Interest Expense	−52.50%	−10.53%
Pre-Tax Income	258.47%	−77.17%
Provision for Income Taxes	213.66%	−83.69%
Net Income	288.34%	−73.66%

Devonport Corporation
Percentage Changes in Balance Sheets
December 31

	1985	1986
Assets		
Current Assets		
Cash	−12.11%	−68.60%
Accounts Receivable	14.06%	28.33%
Inventories	0.46%	−5.00%
Total Current Assets	−0.47%	−17.06%

(Continued on next page)

	1985	1986
Property & Equipment		
Cost	26.96%	21.24%
Accumulated Depreciation	44.28%	33.36%
Net Book Value	22.08%	17.20%
Total Assets	4.70%	−7.91%
Liabilities & Equity		
Current Liabilities		
Accounts Payable	5.73%	−8.20%
Income Taxes Payable	213.66%	−83.69%
Total Current Liabilities	13.01%	−15.54%
Long-Term Notes Payable	−66.67%	−10.00%
Total Liabilities	−9.20%	−14.97%
Equity		
Common Stock	0.00%	0.00%
Retained Earnings	182.27%	17.01%
Total Equity	84.73%	12.08%
	4.70%	−7.91%

Devonport Corporation
Ratio Analyses

	1984	1985	1986
Working Capital	98,781	46,027	31,520
Current Ratio	1.01	.89	.84
Quick Ratio	0.57	0.44	0.16
Debt Ratio	85.20%	73.89%	68.22%
Equity Ratio	14.80%	26.11%	31.78%
Inventory Turnover		6.89	3.00
Days in Inventory		53	122
Accounts Receivable Turnover		8.30	5.07
Average Days to Collect Receivables		44	72
Book Value Per Common Share	18.69	34.52	38.69
Return on Assets		12.25%	3.29%
Return on Equity		59.52%	11.39%
Times Interest Earned	4.78	29.49	8.27

CHAPTER **18**

Cost Accounting Overview

Introduction

Cost accounting identifies, gathers, and measures information about costs. It is used to perform the following functions:

- Determine the cost of products
- Establish control procedures
- Determine inventory values
- Provide data to help make choices among alternative courses of action
- Help management establish plans and budgets

The basic process moves along the following path:

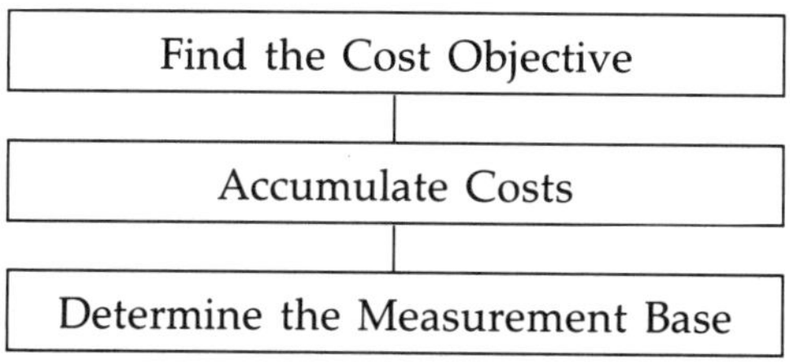

Understanding the Differences Between Financial and Cost Accounting

There are a number of fundamental differences:

Financial Accounting	*Cost Accounting*
Required Methods Proscribed by GAAP	Based on management's needs

(*Continued on next page*)

Financial Accounting	*Cost Accounting*
Data used	
Historical	Historical and projected
Accrual	Accrual and Cash
Timing of information	
Predetermined intervals	When needed

Note: As the above shows, the data produced by the cost accounting system does not have to be reported in accordance with GAAP.

Plus: It may be better for management purposes not to integrate the cost accounting system with the general ledger.

For example, direct, variable or activities-based costing may be very useful for cost and managerial accounting purposes. However, these methods are not allowable under GAAP, which requires full absorption costing.

Be Aware: While the cost accounting system provides valuable information to help run the business, it also furnishes the key data to record net income and inventories for financial statement purposes.

Cost Accounting Terminology

The following terms will be used throughout the cost accounting chapters:

Conversion Costs. Costs required to convert raw materials into finished product. Includes direct labor and overhead.

Direct Costing. A method which uses only variable costs; materials, direct, labor and variable overhead. Also known as Variable Costing.

Direct Costs. Costs that are directly used for the product. These would include materials, direct labor and variable overhead.

Fixed Costs. Costs, that, within a relevant range do not vary with the objective.

Full Absorption Costing. Includes direct materials, direct labor, variable overhead, and non-variable overhead.

Note: The full absorption method is proscribed by GAAP.

Full Costs. All costs including manufacturing, general and administrative, and selling. These are useful for making product pricing decisions.

Remember: It's the market place that determines the product prices.

Indirect Costs. Costs not clearly identified with the cost objective. Often, they are classified as indirect because the benefits of specifically accounting for them are less than the information costs.

Examples: Supplies used in the product (e.g. glue, nails). Fringe benefits (e.g. payroll taxes, employee insurance).

Manufacturing Costs. All costs required to manufacture a product.

Non-Manufacturing Costs. All other costs.

Overhead. All other costs of the manufacturing process. Overhead can be fixed, variable and/or semivariable. It is assigned to the cost objective by allocation. See Chapter 19.

Period Costs. Expenses for the period.

Prime Costs. Direct material and direct labor.

Product Costs. Costs attached to the product.

Semivariable Costs. Expenses that have fixed and variable elements. In direct costing, these elements have to be separated.

Varible Costing. See direct costing.

Variable Costs. Costs that do vary with the cost objective. These may include direct material, direct labor, variable overhead, and variable selling and general and administrative expenses.

How to Identify the Cost Objective

The cost objective defines the reasons why costs are being measured. This concept is important because it focuses on the purposes why costs are accumulated. The following list of procedures should help you get a better handle on cost objectives:

1. Understand the company's mission.

2. Define the firm's product line:
   - tangible characteristics
   - intangible characteristics
   - pricing and market structure.

3. Analyze the company's organization structure.

4. Examine the present cost accounting system.

5. Talk to management and define their needs.

How to Set Up a Useful Cost Accounting System by Identifying the Cost Flows

1. *Diagram the Cost Flows*

The following diagram shows how costs flow into the product and are eventually expensed as period costs.

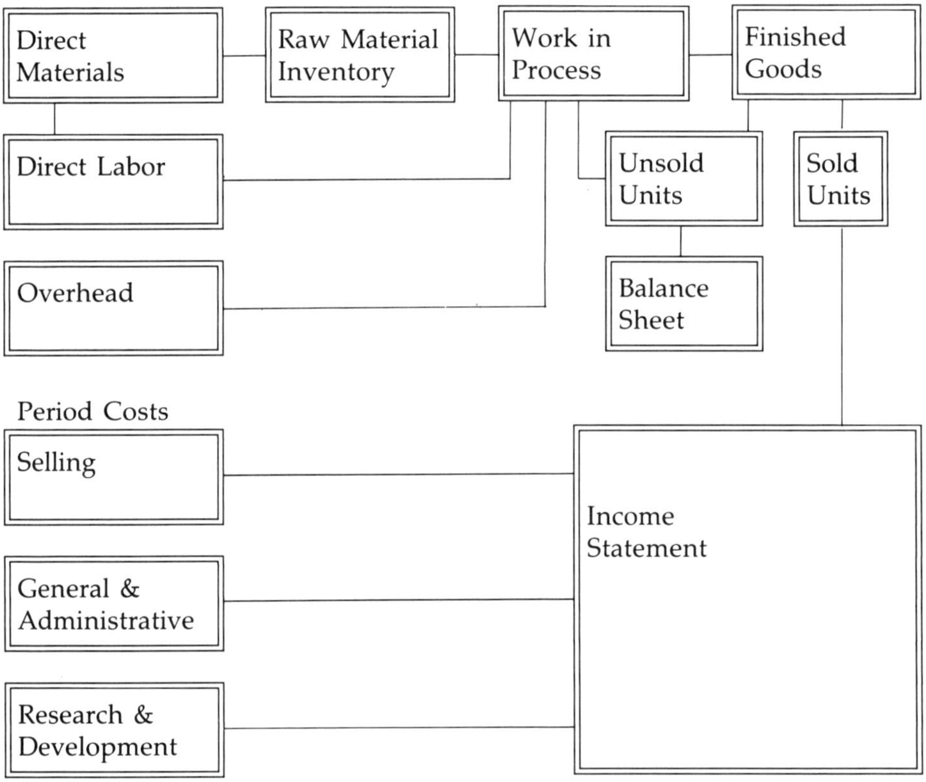

2. *Determine the Cost Objective*

3. *Develop Cost Classifications*

- By function/activity
- By product
- By department

4. *Design the Chart of Accounts*

The account number, itself, should be constructed to classify entries by a variety of cost objectives and functions. Its flexibility will, of course, be dependent upon the data processing system you use.

Attention: Determine your reporting needs first. Then select the DP system that will do the job.

Tip: The advent of improved and less expensive data processing hardware and software gives the user the option to collect a wide array of data and use the various segments as needed.

Account Format

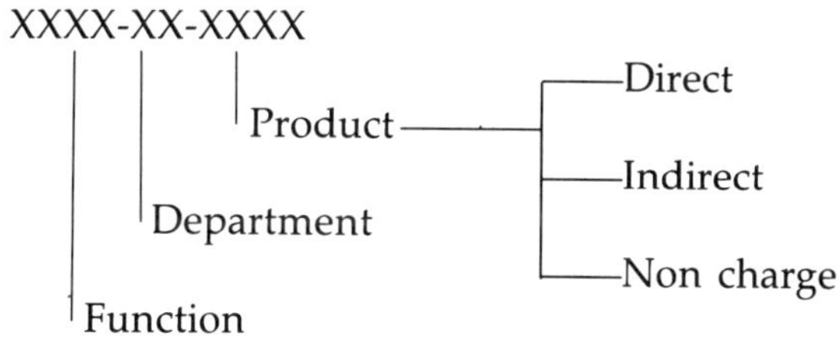

Chart of Accounts by Function

OVERHEAD

Indirect Materials

5505 Factory supplies
5510 Lubricants
5515 Small parts

Indirect Labor

5605 Data processing
5610 Material control
5615 Receiving
5620 Supervision

Quality

5705 Inspection
5710 Overtime
5715 Receiving inspection
5720 Re-work
5725 Sales returns

Other Indirect

5805 Depreciation
5810 Insurance—property
5815 Insurance—workman's compensation
5820 Maintenance
5825 Property tax
5830 Rent
5835 Small tools
5840 Sundry
5845 Utilities

SELLING EXPENSES

6005 Advertising
6010 Commissions
6015 Depreciation
6020 Entertainment
6025 Freight out
6030 Insurance
6035 Payroll taxes
6040 Postage
6045 Printing
6050 Rent
6055 Sales salaries
6060 Samples
6065 Sundry
6070 Taxes
6075 Telephone
6080 Travel
6085 Warehousing

ADMINISTRATIVE EXPENSES

7005 Accounting
7010 Depreciation
7015 Insurance
7020 Legal
7025 Office salaries
7030 Office supplies
7035 Payroll taxes
7040 Postage
7045 Rent
7050 Sundry
7055 Taxes
7060 Telephone
7065 Uncollectible accounts

RESEARCH AND DEVELOPMENT

8005 Courses and seminars
8010 Engineering and design salaries
8015 Materials
8020 Outside consulting
8025 Patent costs
8030 Payroll taxes

Reporting for Manufacturing Companies

The following is the preferred format for the cost of manufacturing section of the income statement.

Cost of Goods Sold Equation

Line #	*Account*	*Equation*
1	Direct Materials	
1a	Beginning Inventory	
1b	Purchases	
1c	Material Available for Use	1c = 1a + 1b
1d	Ending Direct Materials Inventory	
1e	Materials Consumed	1e = 1c − 1d
2	Direct Labor	
3	Overhead	
4	Total Manufacturing Costs	4 = 1e + 2 + 3
5	Work in Process Inventory, Beginning	
6	Less: Work in Process, Inventory − Ending	
7	Cost of Goods Manufactured	7 = 4 + 5 − 6
8	Finished Goods Inventory, Beginning	
9	Cost of Goods Available for Sale	9 = 7 + 8
10	Finished Goods Inventory, Ending	
11	Cost of Goods Sold	11 = 9 − 10

The Four Cost Accumulation Methods

The following diagram illustrates the differences.

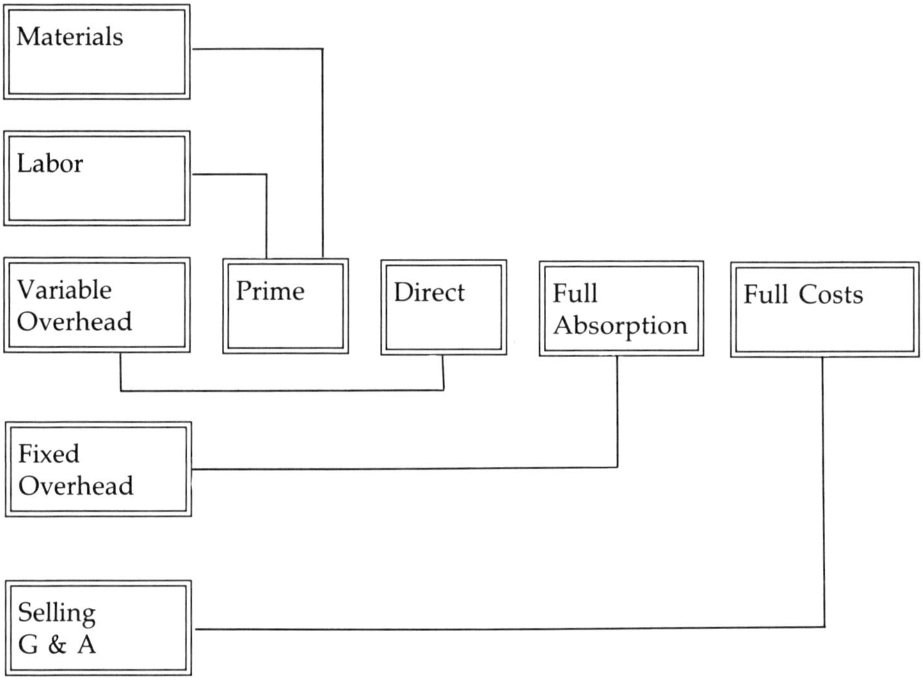

Or,
Prime Costs = Materials + Labor
Direct Costs = Prime + Variable Overhad
Full Absorption = Direct Costs + Fixed Overhead
Full Costing = Full Absorption + Selling + G&A

The following will illustrate the differences between the three approaches:

Number of Units 5,000

Variable costs are applied to the cost objective on a per unit basis (5,000 units.)

	Variable	Fixed
Direct Materials	$10.00	
Direct Labor	5.00	

(Continued on next page)

	Variable	Fixed
Factory Overhead	7.50	$10,000
Selling Expenses	2.50	8,000
General & Administrative Expenses		32,000
Total	$25.00	$50,000

	Prime	Variable	Full Absorb	Full
Direct Materials	$50,000	$50,000	$50,000	$50,000
Direct Labor	25,000	25,000	25,000	25,000
Factory Overhead		37,500	47,500	47,500
Selling				20,500
General/Administrative				32,000
Total Costs	$75,000	$112,500	$122,500	$175,000
Per Unit	$15.00	$22.50	$24.50	$35.00

Note: Absorption costing is required by both GAAP and IRS regulations.

Why Direct Costing May Provide Better Management Information

For a number of manufacturing companies, direct costing, which separates manufacturing costs into its fixed and variable components, is the method of choice. Why?

1. It is more consistent with decision making. Many management decisions are based on per unit changes (increments) resulting from alternative plans.
2. Full absorption costing requires fixed costs to be applied to production on a predetermined level of activity.
3. Variable costing removes the effect of inventory changes.

Example:

Sales Price	$50.00
Direct Costs	$22.50
Fixed Costs	$10,000

	Year 1		Year 2	
	Direct	Full Absorption	Direct	Full Absorption
Units Produced	5,000	5,000	7,000	7,000
Units Sold	4,000	4,000	8,000	8,000
Sales	$200,000	$200,000	$400,000	$400,000
Beginning Inventory			22,500	24,500
Direct Costs	112,500	112,500	157,500	157,500
Fixed Costs		10,000		10,000
	112,500	122,500	180,000	192,000
Ending Inventory	22,500	24,500	0	0
Cost of Goods Sold	90,000	98,000	180,000	192,000
Contribution (1)	110,000		220,000	
Gross Profit				
Fixed Costs	10,000		10,000	
Gross Profit	$100,000	$102,000	$210,000	$208,000
Cost of Goods Sold Per Unit (2)	$22.50	$24.50	$22.50	$24.00

Comments

1. When just the variable segments are used in the computation of cost of goods sold, the amount left over is considered a "contribution" to fixed costs. This is useful when doing incremental cost or breakeven analysis.
2. The per unit amount in the direct costing example is the same regardless of the inventory levels.

Three Ways to Differentiate Between Fixed and Variable Costs

The expenses have to be separated into their fixed and variable components in order to use direct costing. The methods are:

1. Statistical Scattergraph Method
2. High-Low Points Method
3. Single regression
4. Multiple regression

Each of these methods will be presented in turn. And, some of them are mathematically superior to the others. But, when it's all said and done, you have to rely on your judgment. In other words, ask yourself: **DOES IT MAKE SENSE**.

Example: Assume you are trying to break out the fixed and variable components of utilities expense. You want to determine how much this expense will vary with changes in direct labor hours, pounds of materials purchased, or machine hours. The information is tabulated below:

	Utilities	DL Hours	Material Pounds	Machine Hours
January	2,520	84	74	40
February	2,480	83	102	43
March	2,080	74	88	40
April	2,750	113	99	58
May	2,330	97	93	40
June	2,690	91	109	42
July	2,480	95	76	49
August	2,610	117	102	62
September	2,910	116	122	54
October	2,730	103	107	48
November	2,760	120	101	65
December	2,110	78	62	43

Procedure

To compute the fixed and variable portions of any semivariable expense, the following steps are recommended:

1. Select the applicable expense to be analyzed. (the dependent variable)
2. Determine the level of activity (the independent variable(s)) that best predicts the behavior of the dependent variable.
3. Use the relationship to obtain the slope of the line and derive the following equation:

$$Y = a + bx$$

where:

Y = dependent variable

a = fixed element of expense

b = coefficient of change. That is the amount of change for each unit of X

x = independent variable

4. Compute how closely the equation predicts the behavior of y.

Techniques

1. *Statistical Scattergraph Method*

At each level of activity of X, the value of Y is plotted. Next, a straight line is drawn, that, in our perception, best approximates the items plotted. The following graph pictures the direct labor hours/utility cost relationship:

Utility Cost Behavior
Relative to Direct Labor Hours

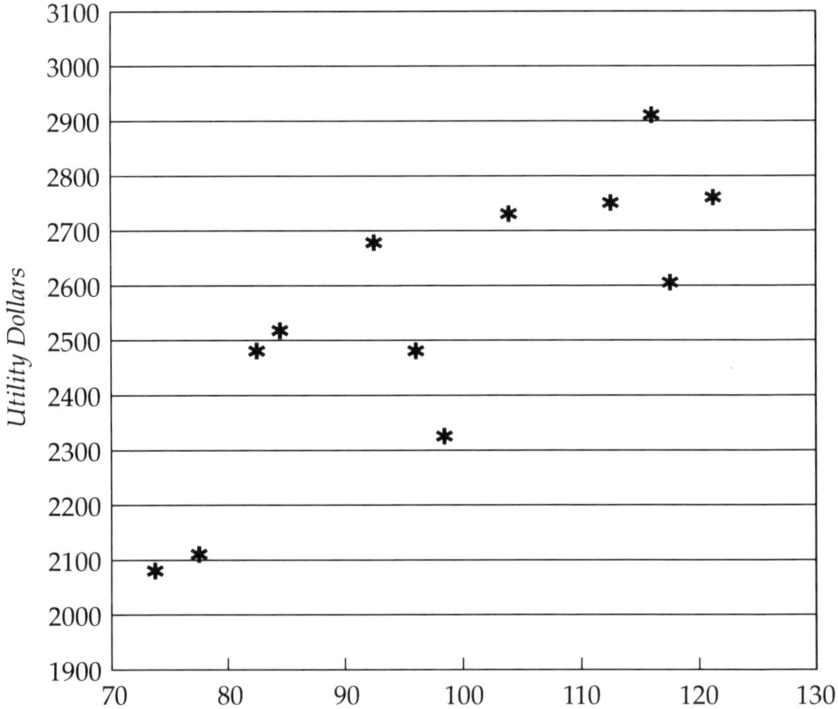

How to find the slope of a line. The slope of the line represents the variable portion of the cost. It will measure the amount of change in Y for each unit of change in X. To derive this slope, find two points, read the values for x and y, and construct the following matrix:

	X	
Y	2,000	0
	2,900	116

The equation, $Y = a + bX$ and is computed as follows:

$$\frac{\text{Change in } Y}{\text{Change in } X} = \frac{2{,}900 - 2{,}000}{116 - 0} = \frac{900}{116} = 7.76$$

The resulting equation is:

$$Y = \$2{,}000 + 7.76X$$

2. *The High/Low Points Method*

$$\frac{Y \text{ at } X \text{ highest value} - Y \text{ at } X \text{ lowest value}}{X \text{ highest value} - X \text{ lowest values}}$$

	August (High)	**December (Low)**	**Difference**
(A) Utilities Expense	$2,760	$2,080	$680
(B) Direct Labor Hours	120	74	46
Variable Portion (A/B)			$14.78

Fixed Portion

Total Utility Costs	$2,760	$2,080
Less: Variable Portion	1,774	1,094
Fixed	$986	$986

This yields the following equation:

$$Y = 986 + 14.78X$$

Caution: The high/low points method may give poor data because the computation is based on two extreme points. It does not provide for other variations in activity.

3. *Single Regression*

Regression analysis employs the statistical technique "method of least squares" to derive an equation that will show the smallest deviation between the predicted value of the dependent variable and its actual amount.

Constructing a regression equation. To construct this equation, use the following procedure: The above example will illustrate this process.

a. *Select the dependent variable* (Y). This is the cost whose behavior we want to predict.

For example, utilities.

b. *Choose the independent variable.* This is the factor that is being considered as a predictor of Y, the dependent variable.

For example, direct labor hours.

c. *Head up the columns of a worksheet as follows:*

column	*title*	*from example*
(1)	Y	Utilities
(2)	X	Direct Labor Hours
(3)	X^2	
(4)	$X*Y$	
(5)	Y^2	

c. *Square each item in column 2 and enter it in column 3.*

d. *Multiply each value in column 1 by its corresponding value in column 2 and enter it in column 4.*

e. *Add each column.*

The following tabulation will be used for illustration:

(1) Utilities Y	(2) DL Hours X	(3) X²	(4) XY	(5) Y²
2,080	74	5,476	153,920	4,326,400
2,110	78	6,084	164,580	4,452,100
2,480	83	6,889	205,840	6,150,400
2,520	84	7,056	211,680	6,350,400
2,690	91	8,281	244,790	7,236,100
2,480	95	9,025	235,600	6,150,400
2,330	97	9,409	226,010	5,428,900
2,730	103	10,609	281,190	7,452,900
2,750	113	12,769	310,750	7,562,500

(Continued on next page)

	(1) Utilities Y	(2) DL Hours X	(3) X^2	(4) XY	(5) Y^2
	2,910	116	13,456	337,560	8,468,100
	2,610	117	13,689	305,370	6,812,100
	2,760	120	14,400	331,200	7,617,600
Totals	30,450	1,171	117,143	3,008,490	78,007,900

f. *Compute sum of squares (SST) of Y as follows:*

$$SST = \frac{\left(\sum Y\right)^2}{n} - \sum Y^2$$

or

$$SST = \frac{\sum (column\ 1)^2}{n} - \sum (column\ 5)$$

From example:

$$30{,}450^2 - \frac{78{,}007{,}900}{12} = 741{,}025$$

g. *Compute sum of cross products (SCP) as follows:*

$$SCP = \sum XY - \frac{\sum X \times \sum Y}{n}$$

or

$$SCP = \sum column\ 4 - \frac{\sum column\ 1 \times \sum column\ 2}{n}$$

From example:

$$3{,}008{,}490 - \frac{(30{,}450 * 1{,}171)}{12} = 37{,}078$$

h. *Calculate sum of squares, X (SSX):*

$$SSX = \sum X^2 - \frac{\left(\sum X\right)^2}{n}$$

or

$$\sum column\ 3 - \frac{\sum column\ 2^2}{12}$$

From example:

$$117{,}143 - \frac{1{,}171^2}{12} = 2{,}873$$

i. *Calculate "b" coefficient as follows:*

$$b = \frac{SCP}{SSX}$$

From Example:

$$b = \frac{37{,}078}{2{,}873} = 12.91$$

j. *Calculate "a" as follows:*

$$a = \overline{Y} - b\overline{x}$$

or

$$a = \sum \frac{column\ 1}{n} - b * \frac{\sum column\ 2}{n}$$

From example:

$$\overline{Y} = \frac{30{,}450}{12} = 2{,}537.5$$

$$\overline{X} = \frac{1{,}171}{12} = 97.6$$

$$a = 2{,}537.5 - 12.91 * 97.6 = 1{,}278$$

k. *This yields the following equation:*

$$Y = a + bx$$

From example:

$$Y = 1{,}278 + 12.91X$$

4. *Multiple Regression*

When single regression is used to calculate the dependent variable (Y), any resulting prediction is based on the action of just one ingredient (X). Multiple regression, on the other hand, may use many independent variables. This is logically superior because any activity may be affected by many influences.

In other words. Utility expenses may vary because of changes in the number of direct labor hours *and* pounds of materials purchased and machine hours used.

While the multiple regression equations can be calculated by hand, the process is extremely tedious. Fortunately, there are computer programs to do this work easily.

Varibles used:

$X1$ = Direct Labor Hours

$X2$ = Pounds of Raw Materials Purchased

$X3$ = Machine Hours

If we use all of these we derive the following equation:

$$Y = 1{,}105 + 12.08X1 + 5.48X2 - 5.431X3$$

However, if the above calculation is used literally, every time an hour of machine time is used, the predicted utility value will drop by \$5.43. Therefore, refinement is needed to produce the following formula:

$$Y = 1{,}082 + 8.95X1 + 6.152X2$$

How to Know How Well Your Equation Will Predict Cost Behavior

The regression technique provides a number of gauges to help determine just how well the equation will predict cost actions.

Correlation. The coefficient of determination is a widely used measure of the goodness of fit of the regression line. It ranges from:

0 = no fit
to 1 = perfect fit

Its formula is $= r^2 = \dfrac{\text{Explained variation}}{\text{Total Variation}}$

or $$\frac{SSR}{SST} = \frac{b(SCP)}{SST}$$

The total variation is the sum of all the differences between the arithmetic mean (the average) of Y and the actual amounts. The explained variation is the difference between the average and the calculated amounts (as derived from the regression equation). Therefore, the higher the proportion of explained variation, the better the equation will predict behavior.

From examples:

Single Regression $Y = 1{,}278 + 12.91X$

$$\frac{SSR}{SST} = \frac{b(SCP)}{SST} =$$

$$\frac{SSR}{SST} = \frac{b(SCP)}{SST} \quad \frac{12.91 * 37{,}078}{741{,}025}$$

$$r^2 = .646$$

Multiple Regression $Y = 1{,}082 + 8.95X1 + 6.152X2$

$$r^2 = .746$$

This shows that the multiple regression equation is a better predictor.

The Standard Error of the Estimate calculates the amount of deviations of the various data points about the regression line. The lower this number, the better the predictor.

The following equation is used:

$$Syx = \sqrt{\frac{SSE}{n - v}}$$

Where n = number of observations
v = number of variables. In single regression, $n = 2$

In the previous calculations, the following standard errors have been derived:

Single Regression	±\$162.03
Multiple Regression	±\$151.34

Single regression is calculated as follows:

a. Compute SSE

$SSE = SST - SSR$

From Example $SSE = 262{,}507$

b. Compute the equation

$$\sqrt{\frac{SSE}{n - 2}} = \sqrt{\frac{262{,}507}{10}} = 162.03$$

Note: Predictability is not always enhanced by the addition of more variables. Why? Because regression theory assumes that all of the errors are independent of each other, or errors identified by each additional variable have no impact on the others. However, there are cases when any one independent variable may actually affect the outcome of others. In this case, its inclusion becomes useless.

Example: Assume two independent variables are used; direct labor and workman's compensation insurance. Obviously, the dollars spent for direct labor will affect workman's compensation insurance.

The Durbin Watson (DW) statistic provides an indication of this condition. To avoid this or *autocorrelation,* look for a DW of from 1 to 2.

Note: DW calculation is very involved. Fortunately, various computer programs easily supply this number.

From example, the DW for the multiple regression is 1.48 which is well within limits.

Predictability Summary

Use the following checklist to judge the validity of various regression equations:

1. Which of the proposed equations yields an r^2 closest to 1?
2. Which provides the lowest *Syx*?
3. Does the DW statistic fall within 1 and 2?
4. Does the equation make sense?

CHAPTER 19
Cost Allocation

Introduction

The cost allocation process apportions costs to objectives. This information is used for a variety of reasons including:

- Product pricing
- Financial statement preparation
- Differential cost analysis
- Break even analysis
- Compensation

While it is relatively easy to apply direct costs to a product, department or other cost objective, indirect costs must be apportioned to the applicable objective by some form of allocation.

This chapter will cover the following:

- Key terminology of cost allocation
- Allocating indirect costs
- How to allocate costs—a seven step procedure
- How to calculate overhead variance
- Allocating costs to departments
- Service center costs.
- Joint and by products
- Activities Based Costing system (ABC).

Key Terminology of Cost Allocation

Activities Based Costing: A method to accumulate product costs and other information based on the actual activities required to manufacture the product or achieve other goals.

Allocation base: A measure that can be directly associated to and approximates the common cost shared by two or more cost objectives. Direct labor hours have been used as an allocation base to apportion overhead to products. However, ABC is increasingly used to apportion costs from multiple activities.

Applied overhead: Overhead assigned to a cost objective by using a calculated rate.

Controllable costs: A cost that can be influenced by a manager in the short run.

Cost objective: Any purpose for which a cost is assigned.

Differential costs: Costs that change in response to a particular course of action.

Direct costs: Costs that vary with some allocation base.

Discretionary costs: Costs that are hard to relate to outputs.

Dual rate method: An allocation method that separates costs into their fixed and variable components.

Fixed costs: Costs that do not vary as volume changes within a relevant range.

Joint costs: Cost of a process that produces two or more outputs.

Indirect costs: Costs that do not vary directly with an allocation base. They are often referred to as support costs.

Life-cycle costing: A method of accumulating costs for activities over the entire life cycle of a product. This may cover periods in excess of a year.

Noncontrollable costs: Costs that cannot be influenced or changed by a particular manager.

Predetermined overhead rate: An amount obtained by dividing total estimated overhead for the next period by the overhead allocation base.

Relative sales value method: Joint cost allocation based on the proportional net sales values at the split off point.

Responsibility accounting: A system of reporting revenues and costs in the organizational segment that has the responsibility.

Allocating Indirect Costs—An Overview

The following equation is used:

$$\text{Costs Applied} = \frac{\text{Indirect Costs}}{\text{Base}}$$

The following seven-step procedure is commonly utilized:

How to Allocate Costs—A Seven Step Procedure

The path pictured below will help you effectively allocate indirect expenses:

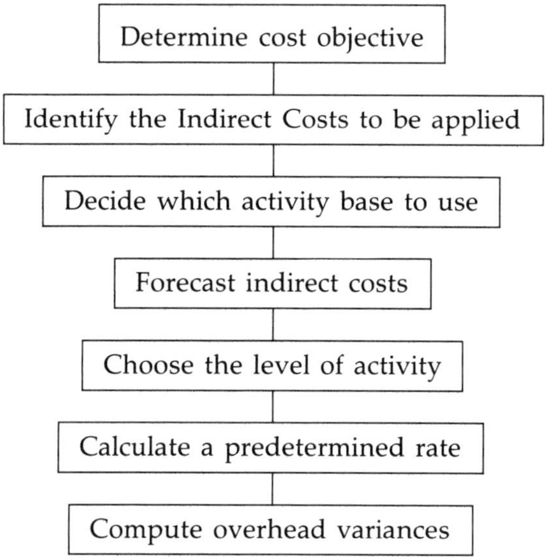

1. *Determine Cost Objective*

The cost objective is the reason why expenses are gathered. Cost accounting is a method of assigning amounts to:

Products

Divisions

Departments

And, each objective will absorb costs from the various pools in different ways and amounts.

2. *Identify the Indirect Costs to Be Applied*

These are the outlays that have some indirect bearing on measured cost objective.

For example: if Department A is our cost objective, the amount of rent applicable to that department would be an allocated indirect cost.

3. *Decide Which Activity Base to Use*

An activity base is a function or action which initiates and drives the costs.

For example, the number of direct labor hours used will drive not only the direct payroll costs but items of indirect overhead as well.

Note: One of the major weaknesses of traditional cost accounting has been its tendency to allocate most indirect costs to an objective on the size of only one activity base.

Solution: Activity based costing, which will be discussed at the end of this chapter, is a multiple allocation method that provides better information.

Don't forget the cost benefit equation. That is, the value gained by allocating multiple cost bases should be greater than the costs to accumulate data.

Some examples of multiple cost bases are shown below:

Type	**Description**	**Comments**
Physical Output	Est Indirect Cost / Estimated Units of Production	Allocation problems if more than one product produced
Direct Materials	Est Indirect Cost / Estimated material cost	Limited use because most overhead components are not material oriented
Direct Labor Costs	Est Indirect Cost / Estimated Direct Labor $'s	Different wage rates and scales will distort allocation
Direct Labor Hours	Est Indirect Cost / Estimated Direct Labor Hours	If production is labor oriented, seems to be the most logical single base
Machine Hours	Est Indirect Cost / Estimated Machine Hours	If production is highly automated, may be the most logical single base

4. *Forecast Indirect Costs*

Inasmuch as the predetermined rate uses an estimated figure for the indirect costs to be applied, it is important to carefully project these expenses.

Note: For purposes of full absorption costing, the expenses will include both the variable and fixed portions.

The following procedure is useful:

a. Examine the prior period's expenses
b. Determine if any trends exist which should be expected to continue.

For example, assume the following past factory overhead expenses:

Factory Overhead

Year	Amount	% Change
1979	27,700	
1980	19,600	−29.2%
1981	15,600	−20.4%
1982	13,900	−10.9%
1983	14,700	5.8%
1984	14,900	1.4%
1985	15,500	4.0%
1986	19,500	25.8%
1987	24,500	25.6%
1988	26,000	6.1%
1989	25,900	−0.4%

Prediction Based on

Percent Change 24,864

This is calculated as follows:

25,900 * (1 − .04)

Moving Average

Three-year moving average, for the prediction

$$\frac{24{,}500 + 26{,}000 + 25{,}900}{3} = 25{,}467$$

Weighted Moving Average

We have weighted the prior years as follows:

3 years back	1/6
2 years back	2/6
1 year back	3/6

In this way, greater importance is placed on the most current prior year.

$$24{,}500 * 1/6 + 26{,}000 * 2/6 + 25{,}900 * 3/6 = 25{,}700$$

c. Adjust trend prediction by other information:

- Estimated level of economic activity.
- Changes in company's plans or organizational structure which may affect indirect expenses.

5. *Choose the Level of Activity*

The activity level selected should be most representative measure of the company's operations.

- *Normal Capacity:* A long-term approach. Based on a time frame sufficient to develop a utilization of the physical plant to level out the highs and lows that occur in every business venture.
- *Expected Actual Capacity:* Used for short-term allocation. The rates are derived from expected actual output for the next production period.

For Example: Assume the following:

Year	1	2	3	4
Overhead	$175,000	$178,000	$172,000	$185,000
Hours	145,000	152,000	165,000	174,000
Rate			3-year	Current Year
Rate to be applied			$1.14	$1.06

The three-year average rate of $1.14 evens out the highs and the lows. However, the rate of $1.06 in year 4 may be a better measure of current operations.

Note: The following factors should be appraised when estimating the activity volume:

- Economic activity levels
- Change in company's marketing
- Change in company's capacity

6. *Calculate a Predetermined Rate*

The predetermined rate equals

$$\frac{\text{Estimated Indirect Costs}}{\text{Estimated Level of Activity}}$$

The predetermined rate should be adjusted to reflect estimated units of activity computed on the best information available.

For example, let direct labor hours be the base. The following calculation will enables you to determine the *chargeable* hours:

Days per Year		365
Less Weekends	52	(104)
Total Workdays		261
Exclusions:		
Vacation	10	
Holidays	8	
Average Sick Days	3	
Days in training	5	(26)
Net Days		235
Hours in Year (@ 8)		1,880
Less: Idle time, etc.	10.00%	(188)
Net Hours Estimated per Employee		1,692
Number of Employees		125
Total Estimated Direct Hours		211,500

In the following illustration, the activity rate is used to calculate a pre-determined overhead rate:

	Fixed	**Variable**	**Total**
Depreciation	$ 12,000		$ 12,000
Factory Supplies		$25,000	25,000
Group Insurance	3,000	9,000	12,000
Indirect Labor	10,000	50,000	60,000
Payroll Taxes		65,000	65,000
Repairs and Maintenance	16,000	4,000	20,000
Supervision Salaries & Indirect Labor	125,000	10,000	135,000
Utilities	4,000	10,000	14,000
Workman's Compensation Insurance		8,000	8,000
Total Estimated Overhead	$170,000	$181,000	$351,000
Estimated Direct Labor Hours	211,500	211,500	211,500
Rate per Direct Labor Hour	$ 0.8038	$ 0.8558	$ 1.6596

6. *Analyze Variances*

The accuracy of indirect expense allocation is, of course, dependent upon

- Overhead
- Activity level

Because both GAAP and IRS regulations require that amounts assigned to period and product costs be based on actual transactions, the differences between the totals assigned and the true costs should be accounted for.

However, it is not enough to only adjust to actual and forget about the differences. The variances may be caused by factors that, if left unchecked, could harm the company.

There are two forms of exception that should be investigated:

Spending Variance: Due to budget or expense factors

Idle Capacity Variance: Due to volume or capacity factors

How to Calculate Overhead Variances

Consider the following:

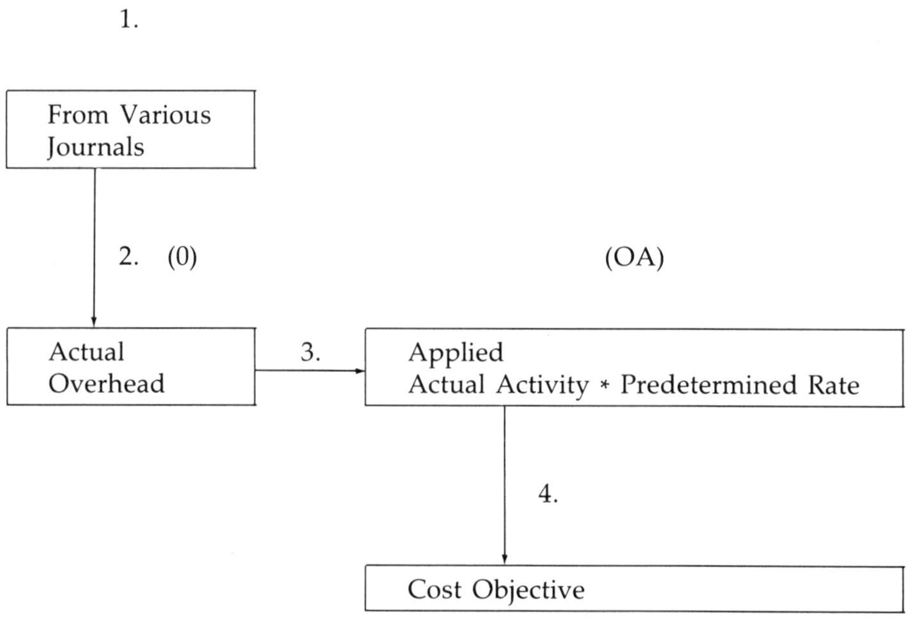

1. Actual expenses are accumulated in the various journals.
2. These are charged to the proper overhead accounts.
3. An account entitled "Overhead applied" is credited as the respective activity occurs.
4. The overhead applied is charged to the assorted cost objectives.

The differences between items 2 and 3 are accounted for as *underapplied* or *overapplied*. To complete the work, this variant is analyzed as follows:

The following equations are used:

Let

O = Actual Overhead
OA = Overhead Applied
F = Fixed Overhead (Budgeted)
U = Units (Hours)
R = Rate
VR = Variable Rate
OA = U * R

1. Total variance = $OA - O$
   If $OA > O$, then overhead is over applied
   If $O > OA$, then overhead is under applied
2. Spending Variance
   $O - (F + (U * VR))$
   If > 0, then unfavorable
   If < 0, then favorable
3. Idle Capacity Variance
   $(F + U * VR) - OA$
   If > 0, then unfavorable
   If < 0, then favorable

Example: The actual overhead versus the budgeted overhead is shown below. During the period the company charged 220,000 hours.

Remember: The following rates were calculated in the previous section:

Variable rate per hour	\$0.8038
Fixed rate per hour	\$0.8558
Total rate per hour	\$1.6596
Estimated direct labor hours	211,500

Total Variance (OA − O)

	Budgeted	**Actual**
Depreciation	\$12,000	\$12,000
Factory Supplies	25,000	23,465
Group Insurance	12,000	9,874

(Continued on next page)

	Budgeted	Actual
Indirect Labor	60,000	65,433
Payroll Taxes	65,000	66,987
Repairs and Maintenance	20,000	19,432
Supervision Salaries & Indirect Labor	135,000	138,745
Utilities	14,000	15,666
Workmans' Comp Insurance	8,000	9,456
Total	$351,000	$361,058
Actual Hours		220,000

Total variance = *OA* − *O*	
OA = *U* * *R* (220,000 * $1.6596)	$365,106
O =	361,056
Overapplied	$ 4,050

This will appear on the general ledger as follows:

	Debit/(Credit)
Actual overhead accounts	$361,058
Overhead applied	$(365,106)

Comment: The company spent $361,058 but charged $365,108 to production. This resulted in an over allocation of $4,050.

Spending Variance

O		361,058
F	170,000	
U * *VR* (220,000 * .8558)	188,276	358,276
Unfavorable		$2,782

Comment: The spending variance is caused by the difference between the actual manufacturing overhead and the amount that had been estimated to be spent at the volume attained. Since the company spent more than estimated, here is an unfavorable variance of $2,784.

Idle Capacity Variance

$F + U * VR$		\$358,276
Applied		
U	220,000	
R	\$1.6596	365,108
Favorable		(\$6,832)

or:

Actual Hours Used	220,000
Budgeted hours	211,500
Actual hours over budgeted	8,500
Predetermined fixed overhead rate	.8038
Favorable	(6,832)

Comment: This variance is caused by the difference between actual and estimated volumes of activity. Inasmuch, as the firm used more hours of production (220,000 − 211,500), the difference is favorable because the higher volume reduced the amount of idle capacity.

Summary of Variances		
Spending Variance	\$2,782	Unfavorable
Idle Capacity Variance	(6,832)	Favorable
Total	\$(4,050)	

Disposition of Over- and Underapplied Overhead

1. *Prorate the adjustment between work in process, finished goods, and cost of goods sold:*

Illustration:

		%
Work in Process	45,000	6%
Finished Goods	55,000	7%
Cost of Goods Sold	700,000	88%
	800,000	100%

	Debit	Credit
Overhead applied	4,050	
Work in Process		228
Finished Goods		278
Cost of Goods Sold		3,544

2. *Assign the entire amount to cost of goods sold:*

	Debit	Credit
Overhead applied	4,050	
Cost of Goods Sold		4,050

Allocating Costs to Departments

A company can improve the value of its information by allocating indirect costs to departments. This will not only provide better expense control but will also help to gauge a manager's performance.

Careful: If expenses are allocated that are not controllable by the individual manager, serious morale problems can result. This will be covered under "Responsibility Accounting" in Chapter 23.

How to Allocate Indirect Expenses to Departments

Certain expenses are shared by all departments, and cannot be specifically charged to any one section. They must therefore be prorated. The following proration bases are commonly used:

Type of Cost	Allocation Basis
Accounting	Service Hours
Advertising	Sales Dollars
Building & Grounds	Floor Space
Data Processing	Number of Documents
Depreciation—Building	Square Footage
Engineering	Service Hours
Insurance—Property	Square Footage
Insurance—Workmans Comp	Department Payroll
Materials Handling	Number of Items
Medical Facilities	Number of Cases
Personnel Department	Number of Employees
Property Tax	Square Footage

Type of Cost	Allocation Basis
Purchasing	Number of Orders
Rent	Square Footage
Repairs	Square Footage
Telephone	Number of Instruments
Utilities	Floor Space

How to Allocate Service Center Costs

A service center is organized to provide support to other segments of the organization including producing as well as non-producing departments.

Examples: Accounting department, maintenance department

The allocation bases for their expenses are displayed in the previous chart. The following describes and illustrates three methods of apportionment:

1. *Direct Method:* Expenses allocated only to producing departments. While this method avoids clerical work, it can only be justified if service departments do not aid other support departments.

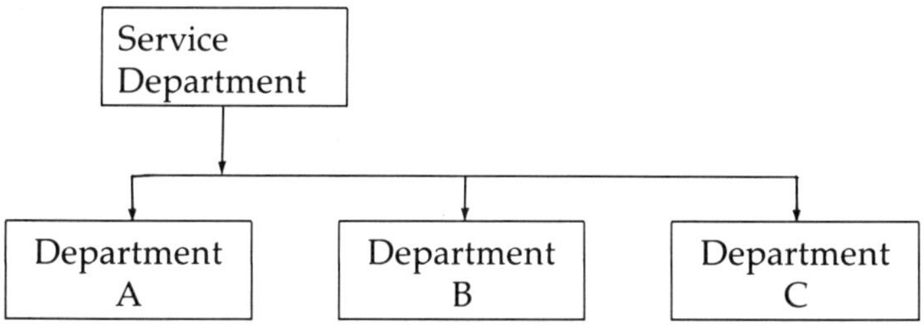

2. *Sequential Method:* Transfers support costs to other service departments as well as producing departments.

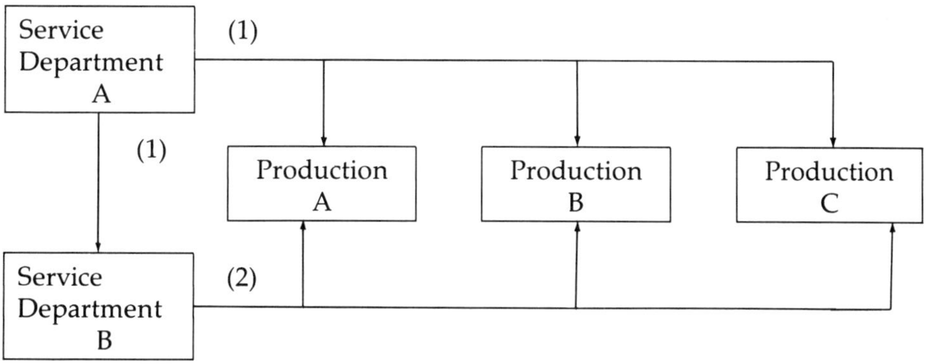

The process works something like this:

(1) Service department A allocates all of its costs to users. These users include Service Department B plus operating departments.

(2) Service department B allocates all of its costs (which include distribution of Department A costs) to producing departments.

When this approach is used, a decision must be made as to which service department should be closed first. The most common process closes the departments in descending order, i.e., the largest department first.

3. *Reciprocal Method:* Since these departments also serve each other, the total cost of any supporting area actually includes a portion of all of the other service departments.

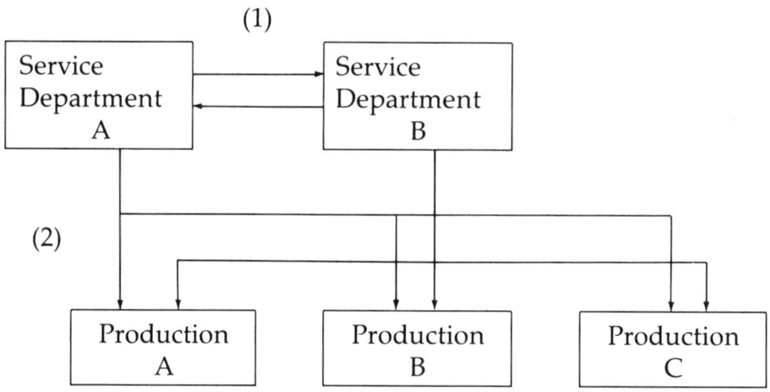

(1) The service department costs are cross allocated using simultaneous equations or matrix algebra.

(2) The allocated costs are then apportioned to the production departments.

Illustration

The Tama Corporation has two service departments:

Department	*Basis of Allocation*
Building maintenance	Square footage
Personnel	Number of employees

And three production departments; A, B, C.

The costs and outputs of these departments are shown below

	Personnel	Building Maint.	Production Department A	B	C
Costs	$6,000	$7,500			
Employees		25	35	30	10
Square Feet	2,000		10,000	5,000	3,000

1. *Direct Allocation:* Interactions among service departments are ignored. Therefore the costs are allocated directly to the producing departments.

Personnel		46.67%	40.00%	13.33%
	$6,000	$2,800	$2,400	$800
Building Maint		55.56%	27.78%	16.66%
	7,500	4,167	2,083	1,250
Total	$13,500	$6,967	$4,483	$2,050

2. *Sequential:* Inasmuch as each service department provides something to the other, there is no natural order to sequentially allocate their costs. The step down method allocates the department that incurs the most expenses first.

Personnel	Building Maint.	A	B	C
$6,000	$7,500			
10.00%		50.00%	25.00%	15.00%
$750	(7,500)	$3,750	$1,875	$1,125
6,750	0	3,750	1,875	1,125
(6,750)		3,150	2,700	900
0	0	$6,900	$4,575	$2,025

3. *Reciprocal Allocation:* This technique allocates the costs between departments by using simultaneous equations. Therefore, arbitrary assumptions about the sequence in which these costs are distributed are not necessary.

The following equations are used:

Let P = Personnel department
Let B = Building maintenance department

$$P = 6{,}000 + .10B$$
$$B = 7{,}500 + .25P$$

$$P = 6{,}000 + .10(7{,}500 + .25P)$$
$$P = 6{,}000 + 750 + .025P$$
$$.975P = 6{,}750$$
$$P = 6{,}923$$

Therefore, substituting for B

$$B = 7{,}500 + .25P$$
$$B = 7{,}500 + .25 * 6923$$
$$B = 9{,}231$$

The amounts to be allocated from B and P now total \$16,154, which are allocated as follows:

		A	B	C
Personnel		35.00%	30.00%	10.00%
Building Maintenance		50.00%	25.00%	15.00%
Personnel	\$6,923	2,423	2,077	692
Building Maintenance	9,231	4,616	2,307	1,385
	\$13,500	\$7,039	\$4,384	\$2,077

How Costs Are Traditionally Allocated When Joint and Byproducts Are Produced

Joint Costs

Costs that arise from the common manufacturing of products produced under the same process. These costs flow as follows:

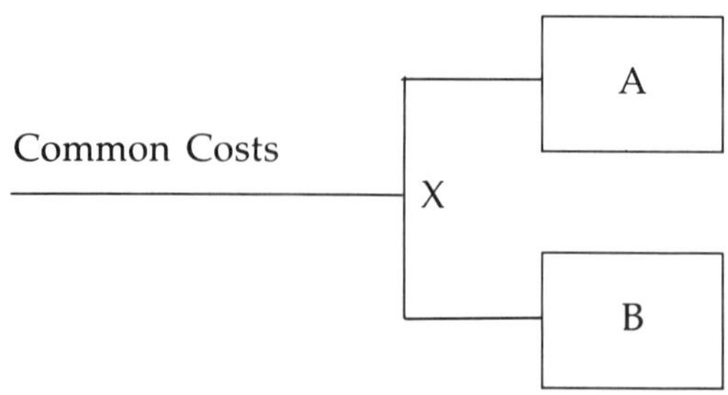

The common costs support products A and B up to the point X. These are next allocated to each of the products by utilizing one of the following methods:

Method	**How Calculated**	**Comments**
Market value or sales value	Relative market value of the individual products	One product may sell for more than the other because it costs more to produce it.
Quantitative or physical unit	Physical measurement	Costs are affected by physical measurement
Average unit cost	Joint production cost divided by total number of units produced	Only useful if all units produced are measured in terms of the same unit
Weighted average	on predetermined standards	Weighting based on size of unit, difference in type of labor, and so on.

Using the Market Value Method

1. Accumulate common costs used to produce all joint products.
2. Compute relative sales value of each item.

Relative Sales Value =

Market Value per Unit * Units Produced = Total Market Value
Relative Sales Value = Total Market Value − Additional Costs

3. Allocate common costs to each product on basis of relative sales value.

Common Costs $120,000

Product	**Market Value Per Unit**	**Units Produced**	**Total Market Value**	**Costs After Split-Off**	**Net Market Value**
A	$1.50	5,000	$7,500	$1,500	$6,000
B	$0.50	8,000	4,000	500	3,500
C	$3.25	4,000	13,000	2,500	10,500
			$24,500	$4,500	$20,000

	Net Market Value	%	Allocation
A	$6,000	30.00%	$36,000
B	3,500	17.50%	21,000
C	10,500	52.50%	63,000
	$20,000	100.00%	$120,000

Byproducts

A byproduct is generally something that is produced simultaneously with the major production but has relatively little value. There are two acceptable ways to cost by-products:

1. *No Joint Production Cost is allocated:*
   Any revenues generated by selling by product is either credited to the income or to the cost of the main product.

Presentation alternatives:

- Other income
- Additional sales revenues
- Deduction from cost of goods sold
- Deduction from total manufacturing costs

Note: The amount may be reported at net after additional processing costs, marketing, and general and administration costs.

2. *A portion of the joint production cost is allocated to the by-product.*

How to Get Better Information by Setting Up an Activities-Based Costing System (ABC)

In the past, most companies used a single allocation base to apportion their overhead costs. Why? Because, information gathering costs were prohibitive. The introduction of the computer to the factory has allowed accountants to gather and allocate costs with much more ease.

ABC gathers product costs by the activities actually required to manufacture the goods. This method, still in its infancy, has been designed to alleviate the shortcomings of traditional indirect cost allocation methods, which quite often, follow direct labor hours.

Some of the traditional method shortcomings are:

1. In increasingly automated factories, direct labor is becoming less important in the production process.
2. Many companies produce a wide array of units in different lot sizes and configurations. The traditional methods fail to accurately apportion various cost drivers to diverse products.

For example, assume a company manufactures two products, A and B. The only indirect costs are set up expenses. Under the traditional method, indirect costs of $80,000 are allocated on the basis of direct labor hours. As a result the data would show that product B (which has a higher markup) is more profitable than A.

But, set-up costs have to be incurred every time a new order is started. Since Product B is sold in small lots, it requires more than double the number of orders than A. If we were to, instead, allocate these indirect costs by the activity that drives them, we would apportion 70% to B and only 30% to A. We would find that product B is only marginally profitable. In fact, it probably does not contribute enough to cover other variable costs or fixed expenses.

	Traditional		**Activity Based**	
Product	**A**	**B**	**A**	**B**
Units Sold	10,000	1,000	10,000	1,000
Number of Orders	30	70	30	70
Hours Per Unit	3	3	3	3
Total Hours	30,000	3,000	30,000	3,000
Sales Price	$50.00	$75.00	$50.00	$75.00
Sales	$500,000	$75,000	$500,000	$75,000
Direct Costs	150,000	15,000	150,000	15,000
Indirect Costs	72,727	7,273	24,000	56,000
Total Costs	222,727	22,273	174,000	71,000
Gross Profit	$277,273	$52,727	$326,000	$4,000
Gross Profit Pct	55.45%	70.30%	65.20%	5.33%

Setting Up the System

1. *Identify the categories of manufacturing overhead.*

For example, purchases, support activities, and production control.

2. *Define and separate the important activities.*
For example: Purchasing requires the following activities:

Bidding
Negotiating
Buying
Documentation
Storage
Handling

3. *Analyze the components of each product to determine the amount of each activity used by that product.*

The ABC method requires accountants to understand production processes and operations better. You will have to go out on the floor, talk to people and get the information you need to build a base of activities that drive the various costs.

A computer system, which is programmed for manufacturing control and contains a good data base management program, will help.

CHAPTER 20

Cost Accounting Systems

Introduction

This chapter discusses the two major cost systems presently in use:

- Job Order
- Process

A Comparison Between Job Order and Process Cost Systems

The following chart contrasts the two:

	Job Order	**Process**
Type of Product	Identifiable units or groups of units	Homogeneous products
Product valuation	higher	lower
Quantity of units	lower	higher
Industry example	machine shop	breakfast cereal
Objectives	identify output in terms of individual or groups of homogeneous units	develop unit cost for homogeneous units produced
Costs accumulated by	job	department
Method of accumulation	job order cost sheet	cost of production report

How to Set Up a Job Order Cost System

Job order costing is used to account for the flow of costs into specific, identifiable jobs. The costs will remain in work in process or finished goods inventory until the goods are shipped.

The unit of accumulation is the job order cost sheet which should be designed to account for the following flow of its components:

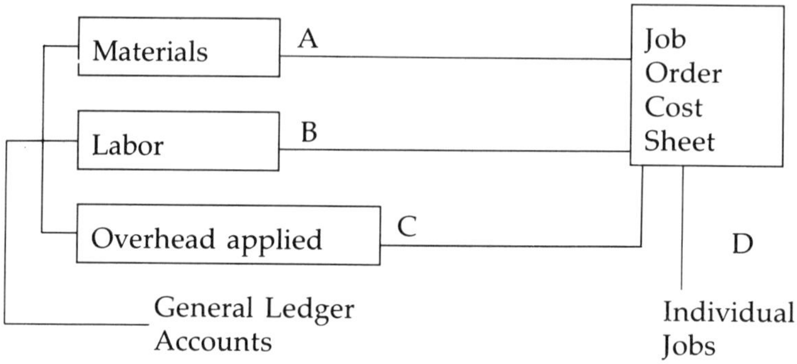

Setting Up the System

1. Define the nature of the jobs that have to be accounted for.

    Customer

    Type of job

    Special requirements

2. Develop a numbering system to accumulate costs by job.
3. Design a job order cost sheet (see below).
4. Work with the manufacturing and purchasing department to prepare a complete bill of materials for each job.

    Establish standard prices

    Establish standard quantities

5. Set up labor cost monitoring system. This should inclue:

    Time keeping

    Coding of labor hours by job

6. Analyze overhead and cost drivers to determine the best methods to allocate indirect costs to each job.
7. Establish monitoring procedures.

Cost Accumulation

A. *Materials*

To account for material costs, we use a perpetual inventory system. The following series of entries is used:

	Debit	Credit
1. Purchase of materials		
Raw Materials Inventory	XXX	
Accounts Payable		XXX
2. Issue of materials to job		
Work in process Inventory	XXX	
Raw Materials Inventory		XXX

Note: This category includes sub-contracted services.

B. *Labor*

Labor is accumulated by time cards designed to collect this data.

C. *Overhead*

Overhead is applied to the jobs. See Chapter 19 for details about overhead allocation.

D. *Individual Job Cost*

These are maintained as subsidiary ledgers which support the account Work in Process Inventory.

Using the Job Cost Sheet

The job cost sheet should be designed to follow the work through all its phases.

JOB ORDER COST SHEET

- Customer Name
- Job Number
- Part Name
- Part Description
- Date Started
- Number of Units
- Shipping information
    - Date shipped
    - Number of units

- Direct Labor
    - Date
    - Employee Number
    - Department Number
    - Time
    - Straight time rate
    - Overtime rate
    - Total labor cost

(Continued on next page)

JOB ORDER COST SHEET

Materials
- Date received
- Date ordered
- Description
- Purchase order number
- Quantity
- Unit price
- Amount

Special Supplies and Tools
- Date received
- Date ordered
- Description
- Purchase order number
- Quantity
- Unit price
- Amount

Completed Job Report—Estimate versus Actual
- Direct materials
- Direct labor
- Special Supplies and tools
  - Total Direct Cost
- Manufacturing overhead applied
- General and Administrative
  - Total Cost
- Freight and Miscellaneous
- Invoice Price

Process Cost Accounting

Setting Up the System

1. Define characteristics of production operation including:

   Products manufactured

   Work flow through departments

   Method of measuring

2. Set up departmental costing for materials, labor, and overhead.

3. Choose method to account for flow—Average or FIFO.
4. Accumulate costs by department.
5. Cost of production report.
6. Compute equivalent units.
7. Calculate costs of inventory and products sold.

The Process Cost Flow

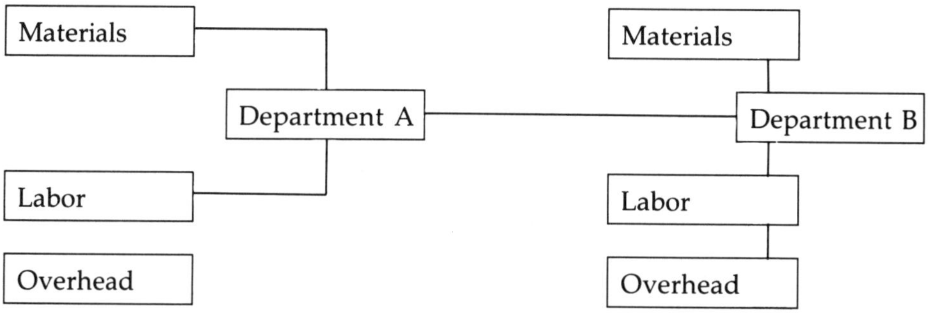

As the above illustrates, there are four components to a process cost system:

1. Materials
2. Labor
3. Overhead
4. Prior Department Cost

Materials, labor, and overhead can be added in any department. The prior department cost to department B (above) equals the amount transferred from B.

The Cost of Production Report

Company Name ______________________
Department ______________________

Period Ended ______________________

A. Quantity To Be Accounted For
Units received from prior department
Beginning work in process inventory
Units started in process
Total quantity to be accounted for

(Continued on next page)

The Cost of Production Report

B. Quantity Accounted for
Units transferred to next department
Units still in process
Units lost in process
Total quantity accounted for

****

C. Costs to Be Accounted For—
Costs from preceding department
(Transferred in)
Beginning work in process inventory
Costs added by department
Materials
Labor
Factory Overhead
Total costs to be accounted for

D. Costs Accounted For as Follows
Transferred to next department
Work in process ending inventory
Total cost accounted for

Key to Symbols

A & C Quantity and Costs to Be Accounted For: These are the units and costs that are being brought into the process, and includes beginning work in process, and transfers in.

B & D Quantity and Costs Accounted For: This is what results from the production process.

The following equalities must be observed:

$A = B$
$C = D$

To Be Accounted For		*Accounted For*
Received from prior department Beginning work in process inventory Started in process	=	Transferred out Ending inventory Lost in process

Equivalent Units

These are the number of units which could have been completed entirely with the inputs in the current period. Because the components displayed above may be put into the production process at varying times, the amount of equivalent units may be different for each. The number of equivalent units (EU) is computed as follows:

$$EU = \text{Number of units} * \text{Percent complete}$$

Example: The Department A production report has accounted for 175,000 units which are 100% complete as to materials and 50% complete as to labor and overhead. The equivalent units of production are calculated as follows:

	# Units	% Complete	Equivalent Units
Materials	175,000	100.00%	175,000
Labor/Overhead	175,000	50.00%	87,500

If the following costs were incurred during the period:

Costs	Total
Material	525,000
Labor/Overhead	481,250

By dividing by the number of equivalent units, these costs per unit result:

Material	3.00
Labor/Overhead	5.50

Assuming an ending inventory of 50,000 units, we derive the following carrying value:

Material	50,000 @ $3.00	$150,000
Labor/Overhead	25,000 @ $5.50	137,000
Total Ending Inventory		$287,500

How to Account for Lost Units (Spoilage)

If the loss is a normal factor of production, it may be accounted for in one of two ways:

1. Allocated among the costs of the good units

$$\frac{\text{Total Costs}}{\text{Total Units} - \text{Lost Units}} = \text{Cost per unit}$$

2. Accounted for separately

$$\frac{\text{Total Costs}}{\text{Total Units}} = \text{Cost per unit}$$

$$\text{Lost Unit Cost} = \text{Cost per unit} * \text{Lost units}$$

For example, assume 5,000 units were put into production, and 500 units were spoiled. The total manufacturing cost was $90,000.

	1.	2.
Total Costs	$90,000	$90,000
Total Units	5,000	5,000
Lost Units	(500)	
Net Units	4,500	5,000
Cost per Unit	$20.00	$18.00
Cost of Production	$90,000	$81,000
Lost Unit Cost		9,000
	$90,000	$90,000

Cost of Production Report Illustrated

	Physical Units	Equivalent Units %	Materials	%	Labor & OH
Department A					
Units to Be Accounted For					
Beg Inventory	30,000				
Started	270,000				
	300,000				
Units Accounted For					
Transferred out	250,000	100%	250,000	100%	250,000
Ending Inventory	50,000	100%	50,000	50%	25,000
	300,000		300,000		275,000

Costs to Be Accounted For		Materials	Labor & Overhead
Beg Inventory	$ 60,000	$ 30,000	$ 30,000
Started	540,000	420,000	120,000
	$600,000	$450,000	$150,000
Unit costs		$1.50	$0.55
Costs Accounted For			
Transferred out		$375,000	$136,364
Ending Inventory		75,000	13,636
		$450,000	$150,000

Materials Added During Production

Options:

1. The unit cost is increased if these materials add to the total value of the product but the number of units stay the same.
2. Or, the added ingredients may increase the number of units and, consequently, change the per unit cost.

Accounting for Beginning Work in Process Inventories

Depending upon the cost flow selected the method of accounting for these beginning costs will vary:

Method	**FIFO**	**Weighted Average**
Description	Beginning inventory costs are kept separate from the new costs required to complete the work in process inventory	Beginning inventory costs are added to the new period costs
Equivalent Units	Units accounted for in cost of production report minus beginning inventory at previous percent of completion	Units accounted for in cost of production report

Note: If the company uses LIFO, the accounting procedure used will be similar to FIFO.

The Cost of Production Report

Illustration: The following information is pertinent for the second production department of the Patrick Corporation:

Beginning Inventory	
Units	5,000
Costs from preceding department	$7,000
Materials in process	$0
Labor in process	$1,200
Factory overhead in process	$900

Quantity Schedule	
Units to be accounted for	
Units in process at beginning (40% labor and overhead)	5,000
Received from prior department	45,000
Total Units to be Accounted For	50,000

Quantity Schedule	
Transferred to next department	48,000
Ending Inventory (70% labor and overhead)	2,000
Total Units Accounted For	50,000

Cost Data	
Costs from prior department	$60,000
Cost added by department	
Labor	$20,000
Overhead	$15,000

WEIGHTED AVERAGE

	Materials	Labor & Overhead
Equivalent Units		
Transferred Out	48,000	48,000
Work in process—ending	2,000	1,400
	50,000	49,400

Costs to Be Accounted For

			Per Unit
Costs from preceding department			
Work in process—beginning		$7,000	
Costs transferred in		60,000	
		$ 67,000	$1.340
Costs Added by Department			
Work in process beginning inventory			
Labor		$ 1,200	
Overhead		900	
Costs Added during period			
Labor		20,000	0.429
Overhead		15,000	0.322
Total Costs Added		37,100	0.751
Total Costs to Be Accounted For		104,100	2.091
	Units		
Transferred to Next Department	48,000	$100,369	2.091
Work in Process Ending Inventory			
Preceding Department	2,000	$2,680	1.340
Labor	1,400	601	0.429
Overhead	1,400	450	0.322
		3,731	
Total Costs Accounted For		$104,100	

FIFO

Equivalent Units	Materials	Labor & Overhead
Equivalent Units		
Transferred Out	48,000	48,000
Less: Beginning Inventory		5,000
Started and Finished this Period	48,000	43,000
Beginning Inventory (this period)		3,000
Work in process—ending	2,000	1,400
	50,000	47,400

Costs to Be Accounted For

	Units		Per Unit
Work in process—beginning		$9,100	
Costs transferred in		60,000	$1.333
		69,100	
Costs Added during period			
Labor		20,000	0.422
Overhead		15,000	0.316
Total Costs Added		35,000	0.738
Total Costs to Be Accounted For		$104,100	$2.072
Costs Accounted For			
Transferred to Next Department	Units		
From Beginning Inventory			
Inventory Cost		$9,100	$0.422
Labor	3,000	1,266	0.316
Overhead	3,000	949	
		$ 11,315	
From Current Production			
Units Started and Finished	43,000	89,084	
Work in Process Ending Inventory			
Cost from preceding department	2,000	2,667	
Labor	1,400	591	
Overhead	1,400	442	
		3,700	
Total Costs Accounted For		$104,100	

CHAPTER 21

Cost Accounting for Control Purposes

Introduction

To control, management sets up a process to measure and correct activities in order to assure that events conform to plan. Some of the accounting methods are:

- Flexible budgets
- Standard cost systems

As the following diagram illustrates, there are three elements to a well designed control system:

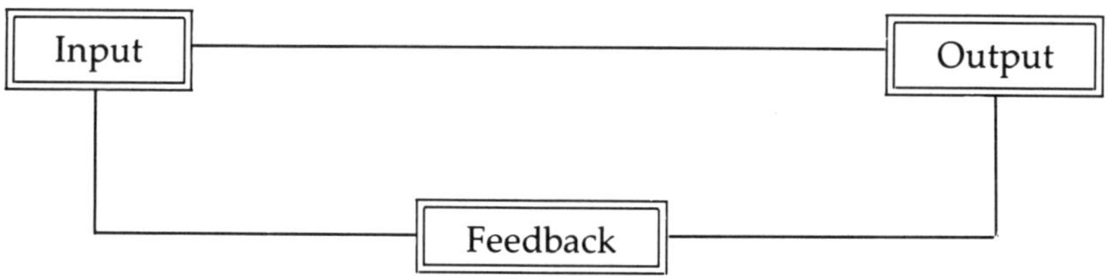

Activities are inputted throughout the process. You hope the result will be what you want. To attain a better chance of that happening, it is useful to build in mileposts or checkpoints along the way.

Feedback: Provided by the various mileposts or checkpoints. It should allow managers to learn about problems before its too late. Remember, good feedback comes from timely accurate information.

Designing the Control System

1. *Determine why the information is to be gathered.* The major job of an organization is to get its product and/or service produced and out the door with the most feasible combination of resources. The control system should not delay that process.

Therefore, each time you institute or recommend a control procedure, ask yourself, "Why?"

Remember: The cost benefit equation.

2. *Select the applicable items to be compiled.* Only those components that will affect management's actions should be used. Furthermore, each of these components should be within control of the responsible manager.

   Related Topics

   Responsibility Accounting—Chapter 22
   Differential Costs—Chapter 23

3. *Select and calculate the standards against which performance is to be judged.* The standards will come out of plans constructed by management, and, should consist of verifiable goals or objectives that can be stated in quantifiable terms.
4. *Build in estimates in order to provide rapid information.* Accuracy might have to be sacrificed in order to obtain feedback. As previously stated, feedback is only useful if it is timely.

   Suggestion: Relevant information must be timely. However, to get data quickly, reliability often has to be sacrificed. You must straddle a fine line between these two contrary needs.

   Example: Inventory taken and priced under the guidelines established by GAAS is more reliable than a computed account or one calculated with standards or estimates. However, the information derived from the more accurate version may be too late to provide useful feedback.

   Caution: In most cases, GAAP considers reliability more important than relevance.

   However: The control procedures presented here are used for the internal purposes of management and do not have to reflect GAAP.

5. *Establish methods to measure performance.* The accounting system should provide the information to do this.
6. *Make sure the information is communicated to the right people.* The right people, of course, are those capable of using it to make management decisions.

7. *Set up systems to control deviations.* The key ingredients are:
   - Timely feedback
   - Communication of deviations to persons in the organization that can take corrective action.
   - Re-defining standards, if necessary.

How to Use Flexible Budgets to Explain Deviations

Chapter 24, describes methods that management uses to reduce its planning activities to numbers by preparing forecasts and budgets. A flexible budget is a useful *control* device.

Management by Exception (MBE)

Once the company's executives have established their organization's goals, strategies and tactics, a follow-up system is needed to determine that activities are proceeding according to plan. The MBE practice shows where the significant deviations have occurred.

For example, it is more useful to say, "A company spent $1,200 or 12% over budget," than to merely present the results.

How the Flexible Budget Enhances MBE

When a company experiences deviations from its planned objectives, the differences may be caused by changes in:

- Sales prices
- Volume
- Mix
- Cost elements

The Impact of Volume

The forecasts that are initiated at the beginning of the period report differences caused by changes in volume.

For example, assume that CSUN Enterprises budgets $100,000 direct labor based on the following forecast:

Units	10,000
Hours per unit	2
Hourly rate	$5.00
Total Labor	$100,000

At the end of the period, the company had produced 15,000 units and the actual labor costs totaled $138,000, or $38,000 over budget. However, a flexible budget analysis would have shown that CSUN actually spent $12,000 less than budget.

Units	15,000	
Hours per unit	2	
Hourly rate	$5.00	
Total Labor	$150,000	
Budgeted Labor at Volume Level		$150,000
Actual Labor		138,000
Favorable Variation		$ 12,000

The Flexible Budget Procedure

As the following represents, there are three components to the process:

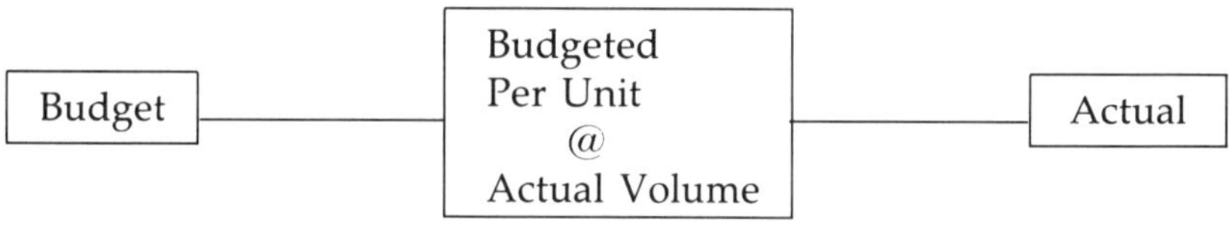

How to Use the Four-Level Variance Analysis Technique

The following is a systematic way to analyze the variances computed from each period's financial results.

Level 0: Difference between budgeted and actual net income.

Level 1: Difference between components of budgeted and actual net income.

Level 2: Impact on profits caused by changes in level of business activity, costs, prices, and operating efficiencies. It is made up of two components:

- *Sales activity variance.* Measures differences caused by incorrectly estimating the actual level and mix of sales.
- *Cost/price/efficiency variance.* Depicts differences between expected profits at the volume attained and the actual profits realized at these volumes.

Level 3: Provides greater detail to level two variances.

Sales activity variance supported by:

Sales volume variance

Changes in contribution margin caused solely by variations in physical units sold

Sales mix variance

Changes caused solely by different product mixes than anticipated.

Cost/price/efficiency variance explained by

Sales price variance

Difference between budgeted and actual selling prices.

Variable cost variance

Difference between actual variable costs and the amount budgeted at sales levels realized.

Period cost variance

Contrast between budgeted and actual fixed costs.

Level 4: Analyzes the contrasts disclosed in Level 3 in greater detail:

Sales volume variance

Market size variance

Differences due to changes in overall industry sales

Market share variance

Differences due to changes in company's market share

Sales mix, sales price, and variable cost variances

Analyzed by product

Period cost variance

Divided into components, e.g., general and administrative, selling

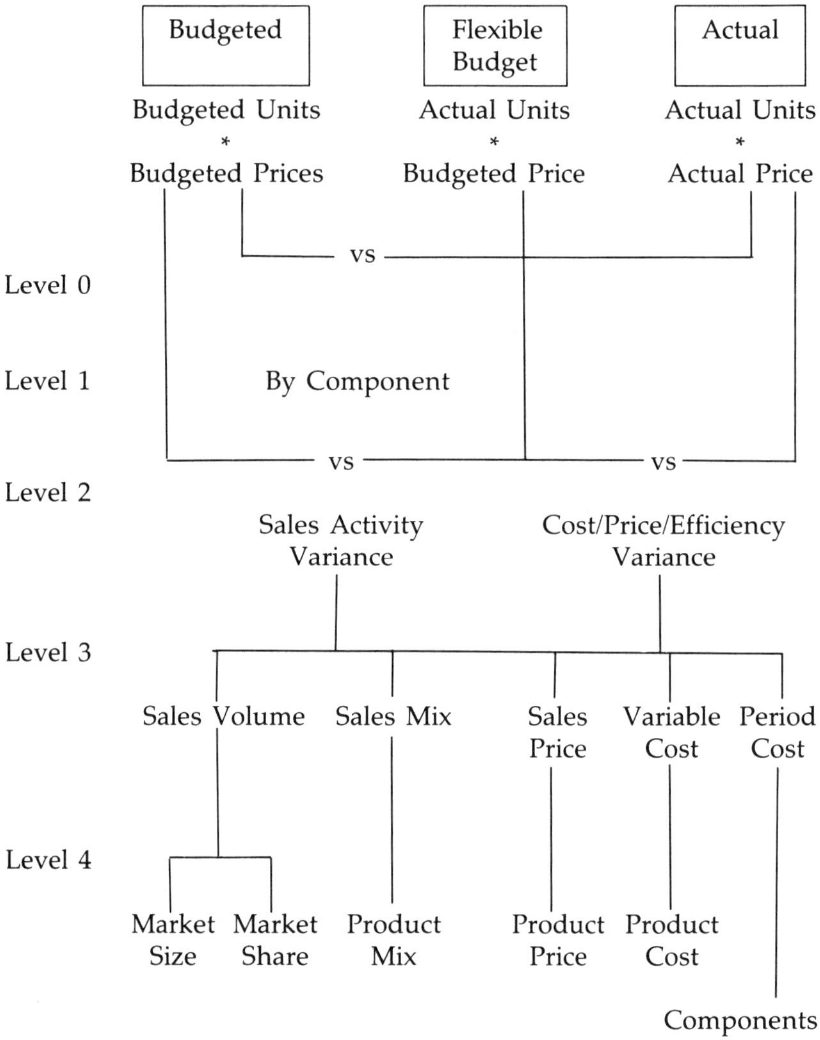

Computation Equations

Keys to Symbols

P = Profit
A = Actual
FB = Flexible Budget
B = Budget
R = Revenues
V = Variable Costs
F = Fixed Costs

$X_1, X_2, \ldots \ldots X_n$
C = contribution margin
U = units sold

Level 0

$AP - BP$

Level 1

Components of $AP - BP$

Level 2

Sales Activity Variance = $FBP - BP$
Cost/Price/Efficiency = $AP - FBP$

Level 3

$$\text{Average Contribution Rate} = C = \frac{CX_1 + CX_2 + \cdots + CX_n}{U}$$

Sales Volume Variance (For each product (X))

$$\left(\begin{matrix}\text{Budgeted Units}\\ \text{By product}\end{matrix} - \begin{matrix}\text{Actual Units}\\ \text{By products}\end{matrix}\right) * C$$

Sales Mix Variance

$$\text{Changes in Units} * \left(\begin{matrix}\text{Contribution}\\ \text{Each Product}\end{matrix} - \begin{matrix}\text{Contribution}\\ \text{Average}\end{matrix}\right)$$

Sales Price Variance = $AR - FBR$
Variable Cost Variance = $AV - FBV$
Period Cost = $AF - BF$

Level 4

Market Size Variance =

$$\left(\begin{matrix}\text{Actual}\\ \text{Total Market}\end{matrix} - \begin{matrix}\text{Expected}\\ \text{Total}\\ \text{Market}\end{matrix}\right) * \begin{matrix}\text{Expected}\\ \text{Market}\\ \text{Share}\end{matrix} * C$$

Market Share Variance =

$$\left(\begin{matrix}\text{Actual}\\ \text{Market}\\ \text{Share}\end{matrix} - \begin{matrix}\text{Expected}\\ \text{Market}\\ \text{Share}\end{matrix}\right) * \begin{matrix}\text{Actual}\\ \text{Market}\\ \text{Volume}\end{matrix} * C$$

Illustrated

The Sydney Corporation has prepared the following budget for the month of March, 1990:

Sydney Corporation
Budget
March, 1990

	Units	Per Unit	
Sales			
Product A	2,000	$3.00	
Product B	1,000	$5.00	
Variable Costs			
Product A		$1.50	
Product B		$2.00	
Sales			$11,000
Variable Costs			5,000
Contribution			6,000
Fixed Costs			
Selling		2,000	
General & Administrative		3,500	
Total Fixed Costs			5,5000
Net Income			$500

In addition to the above, it has also estimated the industry will sell 60,000 units of which the Sydney Corporation would capture 5% of the market.

The Company has approximated a profit of $500 on sales of $11,000. However when the month of March was closed, it had actually shipped $22,000, double the projected volume, but had recorded a loss of $3,375. See below.

Only 40,000 units were sold in the industry.

Sydney Corporation
Statement of Income (Actual)
For the Month of March, 1990

	Units	Per Unit
Sales		
Product A	500	$3.50
Product B	4,500	$4.50

	Units	Per Unit
Variable Costs		
Product A		$1.75
Product B		$3.50
Sales		$22,000
Variable Costs		16,625
Contribution		5,375
Fixed Costs		
Selling	$4,000	
General & Administrative	4,750	
Total Fixed Costs		8,750
Net (Loss)		$(3,375)

A four level variance analysis was prepared.

To begin to analysis the discrepancy, Sydney's accountant prepared a flexible budget at the level of the actual units shipped.

Sydney Corporation
Flexible Budget of Actual Units
March, 1990

	Units	Per Unit
Sales		
Product A	500	$3.00
Product B	4,500	$5.00
Variable Costs		
Product A		$1.50
Product B		$2.00
Sales		$24,000
Variable Costs		9,750
Contribution		14,250
Fixed Costs		
Selling	2,000	
General & Administrative	3,500	
Total Fixed Costs		5,500
Net Income		$ 8,750

A four level variance analysis was prepared.

LEVEL 0

The following evaluation discloses the difference between the budgeted and actual results.

Actual Net Income	($3,375)
Budgeted Net Income	500
Variance (U)	($3,875)

LEVEL 1

	Actual	Budget	Difference
Sales	$22,000	$11,000	$11,000
Variable Costs	16,625	5,000	11,625
Contribution	5,375	6,000	(625)
Fixed Costs			
Selling	4,000	2,000	2,000
General & Administrative	4,750	3,500	1,250
Total Fixed Costs	8,750	5,500	3,250
Net Income	$(3,375)	$500	$ (3,875)

By breaking down the differences by components, we can see that the Company had $11,625 variable costs while sales only increased by $11,000. Furthermore, fixed expenses exceeded budget by $3,250.

LEVEL 2

The above shows that sales volume in excess of budgeted levels accounted for a profit of $8,250 in excess of the profit plan. However, sales in this quantity should have yielded a profit of $8,750. In reality, Sydney lost money at this level.

Sales Activity Variance		
Flexible Budget Net Income	$8,750	
Budgeted Net Income	500	
Variance (Favorable)		$8,250
Cost/Price/Efficiency Variance		
Actual Net Income	(3,375)	
Flexible Budget Net Income	8,750	
Variance (Unfavorable)		(12,125)
Total Variance (Unfavorable)		(3,875)

LEVEL 3

At this point we dissect the variances disclosed in Level 2.

Finding the Weighted Average Contribution per Unit

Contribution Margin per Unit

	Units	Contribution *Per Unit*	*Total*
A	2,000	$1.50	$3,000
B	1,000	$3.00	3,000
	3,000		$6,000
Per Unit			$2.00

Sales Volume Variance

Units shipped in excess of budgeted amounts contributed $4,000 to profit.

Units	**Actual**	**Budget**	**Difference**	
A	500	2,000	(1,500)	
B	4,500	1,000	3,500	
	5,000	3,000	2,000	
Contribution per Unit			$2.00	
Total Sales Volume (Favorable)				$4,000

Sales Mix Variance

The following shows that by changing the mix from products yielding less than the average contribution to those which generate a higher return, the company will improve its profits.

Units	**Unit Diff**	**Contribution Wtd Ave**	**Contribution Individual**		
A	(1,500)	$2.00	$1.50	750	
B	3,500	$2.00	$3.00	3,500	
Sales Mix Variance					4,250
Total Sales Activity Variance					$8,250

Cost/Price/Efficiency Variance

The actual revenues and variable and fixed expenses are next compared to the amounts resulting from actual units times quantity shipped.

Sales Price Variance	
Actual Revenues	$ 22,000
Budgeted Revenues at Actual Sales Levels	24,000
Total Sales Price Variance (Unfavorable)	(2,000)
Variable Cost Variance	
Actual Variable Costs	16,625
Budgeted Variable Costs at Actual Volume	9,750
Total Variable Cost Variance (Unfavorable)	(6,875)
Period Cost Variance	
Actual Fixed Costs	8,750
Budgeted Fixed Costs	5,500
Total Period Cost Variance (Unfavorable)	(3,250)
Total Cost/Price/Efficiency Variance (Unfavorable)	$(12,125)
Level 3 Summary	
Sales Activity Variance (Favorable)	8,250
Cost/Price/Efficiency Variance (Unfavorable)	(12,125)
	$ (3,875)

LEVEL 4

The following schedules show the impact of industry factors on Sydney Corporation.

Market Size Variance

Market research had predicted 60,000 total unit sales by the industry. However, actual results fell short by 20,000 units. This hurt the Sydney's performance by $2,000.

Actual Total Market	40,000	
Expected Total Market	60,000	
	(20,000)	
Expected Market Share	5.00%	(1,000)

Budgeted Contribution Per Unit (Unfavorable)		$2.00	(2,000)

Market Share Variance

However the company's market share climbed from 5% to 12.5% contributed $6,000 to its profit.

Actual Market Share	12.50%		
Expected Market Share	5.00%		
	7.50%		
Actual Market Volume	40,000	3,000	
Budgeted Contribution Per Unit		$2.00	6,000
Total Sales Volume Variance (Favorable)			4,000

Product Mix Variance

This is another exposition of the sales mix variance presented in Level 3.

Units	Unit Diff	Contribution Wtd Ave	Contribution Individual		
A	(1,500)	$2.00	$1.50	$750	
B	(3,500)	$2.00	$3.00	3,500	
Total Product Mix Variance (Favorable)					4,250

Product Price Variance

This allows additional tracing of the impact on profits due to price changes. As you can readily see a $0.50 per unit drop in Product B was responsible for a $2,250 profit erosion.

	Actual Units	Actual Price	Budgeted Price		
A	500	$3.50	$3.00	$ 250	
B	4,500	$4.50	$5.00	(2,250)	
Total Product Price Variance (Unfavorable)					$(2,000)

Product Cost Variance

This schedule evaluates the effect on net income by variable cost fluctuations for specific products. It is evident that $1.50 per unit additional variable costs for product B significantly wrecked the profit plan set by the company. In fact, it appears to be the key contributor.

	Actual		Budgeted	
	Units	**Cost**	**Cost**	
A	500	$1.75	$1.50	(125)
B	4,500	$3.50	$2.00	(6,750)
				$(6,875)

Period Cost Components

At this point we compare various fixed cost components at actual to the budgeted amounts. The concept of MBE is applied to zero in on the most material items.

	Actual	**Budget**		
Selling	4,000	2,000	$(2,000)	
General/Admin	4,750	3,500	(1,250)	
Total Fixed	8,750	5,500		(3,250)
Total Period Cost Variance (Unfavorable)				(3,875)

How to Set Up and Use a Standard Cost System

Definitions

Standard Costs: The anticipated cost of producing and/or selling a unit of output.

Standard Cost System: An accounting system in which products are costed using standard rather than actual costs.

Uses of Standard Costing

- To establish budgets
- To control costs
- To promote cost reduction
- To simplify the accounting procedures

- To assign costs to product
- As a basis to set bids and prices

The system is explained by means of the following T accounts:

Direct Materials		**Work in Process**
Actual Costs	Applied @ Predetermined Rate	Standard Direct Materials
Direct Labor		
Actual Costs	Applied @ Predetermined Rate	Standard Direct Labor
Manufacturing Overhead		
Actual Costs	Applied @ Predetermined Rate	Standard overhead rate * standard input for volume achieved

Variances

These are the differences between actual and standard costs. Analysis of these variances is an important control area. In fact, to many, it is standard costing's raison d'etre.

How Are Standard Costs Applied

By using the following equation:

$$\frac{\text{Predetermined Costs}}{\text{Activity Level}}$$

The preferred level is the *normal* rate of activity utilizing the following data:

- Previous volume

- Work force
- Holidays, vacations
- Idle time
- Training time
- Learning curve

Estimating Components (Direct material, Direct Labor Manufacturing Overhead)

Component	**Cost**	**Activity Base**
Direct Materials	Bills of material Purchase orders Prior costs	Engineering estimates Yield after lost units Bill of materials
Direct Labor	Prior costs Union contracts	Prior history Time and motion studies Adjusted for learning curve
Manufacturing Overhead	Prior history Cost estimates based on present conditions	See Chapter 19, Cost Allocation

Caution: Poorly established labor time standards may cause serious behavioral problems.

Because: If goals are set too high, employees may become discouraged.

But: If targets are set too low, then workers may tend to only achieve what's expected of them.

How to Compute and Account for Variances

A variance is a difference between the standard and actual cost—materials, labor, and overhead.

Direct Material and Labor

The following diagram will explain the flow of standard costs and their related variances to these components:

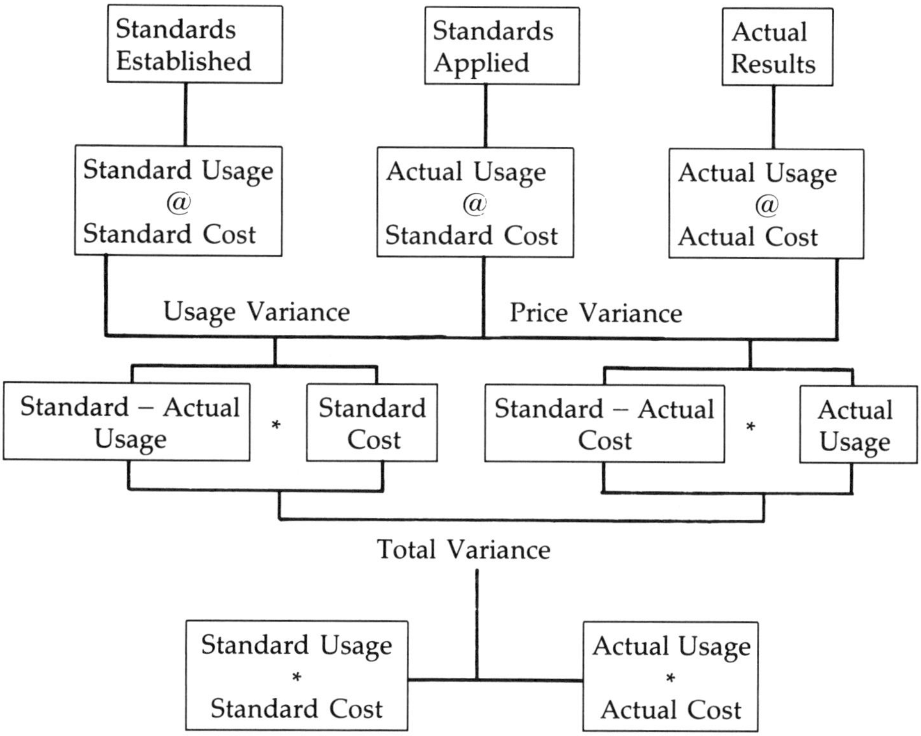

Interpreting Direct Material and Direct Labor Variances

Type	**Reason**
Direct Material Usage	Spoilage Theft Standards cannot be determined Erroneous estimates
Direct Material Price	Different quantities purchased New vendors Different purchase terms Supply and demand effect on prices Effect of inflation Improper standard setting
Direct Labor Usage	Learning curve differences Equipment breakdowns Motivation problems Production bottlenecks Improper standard setting

Type	Reason
Direct Labor Price	Different employee mix than anticipated Impact of new wage contracts Different overhead than anticipated Envisioned cost of living adjustments different Improper standard setting

Overhead Variances

In a standard cost system, overhead is applied to production on the basis of standard inputs. Therefore, the overhead follows these inputs as established by predetermined calculations. If, as is usually the case, there are differences, then, variance analysis should be conducted.

Note: See discussion on Activity Based Costing in Chapter 20.

Determining Standard Overhead Rates

There are two predetermined standard rates:

1. Variable Rate $(VOR) = \dfrac{\text{Predetermined Variable Overhead}}{\text{Normal Operating Activity}}$
2. Fixed Overhead $(FOR) = \dfrac{\text{Predetermined Fixed Overhead}}{\text{Normal Operating Activity}}$
3. Standard Overhead $(SOR) = VOR + FOR$

The Three Overhead Variances

Type	Responsibility	Information Disclosed
Spending	Department manager	Ability to keep controllable expenses within budgetary limitations
Efficiency	Department manager	Inefficiencies, labor problems, operational changes, new technology, new materials
Idle Capacity	Executive management	Under utilized capacity

Computing Overhead Variances

1. *Spending*

   Actual Factory Overhead − (*VOR* * Actual Hours) − Budgeted Fixed Costs

2. *Efficiency*

   Actual Hours * *SOR* − Standard Hours * *SOR*

3. *Idle Capacity*

   Normal Capacity Hours * *FOR* − Actual Hours * *FOR*

Standard Costs Illustrated

The Beth Corporation has developed the following standard costs for the month of May, 1990:

Standard Unit Cost

	Quantity	Unit	@	Total
Direct Materials	4	lbs	$3	$12
Direct Labor	2	hrs	9	18
Variable OH	2	hrs	2	4
Fixed OH	2	hrs	5	10
				$44
Budgeted Fixed Factory Overhead				$120,000
Budgeted Activity Level				
Fixed OH per Hour				$5
Budgeted Hours				24,000

At the conclusion of the period, the actual data was accumulated and the following results were noted:

	Quantity	Unit	@	Total
Production	10,000	unit		
Direct Material	50,000	pound	2.98	149,000
Materials Used	41,500	pound		
Direct Labor	21,000	hours	9.36	196,560
Factory Overhead				
Variable				41,000
Fixed				117,000

Variances

I. Material

		Quantity	Unit	@	Total
Total					
Actual		41,500	pound	$2.98	$123,670
Standard					
Units	10,000				
@	4	40,000		3.00	120,000
Total Variance		1,500		−0.02	$ 3,670

Usage

Variance in Pounds	1,500	
Standard Cost	$3.00	
Unfavorable		$ 4,500

The Company used more materials than estimated and a negative variance results.

Price

Variance in Price	$−0.02	
Actual Pounds	41,500	
Favorable		(830)
		$ 3,670

However, a .$.02 per pound price reduction yields a favorable price variance.

II. Labor

		Quantity	Unit	@	Total
Actual		21,000	hours	$9.36	$196,560
Standard					
Standard					
Units	10,000				
	2	20,000	hours	9.00	180,000
Variance		1,000		$0.36	$ 16,500

II. Labor

	Quantity	Unit	@	Total
Usage Variance				
Variance in Hours			1,000	
Standard Cost			9.00	
Unfavorable				$9,000

Actual hours needed to produce the product exceeded standards. And, consequently, a negative variance resulted.

Price Variance				
Variance in Price		0.36		
Actual Hours		21,000		
Unfavorable				7,560
				16,560

In addition, per hour labor rates were greater which results in a negative price variance.

III. Overhead

	Quantity	Unit	@	Total
Actual				
Variable				$ 41,000
Fixed				117,000
				158,000
Standard				
To Production	20,000		7.00	140,000
Total Variance (Unfavorable)				18,000

Spending Variance				
Actual Overhead			$158,000	
Fixed Overhead Budgeted		120,000		
Variable Overhead				
Actual Hours	21,000			
Variable OH Rate	2.00	42,000	162,000	
Variance (Favorable)				(4,000)

The company spent more than the budgeted fixed expenses and the standard cost for the actual labor hours worked resulting in a negative spending variance.

Efficiency Variance

Actual Hours	21,000		
Standard OH Rate	$7.00	$147,000	
Overhead Charged to Production			
Units	10,000		
Hours per Unit	2		
Rate per Hour	$7.00	140,000	
Variance (Unfavorable)			7,000

More hours were required to produce the units than estimated resulting in a negative efficiency variance.

Idle Capacity Variance

Normal Capacity			
Hours	24,000		
Fixed Overhead Rate	5.00	120,000	
Actual Usage			
Hours	21,000		
Fixed Overhead Rate	5.00		
Actual Usage		105,000	15,000
Total (Unfavorable)			$18,000

Beth's overhead structure is based on a capacity of 24,000 hours. However, only 21,000 hours were actually employed. The unused time results in an unfavorable variance.

Variance Analysis Summary

		Materials	**Labor**	**Over-head**
Actual		$123,670	$196,560	$158,000
Standard		120,000	180,000	140,000
Variance	$38,230	$ 3,670	$ 16,560	$ 18,000

	Materials	Labor	Over-head
Usage	$ 4,500	$ 9,000	
Price	(830)	7,560	
Spending			(5,000)
Efficiency			7,000
Idle Capacity			15,000
Total Variances	$ 3,670	$ 16,560	$ 18,000

Recording Standard Cost Entries

There are three phases of bookkeeping under a standard cost system:

1. The costs are recorded as they are incurred at their actual amounts.
2. Production is charged at standard usage and costs.
3. Variances are recorded.

From above example:

	Debit	Credit
RECORDING COSTS		
Raw Materials Inventory	149,000	
Accounts Payable		149,000
To record purchase of 50,000 pounds of raw material @ $2.98 per pound		
Direct Labor	196,560	
Cash/Accrued Expenses		196,560
To record actual direct labor in month, 21,000 hours @ 9.36		
Manufacturing Overhead	158,000	
Cash/Accounts Payable		158,000
To record actual manufacturing costs		
CHARGING TO PRODUCTION		
Work in Process	440,000	
Raw Materials Inventory		120,000
Direct Labor		180,000
Manufacturing Overhead		140,000

(Continued on next page)

	Debit	Credit
RECORDING VARIANCES		
Materials Price Variance	4,500	
Materials Usage Variance		830
Direct Labor Price Variance	9,000	
Direct Labor Usage Variance	7,560	
Overhead Spending Variance		4,000
Overhead Efficiency Variance	7,000	
Idle Capacity Variance	15,000	
Work In Process		38,230
To Charge Variances to operations as per following schedule		

Alternative

Some companies prefer to record variances as a function of purchasing. If Beth had elected that treatment, the following variance would have resulted.

Purchase at Actual		$149,000
Purchase at Standard		
Pounds	50,000	
Price per Pound	$3.00	
Total at Standard		150,000
Favorable Variance		$ (1,000)

CHAPTER 22

How to Use Cost Accounting to Evaluate Performance

Introduction

The modern corporation is too complicated to be effectively run by just one person. It makes more sense to divide and decentralize the management tasks among departments and divisions. To properly gauge the various managers' performances, a system has to be installed that will

1. Define the area of responsibility
2. Accumulate the pertinent items into that area
3. Set performance standards

Chapter 22 provides evaluation methods by addressing the following issues:

- Responsibility accounting
- ROI
- Cost of capital
- Transfer pricing

How to Establish an Appraisal System

In order to evaluate performance, standards should be established against which the applicable persons' work will be judged. To do this, it is imperative that all managers of the corporation, from the most senior to the most junior be involved in the process.

The Mission Statement

Every business has a basic function or task assigned to it by society. The statement's purpose is to answer these questions:

What is our business?

What should it be?

Who are we?

Who are our customers?

What do they want from us?

Planning Steps

1. *Become aware of opportunities.* Take a preliminary look at future possible opportunities and your firm's ability to perceive them clearly and completely.
2. *Study the environment.* Try to understand the internal and external environment. It underlies and affects the entire planning process.
3. *Determine alternative courses.* What you want to do here is to not only uncover but find the most promising alternatives.
4. *Evaluate alternative courses.* Decision theory and operations research are effective methods.
5. *Select a course of action.*
6. *Formulate derivative plans.* These are subtasks that should support your major plan.
7. *Numberize plans by preparing budgets.* The budgeting process will be covered in detail in the Managerial Accounting Section of this book. The budgets derived may take several forms:

By Time	By Type	By Financial Statement
Short term	Static budget	Income statement
Intermediate term	Variable budget	Balance sheet
Long term	Capital investment budget	Cash flows

How to Recognize and Use Responsibility Centers

A responsibility center is used to gather and report elements of income, expense, assets, and liabilities that are within the control of designated management. A major task of a firm's organization is to determine the scheme of departmentation or decentralization that will best fulfill its goals and strategies. Common forms of decentralization are:

- By function
- By product
- By area
- By customer

There are many benefits to effective decentralization of management which include:

- Faster response to problems and opportunities
- Better use of executives' time
- Reduction of problems to manageable size
- Improved training opportunities for new supervisors.

In spite of these benefits, thoughtless division may be very harmful because many managers may try to maximize their performance at the expense of the organization.

Classification of Responsibility Centers

Type	**When Used**	**Responsibility/ Measurement**
Standard Cost	When there is a well defined and measurable inputs and outputs	Efficient uses of resources (See Standard Costing)
Revenue	Marketing activities	*Alternatives:* Gross Revenues: if selling prices can be set in department. Physical volume: if prices can not be set in department
Discretionary	Non measurable outputs produced. e.g. general and administrative control, research and development	Compare to other companies, prior performance, and to budget.

(Continued on next page)

Type	When Used	Responsibility/ Measurement
Profit	Product lines, and other forms of limited decentralization	Net income
Investment	Subsidiary, division	Responsible for profit, working capital, physical assets. ROI computation commonly used.

How to Set Up Responsibility Accounting Systems

Any accounting reports used to measure managers' effectiveness should be based only upon the revenues and costs within their control. As the following diagram illustrates, the scope of controllable costs decline as the administrator's distance from the top increases:

A. CEO

B. Division Manager

C. Line Manager

D. Department Manager

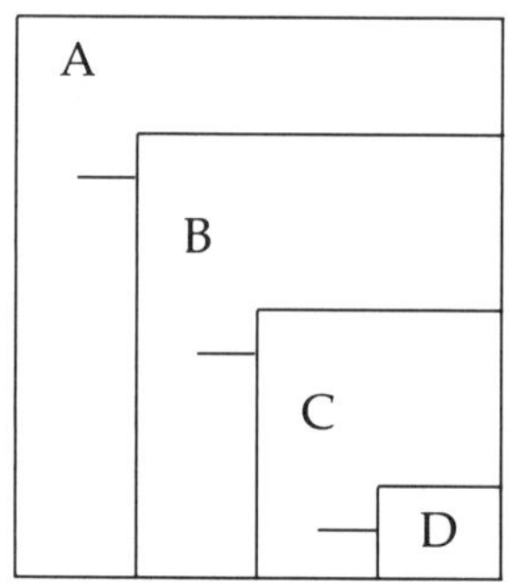

Purposes of Responsibility Accounting System

1. To communicate what is expected of manager.
2. To provide data to managers to allow them to know if any corrective actions are required.
3. To provide information useful for evaluation.

Responsibility Accounting Set Up Procedures

1. Define manager's function and scope of responsibility.
2. Make sure that the executive that will be judged is given an opportunity to participate in the process.

3. Prepare a list of assets, revenues, and expenses controllable at the particular manager's level.
4. Establish a budget as a control device to spot deviations.
5. Prepare statements that exclude any items that do not fall within that particular manager's control.

Example of Responsibility Reporting

The following is a typical departmental income statement:

	Budgeted	**Actual**	**Within Department Control**
Variable Costs			
Materials	$405,000	$437,549	$338,040
Labor	180,000	184,354	149,805
Fixed Costs			
Depreciation	5,000	5,000	
Insurance	1,250	1,343	
Rent	4,500	4,500	
Repairs/Maintenance	750	987	987
Share of General and Administrative	2,500	2,500	
Supervision & Indirect Labor	10,000	11,243	11,243
Supplies	2,000	1,946	1,946
Utilities	1,200	1,347	1,347
	$612,200	$650,769	$503,368

Variable Cost Standards

	Budgeted Units	**@**	**Actual Usage**
Materials	4,500	90	3,756
Labor	12,000	15	9,987

As we know, there are two variable cost components:

The number of units

The rate per unit

Note: In a producing department like this, the ability of the manager to affect the rates per unit (e.g. prices of materials, or labor rates) is limited.

Although variable costs exceeded budget, department management actually kept the usage of these items down. This is portrayed in column 3.

Also, executives at this level should not be held responsible for all fixed costs, including, of course, rent and share of corporate general and administrative expenses. Therefore, they are only charged with fixed costs that they can control.

Using ROI to Judge Performance

Return on Investment (ROI) is a common measurement of short-term performance of an investment center. Since it is frequently used, its value lies in its ability to judge management's performance as compared to:

1. Other periods
2. Other divisions of the firm
3. Other companies

Alternative Measurements

On Net Book Value:

$$ROI = \frac{\text{Net Income}}{\text{Average Assets}}$$

This is the conventional ROI measurement technique. It is used in practice because it is easy to apply.

However, the denominator used is the net book value of the assets, which, of course, declines over time. Thus, all else being equal, the ROI would be expected to increase each subsequent year. *For example:*

Net Annual Income	10,000
Asset Cost	100,000
Depreciation per Year	20,000

Year	Average Assets	Net Income	ROI
1	90,000	10,000	11.11%
2	80,000	10,000	12.50%
3	70,000	10,000	14.29%

ROI should not increase merely because assets get older.

Proponents of this method argue that the reduction in net book value is usually matched by increases in repairs and maintenance costs that are associated with that asset.

On Original Cost:

$$\frac{\text{Operating Income before Depreciation}}{\text{Average Total Assets at Original Cost}}$$

There are a number of arguments in favor of using original cost. These are:

- Assets are acquired for long term use.
- The gross assets "figure" is a better comparison to other companies.

Example:

Devonport Corporation
Comparative Balance Sheets
December 31

	1984	1985	1986
Assets			
Current Assets			
Cash	$220,505	$193,811	$ 60,853
Accounts Receivable	170,578	194,555	249,675
Inventories	95,645	96,081	91,277
Total Current Assets	486,728	484,447	401,805
Property and Equipment			
Cost	185,444	235,444	285,444
Accumulated Depreciation	40,798	58,861	78,497
Net Book Value	144,646	176,583	206,947
Total Assets	$631,374	$661,030	$608,752
Liabilities & Equity			
Current Liabilities			

(Continued on next page)

Devonport Corporation
Comparative Balance Sheets

December 31	1984	1985	1986
Accounts Payable	$374,345	$395,789	$363,333
Income Taxes Payable	13,592	42,631	6,952
Total Current Liabilities	387,937	438,420	370,285
Long-Term Notes Payable	150,000	50,000	45,000
Total Liabilities	537,937	488,420	415,285
Equity			
Common Stock (5,000 shares)	50,000	50,000	50,000
Retained Earnings	43,437	122,610	143,467
Total Equity	93,437	172,610	193,467
	$631,374	$661,030	$608,752

Devonport Corporation
Comparative Statements of Income

	1984	1985	1986
Sales	$1,500,918	$1,538,441	$1,125,689
Cost of Goods Sold	780,477	661,530	281,423
Gross Profit	720,441	876,911	844,266
Operating Expenses			
Selling	225,092	295,766	375,069
General & Administrative	452,370	455,066	437,563
Total Operating Expenses	677,462	750,832	812,632
Operating Income	42,979	126,079	31,634
Interest Expense	9,000	4,275	3,825
Pre Tax Income	33,979	121,804	27,809
Provision for Income Taxes	13,592	42,631	6,952
Net Income	$ 20,387	$ 79,173	$ 20,857

On Net Book Value:

$$\text{ROI} = \frac{\text{Net Income}}{\text{Average Assets}}$$

	Beginning Assets	Ending Assets	Average Assets	Net Income	ROI
1985	631,374	661,030	646,202	79,173	12.25%
1986	661,030	608,752	634,891	20,857	3.29%

On Original Cost:

$$\frac{\text{Operating Income before Depreciation}}{\text{Average Total Assets at Original Cost}}$$

	Beginning Assets	Ending Assets	Average Assets	Operating Income	ROI
1985	631,374	661,030	646,202	126,079	
Depreciation	40,798	58,861	49,829	18,063	
			696,031	144,142	20.71%
1986	661,030	608,752	634,891	31,634	
Depreciation	58,861	78,497	68,679	19,636	
			703,570	51,270	7.29%

On Net Income:

	Beginning Assets	Ending Assets	Average Assets	Net Income	ROI
1985	631,374	661,030	646,202	79,173	
Depreciation	40,798	58,861	49,829	18,063	
			696,031	97,236	13.97%
1986	661,030	608,752	634,891	20,857	
Depreciation	58,861	78,497	68,679	19,636	
			703,570	40,493	5.76%

How to Calculate Cost of Capital in Order to Find the Minimum Desired Rate of Return

How to Find the Minimum ROI

Like so many ratios, ROI should not be used in a vacuum. Instead, additional data can be helpful. The *Incremental* rate of return shows whether the company is obtaining a ROI sufficient to cover its cost of capital, and would be calculated as follows:

$$\text{Incremental ROI} = \text{ROI} - \text{Cost of Capital}$$

Cost of Capital Defined

The minimum rate of return that a project must earn in order to avoid diluting the market value of the company.

It is computed as the weighted average of the funds used to capitalize the firm which inculde:

- Bonds payable
- Common stock
- Preferred stock
- Retained earnings

Steps

1. *Determine the cost of capital on interest bearing debt:*

$$k_d = (\text{Interest paid/average debt balance}) * (1 - \text{tax rate})$$

2. *Determine cost of capital on preferred stock:*

$$k_d = \frac{\text{Dividends}}{\text{Proceeds from preferred stock}}$$

3. *Determine cost of capital on common stock:*

$$k_e = \left(\frac{\text{Dividends}}{\text{Proceeds from common stock} + \text{retained earnings}}\right) * (1 + g)$$

Note: g = anticipated growth rate

4. *Calculate the capital weighting.*
5. *Compute the weighted average cost of capital.*
6. *Establish the incremental rate of return.*

Example:

The Morris Company has the following structure:

	Beginning	Ending	Average
Debt	100,000	200,000	150,000
Equity			
Preferred Stock	50,000	50,000	50,000
Common Stock	100,000	100,000	100,000

	Beginning	Ending	Average
Excess Paid in Capital on Common Stock	250,000	250,000	250,000
Retained Earnings	50,000	75,000	62,500

Tax Rate	40%
Interest Paid	$12,000
Preferred Dividend Rate	8%
Common Dividends Paid	$50,000
Dividend Growth Rate	10%

1. *Cost of Debt*

After Tax Interest Cost

Total Interest	$12,000
Tax Rate	40%
	$ 7,200

Cost of Debt $\frac{\text{After Tax Interest}}{\text{Average Debt}} = \frac{7{,}200}{150{,}000} = 4.80\%$

2. *Cost of Preferred* = 8%

3. *Cost of Common Equity*

Average

Common Stock	100,000
Excess Paid in Capital	250,000
Retained Earnings	62,500
Total	412,500

Cost of Common Equity $\frac{50{,}000}{412{,}500} = 12.12\%$

Growth Rate 10.00%

Common Rate (12.12% * 1.10) 13.33%

4. *Cost of Capital Weighting*

	Amount	% of Total	Rate	% * Rate
Debt	150,000	24.49%	4.80%	1.18%

(*Continued on next page*)

	Amount	% of Total	Rate	% * Rate
Preferred Stock	50,000	8.16%	8.00%	0.65%
Common Equity	412,500	67.35%	13.33%	8.98%
Total	612,500	100.00%		

5. *Cost of Capital* 10.81%

6. *Establish the Incremental Rate of Return*

This equals

$$\text{Incremental ROR} = \text{ROI} - \text{Cost of Capital}$$

For 1986, the incremental rates would be:

	ROI	Cost of Capital	Incremental Rate
On Net Assets	12.25%	10.81%	1.44%
On Gross Assets	13.97%	10.81%	3.16%

How to Avoid Being Taken in by ROI Computations

While the ROI computation is a widely utilized measurement tool, there are certain inherent dangers:

1. It emphasizes short term decision making at the expense of long run goals.

Example:

A manager is judged on this year's results. If the ROI is good, he or she gets a bonus, more status, and lots of perks. The preliminary numbers are shown below:

Net Income	$30,000
Net Assets	$200,000
ROI	15.00%

The manager is pondering two separate courses of action:

A. Improve future production efficiency by purchasing $50,000 of equipment.

B. Fix the present facilities which are seriously in need of repair. The estimated cost is $10,000.

The following analyses show that either of these expenditures will decrease the ROI.

Net Income	$ 30,000	$ 30,000
Repairs		10,000
Adjusted net income	30,000	20,000
Net Assets	$200,000	$200,000
Additional Equipment	50,000	
Total	$250,000	$200,000
ROI	12.00%	10.00%

If the manager's performance is judged solely on ROI, will the needed improvements be made?

2. It can create situations where the department or divisions goals aren't congruent with those of the organization. This quandary is often seen in transfer pricing situations.

How to Compute the Best Transfer Price

A transfer price is defined as the value used for internal reporting purposes which is assigned to goods moving from one part of a company to another. There are many factors that should be considered in setting the amount. But the aim is the following:

- To establish divisional autonomy
- While, at the same time, to encourage managers to take actions consistent with company goals.

There are four general prices that are commonly used:

- Market prices
- Cost
- Negotiated prices between division
- Central intervention by top management

Conditions and Pricing Alternatives

Conditions	**Alternative**
Perfectly competitive market	Market price – (selling, distribution and collection expenses)

Conditions	**Alternative**
Outside market not perfectly competitive	Negotiated transfer pricing
No external market	Incremental cost of production or increment cost + fixed fee to recover fixed costs
No outside market price and capacity constraints	Central intervention

CHAPTER 23

Using Accounting to Make Decisions

Introduction

This chapter presents an overview of the various ways accounting data is used to make decisions. It will cover the following:

- The scientific method of problem solving
- Operations research practices
- Differential cost analysis
- Decision making under conditions of uncertainty

Financial Accounting Versus Managerial Accounting

The following table will show the uses of and the differences between these two.

	Financial Accounting	**Managerial Accounting**
Data Generating methods	In accordance with GAAP	According to managers' needs
Time frame	Historical	Historical and future
Accounting concepts used	Accrual	Accrual and cash
Time frame for recording data	Predetermined intervals	As needed
Impact on employee behavior	Not important	Very important

How to Use the Scientific Method to Solve Problems

As managers, our days are filled with a variety of problems and opportunities, some of which may be very complicated. And, at any time, they may seem to us to be unsolvable. The ensuing road map is a way to look at most of the perplexities and unravel them into a meaningful, effective plan of attack:

1. Define the problem or opportunity
2. Determine which alternative solutions exist
3. Eliminate alternatives
4. Quantify possible results
5. Consider qualitative factors
6. Make a decision:
7. Get feedback, and make changes as necessary

1. *Define the Problem or Opportunity*

The first step to solving any problem or exploiting any opportunity is to recognize that it exists. Unfortunately, we spend a good part of our day putting out fires. And, because of this, we never take the time to explain or understand their root causes. Instead, we go on to the next crisis. As managers we must heighten our sense of our environment, and keep our antenna out for various stimuli that tell us of impending problems and opportunities.

How do we do that? The following quick problem and opportunity recognition guide will show you how:

- Keep lines of communication open with others in your organization.
- Form a support group with others who have similar businesses and problems. Often, the professional societies are a good place to start.
- Make sure the company's accounting system is performing as it should. It should be able to warn you about situations before they become too critical.
- Try to schedule quiet time for yourself. The office is not the place. Get away to a park, to the beach, somewhere close, where you can gather your thoughts and plan appropriate actions.
- Once a year, conduct a long-range planing session with your partners, managers, and other key employees. Try to discuss

where your organization should be in the future and how it plans to get there.

2. *Determine Which Alternative Solutions Exist*

There are answers to every problem and opportunity. Sometimes, quite a number of them. The trick is to find the one that works best.

List all the alternatives no matter how silly they may seem. Don't leave any out. Later, you can narrow down your list.

Suggestion: Use brainstorming.

Brainstorming has been found to be an excellent way to see beyond the status quo and find alternative ways to solve difficult problems. The typical brainstorming session gathers a number of people (about 4 to 8) who want to solve a problem. They are cloistered away in a setting that will encourage them to let their thoughts roll. Some rules are necessary:

1. Nothing is out of bounds. No idea, no matter how foolish it may seem, should be suppressed.
2. The purpose is to generate ideas, not to evaluate them.
3. Have someone list the ideas as they occur.
4. Limit the session to 15 to 20 minutes.

Note: It is important to keep an open mind. Some of these alternatives could affect your job or your position with the client.

3. *Eliminate Alternatives*

At this point you should be able to work through the list that has been generated and reduce it down to a few choices. This cannot be done all at once. You will have to make some preliminary decisions. Use the following as initial guides:

- If something is a significant departure, it may have a more profound influence than you might want.
- Think about the repercussion on the company's well being, its profits, and its resources. This is a preliminary review. You will do analysis by quantification later.

Try to pick three possible options.

For example, we are considering a new product line. It will require capital expenditures. Three options are:

- Buy the equipment

- Lease the equipment
- Abandon the idea

4. *Quantify Possible Results*

By using a combination of operations research, differential evaluation, and other managerial accounting techniques, the expected hard-dollar costs or benefits of each choice can be understood.

The time frame should also be reviewed:

- When will it be started?
- How long will it take?

5. *Consider Qualitative Factors*

Accountants have a tendency to try to reduce everything to its dollars and cents, or its bottom line. By relying solely on these criteria, we tend to short change the analytical process. There are many determinants that just do not lend themselves to a quantification process.

Example: A new process is projected to yield a substantial cost savings. However, its implementation will require major changes in the work routines. The company's employees have always done their jobs in a certain way. The proposed modification might seriously harm morale.

A listing of non-quantifiable consequences:

- Reduced employee morale
- Harm to company's image
- Adverse social results
- Government action

6. *Make a Decision*

The combination or quantitative and qualitative factors discussed above will point to the perceived best course. But, when it's all said and done, it's the manager who must make the decision. And, that resolution is dependent upon his/her judgment, which is affected by experience, and temperament.

7. *Get Feedback and Make Changes as Necessary*

No decision, once made, should be etched in stone. Conditions change and some of these new circumstances will reveal that

- Some ingredients of the proposed course of action need to be changed.
- The entire plan is wrong.

It is important to build an accounting system that will provide quick feedback when activities are not proceeding according to plan. You have to be able to realize this soon enough to be able to make meaningful changes.

Furthermore, and most important, do not tie your ego into its success. It may not be right. It is better to recognize that fact and go on to something else.

How to Use Operations Research

Operations research (OR) is that body of knowledge which uses quantitative approaches to decision making. While there is math involved, many of the techniques are available through off-the-shelf computer programs.

The OR process flows as follows:

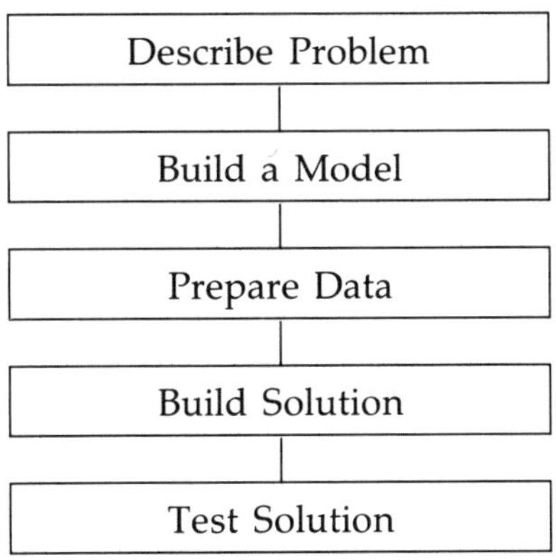

1. *Problem Definition*

The general problem description should be translated into a well-defined paradigm which can be approached mathematically.

2. *Build a Model*

The model will depict a managerial situation by mathematical symbols and expressions.

For Example:

Profits could be represented by

$$P = S - E$$

Where P = profits
S = sales
E = expenses

3. *Prepare Data*

Define the inputs that will be needed to arrive at a solution.

For Example:

The determination of profit will need the following inputs: Sales price per units, number of units, variable costs per unit, fixed costs.

4. *Build Solution*

Attempt to define the values in the decision variable which provides the best or optimal solution.

5. *Test Solution*

Before the solution model is accepted it must be tested by running previous data on the algorithm derived to determine if the results match or are within an acceptable range of previous experience.

OR Models

There are two major classifications:

Type	**Description**	**Uses**
Deterministic	All uncontrollable outputs are known	Linear programming Inventory control
Probabalistic (Stochastic)	Uncontrollable input is uncertain and subject to variation	–Statistical analysis –Regression –Decision trees –Simulation

Differential Cost Analysis

Differential costs are those expenditures that change in response to alternative courses of action.

For Example: If a company is deciding if it wants to manufacture a new product, any costs that may change as a result of that decision are differential. These could include direct labor, materials, and variable overhead. However, it could also contain additional rent if greater capacity is needed.

While the accounting process is all inclusive, certain items should be excluded from the analysis:

- Those that will be the same regardless of whichever alternative is chosen.
- Past costs, also known as sunk costs.

Using Cash Flows

While cash flows and accrual-based income are the same over the life of an enterprise, the cash generated by the various choices is more important. A company cannot spend accrual based income.

The Effect of Depreciation

Various depreciation methods will affect the company's income tax liability and cash flow. Therefore, it should be considered to that extent.

Illustration

The Janice Company manufactures one product, Brand X which uses a sub-assembly, SA. It presently uses 5,000 SAs which are manufactured, along with other parts, in its assembly department. The portion of costs required to manufacture SA are shown in a separate column. These are the costs that will be affected by the decision.

Assembly Department Costs	**Total**	**SA**
Materials	$ 67,500	17,500
Direct Labor	50,000	28,000
Indirect Labor	20,000	6,000
Utilities	8,800	300
Depreciation	10,000	
Property taxes & Insurance	8,000	
Payroll taxes	9,800	
Other	5,000	500
	$179,100	$52,300

If SA is purchased from an outside vendor, the related expenditures are shown below. In addition, certain equipment, now used in the manufacturing process, will be sold at its net book value of $5,000.

Per Unit	
Purchase price	$8.00
Freight	0.50
	$8.50
Fixed Costs	$5,000

The ensuing schedule evaluates the best course of action. This is shown this on pre-tax and after tax bases.

		Pre Tax	After Tax
Costs Avoided if Purchased			
Direct Costs in Assembly		$52,300	
Property taxes & insurance		1,000	
		53,300	53,300
Sale of Equipment		5,000	5,000
Costs of Outside Purchase			
Variable costs		(42,500)	(42,500)
Fixed Costs		(5,000)	(5,000)
Cash Flow		10,800	10,800
Tax Effect			
Cash Flow from Above	$10,800		
Less: Sale of Equipment	(5,000)		
Add: Depreciation Decrease	1,000		
	6,800		
Tax Rate	40.00%		(2,720)
Net Differential Cash Flow		$10,800	$8,080

Where the effect of income taxes is not considered, depreciation will not be an ingredient in the computation.

CHAPTER 24

Forecasting and Budgeting

How to Understand the Overall Forecasting Process

The primary task of management is to plan. That function encompasses the various activities which should be addressed in the following order:

1. Purpose or mission	What is our business
2. Objectives	Where are we going
3. Strategies	How to get there
4. Policies	Guides to action
5. Procedures/Rules	Details or guides
6. Programs	Detailed tasks

Where Does the Profit Plan Fit In?

The profit plan enables these activities to be converted into numbers. The numbers, which are usually presented in financial statement form, will reflect management's aims and help to show whether the organization is moving in the right direction.

Participative Budgeting

It is an obvious fact that people will work better within a organization when they have some say in its operation. Quite often the best data comes from the so called lower level employees who work with the systems and procedures on a day-to-day basis.

What Is the Optimum Forecasting Period?

A management system set up in accordance with the activities chart pictured above, must, by necessity, try to include a multiyear time frame, long enough to see the plans materialize. A forecast, or a numberized business plan, should cover these goals and planned actions over its entire span.

However, it is axiomatic that the farther into the future we try to see, the more cloudy our view becomes. Thus, one budget alone, will not suffice for the entire time horizon. We should, instead, look at this process as comprised of three horizons:

Short Term: one year or less

Intermediate Term: From one through five years

Long Term: Over five years

Preparing the Master Budget

Schematically, the master budget consists of the following:

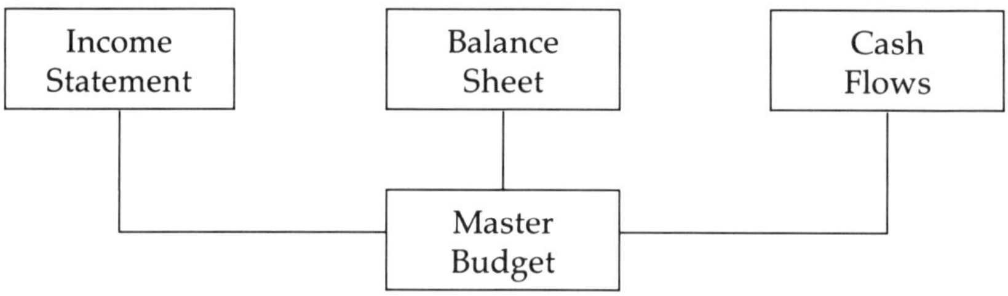

As you can see, the forecasted statements correspond to the package produced by the accounting system. Generally, the same rules of accumulating and reporting information will apply to the budgetary process. However, we use projected rather than historical information.

A Step-by-Step Procedure to Build the Budgets

1. Decide on the time span to be covered.
2. Formulate forecasting assumptions. For example:
   a. rate of inflation
   b. growth percentage
   c. income taxes
   d. money costs

3. Project the Statement of Income
   a. Forecast Sales (See next section)
      1. By units
      2. By dollars
   b. Forecast Units to Produce or Purchase

Production or Purchases	= Ending Inventory + Sales −	Beginning Inventory

Note: Various methods to calculate inventory levels will be covered in Chapter 28.

   c. Estimate future materials cost by equation

Units forecast * Estimated price per Unit

   d. Estimate future labor

Note: Both material and labor amounts may be developed with the same techniques utilized for pricing or bidding.

   e. Use projected sales units and dollars to predict variable selling costs, including commissions, freight out, bad debts.
   f. Use projected materials purchased or usage to figure variable factory overhead expenses.
   g. Estimate fixed costs by referring to prior financial information and modifying it for:

      costs of added capacity
      effects of assumptions
      changes in operations

   h. Approximate financing expenses by examining cash flow requirements.

Note: The discussion at the end of this chapter presents a method to prepare forecasts by using electronic spreadsheets. Interest expense is, of course, a function of borrowing. The techniques presented will help you derive the best mix of financing versus owner investment.

   i. Compute future depreciation on assets on hand and on anticipated acquisitions.

j. Put all of the above into an income statement format.

k. Calculate income taxes by using your best guess of prospective income tax rates.

4. Project cash flows

   a. Convert income statement items to cash flows. The projections should be presented in the same format as on the income statement.

Note: Refer to Statement of Cash Flows discussion in Chapter 3.

Account	**Conversion Procedure**
Collections on sales	Accounts receivable beginning + Sales − Accounts Receivable ending, or Collection Schedule (see below)
Payments for Purchases	Accounts payable beginning + Purchases − Accounts payable ending
Beginning and ending inventories	Already considered in purchase calculations
Depreciation	Not included
Provision for bad debts	Not included
Other expenses	Generally the same as the income statement unless there is a major difference in beginning and ending payables
Provision for income taxes	If company pays estimates on timely basis, income tax payments are .25 * prior year's tax + .75 * current year's tax

Example: How to calculate accounts receivable collections

The Smith Company has the following collection experience:

Month of Sale	60%
One Month After	25%
Two Months After	10%
Three Months After	3%
Total	98%

We apply these percentages to the projected sales for the months March–April, 1990.

Projected Sales	**January** **$60,000**	**February** **$65,000**	**March** **$55,000**	**April** **$90,000**
Collections				
January Sales	36,000	15,000	6,000	1,800
February Sales		39,000	16,250	6,500
March Sales			33,000	13,750
April Sales				54,000
Total	$36,000	$54,000	$55,250	$76,050

Note: This procedure may also be used to schedule payments for purchases and other expenses.

b. Calculate financing and investing cash flows.

5. Prepare Projected Balance Sheets. The following chart is a guide through the components: The general equation is beginning balance + statement of income + cash flow.

Account	**Statement of Income**	**Cash Flow Projection**
Cash		± Net Cash Flow
Accounts Receivable (Net)	Sales − Bad Debts	− Collections
Property & Equipment		+ Acquisitions − Sales
Accumulated Depreciation	+ Current Depreciation	
Other Assets		+ Acquisitions − Sales
Accounts Payable	+ Purchases	− Payments
Accrued Expenses	+ Expenses	− Payments
Notes Payable		+ New Loans − Repayments
Income Taxes Payable	+ Provision	− Payments
Common/Preferred Stock		± Financing Cash Flows
Retained Earnings	+ Net Income	− Dividends

How to Predict Sales

It has often been said, "Nothing happens until somebody sells something." The same is true when you prepare forecasts. And this is where you have to start. This section will provide some tips to project revenues.

Top Down Analysis

As was previously stated in Chapter 16, in order to be able to analyze and understand a particular firm, you have to, first, attempt to perceive the organization in its envirionment. Top down forecasting does just that in the following order:

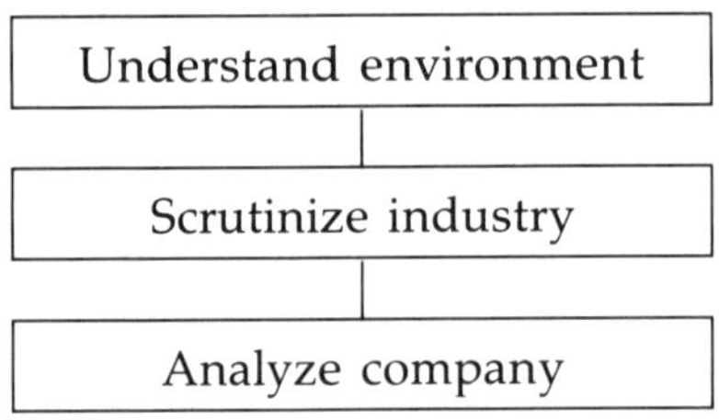

Environmental influences

- Economic conditions
- Political
- Social
- Cultural
- Demographics
- Technological

Industry

- Rate of change
- Expanding or declining
- Capital intensity
- Rate of technological obsolescence

Company

- Management and staff
- Capacity

- Financial strength
- Ability to adapt to change

Forecasting Components—Units, Price

These components are utilized in two ways:

1. *Sales = Forecasted Units * Forecast Per Unit Price*
   The data that follows can be used to project both of these components. The price will be influenced by a combination of various economic factors and the company's specific marketing strategies.
2. *Total Sales*
   Related to techniques discussed below.

Sales Projection Methods

Qualitative:

Product of the opinions and experience of knowledgeable individuals

- *Jury of Executive Opinion.* This technique uses the hunches and guesses of top management. A commonly used method, it is the old "seat of the pants" approach. However, experience, taken by itself, does not always account for all of the pertinent factors and influences. Sometimes it tends to favor emotion over good sound business logic.
- *Sales Force Composite.* When this technique is used, the sales force is convassed for their individual estimates of sales they each expect in the coming period(s). However, as we all know, salespeople have a tendency to "low ball" their estimates in order to look good later on.
- *Customer Canvassing.* Customers are asked to project how much they expect to buy in the next period. Their individual responses are then totaled to provide a comprehensive projected sales picture. There are inherent weaknesses in this approach:
  (1) It will only work when the bulk of the sales are divided between a few large customers, and
  (2) Buyers may submit inflated figures in order to be able to bargain for lower costs.

- *Delphi Technique.* This method has had some scientific validation. It works as follows:
  1. A panel of inside and outside experts are anonymously asked to forecast what they think will happen.
  2. The answers are compiled and the composite results are fed back to the panel members.
  3. The panel members digest this new data and make further estimates. This process may be repeated a number of times.
  4. A consensus is attained.
- *Quantitative Forecasting.* Uses numerical data.

Time Series

When time series anayses are used, observations are taken at successive previous points in time and then extrapolated to the future. Although the data may show random fluctuations, the series may still display some gradual pattern. Based on this pattern, we are able to project future behavior.

It is beyond the scope of this book to fully explain time series. However, there are computer programs that are effective and relatively easy to apply.

Regression Analysis

This technique takes the form

$$Y = A + bx_1 + bx_2 \cdots + bx_n$$

Where Y = the dependent variable – sales
A = the minimum dollar amount
$x_1 \cdots x_n$ = independent variable
b = coefficient or value of independent varible which will influence the actions of the dependent variable

Sample of Independent Variables

- Leading economic indicators
- Rate of inflation
- Industry trends
- GNP
- Disposable personal income
- Population
- Specific industry trends

Note: See discussion on Cost Behavior in Chapter 18.

There Is No One "Best" Method

A combination of qualitative and quantitative techniques is the most effective way to forecast sales. Use the quantitative methods first to arrive at numerical findings. Then utilize management's experience to answer the question: "Do the projections *feel* right?"

How to Use an Electronic Spreadsheet to Prepare Forecasts

The following procedure is used:

• A *shell* is set up. The shell is a series of assumptions which are coupled with financial statement formats. The assumption screen will look like this

ASSUMPTIONS (000's)			
Sales	a.	Gross Profit %	j.
Selling Expenses	b.	Growth Rate	k.
General Administrative	c.	Inflation rate	l.
		Income tax rate	m.
Days		Earnings on Cash	n.
To collect receivables	d.	Dividend Payout	o.
To turn inventories	e.	Amount to Start	p.
To pay bills	f.	Leverage %	q.
Equipment Purchased		Borrowing	r.
Amount	g.	Amount	
Method	h.	Years to Repay	
Life	i	Interest Rate	

Key to Assumptions

a, b, c.–Initial year amounts

d, e. f.–Calculated on turnover ratios. Uses company's experience and policy

g. h, i.–Computes depreciation and cash flow required for equipment purchases

j.–Previous or projected rate

k.—Estimated rate of sales growth

l.–Based on economic data

m.–Use current marginal tax. Program can be modified to utilize tax tables.

n.–Incremental interest rate. Computes income on average excess cash. Will also show interest expense on cash shortage.

o.–Expressed as a percentage of net after tax income

p.–Estimated starting funding needed

q.–Percentage of funding requirements to be supplied by borrowing

r.–Enter interest rate, repayment term. Calculates payments, interest, current and long term balances

• Financial statement formats are prepared which incorporate these assumptions.

• "What if" analyses are performed for a variety of assumptions. Their effects may be presented on one screen:

YEAR	**1**	**2**	**3**
EQUITY			
NET INCOME			
CASH FLOW			
RETURN ON EQUITY			
BALANCE SHEETS			
Assets	$	$	$
Liabilities			
Equity			
	$	$	$
INCOME STATEMENT			
Net Income	$	$	$
STATEMENT OF CASH FLOWS			
Net Cash Flow	$	$	$

• Detailed forecasts are portrayed on succeeding screens.

TABLE OF CONTENTS

ASSUMPTIONS (000's)

Year 1		**Gross Profit %**	40.00%
Sales	$250,000	Growth Rate	10.00%
Selling Expenses	$25,000	Inflation rate	8.00%
General Admin	$50,000	Income tax rate	40.00%
		Earnings on Cash	5.00%
Days		Dividend Payout	25.00%
To collect receivable	45	Amount to Start	$200,000
To turn inventories	60	Leverage %	40.00%
To pay bills	50		
		Borrowing	
Equipment Purchased		Amount	80,000
Amount	$150,000	Years to Repay	15
Life	10	Interest Rate	10.00%

****

YEAR	1	2	3	4	5
EQUITY	$120,949	$124,776	$131,054	$140,161	$152,462
NET INCOME	$1,265	$5,103	$8,370	$12,143	$16,401
CASH FLOW	$42,840	$12,873	$17,534	$20,077	$22,906
RETURN ON EQUITY		1.04%	1.64%	2.24%	2.80%

Year	1	2	3	4	5
	BALANCE SHEETS				
Assets	$234,090	$237,588	$246,309	$258,192	$273,585
Liabilities	$113,141	$112,812	$115,255	$118,032	$121,124
Equity	120,949	124,776	131,054	140,161	152,462
	$234,090	$237,588	$246,309	$258,192	$273,585
	INCOME STATEMENT				
Net Income	$ 1,265	$ 5,103	$ 8,370	$ 12,143	$ 16,401
	STATEMENT OF CASH FLOWS				
Net Cash Flow	$ 42,840	$ 12,873	$ 17,534	$ 20,077	$ 22,906

Year	1	2	3	4	5
	STATEMENT OF INCOME				
Sales	$250,000	$275,000	$302,500	$332,750	$366,025
Cost of Goods Sold	150,000	165,000	181,500	199,650	219,615
Gross Profit	100,000	110,000	121,000	133,100	146,410
Operating Expenses	97,891	103,637	109,836	116,525	123,741
Operating Income	2,109	6,363	11,164	16,575	22,669
Interest on Cash		2,142	2,786	3,663	4,666
Pre-Tax Income	2,109	8,505	13,949	20,238	27,335
Income Taxes	844	3,402	5,580	8,095	10,934
Net Income	$ 1,265	$ 5,103	$ 8,370	$ 12,143	$ 16,401

Year	1	2	3	4	5
COST OF GOODS SOLD					
Beginning Inventory	$ 0	$ 25,000	$ 27,500	$ 30,250	$ 33,275
Purchases	175,000	167,500	184,250	202,675	222,943
Merchandise Avail	175,000	192,500	211,750	232,925	256,218
Ending Inventory	25,000	27,500	30,250	33,275	36,603
Total	$150,000	$165,000	$181,500	$199,650	$219,615
OPERATING EXPENSES					
Selling	$ 25,000	$ 27,000	$ 29,160	$ 31,493	$ 34,012
General and Administrative	50,000	54,000	58,320	62,986	68,024

Year	1	2	3	4	5
Depreciation	15,000	15,000	15,000	15,000	15,000
Interest	7,891	7,637	7,356	7,046	6,705
Total	$ 97,891	$103,637	$109,836	$116,525	$123,741

Year	1	2	3	4	5
Assets					
Current Assets	$ 99,090	$117,588	$141,309	$168,192	$198,585
Property & Equipment	135,000	120,000	105,000	90,000	75,000
	$234,090	$237,588	$246,309	$258,192	$273,585
Liabilities					
Current	$ 38,246	$ 40,877	$ 46,590	$ 52,978	$ 60,060
Other	74,895	71,935	68,666	65,053	61,063
	113,141	112,812	115,255	118,031	121,123
Equity	120,949	124,776	131,054	140,161	152,462
	$234,090	$237,588	$246,309	$258,192	$273,585
Current Assets					
Cash	$ 42,840	$ 55,713	$ 73,247	$ 93,324	$116,229
Accounts Receivable	31,250	34,375	37,812	41,593	45,753
Inventories	25,000	27,500	30,250	33,275	36,603
Total Current	$ 99,090	$117,588	$141,309	$168,192	$198,585
Property & Equipment					
Cost	$150,000	$150,000	$150,000	$150,000	$150,000
Less: Accum Deprec	15,000	30,000	45,000	60,000	75,000
	$135,000	$120,000	$105,000	$ 90,000	$ 75,000
Current Liabilities					
Notes Payable	$ 2,679	$ 2,961	$ 3,270	$ 3,612	$ 3,990
Accounts Payable	34,723	34,514	37,740	41,271	45,136
Income Taxes Payable	844	3,402	5,580	8,095	10,934
	$ 38,246	$ 40,877	$ 46,590	$ 52,978	$ 60,060
Equity					
Contributed	$120,000	$120,000	$120,000	$120,000	$120,000
Retained Earnings	949	4,776	11,054	20,161	32,462
	$120,949	$124,776	$131,054	$140,161	$152,462
Retained Earnings					
Beginning		$ 949	$ 4,776	$ 11,054	$ 20,161
Net Income	1,265	5,103	8,370	12,143	16,401

(*Continued on next page*)

Year	1	2	3	4	5
Less Dividends	(316)	(1,276)	(2,092)	(3,036)	(4,100)
	$ 949	$ 4,776	$ 11,054	$ 20,161	$ 32,462

Year	1	2	3	4	5
STATEMENT OF CASH FLOWS					
Operating Cash Flows	($4,419)	$ 16,828	$ 22,586	$ 26,383	$ 30,618
Investing Cash Flows	(150,000)	0	0	0	0
Financing Cash Flows	197,259	(3,955)	(5,052)	(6,305)	(7,713)
Net Cash Flows	42,840	12,873	17,534	20,077	22,906
Cash, Beginning		42,840	55,713	73,247	93,324
Cash, Ending	$ 42,840	$ 55,713	$ 73,247	$ 93,324	$116,229

Year	1	2	3	4	5
OPERATING CASH FLOWS					
Net Income	$ 1,265	$ 5,103	$ 8,370	$ 12,143	$ 16,401
Add back: Deprec	15,000	15,000	15,000	15,000	15,000
Changes in:					
Accounts Receivable	(31,250)	(3,125)	(3,438)	(3,781)	(4,159)
Inventories	(25,000)	(2,500)	(2,750)	(3,025)	(3,328)
Accounts Payable	34,722	(208)	3,226	3,531	3,865
Income Taxes Payable	844	2,558	2,178	2,515	2,839
Total	($4,419)	$ 16,828	$ 22,586	$ 26,383	$ 30,618

Year	1	2	3	4	5
INVESTING CASH FLOWS					
Purchases of Equip	($150,000)	$ 0	$ 0	$ 0	$ 0
Total	(150,000)	0	0	0	0
FINANCING CASH FLOWS					
Borrowing (Repay)	$ 77,575	($2,679)	($2,960)	($3,271)	($3,613)
Sales of Corp Stock	120,000	0	0	0	0
Dividends Paid	(316)	(1,276)	(2,092)	(3,036)	(4,100)
	$197,259	($3,955)	($5,052)	($6,305)	($7,713)

CHAPTER 25

How to Prepare Your Client's Business Plans

Introduction

This chapter will cover the following:

- What business plans are and why they are written
- What a business plan contains
- The art and science of planning
- The business planning team
- Ingredients of business plans
- Using the business plan
- How to get paid for your services

What Is a Business Plan?

A business plan is an in-depth analysis of an enterprise. As such, it is a road map of the activities needed for success. As we will discuss in the next section, the primary role of management is to PLAN. Therefore, its major aim is to reduce management's goals and aspirations to writing.

As your client's business grows, the plan will help it coordinate the tasks and marshall the resources that will be needed to reach these goals.

- *What should it do?*
  It should define your client's reason to be by answering the five W's:
- *Who are we?*
- *What*
  is our purpose?
  are our products and/or services?

markets are we going to penetrate?
profit margins do we expect to achieve?

- *Why* are we in business?
- *Where* will we operate/sell? locally?, regionally?, nationally?
- *When* will we start?, introduce a new product?, expand?

What Does It Contain?

1. *Description of the Business:* This may be the most difficult segment to prepare. Because, it forces your client to focus on the basic reasons for going into business. All too often, major mistakes could have been avoided, if the *real* purpose or mission was clearly defined in the beginning.
2. *The Market Plan:* If the growing business is to be successful, its management must understand its environment, its product and its competition. The marketing plan will use these factors to forecast demand and total revenues.
3. *The Production and Facilities Plan:* Its function is to analyze the firm's capacity and its ability to service its present and prospective customers in the most efficient manner.
4. *The Financial Plan:* This portion consists of the company's prior and forecasted financial information.
5. *The Organization and Personnel Plan:* Contains descriptions of the firm's management and personnel, lines of authority, and headcounts.

The Art and Science of Planning

The climate of many small and growing businesses is characterized by chaos as their management scurries to put out fires. Planning, if done at all, is concerned with getting through the latest crisis.

Suggestion: In order to plan successfully, management must try to distance itself from the ongoing crises, and, wholeheartedly commit itself. Many companies conduct long-term planning sessions off premises.

The planning process should include:

1. An examination of the objectives management wants to accomplish

2. The actions that must be taken in order to fulfill those objectives
3. Who is responsible. While top management has the primary responsibility for planning, it is something that should involve everyone.

Planning to Plan—Steps:

1. Search for opportunities
2. Set objectives
3. Study the environment
4. List alternative courses of action
5. Evaluate the alternatives
6. Select the best course of action
7. Determine what must be done to get there
8. Quantify plans by budgeting

Note: Make sure you continually remind your client that business planning is a long ongoing procedure over a lengthy time period. Results won't come immediately.

The Business Planning Team

This job takes more than just you and your client. There are other important players.

1. The company's bankers
2. Legal counsel
3. Marketing and research specialists
4. The client's functional management incuding production, marketing, and human resources

Don't forget the rank and file employees.

Your Role as Quarterback

You will certainly do much of the financial work. But, your major function should be to monitor and coordinate the others.

While proper attention to the following topics requires expertise that may be beyond your expertise, as quarterback you should understand the components.

The Marketing Plan

It is important to resolve the marketing issue before anything else is done. This includes the following:

1. Estimating market size
2. Identifying current and prospective customers
3. Selecting target markets
4. Scouting the competition
5. Developing marketing strategy
6. Establishing pricing
7. Building sales projections

The Production and Facilities Plan

The company's goal is to design its operations to simplify and standardize its production processes.

Note: This is not only a manufacturing problem. These questions must be solved whether the firm is a restaurant, retailer or distributor.

There are two components:

- Production management
- Capacity analysis

Components of production management

1. Materials and other resources needed to produce the product
2. Plant layout
3. Product throughput
4. Technology
5. Product mix

Capacity analysis

1. Analyze existing capacity
2. Predict future requirements
3. Identify alternative ways to modify capacity
4. Compute the costs

The Management and Personnel Plan

The company's management and employees are the glue that holds all of the other compounds together. The following should be prepared and analyzed for this portion:

1. The company's organization chart
2. Task descriptions of the jobs of chief executive officer, heads of marketing and production, chief financial officer or controller, and other key managers.
3. Headcount by major categories
4. Provisions for training
5. Provisions for expanding

The Financial Plan

This portion should, of course, put all the other segments into financial statement format. While we are usually concerned about GAAP, we must think, first, of the client's needs even though certain *internal* information may not conform.

Warning: Make sure that you protect yourself by following the full disclosure rules and drafting the necessary disclaimers.

Historical Financial Information

1. Comparative statements of income and retained earnings
2. Comparative balance sheets
3. Comparative statements of cash flows
4. Ratio analyses

Prospective Financial Information

1. Forecasted statements of income
2. Forecasted or pro forma balance sheets
3. Forecasts of cash flow
4. Projected ratio analyses
5. Projected uses of proceeds of loans or securities sales

Comparative statements should utilize a time horizon long enough to allow the reader to see developing trends and the resolution of various plans and strategies.

Putting It All Together

First and Foremost—Consider the Reader

Whether the users are inside management, creditors, or investors, their time is probably limited. Therefore, you want to provide them a broad overview. The following information should be prominently displayed.

1. *Characteristics of the company and its industry*
   - What the firm does
   - How it fits into its industry
   - Industry trends
2. *Latest balance sheet, income statement, statement of cash flows, and financial summary*
3. *What is different?*
   - What is unique about company, its product, its management?
   - What are its goals?
   - What does it need to do to accomplish these goals?

How to Use the Business Plan

The Internal Users Are the Most Important

To a growing enterprise, a business plan is essential whether or not financing is needed. The plan should be the keystone the company will use to control its business and operations.

It is valuable to the internal users because:

1. It puts the firm's goals and aspirations into written form.
2. It will be the pivotal document to monitor the organization's progress towards these goals.

Control Procedures

1. Establishment of standards
2. Performance measurement
3. Correction of deviations

Opportunity

You can help your client monitor performance by establishing operational audit procedures. If the company cannot afford to do the work in-house, you should be ready to install programs that will periodically review its operations.

External Uses

The external users are looking for reasons to loan or invest money in the company. The following determinants will affect the choice of options:

- How much is needed?
- How will it be used?
- How will borrowed funds be repaid?
- How strong is the company?
- What are its future capital raising plans?

There is an almost endless variety of financing sources. And, a good plan will point to the most favorable combination.

How to Get Paid for Your Services

A business planning engagement is a very expensive undertaking.

- The needs of management have to be established.
- Information must be gathered including market, production, and personnel forecasts.
- Financial statements have to be prepared.

Finally, everything has to be combined into an integrated, meaningful document.

Before starting out, it's important for you and your client to reach an understanding about the terms of the engagement and what your firm's responsibilities are. And, like anything else you do, make sure you get it in writing. A sample engagement letter is presented in the appendix to this chapter.

If you are preparing this plan for a new, growing client, one who is fighting the cash flow battle, any fee discussion is a ticklish subject at best. If he or she is using crisis management, while, at the same time, trying to expand, expect to have to do some hard selling just to get the client to go along with the while thing in the first place.

The Best Ways to Get Paid

1. Do some preliminary analysis to determine if there will be enough cash flow to cover your fee before you even begin discussions.
2. Make sure a good engagement letter is drawn up.
3. Try to divide the task into small, manageable segments each of which will stand on its own. And, establish estimates of progress charges.
4. Do not start the next segment until your previous billings have been collected.
5. Progress bill and collect. You should bill at least once a month, sometimes more often.
6. Make sure you give value for billings rendered.

Exhibits for Chapter 25

1. Business Plan checklist
2. Sample business plan
3. Business plan engagement letter

Exhibit 1

Business Plan Checklist

Supporting Information

1. Is all financial information included?
   - Comparative financial statements
   - Financial ratios
   - Forecasted income statements
   - Cash flow forecasts
   - Pro forma balance sheets
   - Use of proceeds
2. Is necessary supporting data included?
   - Copyrights
   - Equipment lists
   - Facilities descriptions
   - Leases
   - Organization charts
   - Patents
   - Personnel manuals
   - Product descriptions
   - Resumes

History

1. What date was the organization founded?
2. By Whom?
3. Have there been major changes in the following?
   - Facilities
   - Location
   - Personnel
   - Product lines
4. Graph sales and profit trends

Features:

1. Legal business form
2. Nature of the business
3. Strengths and weaknesses
4. What is unique
5. Why business will be profitable

(Continued on next page)

Exhibit 1 (*Continued*)

Industry

1. Graph the industry trends?
2. How would you characterize the competition?
3. What is the overall economic climate?

The Market Plan

1. Define the firm's products and services
2. What is unique about them?
3. How would you characterize the competition?
4. Who is your target market?
   - Age
   - Occupation
   - culture
5. What proportion of sales will be made to a small number of customers?
6. What percentage of the market does the firm hope to capture?
7. What is the growth potential?
8. How long will it take to penetrate the market?
9. How will the products be distributed?
10. What are the tangible features of the product?
11. What are its intangible features?
12. How is it priced?
13. How will the firm promote its products/services?
14. What are its credit policies?
15. What are its customer service procedures?
16. What makes the firm different from the competition?

The Production and Facilities Plan

1. What are the features of your location?
   - Accessibility
   - Area stabilty
   - Permit and licensing requirements
   - Shipping and receiving accessibility
   - Site and building
   - Traffic patterns
   - Visibility
   - Zoning
2. How many square feet are available at your present location?
   - For manufacturing
   - For sales
   - For offices

- For laboratories and research

3. If the building is leased
   - What is the term of the lease?
   - Are there renewal options?
   - Will the landlord make improvements?
4. Is additional space available if needed?
   - At what cost?
   - When do you think it will be needed?
   - Have you budgeted for costs and disruptions caused by moving?
5. What renovations are needed?
   - When?
   - What will they cost?
6. Describe the company's production procedures
   - Space requirements
   - Equipment used
   - Raw materials
7. What are firms present inventory levels, cost and lead times?

Organization and personnel plan

Provide and describe the following:

- Availability of additional personnel
- Division of work
- Educational and personnel data of key personnel
- Employee benefit programs
- Headcount by category
- Key tasks in organization
- Management and business experience
- Organization chart
- Personnel policies
- Recruiting programs
- Resumes of key personnel
- Training programs

Financing

1. How much is required for the project?
2. How will the funds be raised?
3. Will the financing be from debt or equity?
4. How will the funds be used?
5. How will funds be repaid?
6. What percentage of funding will be generated internally?

Exhibit 2

Sample Business Plan[4]

A BUSINESS PLAN

FOR

PORTAS, INC.

SOUTHERN CALIFORNIA

SUBMITTED TO

THE LAST NATIONAL BANK

Jerry Portend
President
123 Nondescript Street
Anywhere, California
(213) 123-4567

---

[4] Ruben, Jay
How to Increase Your Fees by Preparing Your Client's Business Plans
Premier Publishing Company, 1988

TABLE OF CONTENTS

PORTAS, INC.

HISTORY OF THE COMPANY

The company was formed in 1946 by Joseph Portend when he returned from service in the South Pacific. The original business was a hot dog stand on a busy corner. Sales that first year were $16,542. As the years went by, the stand experienced an increasing demand for its home cooked food until, in 1948, Mr. Portend realized that more space was needed. The present restaurant was completed in 1949 as a 3,800 square foot, free standing structure with seating capacity of approximately 110. Upon completion of the new restaurant, Mr. Portend expanded the menu and extended the hours. Cooks and waitresses were hired.

In 1962, Mr. Portend's son, Jerry, entered the business, as a bus boy. As time went by, he learned (by doing) all elements of the business. He has been an integral part of the restaurant ever since, except for his college years when he attended Cornell University and majored in food service management.

Joseph Portend passed away in 1975, and Jerry Portend took over the restaurant's management.

Since that time, Jerry Portend has gradually upgraded the facilities and the menu.

(Continued on next page)

Exhibit 2 (*Continued*) **PORTAS, INC.**

SUMMARY AND DESCRIPTION OF THE BUSINESS

Portas is a coffee shop located in the downtown region of Los Angeles. It has managed to sell high quality food at low prices for the last 40 years. The company has catered to a loyal following and can, at any one time, serve up to 110 people. Its business hours are from 6:00 AM to 10:30 PM, seven days per week.

Over the past five years, three major franchise operations have opened within a one mile radius of the company. These chains sell hamburgers, fried chicken and Mexican products. Operating statistics have shown that their openings have caused practically no loss in sales to Portas.

Portas displays a unique architecture, which dates back to the '40s and has been featured, for this reason, in local newspapers, on television and in architectural books. Mr. Portend believes this form of architecture can benefit the corporation by taking advantage of the nostalgia market. Therefore, he is planning to change the name of the restaurant to American '40s Canteens and plans to run promotions and advertisements built around that time period. After the new name gains identification, Mr. Portend plans to open another store in an area of similar population and demographics.

The following are key financial data:

	1984	1985	1986
Sales (ooo's)	$1,155	$1,228	$1,277
After Tax Income (ooo's)	89	106	160
Net Income Percentage	8	6	7
Return on Investment	25%	26%	30%
Return on Equity	33%	33%	35%

MARKET PLAN

An in-depth analysis of the food service industry competition structure and market segments in the target area has indicated an existence of an undersatisfied target size to warrant exploitation by Portas, Inc. As noted earlier, the market for nostalgia-related items has been increasing, with special interest in times and events related to World War II. Our analysis indicates that this market is un-tapped by others in this industry.

In assessing the nature of the competition in the target market, two separate views must be taken. The first view would be a consideration of restaurants of similar price and quality in the present general area and anticipated location of the second store. In the present location, there are four similar type restaurants, of which three are franchise operations, in a two-mile radius. Three of these began operations within the last five years. However, based on studies conducted by Portas management, they have had little effect on our firm's business.

We have investigated new locations and have used the criteria that the new locations have the same general population and demographic characteristics as the present locale.

Regarding the nostalgia markets, our studies have indicated that, while there are a number of competitors which have devoted their theme to the '50s, we have found none who have built their concept around the period of World War II.

The proposed market plan envisions a two-phase process:

1. Re-decorate our present location and institute an extensive advertising and public relations program around the WW II theme.

2. After one year, open a second store, which will be built around the same features.

This two-pronged program is based upon data gathered from a market study of competition within this area and several target areas. The data collected, as representative of the volume of other restaurants, does not indicate the total capacity of others, nor does it suggest that Portas will necessarily achieve these volumes.

FACILITIES AND LOCATION PLAN

Present Location

Portas is located in a major suburb of Los Angeles with good major street and freeway access. It has 3,800 square feet of space of which 1,900 square feet comprise the dining area.

The building, built in the '40s, is of frame and stucco construction. The company has undergone a program to gradually upgrade the building and kitchen equipment, booths, wiring and plumbing. Therefore, the repairs and maintenance (which is reflected in the financial data) has run higher than comparable newer restaurants.

The land and building are owned by the corporation. There are no liens.

Proposed Location

The company has been investigating a location in another Los Angeles suburb about 15 miles from the present locale.

In our plan, we have decided to lease land approximately the same size as our current site and build a restaurant based on the WW II theme. We have negotiated with a landowner and will be able to lease the land for $4,000 per month for the first five years. Subsequently, the rent will then be increased to $4,000 per month plus 2% of sales. The lease term will be 99 years. The lease contains an option to buy which we will be able to exercise at the end of five years for $235,000 plus an amount each year equal to the CPI annual increase thereafter.

The design necessary to accommodate our proposed theme will not affect the general building construction but only the interior and superficial effects on the outside. Therefore, if the passage of time indicates the end of this trend, we will be able to redecorate with relative ease.

Financing

The company anticipates borrowing the needed funds at 12% interest to be amortized over 10 years. The financing instrument will be a trust deed on our present facilities.

MANAGEMENT AND PERSONNEL PLAN

Management

The firm is under the management of Mr. Jerry Portend, president of Portas, Inc. Mr. Portend is extremely well qualified to manage this operation since he has, since childhood, worked in the restaurant business and has a bachelors degree from Cornell University in food service management.

Mr. Portend, as principal of the firm, has arranged for professional outside support to assist him during the new market implementation phase and to provide a source of

(Continued on next page)

Exhibit 2 (*Continued*)

continuing advice and counsel. The following have agreed to serve as directors and consultants:

William Brisk, PhD	Mr. Brisk has served as a marketing consultant specializing in food service operation for the last 30 years.
John Dough, CPA	Mr. Dough has been a practicing CPA since 1962. He has specialized in restaurant accounting and finance.
Milton Lend	Mr. Lend is the company's banker and advises the company on financial matters.
Harvey Sue, Attorney at Law	Mr. Sue is a Harvard graduate and is the company's legal advisor.

Personnel

At present, the company has 43 employees working in three shifts as follows:

Waitresses	21
Cooks	6
Busboys	9
Hostesses	3
Bookkeeper	1
Managers	3
	43

Many of these employees have been with the company for over 20 years. Wages are standard for the above classifications. In addition, the company provides health and accident insurance coverage for its employees.

We estimate that projected growth in this location can be serviced with a proportional increase in staffing.

Staff for the new location will be employed in the same mix as above.

PORTAS, INC.
STATEMENTS OF INCOME AND RETAINED EARNINGS

	1984		1985	
SALES	$ 1,115,255	100%	$1,227,957	100%
COST OF SALES				
Food	375,536	34%	395,115	32%
Labor	433,368	39%	476,650	39%
Total Cost of Sales	808,904	73%	871,765	71%
GROSS PROFIT	306,351	27%	356,192	29%
OPERATING EXPENSES				
Advertising	4,460	0%	3,110	0%
Accounting	5,110	0%	6,225	1%
Automobile	3,693	0%	7,282	1%
Depreciation	23,097	2%	19,645	2%
Insurance	10,945	1%	16,004	1%
Laundry & Linen	6,680	1%	7,722	1%
Kitchen Supplies	26,435	2%	31,356	3%
Licenses	2,237	0%	764	0%
Office	1,941	0%	2,573	0%
Repairs & Maintenance	26,595	2%	28,462	2%
Salaries-Officer	30,000	3%	37,000	3%
Taxes	8,661	1%	8,942	1%
Telephone	2,531	0%	3,164	0%
Utilities	36,176	3%	37,911	3%
TOTAL EXPENSES	188,561	17%	210,160	17%
OPERATING INCOME	117,790	11%	146,032	12%
Interest Earned	9,240	1%	5,459	
Pre Tax Income	127,030	11%	151,491	12%
Provision for Income Taxes	38,109	3%	45,447	4%
NET INCOME	88,921	8%	106,044	8%
Retained Earnings-Beg.	58,049		146,970	
Retained Earnings-Ending	$146,970		$253,014	

(Continued on next page)

Exhibit 2 (*Continued*)

PORTAS, INC.
BALANCE SHEETS

	1984	1985	1986
ASSETS			
CURRENT ASSETS			
Cash	$ 5,579	$130,895	$314,070
Inventories	15,648	16,463	15,829
Total Current Assets	21,227	147,358	329,899
PROPERTY & EQUIPMENT			
Cost	541,863	541,863	541,863
Less: Accumulated Depreciation	210,008	229,653	249,298
Net Book Value	331,855	312,210	292,565
	$353,082	$459,568	$622,464
LIABILITIES & STOCKHOLDERS' EQUITY			
CURRENT LIABILITIES			
Accounts Payable	42,584	37,650	35,268
Payroll & Sales Taxes Payable	34,480	37,642	37,987
Income Taxes Payable	9,048	11,262	16,621
Total Current Liabilities	86,112	86,554	89,876
STOCKHOLDERS' EQUITY			
Common Stock	120,000	120,000	120,000
Retained Earnings	146,970	253,014	412,588
Total Stockholders' Equity	266,970	373,014	532,588
	$353,082	$459,568	$622,464

PORTAS, INC.
RATIO ANALYSIS

	1984	1985	1986
CURRENT RATIO	0.25	1.70	3.67
QUICK RATIO	0.06	1.51	3.49
INVENTORY TURNOVER	52	54	53
DEBT TO EQUITY	0.32	0.23	0.17
RETURN ON INVESTMENTS	25.18%	26.10%	29.50%
RETURN ON EQUITY	33.31%	33.14%	35.24%

STATEMENT OF CASH FLOWS

Sales	$1,115,255	$1,227,957	$1,277,414
Less: Expenses Paid	974,368	1,060,439	1,038,288
Operating Cash Flow	140,887	167,518	239,126
Interest Income	9,240	5,459	17,799
Income Taxes Paid	(9,948)	(47,662)	(73,749)
Notes Paid	(139,071)		
Net Cash Flow	1,108	125,315	183,176
Cash–Beginning	4,471	5,579	130,895
Ending Cash Balance	$ 5,579	$ 130,895	$ 314,070

(Continued on next page)

Exhibit 2 (*Continued*)

PORTAS, INC.
PROJECTED STATEMENT OF INCOME

	1987	1988	1989	1990	1991
SALES					
Existing	$ 1,469,026	$1,689,380	$ 1,942,787	$2,234,205	$ 2,569,336
New Unit		240,000	600,000	810,000	1,093,500
Total Sales	1,469,026	1,929,380	2,542,787	3,044,205	3,662,836
COST OF SALES					
Food	436,878	573,784	756,207	905,325	1,089,302
Labor	552,785	726,014	956,835	1,145,516	1,378,302
Total Cost of Sales	989,663	1,299,798	1,713,042	2,050,841	2,467,604
GROSS PROFIT	479,363	629,582	829,745	993,364	1,195,232
OPERATING EXPENSES					
Advertising	44,071	57,881	38,142	45,663	54,943
Accounting	6,764	14,205	14,915	15,661	16,444
Automobile	4,821	10,123	10,629	11,161	11,719
Depreciation	20,627	30,627	58,127	58,127	58,127
Insurance	16,083	33,774	35,463	37,236	39,098
Interest		27,258	62,821	58,779	54,225
Laundry & Linen	8,896	18,681	19,615	20,596	21,625
Kitchen Supplies	32,494	68,238	71,650	75,233	78,994
Licenses	1,622	3,407	3,577	3,756	3,944
Office	4,568	9,592	10,071	10,575	11,104
Repairs & Maintenance	34,902	43,977	46,175	48,484	50,908
Rent		48,000	48,000	48,000	48,000
Salaries-Officer	31,500	65,000	65,000	65,000	65,000
Taxes	10,001	21,003	22,053	23,155	24,311
Telephone	2,340	4,915	5,161	5,419	5,690
Utilities	38,116	80,043	84,046	88,247	92,661
TOTAL EXPENSES	256,805	536,724	595,445	615,092	636,793
OPERATING INCOME	222,558	92,858	234,300	378,272	558,439
Interest Earned	3,500	4,138	7,686	13,542	22,433
Pre Tax Income	226,058	96,996	241,986	391,814	580,872
Provision for Income Taxes	67,818	29,099	72,596	117,544	174,262
NET INCOME	$ 158,240	$ 67,897	$ 169,390	$ 274,270	$ 406,610

PORTAS, INC.
RATIOS

Net Profit Percentage	10.77%	3.52%	6.66%	9.01%	11.10%
Return on Investment	18.65%	5.27%	11.60%	15.60%	18.31%
Return on Equity	35.00%	12.01%	24.77%	30.28%	32.63%

FORECAST OF CASH FLOW

	1987	1988	1989	1990	1991
Sales	1,469,026	1,929,380	2,542,787	3,044,205	3,662,836
Less: Expenses Paid	1,508,956	1,757,557	2,213,321	2,578,019	3,009,732
Operating Cash Flow	(39,930)	171,823	329,466	466,187	653,104
Interest Income	3,500	4,138	7,687	13,542	22,433
Income Taxes Paid	(62,125)	(21,824)	(71,069)	(88,158)	(130,696)
Notes Paid		(12,197)	(31,871)	(35,913)	(40,467)
Capital Equipment	(50,000)	(550,000)			
Financing		550,000			
Net Cash Flow	(148,555)	141,940	234,213	355,658	504,374
Cash - Beginning	314,070	165,515	307,455	541,668	897,326
Ending Cash Balance	165,515	307,455	541,668	897,326	1,401,700

(Continued on next page)

Exhibit 2 (*Continued*)

PORTAS, INC.
PRO FORMA BALANCE SHEETS

	1987	1988	1989	1990	1991
CURRENT ASSETS					
Cash	$165,515	$ 307,455	$541,668	$897,326	$1,401,700
Inventories	8,738	11,476	15,124	18,106	21,786
Total Current Assets	174,253	318,931	556,792	915,432	1,423,486
PROPERTY & EQUIPMENT					
Cost	591,863	1,091,863	1,091,863	1,091,863	1,091,863
Less: Accumulated Depreciation	31,889	69,389	69,389	69,389	11,262
Net Book Value	559,974	1,022,474	1,022,474	1,022,474	1,080,601
	$ 734,227	$ 1,341,405	$ 1,579,266	$ 1,937,906	$2,504,087
CURRENT LIABILITIES					
Accounts Payable	$173,455	$ 251,649	$344,871	$ 454,588	$ 603,963
Notes Payable	0	36,272	40,872	46,056	51,897
Payroll & Sales Taxes Payable	12,564	16,500	21,747	26,034	31,326
Income Taxes Payable	16,954	7,275	18,149	29,386	43,566
Total Current Liabilities	202,973	311,696	425,639	556,064	730,752
LONG-TERM DEBT	0	430,558	385,085	339,030	323,913
Total Liabilities	202,973	742,254	810,724	895,094	1,054,665
STOCKHOLDERS' EQUITY					
Common Stock	120,000	120,000	120,000	120,000	120,000
Retained Earnings	411,254	479,151	648,542	922,812	1,329,422
Total Stockholders' Equity	531,254	599,151	768,542	1,042,812	1,449,422
	$734,227	$ 1,341,405	$1,579,266	$1,937,906	$ 2,504,087

PORTAS, INC.
FORECASTED RATIOS

	1987	1988	1989	1990	1991
CURRENT RATIO	0.74	1.02	1.31	1.65	1.95
QUICK RATIO	0.70	0.99	1.27	1.61	1.92
DEBT TO EQUITY RATIO	1.33	1.24	1.05	0.86	0.73

BREAKEVEN ANALYSIS (1988)

Variable Cost Percentage	70.37%
Fixed Costs	
Present Location	222,340
New Location	256,503
Total	478,843
Breakeven Volume	
Present Location	750,353
New Location	865,648
Total	1,616,001

(Continued on next page)

Exhibit 3

Engagement Letter

This letter is to confirm our understanding of the terms and objectives of our engagement and the nature and limitations of the services we will provide.

We will help you prepare your business plan. Our services will be performed with the cooperation of your management team and other experts considered necessary. In accordance with this engagement, we will perform the following services:

1. Help management define its business mission, its goals and its objectives.
2. Analyze and attempt to quantify the company's strengths and weaknesses as they apply to the firm's market position, equipment and facilities, management and employees, and finances.
3. Compile historical financial statements including balance sheets, statements of income, statements of cash flows and financial ratios. These statements will be compiled in accordance with standards established by the American Institute of Certified Public Accountants and contain the standard compilation letter.
4. Compile forecasted Statements of Income and Cash Flows and Pro Forma Balance Sheets.

We will compile in accordance with standards established by the American Institute of Certified Public Accountants, from information management provides, the forecasted balance sheet and related statements of income and retained earnings and cash flows and summaries of significant assumptions and accounting polices of ________________________ for the years ending. We will not express any form of assurance on the achievability of the forecast or on the reasonableness of the underlying assumptions.

If, for any reason, we are unable to complete our compilation of your forecast, we will not issue a report on it as a result of this engagement.

Management is responsible for representations about its plans and expectations and for disclosure of significant information that might affect the ultimate realization of the forecasted results or the information contained in the business plan.

There will usually be differences between the forecasted and actual results because events and circumstances frequently do not occur as expected, and those differences may be material. Our report will contain a statement to that effect.

We have no responsibility to update our report for events and circumstances occurring after the date of our report.

At the conclusion of our engagement, management agrees to supply us with a representation letter which, among other things, will confirm management's responsibility for the underlying assumptions and the appropriateness of the business plan and its presentation.

In order for us to complete this engagement, management must provide assumptions that are appropriate for the business plan. If the assumptions provided are inappropriate and are not revised to our satisfaction, we will be unable to complete the engagement and, accordingly, we will not issue a report on the forecast.

Our fees for these services are based on our standard per diem rates of the staff persons assigned to this engagement. You will be billed monthly. Invoices are payable upon presentation.

If management intends to reproduce and publish the business plan with its forecast and our report thereon, they must be reproduced in their entirety, and all drafts of the document containing the business plan and forecast must be submitted to us for our approval.

If you approve the terms and conditions of this letter, please sign where indicated.

CHAPTER 26

How to Use Break Even Analysis

Introduction

Break-even analysis will help you understand the effect of costs and volume on profit. It will help you answer the question, What do we have to do

- To break even?
- Earn a certain profit?
- Earn a specific profit after taxes?

Furthermore, BE can be used to determine what an organization has to do to obtain certain results in a multiproduct environment.

This chapter will cover the following ramifications of BE:

- Cost and expense classification for break even analysis
- Using Electronic Spreadsheets to Calculate Break Even
- Multiproduct Situations

Fundamental Assumptions

To break even a company must sell enough units to earn sufficient contribution to cover all fixed costs.

Variable costs: Those expenditures that change with sales activity. They include all expense categories (manufacturing, selling and general & administrative).

Contribution: The difference between Sales Price and Variable costs.

Example: If a company's product sells for $100 and the variable costs per unit total $60, its contribution is $40 per unit.

Fixed costs: Costs, that within a relevant range, do not vary with production. A graph of fixed costs would show the following:

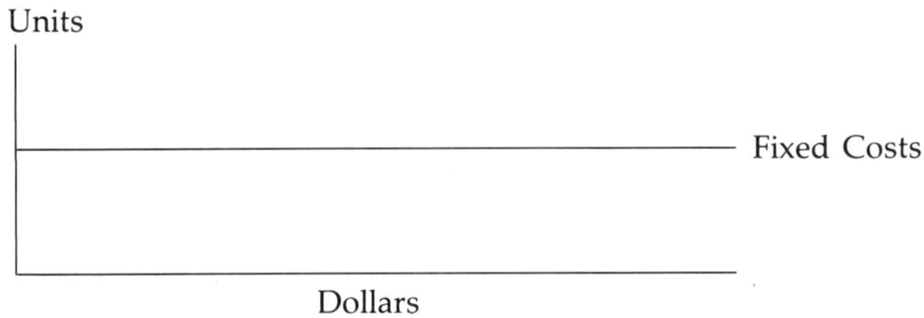

Caution: In the long run, all costs are variable. In the short run, most costs are fixed.

What does this mean? The traditional approach of classifying costs as fixed and variable may not be relevant.

For example, a company needs 1,000 hours of direct labor time to produce 100,000 units per month. If the production falls to 80,000 units, will the direct labor time drop to 800 hours? Probably not. It is not only almost impossible, but impracticable as well to expect to alter payroll as production changes. Once employees are laid off (to accommodate reduced production) it is very costly to recruit, hire, and train new people. Therefore, well-managed companies try to maintain a level of employment to ensure even production.

On the other hand, as a company expands its production, it will also outgrow its facilities. Therefore additional fixed costs, will have to be incurred to continue to produce under the new situations. This will produce the following fixed cost graph:

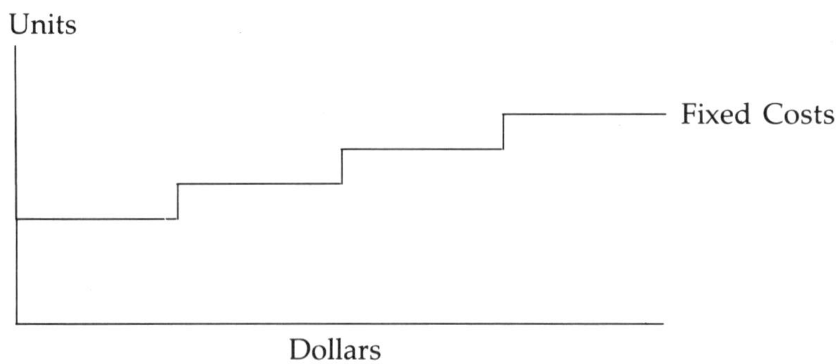

What's the Best Way to Classify Costs and Expenses?

There are few truly variable costs. All other costs are fixed or manageable.

Fixed	Manageable	Variable
Depreciation	Accounting & Auditing	Commissions
Patent Amortization	Advertising	Direct Materials
	Auto Expense	Freight
	Bad Debts	Overtime premium
	Entertainment & Promotion	Royalties
	Fringe Benefits	Scrap
	Insurance	
	Legal	
	Maintenance	
	Office Salaries	
	Officer Salaries	
	Office	
	Payroll Taxes	
	Property Tax	
	Quality Control	
	Receiving	
	Rent	
	Sales Salaries	
	Small Tools	
	Spoilage	
	Supervisor Salaries	
	Supplies	
	Telephone	
	Travel	
	Utilities	

This classification is intended to help you avoid the tendency to lump all costs into fixed and variable categories, because it may incorrectly determine break-even volume. Each of the items in the second column can be managed and should be looked at in this way before constructing any break even charts.

How to Calculate the Break Even Point

To break even a company must sell enough units for the total contribution to be adequate to cover fixed costs. This relationship is expressed as follows:

$$\text{Break-Even Volume} = \frac{\text{Fixed Costs}}{S - VC}$$

$$\text{Break-Even Dollars} = \text{Break-Even Volume} * \text{Sales Price}$$

How to Use Electronic Spreadsheets to Calculate Break Even

The following is a spreadsheet model format:

Columns	C	B	A
After Tax Profit Desired			$
Tax Rate			%
	Adjusted	Changes	Original
Sales Price			
Variable Cost per Unit			
Contribution			
Fixed Costs			
		Change	
Units			
Dollars			

Key to Columns

A—The original cost/volume/price parameters

Note: Profit desired is considered a fixed expense for purposes of break even calculations.

Calculating the Desired "After Tax" Profit

The pre tax profit figures are used in these equations. If you are trying to derive an *after* tax income, you have to make a conversion to income *before* taxes by using the following equation:

$$\text{Pre Tax Profit} = \frac{\text{After Tax Profit}}{1 - \text{Tax Rate}}$$

Sensitivity analysis: This will allow you to calculate the effect of any changes on the pre-computed break even volume and dollar value.

This is a summation of columns A and B.

Illustrations:

I. *How much sales must the company have to break even?*

Sales Price			$100
Varible Cost			60
Contribution			$40
Fixed Costs			$40,000
Break-Even Units	Fixed Costs / Contribution	40,000 / 40	1,000
Break-Even Sales Units * Sales Price			$100,000

Proof:

Statement of Income

Sales	$100,000
Variable Costs	60,000
Contributions	40,000
Fixed Costs	40,000
Profit	0

II. *How Much Business will be needed to earn a profit of $60,000 under the above conditions?*

Profit Desired $60,000

	Adjusted	Changes	Original
Sales Price	$100	—	$100
Variable Cost per Unit	60	0	60
Contribution	$40	$0	$40
Fixed Costs	$40,000		$40,000

Units Required $\frac{\text{Fixed + Profit}}{\text{Contribution}} = \frac{100{,}000}{40}$ 2,500

Sales Required Units * Sales Price $250,000

Graphically, this will appear as follows:

Proof:

Statement of Income

Sales	$250,000
Variable Costs	150,000
Contributions	100,000
Fixed Costs	40,000
Profit	$60,000

III. *Given a 40% tax rate, how much will the company have to sell to earn $60,000 after tax?*

After-Tax Profit	$60,000
Tax Rate	40.00%
Pre-Tax Profit ($60,000/(1−40%))	$100,000
Fixed Costs	40,000
Total	$140,000
Units to Attain Profit	3,500
Sales Required	$350,000

Proof

Statement of Income

Sales	$350,000
Variable Costs	210,000
Contributions	140,000
Fixed Costs	40,000
Pre-Tax Profit	100,000
Income Taxes	40,000
	$60,000

How to Find the Right Break Even Volume in Multiproduct Situations

The general equation uses a weighted average of the individual products' contributions to fixed costs:

$$\text{Profit} = (P_1 - V_2)X_1 + (P_2 - V_2)X_2 \cdots (P_n - V_n)X_{n-F}$$

Illustration:

MIX IN PROPORTIONS

Unit	% (a)	Sales Price	Variable Cost	Contrib.	Weighted Average (b)
A	20.00%	$100	$30	$70	$14
B	70.00%	80	70	10	7
C	10.00%	60	50	10	1
	100.00%	$240	$150	$90	$22
Fixed Costs					$50,000
# Units					2,273 (c)

Key

a. Percent of sales volume
Note: The prior sales volume in dollars could also be depicted.
b. Contribution margin * percentage
c. $50,000/$22

Break Even Sales

Unit	#	Total Sales	Variable Cost	Contrib.
A	455	$ 45,455	$13,650	$31,805
B	1,591	127,273	111,370	15,903
C	227	13,636*	11,340	2,292
	2,273	$186,364	$136,364	$50,000

*rounding adjustment

CHAPTER 27

Using Capital Budgeting to Evaluate Long Term Investment Projects

Introduction

The capital budgeting technique helps the user make decisions about long term investments by comparing the expected returns to the amounts at stake. It considers the following:

1. Initial investment
2. Expected returns
3. Time frame
4. Adjusted cost of capital rate

Inasmuch as these methods contrast the net returns to the applicable investments, their computations have something in common to the customary ROI calculations. (See Chapter 22)

$$\text{ROI} = \frac{\text{Return}}{\text{Investment}} \quad \text{Amended to} \quad \frac{\text{Differential Return}}{\text{Differential Investment}}$$

Because the estimated returns are expected to be received at varying times and in varying amounts, other complications are added to the problem. We attempt to answer the following questions:

1. Will we come out with more than we put in?
2. How long will it take?
3. Will the investment earn a sufficient return?

Example: The Joseph Company is thinking about buying new equipment that will cost \$100,000. The investment is expected to improve profits by \$20,000 per year for the next six years. According to ROI calculations, we expect to earn 20% on our money.

However: Although the firm will earn a total of $120,000 over the next six years, the returns will not be the same each period.

Year	Return
1	$ 5,000
2	15,000
3	18,000
4	20,000
5	28,000
6	34,000
	$120,000

How to Interpret Returns

There are a number of ways returns can be calculated:

- Net Differential Income – Increased revenues, reduced expenditures, additional profits
- Differential cash flow

1. *Net Differential Income:* Generally calculated under GAAP and uses pre tax or after tax income.
2. *Net Differential Cash Flow:* A combination of expected annual cash returns and anticipated returns on the eventual disposal of the underlying assets.

Why Cash Flows? Because, it is a better gauge of investment return than net income. As you know, net income is affected by inventories, uncollected sales, and other items that have to be recognized in certain ways to adhere to GAAP. But, investors are primarily concerned about receiving cash not reported income.

Forget sunk costs. There are certain expenditures that won't change as a result of the action.

For example, if an organization has excess capacity, rent will not be affected as a result of the investment decision. Therefore, it should not be considered.

Using Non-Discounted Methods to Analyze Long-Term Projects

The non discounted approaches do not consider the time value of money. There are two forms:

1. *Differential Return on Assets Employed.* This is generally the ROI equation. The average annual return is divided by the assets invested.

$$\text{ROI} = \frac{\text{Average Annual Return}}{\text{Assets Invested}}$$

$$\text{Average Annual Return} = \frac{\text{Total Return}}{\text{Number of periods}}$$

Illustrated (See Above)

$$\text{Average Annual Return} = \frac{\$120{,}000}{6} = \$20{,}000$$

$$\text{ROI} = \frac{\$20{,}000}{\$100{,}000} = 20\%$$

2. *Years to Recover Investment.* An investment that provides fast returns is usually more highly regarded than one that does not. The years to recover is calculated as follows:

$$\frac{\text{Investment}}{\text{Average Annual Return}}$$

Since the cash flows in the above illustration are uneven, we start from year 1 and add each subsequent flow until the investment is recovered. In this case, that works out to about 5+ years.

Weaknesses of the Non Discounted Methods

By failing to consider the time value of money, these approaches yield incomplete, and often inaccurate information.

Example: Assume, from the facts above, that there are three possible ways returns may be recieved:

Year	A	B	C	D
1	$ 5,000	$ 30,000	$120,000	
2	15,000	3,000		
3	18,000	10,000		
4	20,000	45,000		
5	28,000	20,000		
6	34,000	12,000		$120,000
	$120,000	$120,000	$120,000	$120,000

Obviously, the total repayment is the same under each of the three options. Therefore, the non discounted methods would show that there is no difference. However, most people want to get their money back as soon as possible and would take option B if given a choice. However, if one had to choose between "A" and "B", what would it be? To find the best answer, we must consider the time value of money.

Present Value—An Overview

Definition

Given a specified rate of return, what is the equivalent amount today of some amount which is payable or receivable in the future.

Present Value of a Sum

$$PV = \frac{FV}{(1 + i)^n}$$

Where:

FV = Future value to be received
i = Interest rate
n = Number of periods

Four Ways to Compute the Present Value

1. By using the equation

2. With an electronic calculator
3. By electronic spreadsheet (e.g. the @PV function in Lotus)
4. By tables.

Illustration: A company wants to put enough (PV) away at 12% interest (i) per annum to accumulate to \$10,000 (FV) at the end of five years (n).

$$PV = \frac{\$10{,}000}{(1.12)^5}$$
$$PV = \frac{\$10{,}000}{1.762342}$$
$$PV = \$5{,}674$$

Proof:

Year	Beginning	Interest	Ending
1	5,674	681	6,355
2	6,355	763	7,118
3	7,118	854	7,972
4	7,972	957	8,929
5	8,929	1,071	10,000

Note: As the time to accumulate the sum increases, the present value, or the amount needed to deposit decreases.

Periods	
0	10,000
1	8,929
5	5,674
10	3,220
20	1,037

And: As the interest rate increases, the amount needed to deposit decreases.

Interest Rate	
2.00%	9,057
6.00%	7,473

(Continued on next page)

Interest Rate	
7.50%	6,966
10.00%	6,209
12.00%	5,674
20.00%	4,019

Multiple Compounding Periods

The above equation and illustration assumed that interest would compound annually. When interest is compounded more often, the following adjustments should be made:

Compounding Period	Interest (i)	Time (n)	Illustrated
Quarterly	$i/4$ (or 3%)	$n * 4$ (or 20)	$5,537
Monthly	$i/12$ (or 1%)	$n * 12$ (or 60)	$5,504
Daily	$i/365$	$n * 365$	$5,489

Illustration: Effect of present value calculation on previous example. Assume the interest rate is 12% and the returns are received at the end of each period.

Year	A Return	PV	B Return	PV
1	$ 5,000	$ 4,464	$ 30,000	$26,785
2	15,000	11,958	3,000	2,392
3	18,000	12,812	10,000	7,118
4	20,000	12,710	45,000	28,598
5	28,000	15,888	20,000	11,349
6	34,000	17,226	12,000	6,080
	$120,000	$ 75,058	$120,000	$82,322

Year	C Return	PV	D Return	PV
1	$120,000	$107,143		
2				
3				
4				
5				
6			$120,000	$60,796
	$120,000	$107,143	$120,000	$60,796

By using discounted cash flow analysis, we see that "C" yields the best return while "D" is the poorest.

Present Value of an Annuity

Defined: How much should be deposited now (*PV*), given a certain interest rate (*i*) to receive a specified number of payments (*n*) at the end of each period?

Equation:

$$PV = \frac{\text{Payment}}{\dfrac{(1 + i)^n - 1}{i}}$$

Illustration:

How much has to be invested at 12% in order to earn to be able to withdraw $1,000 per year at the end of the next five years?

0	1	2	3	4	5
PV	$1,000	$1,000	$1,000	$1,000	$1,000

$$PV = \frac{\$1{,}000}{\dfrac{(1.12)^5 - 1}{.12}}$$

$$PV = \$1{,}000 * 3.604776$$

$$PV = \$3{,}605$$

Proof:

Year	Beginning	Interest	Withdraw	Ending
1	3,605	432	(1,000)	3,037
2	3,037	364	(1,000)	2,402
3	2,402	288	(1,000)	1,690
4	1,690	203	(1,000)	893
5	893	107	(1,000)	0

Present Value of a Deferred Annuity

This form of calculation assumes that a sufficient amount of money will be deposited now which will earn interest to some point in the future when withdrawals will begin to take place.

0	Years 0–4	End of Year					
		5	6	7	8	9	10
		Annual Withdrawals					

The present value of a deferred annuity is calculated as follows:

Present Value of a Sum * Present value of an annuity

Illustration: Assume the annuity of $1,000 per year will begin to be paid at the end of the fifth year.

Present Value of Sum	0.567427
Present Value of Annuity	3.604776
Product (1 * 2)	2.045447
Amount to Deposit	$2,045

Proof:

Year	Beginning	Interest	Withdraw	Ending
1–5	2,045	1,559		3,605
6	3,605	433	(1,000)	3,037
7	3,037	364	(1,000)	2,402
8	2,402	288	(1,000)	1,690
9	1,690	203	(1,000)	893
10	893	107	(1,000)	0

How to Use Present Value Analysis to Evaluate Capital Investments

Net Present Value

The difference between the discounted cash flows expected to be received from a project and the amount paid to acquire the project:

If Receipts > Expenditures = Positive and a "Go" decision
If Receipts < Expenditures = Negative and a "No Go" decision

For Example: Assume the company desires a minimum return of 12%. The present value of the following returns are calculated:

	A	B	C	D
Present Value	75,058	82,322	107,143	60,796
Investment	100,000	100,000	100,000	100,000

Net Present Value	(24,942)	(17,678)	7,143	(39,204)

Therefore, all else being equal, only option "C" will earn the required minimum return (12%).

What's the Right Interest Rate?

The rate chosen can make or break a project. For example, take a look at Alternative A under different interest rate assumptions.

Year	A Return	4.00%	7.50%	10.00%	12.00%
1	5,000	4,808	4,651	4,545	4,464
2	15,000	13,868	12,980	12,397	11,958
3	18,000	16,002	14,489	13,524	12,812
4	20,000	17,096	14,976	13,660	12,710
5	28,000	23,014	19,504	17,386	15,888
6	34,000	26,871	22,031	19,192	17,226
	120,000				
Present Value		101,659	88,631	80,704	75,058
Investment		100,000	100,000	100,000	100,000
		1,659	(11,369)	(19,296)	(24,942)

Depending on the interest rate, the results range from a positive net present value of $1,659 to a negative $65,391.

Options:

1. Company's incremental borrowing or lending rate
2. Cost of Capital. See Chapter 22.
3. Cost of Capital adjusted for risk premium. The greater the risk, of course, the higher the premium.

Illustration: The cost of capital rate illustrated in Chapter 22 was 12.1%. Assume the risk premium is 20%.

Cost of Capital	12.10%
Risk Premium	20.00%
Adjusted Rate	14.52%

How to Guess the Rate of Return

It is easy to construct an electronic spreadsheet to guess the rate of return. The layout will appear as follows:

Estimated Rate of Return	8.0715%	(A)
Investment	100,000	
Net Present Value	(0)	(B)

Year	Total	PV
1	10,000	9,253
2	12,000	10,274
3	8,000	6,338
4	17,000	12,462
5	16,000	10,853
6	33,000	20,713
7	25,000	14,520
8	29,000	15,587
	150,000	100,000

Keep substituting rates for "A" until "B" equals zero.

Internal Rate of Return (IRR)

The IRR is the interest rate that equates the inflows and outflows from a capital investment project. By hand, the calculation is extremely difficult. However, it is now easy to do it on a portable calculator or electronic spreadsheet.

Deficiency: The IRR equations assume that excess cash flows are invested at the projects' internal rate of return. By, contrast, NPV computations use the firm's cost of capital rate which is theoretically superior.

However: The IRR is a handy way to judge an investment's return without, first, trying to derive an appropriate rate.

How to Calculate the Depreciation Shield

As you well know, depreciation does not use cash flow. However, because it is deductible for income tax purposes, it should be considered in cash flow computations as follows:

Cash flow from tax savings = Depreciation * (1 − tax rate)

Example:

Amount of Investment in Equipment	200,000
Estimated Life	10
Income Tax Rate	40.00%
Desired Rate of Return	8.00%

Year	Cash Flow	Deprec.	Tax Savings	After Tax Cash Flow	Present Value
1	30,000	20,000	8,000	22,000	27,778
2	40,000	20,000	8,000	32,000	34,294
3	50,000	20,000	8,000	42,000	39,692
4	60,000	20,000	8,000	52,000	44,102
5	70,000	20,000	8,000	62,000	47,640
	250,000	100,000	40,000	210,000	193,506

How to Use Computer Spreadsheet Models for Capital Budgeting

The following program enables us to calculate Net Present Value and Internal Rate of Return on after tax cash flow. As you can see, we've built in the effect of financing and depreciation.

		EXPECTED CASH FLOW	
Client __________			
Project Description __________			
Total Investment			
Property/Equipment			
Other			
		Year	**Amount**
	0	1	0
Cost of Capital Rate		2	
Percentage Financed		3	
Interest Rate		4	
Term (Years)		5	
Tax Rate		6	
Depreciation		7	
Life		8	
		9	
RESULTS		10	
Net Present Value			
IRR			

Example: The Macro Company is considering a long term capital investment. It expects to invest $300,000 into the project, of which, 80% will be covered by financing. The other estimates and assumptions are detailed on screen below.

Client Macro Corporation			
Project Description			
New manufacturing facility			
Total Investment		**Expected Cash Flow**	
Property/Equipment	**200,000**		
Other	**100,000**	**Year**	**Amount**
	300,000	1	40,000
		2	50,000
Cost of Capital Rate	12.00%	3	60,000
Percentage Financed	80.00%	4	70,000
Interest Rate	10.50%	5	80,000
Term (Years)	25	6	90,000
Tax Rate	40.00%	7	100,000
Depreciation		8	110,000
Life	10	9	120,000
RESULTS		10	130,000
Net			$850,000
Present Value	$22,964		
IRR	14.36%		

The NPV and IRR calculations are made on net cash flow after taxes. These computations are performed as follows:

Net Cash Flow

Year	Net After Loan Payments	Taxable	Tax	Net After Tax	Present Value
1	12,808	(5,101)	2,041	14,849	13,257
2	22,808	5,129	(2,052)	20,756	16,546
3	32,808	15,385	(6,154)	26,654	18,971
4	42,808	25,669	(10,268)	32,540	20,680
5	52,808	35,984	(14,394)	38,414	21,797
6	62,808	46,335	(18,534)	44,274	22,430
7	72,808	56,723	(22,689)	50,119	22,671

Net Cash Flow (*Continued*)

Year	Net After Loan Payments	Taxable	Tax	Net After Tax	Present Value
8	82,808	67,155	(26,862)	55,946	22,596
9	92,808	77,634	(31,054)	61,754	22,269
10	102,808	88,166	(35,266)	67,542	21,746
	578,080	413,079	(165,232)	412,848	202,963

The next schedules backs up the previous lead analysis.

NEA After Loan Payments

	From Above	Loan Payment	Net
1	40,000	27,192	12,808
2	50,000	27,192	22,808
3	60,000	27,192	32,808
4	70,000	27,192	42,808
5	80,000	27,192	52,808
6	90,000	27,192	62,808
7	100,000	27,192	72,808
8	110,000	27,192	82,808
9	120,000	27,192	92,808
10	130,000	27,192	102,808

Interest Calculation Schedule

Principal	240,000
Interest	0
Term	25
Payment	2,266
Annual Payments	27,192

Interest and Principal Portions

Year	Balance	Reduce	Payment	Interest	Months Remaining
1	237,909	2,091	27,192	25,101	288
2	235,587	2,322	27,192	24,871	276

(*Continued on next page*)

Interest and Principal Portions (*Continued*)

Year	Balance	Reduce	Payment	Interest	Months Remaining
3	233,010	2,577	27,192	24,615	264
4	230,148	2,862	27,192	24,331	252
5	226,971	3,177	27,192	24,016	240
6	223,444	3,527	27,192	23,665	228
7	219,529	3,916	27,192	23,277	216
8	215,182	4,347	27,192	22,845	204
9	210,355	4,826	27,192	22,366	192
10	204,997	5,358	27,192	21,834	180

Taxable Income Computations

Year	Net Cash	+ Principal	− Deprec.	Taxable
1	12,808	2,091	(20,000	(5,101)
2	22,808	2,322	(20,000)	5,129
3	32,808	2,577	(20,000)	15,385
4	42,808	2,862	(20,000)	25,669
5	52,808	3,177	(20,000)	35,984
6	62,808	3,527	(20,000)	46,335
7	72,808	3,916	(20,000)	56,723
8	82,808	4,347	(20,000)	67,155
9	92,808	4,826	(20,000)	77,634
10	102,808	5,358	(20,000)	88,166

Sensitivity Analysis

The worksheet allows you to see the effect of various combinations of factors. For example, the following presents a picture of financing choices:

Alternative Financing Percentages

Financing Pct	Net PV	IRR
0.00%	122,332	24.11%
10.00%	109,911	22.92%
20.00%	97,490	21.73%
30.00%	85,069	20.52%
40.00%	72,468	19.31%

Alternative Financing Percentages (*Continued*)

Financing Pct	Net PV	IRR
50.00%	60,227	18.08%
60.00%	47,806	16.85%
70.00%	35,385	15.61%
80.00%	22,964	14.36%
90.00%	10,544	13.09%
10.00%	(1,877)	11.81%

CHAPTER 28

How to Solve Management Problems with Deterministic Analysis

Introduction

The variables are known in a deterministic model.

Remember: Before you start, make sure you go through the steps of the scientific method which are summarized below. For a fuller discussion, refer to Chapter 23.

1. Define the problem or opportunity.
2. Determine which alternative solutions exist.
3. Eliminate alternatives.
4. Quantify possible results.
5. Consider qualitative factors.
6. Make a decision.
7. Get feedback, and make changes as necessary.

This chapter is devoted to help you work out the answers to the following:

- How can I maximize my profits or minimize my costs consistent with my available resources?—Linear Programming.
- What are the best ways to manage inventories?
- How do you estimate labor costs when the efficiency per hour improves?—Learning Curve.

Each section of this chapter will be organized as follows:

1. Description of technique
2. Uses
3. How it works
4. Practical application

How to Use Linear Programming to Optimize Resource Use

Description: Mathematical technique that permits the best use of available resources.

Uses: Maximize contribution margin
Minimize costs
Portfolio mix
Transportation problems

How it Works: Linear programming (LP) computation focuses on the desire to maximize profits or minimize costs, subject to certain limitations or constraints.

For example, a company sells Gizmos at a profit of $20 each. There is practically an unlimited demand for this product. However, the plant is only capable of producing 1,000 per month. Therefore, because of this constraint, the contribution is limited to $20,000 per month. This is obviously very easy to see.

However: Companies are faced with the following:

- Different products
- Different profit margins for each product
- Different uses of resources
- Scarce resources

Example: The Dorcus Company manufactures two bags:

		Hours per Bag	
	Contribution per unit	*Sewing Department*	*Finishing Department*
Standard (*X*)	$6	0.70	1.00
Deluxe (*Y*)	$8	1.00	0.83

From the above, it would seem obvious that Dorcus could maximize its profits by manufacturing only the deluxe model (*Y*).

If Dorcus had no constraints, it would drop the standard item and put all its efforts into the deluxe. However, there are various capacity limitations in its two production departments:

Sewing	630 hours
Finishing	600 hours

The aim is to maximize the profit by computing the best mix of *X* and *Y* within, of course, these capacity limitations.

The maximization equation, which is called the "Objective Function," is expressed as

$$MAX \quad 6X + 8Y$$

The capacity constraints impact the equation as follows:

ST (subject to)

$$0.70X + 1.00Y \Leftarrow 630$$
$$1.00X \quad 0.83Y \Leftarrow 600$$

Which produces the following set of equations:

LP Equations
Standard Form

MAX:	$6X + 8Y$
ST:	$.7X + 1Y \Leftarrow 630$
	$1X + .83Y \Leftarrow 600$

How to Solve: There are three methods to find the profit optimization mix that will respect the constraint conditions:

1. Graphical
2. Simultaneous equations
3. Computer

Graphic Solution

1. Calculate the maximum number of each grade bag that could be produced if the other was not manufactured.

Standard	600
Deluxe	630

2. Compute the resulting profit

Max	#	@	$
X	600	6	$3,600
Y	630	8	$5,040

3. Plot that data into a graphical representation.

Linear Programming Graph
Two Variables

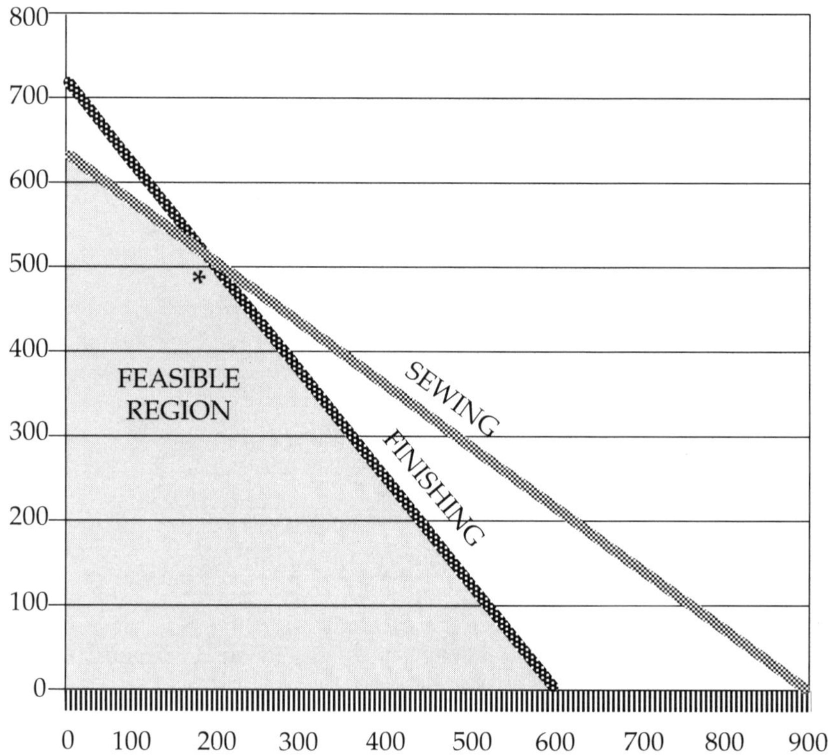

The two diagonal lines represent the production constraints in

- Sewing
- Finishing

Because of these restraints, no bags can be produced in any portion of the graph either to the right or above these lines. Therefore, the optimum production, and mix will be at the point where the lines intersect (*)

$X = 185$ bags
$Y = 500$ bags

Simultaneous Equations

To solve by simultaneous equations, the constraint equations are converted to:

(a) $.7X + Y = 630$

(b) $1X + .83Y = 600$

1. *Isolate* X *and* Y

$$Y = 630 - .7X$$
$$X = 600 - .83Y$$

2. *Solve for* Y

$$Y = 630 - .7(600 - .83Y)$$
$$Y = 630 - 420 + .58Y$$
$$.42Y = 210$$
$$Y = 500$$

3. *Solve for* X

$$X = 600 - .83(500)$$
$$X = 600 - 415$$
$$X = 185$$

By Computer

Computer programs will solve the basic equations and furnish other information besides.

The solution follows:

Dorcus Company—Two-Variable Model

OPTIMAL SOLUTION—SUMMARY REPORT

	Variable	*Value*	*Cost*
1	VAR 1	184.0096	6.0000
2	VAR 2	501.1933	8.0000

Objective Function Value = 5113.60379

The objective function is the total contribution from the computed optimum mix:

Objective Function	**Quantity**	**@**	**Total**
Standard	184	$6	$1,104
Deluxe	501	$8	4,008
			$5,112*

*Rounding Difference

Sensitivity Analysis—Impact of Factor Changes

What happens if one or more of the ingredients of the equations change? Two types of variations are possible:

1. Change in contribution
2. Change in constraints

The LP equations let the user know just how much any of these factors can vary before affecting the objective function.

Dorcus Company—Two-Variable Model

SENSITIVITY ANALYSIS OF COST COEFFICIENTS

	Variable	*Current Coeff.*	*Allowable Minimum*	*Allowable Maximum*
1	VAR 1	6.0000	5.6000	9.6386
2	VAR 2	8.0000	4.9800	8.5714

The objective function will remain the same if the contribution for each bag does not go outside the following ranges:

Standard	\$5.60–\$9.64
Deluxe	\$4.98–\$8.57

Dorcus Company—Two-Variable Model

SENSITIVITY ANALYSIS OF RIGHT-HAND SIDE VALUES

	Constraint	*Type*	*Current Value*	*Allowable Minimum*	*Allowable Maximum*
1	CONSTR 1	⇐	630.0000	420.0000	722.8916
2	CONSTR 2	⇐	600.0000	522.9000	900.0000

This shows how much capacity can be reduced or increased before the objective value would change.

The final analysis of the two variable model portrays the *slack* and the *shadow* price:

Dorcus Company—Two-Variable Model

OPTIMAL SOLUTION—DETAILED REPORT

	Constraint	*Type*	*RHS*	*Slack*	*Shadow Price*
1	CONSTR 1	⇐	630.0000	0.0000	7.2076
2	CONSTR 2	⇐	600.0000	0.0000	.9547

Objective Function Value = 5113.60379

Definitions

Slack: Additional capacity available. There is none in either department.

Sahdow Price: The amount that will be added to the objective function for each unit constraint increase.

LP Problems Which Use More than Two Variables

If an equation requires more than two variables, a graphic solution would be impossible because it would require, as a minimum, a three dimensional presentation. Simultaneous equations, carried out to multi levels, become very difficult at best. Prior to the availability of computer programs, the simplex method, which employed iteration techniques, was used.

Illustration: The Random Corporation manufactures three products, *X*, *Y*, and *Z*. The pertinent production and contribution factors are displayed below:

Department	**Production Time (Hours)**			
Product	**I**	**II**	**III**	**Contribution**
X	2	5	4	$40
Y	2	5	3	$30
Z	4	2	2	$20
Time Available (Hours)	900	400	600	

Equations:

Max: $40X + 30Y + 20Z$

St:

$$2X + 2Y + 4Z \Leftarrow 900$$
$$5X + 5Y + 2Z \Leftarrow 400$$
$$4X + 3Y + 2Z \Leftarrow 600$$

The optimal solution follows:

Random Corporation

OPTIMAL SOLUTION

	Variable	*Value*	*Cost*
1	VAR 1	137.5000	40.0000
2	VAR 2	25.0000	30.0000
4	SLACK 1	500.0000	0.0000

Objective Function Value = 6250.00000

In other words, the best mix would be:

Product	*Quantity*	*@*	*Total*
X	137.5	$40	5,500
Y	25.0	$30	750
			$6,250

The next printout explains why Product Z was not included in the mix:

Random Corporation

SENSITIVITY ANALYSIS OF COST COEFFICIENTS

	Variable	*Current Coeff.*	*Allowable Minimum*	*Allowable Maximum*
1	VAR 1	40.0000	20.0000	60.0000
2	VAR 2	30.0000	20.0000	100.0000
3	VAR 3	20.0000	−Infinity	25.0000

The equation shows the following:

1. Product *Z*'s contribution would have to increase by $5 per unit before Random should allocate any resources to its production.
2. Products' *X* & *Y* would have to drop their individual contribution value to $20 before *Z* would play a part in the mix.
3. The column Allowable Maximum discloses how much more contribution would have to be obtained for either *X* or *Y* before the preferred mix was altered.
4. Department 1 has 500 hours of slack or unused time.

The next two schedules describe the impact of changes on the right hand side (RHS) of the equations.

1. *Slack:* Department I has slack or unused capacity of 500 hours. As the standard cost analysis indicated in Chapter 22 indicates, unused capacity is a negative variance.

How can slack be avoided? By improving the contribution of the various units, especially Product *Z*, including

- Increase prices for Random's products.

- Reduce department capacity—at the same time this will lower costs.

Note: The Random problem considers only production constraints. In many cases, the restriction of the marketplace may have to be worked into the computations.

2. *Shadow Prices:* The shadow price is the effect on the objective function by a 1 hour capacity increase to the limitation previously specified in the RHS. Therefore, each hour increase capacity in Departments II and III will add $2.50 and $8.75 respectively. Inasmuch, as Department I has 500 hours of slack, there are no shadow prices.

Random Corporation
OPTIMAL SOLUTION—DETAILED REPORT

	Constraint	*Type*	*RHS*	*Slack*	*Shadow Price*
1	CONSTR 1	⇐	900.0000	500.0000	0.0000
2	CONSTR 2	⇐	400.0000	0.0000	2.5000
3	CONSTR 3	⇐	600.0000	0.0000	8.7500

Objective Function Value = 6250.00000

The final equation depicts how many hours can be added or subtracted from the capacity of each producing department before the objective function is altered.

Random Corporation

SENSITIVITY ANALYSIS OF RIGHT-HAND SIDE VALUES

	Constraint	*Type*	*Current Value*	*Allowable Minimum*	*Allowable Maximum*
1	CONSTR 1	⇐	900.0000	400.0000	Infinity
2	CONSTR 2	⇐	400.0000	300.0000	900.0000
3	CONSTR 3	⇐	600.0000	160.0000	800.0000

How to Use Managerial Accounting to Control Inventories

Why Inventory Management Is Important

Because of its effect on

- Financial reporting

- Income taxes
- Cash flow considerations

Cash Flow Consideration

A business is judged on its ability to maximize its positive cash flow. As a major component, inventory management is concerned with the following:

1. How much should be held?
2. How often should inventory be ordered?

The Two Major Inventory Costs

	Holding Costs	**Ordering Costs**
Decription	Costs that are dependent upon the size of the inventory	Costs that are dependent upon the number of orders
Example of costs	Capital Insurance Taxes Breakage Rent Pilferage Overhead	Avoiding stock out costs Clerical labor Supplies
Equations	Average Inventory * Average Holding Cost per Unit	Orders per year * Cost per order

A Word About Stock Out Costs

Consider your worst fear in inventory management, "The inventory runs out and production shuts down." To prevent this calamity, safety stocks are carried. But, the holding costs to do this are often prohibitive because space and working capital are seriously impaired.

Inventory Management Example

Holding Cost	5.00%
Cost per Order	$10.00
Demand	250,000
Purchase Cost	$50.00

Quantity per Order	Annual Holding Cost	Annual Ordering Cost	Annual Total Cost
1000	500	2,500	3,000
2000	1,000	1,250	2,250
3000	1,500	833	2,333
4000	2,000	625	2,625
5000	2,500	500	3,000
6000	3,000	417	3,417
7000	3,500	357	3,857
8000	4,000	313	4,313
9000	4,500	278	4,778
10000	5,000	250	5,250

As the following graph discloses

1. The holding cost builds as the size of the average order increases—But,
2. The annual order costs drops because purchases are made less frequently.

The minimum annual total cost is reached at the Economic Order Quantity (EOQ) point, which is where the two lines intersect.

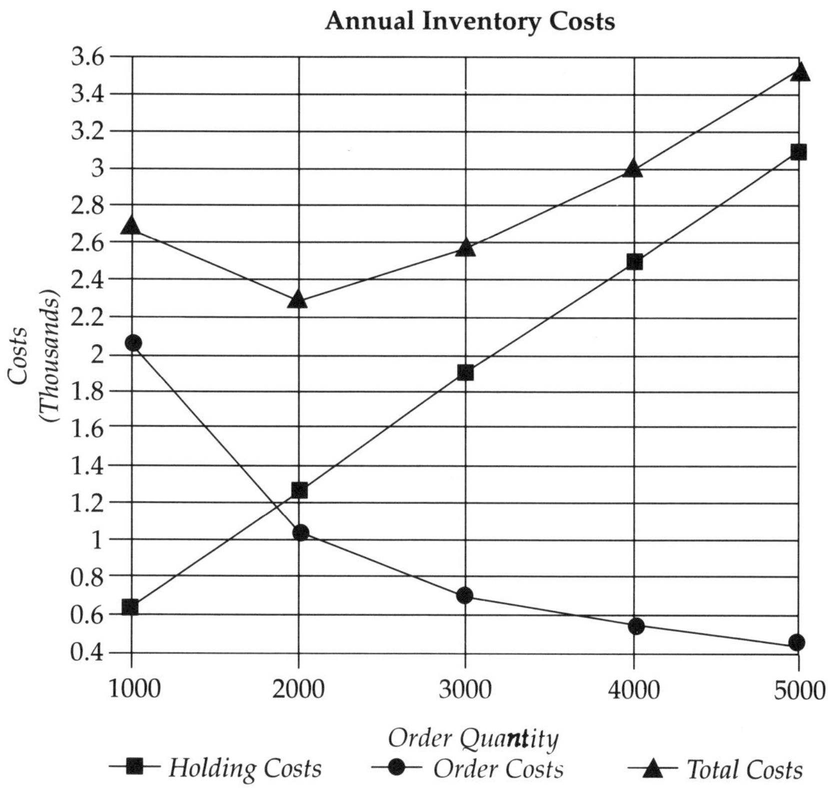

How to Use the Economic Order Quantity (EOQ) Method to Balance Holding and Ordering Costs

It has been theorized that the best order quantity should be an amount that equalizes inventory holding and ordering costs. The following equation is used to calculate the amount

$$EOQ = \sqrt{\frac{2DC_o}{C_h}}$$

Where

Q = Order size
D = Annual demand (units) for the company's product
C_o = Cost of placing one order
C_h = Cost of storing or holding one unit per year

Substituting numbers into the above, we obtain

C_o	\$10.00
C_h	\$2.50
D	250,000

$$EOQ = \sqrt{\frac{2 \times 250{,}000 \times 10}{2.50}}$$

Economic Quantity = 1,414. This translates to 177 orders per year.

$$\frac{250{,}000}{1{,}414}$$

While the computation recommends orders to made about every day, applicable lead times should also be considered. The equation to compute the reorder point with lead time is:

$$r = dm$$

Where

r = reorder point
d = demand per day
m = lead time for a new order in days

The company will place an order when the inventory quantity drops to r.

Just in Time Inventories (JIT)

A JIT system may reduce the inventory holding and ordering problem. Theoretically, when a certain raw material is required, it's supplied by the vendor, right there, on the spot. If this system is properly managed, the buying company does not have to carry any raw materials inventories. However, there are problems.

From the purchaser's viewpoint: If you use a JIT system you theoretically, carry no raw materials inventories. Therefore, you are completely dependent upon the supplier. If that supplier does not have the manufacturing or financial ability to keep you supplied, you could, someday, see your production line grind to a halt as you run out of stock.

From the supplier's viewpoint: Inasmuch as the JIT inventory allows the purchaser to avoid carrying inventories, it, conversely, shifts the burden to the supplier. If you are that supplier, you must carry sufficient stock to immediately satisfy your customer. However, if he or she gets into financial difficulty or tries to play games with you, you could be in deep trouble.

Materials Requirements Planning (MRP)

MRP is most useful for forecasting the amount of raw materials, which are dependent upon outside market demands of finished goods. The method runs on statistical data and provides very useful information. A detailed discussion of the system is beyond the scope of this book. However, there are many varieties of off-the-shelf software which can do the job.

How to Use Learning Curve Analysis to Estimate Labor Costs

For many reasons, the labor cost to make the first unit may be significantly higher than that experienced as more are produced. Many factors may contribute to more efficient performance:

- Increased familiarity by the employees
- Introduction of improved methods
- Product standardization
- Economies of scale

How to Apply: The rate of learning is an exponential function which can only be solved by using natural logarithms. The equation is:

$$\frac{Ln\ (\text{learning curve rate})}{Ln\ (2)}$$

Exponents for various learning curve rates:

70%	−0.5146
80%	−0.3219
90%	−0.152

Mathematical expression:

$$y = ax^b$$

Where

y = average direct labor hours per unit
a = number of direct labor hours for the first unit
x = cumulative number of units produced
b = index of learning ($0 < b < 1$)

What Are the Uses of Learning Curve Analysis

- *Valuing inventory:* Learning curve adjustments can affect the way labor and overhead are applied to inventory. If, at the beginning of the year, a predetermined overhead rate is calculated, and learning curve effects are not built in, distortions may result.
- *Pricing:* Suppose a new product is about to be introduced. If management is using cost-based pricing, its labor cost will probably be based on current hours. However, adjustments should be made for learning curve reductions.
- *Performance evaluation:* Learning curve analysis will help you evaluate differences in work done by experienced versus inexperienced people.

Illustration: A computer manufacturer has estimated that it will take 1,250 hours to produce its first PC. The industry has experienced a learning index of 80%.

A = # of hours for first unit	1,250
B = Index of learning	80.00%

80% Learning Curve

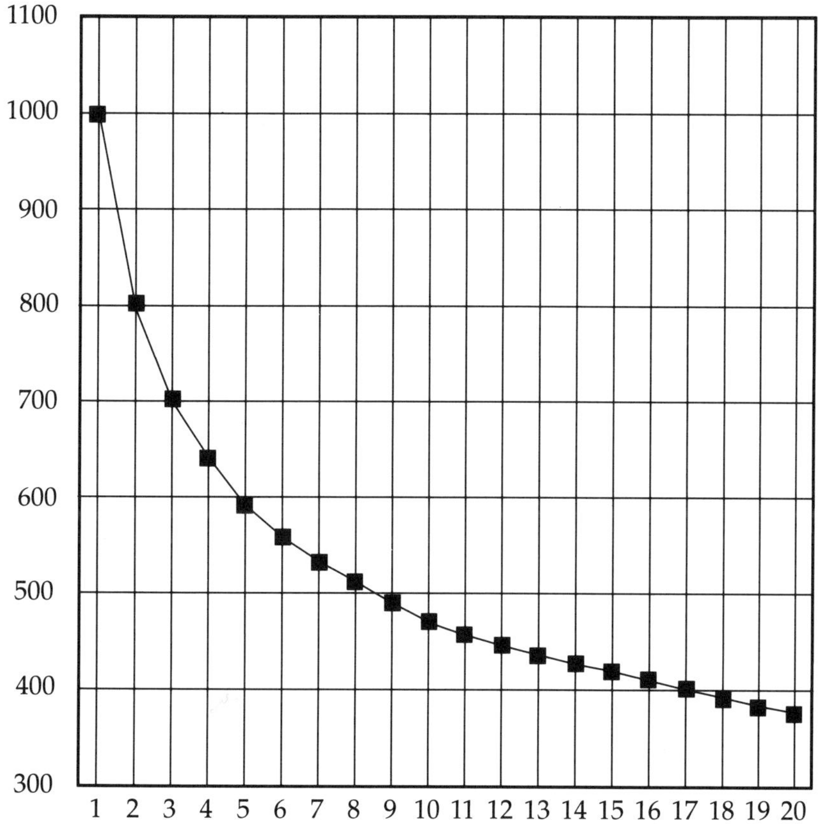

Number of Labor Hours

Unit	Average	Total	Marginal
1	1,250	1,250	1,250
2	1,000	2,000	750
3	878	2,633	633
4	800	3,200	567
5	745	3,723	523
6	702	4,213	490
7	668	4,677	464
8	640	5,120	443
9	616	5,546	426
10	596	5,956	411

As the graph shows, the average labor hours will continue to decline.

CHAPTER 29

How to Use Probability Analysis to Make Decisions

Introduction

Probabilistic models deal with missing or unknown information. After a quick review of probability theory, the following subjects will be presented:

- Using Subjective Probability to Estimate Activities
- Dealing With Uncertainty
- Payoff Tables
- Information Economics
- Computer Simulation

A Short Review of Probability Theory

The probability of an event is the ratio of the number of times the event occurs to the number of times the experiment or the observation is performed when the number of repetitions is very high.

For example, an auditor is confirming accounts receivable. If there are 10,000 accounts outstanding and 300 are estimated to be incorrect, the probability of an error is.03.

$$p = \frac{E}{O} = \frac{300}{10{,}000} = .03$$

This number can never be greater than 1. And, the sum of the probabilities of all observations, also, may not be greater than 1.

For Example: A coin toss

$$\begin{aligned} p(\text{heads}) &= \phantom{\underline{}}.50 \\ p(\text{tails}) &= \underline{.50} \\ & \underline{\underline{1.00}} \end{aligned}$$

How to Use Subjective Probability to Estimate Activities

Subjective probability is really nothing more than an individual's own ideas about the probability of the occurrence of an event. Since this is not based on objective, verifiable numbers, the estimator's conceptions and biases may play a major part. However, as a minimum, subjective estimates do attempt to attach a numerical value, and by so doing, add more validity.

Computing:

Let

p = probability of an event
E = event

A subjective probability of an event is

Estimate $* \; p$.

Then the total is computed to be
Sum $(E * p)_1 + (E * p)_2 + \ldots\ldots\ldots (E * p)_n$

Illustration: Cynthia Simon, sales manager of the Schuster Corporation, is estimating sales for the coming year. From past experience and her perception of next year's economic environment, she expects the following:

Number of Units	p	$P*N$
5,000	0.04	200
10,000	0.10	1,000
15,000	0.20	3,000
20,000	0.30	6,000
30,000	0.20	6,000
40,000	0.10	4,000
50,000	0.06	3,000
	1.00	23,200

In other words, she thinks there will be a 4% chance that the company will sell just 5,000 units. However, she is willing to say that there is a 20% probability that 15,000 units will be shipped in the coming year. The summation of all of these estimates total 23,200 units.

A General Guide to Dealing with Uncertainty

Any problem of this nature should be solved by working through the following steps:

1. *Establish a set of mathematically quantifiable objectives.*
   These can include the following
   a. To try to attain a predetermined profit,
   b. To bring costs down to a certain level,
   c. Or to evaluate a course of action in quantifiable terms.
2. *Determine what actions should be taken.*
   Whatever these are, they should follow the corporate mission and culture, and be attainable within organizational and financial constraints.
3. *Evaluate the various outcomes.*
   List the results in terms of profits, expenses, and resources. Do they make sense? Are they attainable?

Note: In this discussion, and throughout this book, it is extremely important that no matter how mathematically correct the resulting answer, we must always ask ourselves,

"DOES IT MAKE SENSE?"

4. *Assign probabilities to these outcomes.*
   Assigning probabilities is dependent upon a number of factors:
   - Prior history
   - Outside data of the environment, economy, and industry
   - Personal factors of the estimator

Caution: Beware of "Fun with Figures." Accountants love everything to balance. Therefore, we try to avoid making estimates. One way to hide the fact that perceived probabilities are just estimates, is to take the number to many significant digits.

For example, people erroneously think the number 10% is not as good as 10.47456. However, if the preliminary evaluations and judgments were not based on sound reasoning, they will not be much good no matter how far past the decimal point we go.

5. *Compute the likely results by calculating actions and outcomes.* There is an interrelationship between actions and outcomes. An action is a something we plan to do:

Example: We plan to build a new plant.

An outcome is the result of that action. This may be determined by market conditions and other factors beyond our control.

Example: The product will gain/not gain wide acceptance.

A payoff table will be used to help us evaluate the best action in light of varying outcomes and conditions.

6. *Choose the best action.*
7. *Monitor the results of these actions. Do not be afraid to change course.*

How to Construct a Payoff Table

A payoff table takes the following form

Outcomes

Action	s_1 **Good**	s_2 **Bad**
d_1 Spend a lot	r_1	r_2
d_2 Spend a little	r_3	r_4

Where

d = action
r = result
s = condition

Illustration: The Bradley Corporation is making a decision among three alternatives:

$d1$ = Buy a new plant
$d2$ = Lease a new plant
$d3$ = Make no changes

The payoff table estimates the results under two conditions:

$s1$ = There will be high market acceptance
$s2$ = There will be poor (low) market acceptance

The payoff table reveals the following:

		States of Nature Acceptance by Market	
		High	**Low**
		s1	*s2*
Buy New Plant	*d1*	250,000	(50,000)
Leas New Plant	*d2*	175,000	30,000
Make No Changes	*d3*	75,000	40,000

If, for example, the Company decides to acquire a new plant, it will earn $250,000 if the product is accepted by the market. On the other hand, if the market is not ready for what our company is ready to produce, we will lose $50,000.

There are a number of different ways to judge the estimated results.

A. *Maximin* Try to choose the course of action that maximizes the minimum payoff. The company is opting for the more conservative result. And, in this case, the best result will be achieved by making no changes (d3).

Maximum (Maximize minimum payoffs)		**Minimum Payoff**
Buy New Plant	d1	(50,000)
Lease New Plant	d2	30,000
Make No Changes	d3	40,000

B. *Maximax* Go all out and choose the approach the provides the biggest return. Under this decision set, the firm would probably want to buy the new plant.

But New Plant	d1	250,000
Lease New Plant	d2	175,000
Make No Changes	d3	75,000

C. *Regret or Opportunity Loss* This will show what would happen if we predicted a certain state of nature and based our action on that state? The numbers are the lost opportunities resulting from these actions.

	States of Nature Acceptance by Market	
	High	Low
	s1	s2
*d*1	0	90,000
*d*2	75,000	10,000
*d*3	175,000	0

For example, if we thought that market acceptance would be low, we would have chosen to do nothing (make no changes). The opportunity loss of $175,000 is calculated as follows:

Buy New Plant	$250,000
Make no changes	75,000
Opportunity Loss	$175,000

Building in Probabilities to Expected States of Nature

Assume we estimated the following states of nature:

Probability of Acceptance:

High	.40
Low	.60
	1.00

Expected Monetary Value (EMV)

We apply the probabilities to the estimated payoffs for the various states of nature and actions. We find that leasing the plant (*d*2) gives us the best EMV.

	States of Nature Acceptance by Market				
	High	p	Low	p	
	s1	0.40	s2	0.60	EMF
*d*1	250,000	100,000	(50,000)	(30,000)	70,000
*d*2	175,000	70,000	30,000	18,000	88,000
*d*3	75,000	30,000	40,000	24,000	54,000

Expected Opportunity Loss (EOL)

This number is derived by applying the probability to the opportunity losses calculated by the Regret or Opportunity Loss Table. You will see that Option D2 causes the lowest opportunity loss. This would match with the alternative chosen in the EMF calculations.

Expected Opportunity Loss
States of Nature
Acceptance by Market

	High	p	Low	p	
	s1	0.40	s2	0.60	EOL
*d*1	0	0	90,000	54,000	54,000
*d*2	75,000	30,000	10,000	6,000	36,000
*d*3	175,000	70,000	0	0	70,000

Using Information Economics to Compute the Cost of Additional Data

Information is a resource, and, like any other resource, costs money to obtain. Information economics measures its values and the cost to supply it. It is used to evaluate additional audit procedures, quality control measurements, and is useful to examine new markets and investments.

Any decision to seek more information must be based upon

- The environment faced by the decision maker
- Available actions
- Possible outcomes
- Role and cost of information system to signal state of the environment
- Risks of not having sufficient information

Calculating the Benefits of Information

An excellent way to calculate these benefits is to determine the expected value of perfect information (EVPI) and compare that to the costs of obtaining it. Using the previous example, EVPI uses the following payoff table:

	Possible Information		Action and Payoff Before Information is Available	After	Value of Perfect Info	p
(1)	High	s1	75,000	250,000	175,000	0.40
(2)	Low	s2	40,000	40,000	0	0.60
	EVPI				70,000	

(1) If we knew at the beginning that the product would be accepted by the marketplace, we would most likely invest in a new plant. However, we don't know, therefore, we take the more conservative option. The opportunity cost is $175,000, which factored by the probability of high acceptance, results in $70,000.
(2) If, on the other hand, we thought that the acceptance would be low, we would have elected to make no change. This would have been the best payoff of all three actions. There would be no value to this information.

How Much Do We Pay for Information

We pay up to $70,000.

Computer Simulation

It is beyond the scope of this book to do any more than acquaint you with computer simulation as a useful tool to solve many business problems.

Computer simulation, easily utilizes a number of off-the-shelf software products, is a technique to describe the behavior of a real world system. It can be used to analyze the following situations:

- Waiting line models
- Inventory
- Cash flow

This technique uses computer generated random numbers to study the behavior of a business situation. The operating characteristics of the model make inferences about the characteristics of the real condition.

CHAPTER 30
Systems Development

Introduction

A system is a set of elements which operate together to accomplish an objective.

Example: To get to work, you need a car, gas, and a route to get there. Together, these will accomplish your objective.

Note: Nothing in any part of the definition mentions computers or EDP or anything else about the data processing environment. DP is a subset of the larger accounting and office atmosphere.

As the following flow chart illustrates, there are three elements:

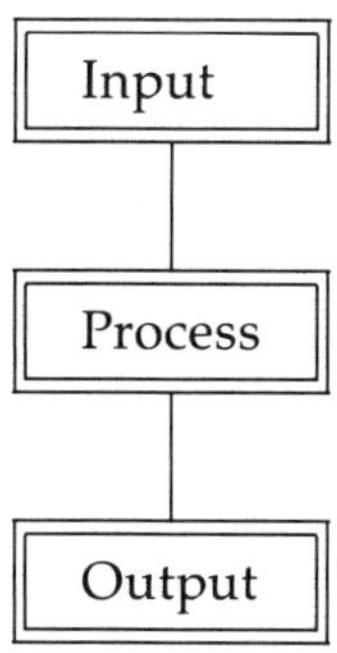

Systems are put into place and are expected to be adaptable to changes as they take place.

This chapter will cover the following elements of systems recognition and design:

- A Step-by-Step Approach to Systems Development
- Defining the Need
- Feasibility Studies
- Systems Proposals
- The Analysis Stage
- Designing the System

- Structured Flowcharts
- Building the System
- How to Save Money by Prototyping
- Installation
- Maintenance and Enhancement
- Systems Development in an EDP Environment

How to Prevent Entropy

Entropy is the decay that takes place over time as variations in usage and requirements alter the needs expressed in a system's original design. This condition is prevented by:

- Realization that the conditions that existed when it was installed won't continue without variance.
- Establishing monitoring and feedback procedures to supply early warning signals of potential breakdown.

A Step-by-Step Approach to Systems Development

1. *Beginning*—Recognize the need
2. *Feasibility*—Write preliminary solution
3. *Analysis*—Prepare approach to solution
4. *Design*—Formulate detailed framework
5. *Building*—Construction
6. *Installation*—Putting it into operation
7. *Maintenance*—Fine tuning and corrections

By breaking the overall project into seven distinct tasks, we avoid jumping off the deep end at the outset. As the program develops, segment by segment, we have the option at progressively greater cost, to either stop or alter our plans.

Defining the Need

A system comes into existence because somebody has a problem. The problem may drain profits, hinder productivity, or cause difficulties in a variety of ways. Situations of this type have three dimensions:

1. The Problem	We cannot get our billing out
2. Indicator	Poor cash flow
3. Reason	Inefficient billing procedure

The Burden of Poor Communication

In many organizations it is said, "Bad news travels down. Good news travels up." Why? Because the management of the firm has created an atmosphere where they only tell employees when they do something wrong. On the other hand, since the workers (or lower management) are afraid that the messenger of bad news will be killed, they only tell their bosses good things. So what happens? Problems are buried under the rug. Then, if there are weaknesses in the system, upper management will certainly not hear about them until it's too late.

As accountants, we are often the worst offenders. We have been lectured from the time we were students that confidentiality must be preserved. And so, we are excessively concerned about secrecy, and hold each bit of information to our bosoms as if it were the rarest mineral.

Example: It is not unusual to find materials' and supplies' prices blanked out on copies of documents.

Even in those corporations where employee ideas are sought, their input is often limited to suggestion schemes that may be poorly implemented. Long implementation delays lead to frustration and result in a loss of interest.

The extent of employee involvement sought in systems improvement can vary according to the overall level of participation desired by the corporation and the degree of interest across the work force.

How to Improve Communications

- *Use clear appropriate language.*
  Let people know what you want in a way that avoids all the buzz words and other multisyllable phrases that we love to use.
- *Establish credibility.*
  No matter how well you employ the services of information specialists, your message will not work unless it's believed. If people think they are being lied to, any meaningful communication attempt will be dead in its tracks.

- *Avoid labels.*
  All too often, as early as childhood, people are assigned labels that follow them throughout their lives. In an organization, as well, employees are often defined by the jobs they hold and any opinion held by a "lowly" employee will be ignored.

Example: "He's just an assembler."

- *Set up training programs.*
  The training function, in many companies, is either neglected or gets lip service and token acceptance, at best. A well-designed educational program, that is supported by top management, can do wonders by allowing the employees to do their jobs better as well as see the bigger picture.

For example, a class covering the company's financial statements and systems to members of the accounts payable department.

Establish communication courses. Communication is something that each of us does. But, few do it well. It is a two-way street where each party functions as a transmitter and receiver of data. Courses in this subject help people open up.

However, for any of this to succeed, it must have the unqualified support of top management.

How to Conduct a Feasibility Study

A well-conducted feasibility study will yield a preliminary solution to the problem. It is less detailed and, therefore, less costly than a full blown systems design. The process flows as follows:

1. Gather information
2. Devise alternatives
3. Evaluate choices
4. Select preferred option
5. Prepare proposal

1. *Information Gathering.* You should focus on two subjects here:

a. A description of the present situation or system

b. The problems

To get this information, you must go to the trenches and interview the people who are directly involved with the present situation and most closely feel the effects of the problem. Your interview should be well planned and expeditiously carried out.

Before the Interview: Planning is the key. You should carefully

a. Get information about the jobs, backgrounds, and temperaments of the interviewees.

b. Schedule your appointments at a convenient time where you will be free from interruption.

c. Carefully prepare questions. They should be open ended to allow the subject latitude to expand upon your queries.

Note: Avoid close ended questions.
Example: "Do you like the present system?"
Better: "What do (or don't) you like about the present system?"

2. *During the Interview.*

a. Show respect, be on time, and do not go over your allotted time.

b. Watch for body language. Often, it will reveal tell tale signs of the "real" situation.

Examples:

Body Language	*Meaning*
Folding Arms, Crossing Legs	Doesn't want to hear. Closed to ideas and questions.
Smiles, Open Arms	Listening, attentive, receptive
Nodding head	Questions registers in mind Cooperation, agreement
Eyes glaze	Doesn't understand you

c. If possible, use a tape recorder.

d. Draw pictures. If you are trying to understand a system, a flow chart is very helpful.

e. At the conclusion of interview, work on a joint summarization of your findings.

3. *After the Interview.*

a. Write up and integrate all the responses.

b. Review with management.

List Alternatives

At this point, the solution may be very obvious. All too often, you might not have a clue how to recommend the best possible answer to management and the various user groups. In this latter case, it's wise to go on a search for options. Brainstorming (Chapter 23) and the Delphi technique (Chapter 24) are useful.

Evaluate Options

The job here is to develop criteria. These criteria should be evaluated by quantitative as well as qualitative factors.

Quantitative factors:

a. Cost
b. Error rate
c. Profitability
d. Savings

Qualitative factors:

a. Flexibility/Adaptiveness
b. Mobility
c. Security
d. Beauty
e. Effect on morale
f. Acceptance

Choose the Best

There are many techniques available to management accountants. Many of these are discussed in other chapters of this book. Some of these are:

Net Present Value—Chapter 27

Return on Investment—Chapter 22

Write a Proposal

This final result of your feasibility study will be discussed in the next section.

How to Prepare a Systems Proposal

This section of the chapter presents some of the contents that should be included, or at least considered, in drafting a proposal.

Who's the User?

You can waste a great deal of time by preparing a proposal for somebody in the organization who does not have decision making authority. Before you start, it is very important to be able to identify those persons and to discern just what and how much control they have.

Sample Contents of Proposal

1. Statement of needs
   a. List in order of priority
   b. Show that they are acceptable to the organization
2. Statement of goals
   a. Illustrate your ability to accomplish them
   b. Explain that there is a clear agreement between you and management.
   c. Make sure that none are self defeating or contradictory to the purpose of project.
3. Statement of objectives
   a. Decide how specific you want them at this point. The proposed feasibility study may be the first step to better definition.
   b. Show how behavior will be modified.
   c. Present the criteria for judging the results.
   d. Discuss methods to evaluate interim outcomes.
4. Projects concept
   a. Inputs
      (1) Needs of organization.
      (2) Your capabilities.
      (3) Description of the present state of the art.

(4) Short description of your understanding of the objectives.

b. Procedures

(1) Identify the tasks to be accomplished.
(2) Provide a description of the task sequence to be followed.
(3) Process of modifying the tasks as the project progresses.

5. Procedures narrative
   a. Illustrate each procedure with flow diagrams.
   b. Specify any unique features.
   c. Describe how client management will be utilized and kept informed.
   d. Describe terminal objectives.
6. Project timeline
   a. Include timeline worksheet
   b. Use PERT/CPM.
   c. Plot significant milestones.
7. Personnel Loading
   a. Detail labor days/hours required.
   b. Calculate average labor time.
   c. Schedule time by individual over total project.
8. Capabilities
   a. Describe your experience.
   b. Provide resumes of key individuals.
   c. Portray your organizational structure.
   d. Summarize why you can do the job.

A Sample Proposal in Letter Form

John Blank, CEO
The Blank Company

Dear Mr. Blank:

This is an informal proposal to the Blank Company to develop a **Computer Simulation Training Program**.

The Program

1. A typical operation would be developed as a computer simulation.
2. Managers would then either play either against the computer or other teams.
3. The players would try various approaches to marketing, inventory policies, cost controls, and personnel to attain the winning results.
4. The simulation program would bring various economic permutations into the scenario.
5. The game would be constructed so results could be seen over a relatively long time frame.
6. Detailed accounting reports would be generated to chart the results.

Our Project Team

Gus Jones, PhD.

Dr. Jones is a professor of Management Science at California State University. In addition to serving as the associate dean at the School of Business and Management, he has extensive publishing and consulting credits. Detailed resume follows.

Jay Ruben, MS, CMA, CPA

Mr. Ruben is a professor of Accounting at California State University–Northridge. Mr. Ruben has over 30 years of public accounting experience and has written and lectured substantially. Detailed resume follows.

Other Resources

Specialized industry accounting specialists, marketing, and finance experts.

The Development Process

We propose a systems approach to this process which will encompass the following steps:

1. *The Initiation Stage:* This stage of our process will analyze your needs by examining the present environmental condition, the desired revised condition and the forces required to modify bring about the change.
2. *Feasibility Study:* To conduct this study, we will interview management and prospective participants to gather information needed to derive a listing of preliminary goals. From this we will develop criteria, evaluate alternative methods to achieve the intended results. The feasibility study will present the preferred alternatives and the reasons for their selection.

3. *Systems Analysis:* We will review the user and system requirements, review the system for other constraints, and make any modifications that are required.
4. The Simulation Program will be designed.
5. Manuals and other instructional materials will be written.
6. Beta testing will be done with a select group.

We will perform the initiation and feasibility studies before we proceed further. We estimate our fee for services up to this point to be $25,000. At the conclusion of these stages, we will meet with you and formalize the work and the fee structure for the next steps.

Terms of Agreement

This proposal will expire August 31, 1990.

After August 31, the proposal may be renewed or extended by mutual agreement of the parties hereto.

Our team shall not, during the term of this agreement or afterward, use or disclose any confidential information of the company obtained from or through the services specified in this agreement, nor display for any purpose any letter, report or any copy or reproduction thereof belonging to Company without written authorization, unless the documents have been previously published. The term confidential information used in this paragraph shall mean information, particularly within the knowledge of Company, and its representatives, employees, and those in privy with it, which is not available to the public and is subject to protection as property under recognized principles.

Either of the parties hereto may cancel this agreement on thirty (30) days written notice.

If the above set forth proposal is in accordance with your understanding of our agreement, please sign and return the enclosed copy of this proposal along with initial deposit ($5,000) to our office.

SIGNATURES

The Analysis Stage

At this point management would have read your proposal. If the decision is to go, then you can proceed to put together the needed resources. This includes the following:

1. Assemble your team. The team should include internal personnel as well as consultants.
2. Prepare detailed scheduling forecasts.
3. Build detailed budgets of costs.

Designing the System

Detailed plans for everything we intend are developed in this stage. Personnel and other resources are assigned to the task.

To start, we put together a logical plan. In so doing, there are two options:

1. Top Down—concentrate on the overall picture.
2. Bottom Up—start with segments and go for immediate solutions.

In the design phase, the various coordination processes should be delineated. These include:

1. Methods of controlling the quality of the work as it progresses.
2. Implementation of budgets and putting into place various monitoring systems.

There are various ways of describing the process. Some of these include very detailed flowcharts where you must use a dictionary to identify and remember the symbols. A better method uses structured flowcharts.

How to Prepare Structured Flowcharts

A structured chart is a graphic representation of the relationships between the various modules within a system.

The structured flowchart uses the following symbols

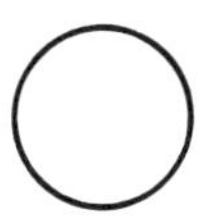
Process or data transformation

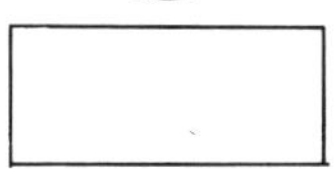
External entity

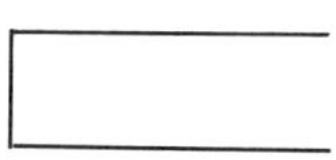
Data Store

Data Flow

When we use this method, we first broadly lay out the overall system and then work down by sub-step to each component.

For Example:

Overall System

1 = Feasibility Study
2 = Analyze the System

2 = Analyze the System
  2.1 = Study the Current System
  2.2 = Model the New System Requirements

These can be further de-constructed.

For example:
  2.1 = Study the Current System
Then
  2.1A = Interview the users
  2.1B = Obtain documentation

The following is an example of a structured flowchart constructed in three levels:

Structured Flowchart

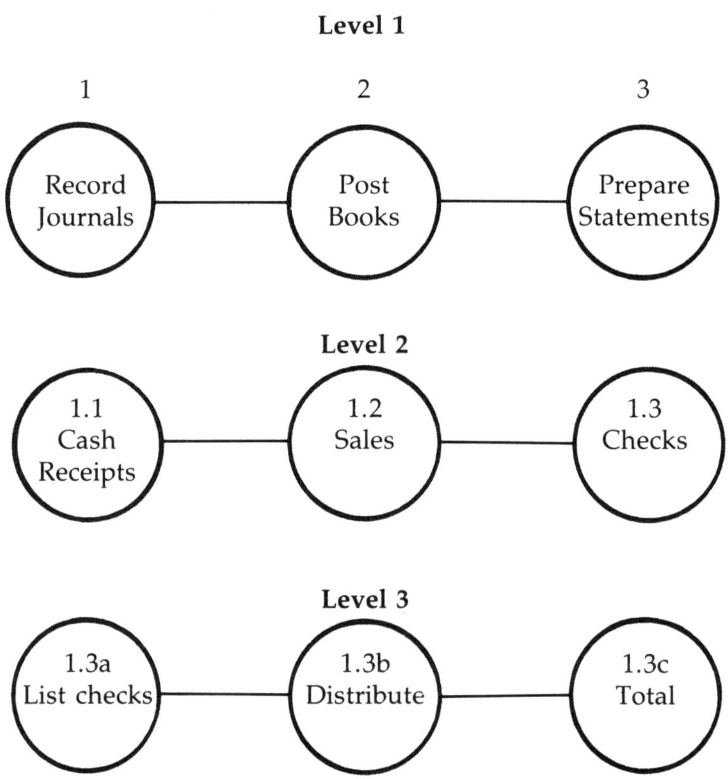

Exhibit 30-1

Building the System

At this phase, the analysis and design has been accomplished and we can now bring all the parts together. There are four activities in this stage:

1. Construction
2. Coordination
3. Testing
4. Preparation of user training manuals.

System Construction

When we construct the system, we bring all the parts together.

For example, assume a sales, accounts receivable system. This may require acquiring software and hardware.

What Has to Be Done?

1. Vendors have to be interviewed.
2. Purchases are made.
3. Contracts are prepared and reviewed.

Coordination

The teams should be working by now. The job of the systems manager is to see that the mandate previously established is followed and the people are doing their work. Some tools that should be considered at this point are:

1. Staff meetings.
2. Review of time budgets.
3. Problem resolution.
4. Logging the process.

Testing

Checking should be performed at various times throughout the entire building period. The following types of procedures can be used individually or in concert:

a. *Logical:* Try to anticipate the probable uses for the system and verify that it is capable of performing these tasks.

For example, if you want the system to age the accounts receivable, you may want to run sample transactions and see if the results agree with your predetermined check figures.

b. *Limit:* To determine that the system will provide signals when limits have been breached.

For example, assume that a customer, Larsen Manufacturing, is only allowed open credit of $1,000. Enter invoices that will exceed that ceiling.

Training Manuals

Training manuals should be provided by the various vendors and then adapted by you to handle the organization's specific requirements. These should include:

1. *Operational information.* Instructions to run the system. This data should be prepared for all users.

Example: Data entry operators, data users, auditors

2. *Technical descriptions including flowcharts.*
3. *Descriptions and outlines for training courses.*

How to Save Money by Prototyping

A *prototype* is an experimental version of the system. It is used when the requirements are difficult to specify in advance, and/or may change significantly during development.
Examples:

- Converting a portion of the inventory to an MRP system.
- Automating only one department.

It saves money, because by building only a portion of the complete project, the organization can try out ideas without incurring large costs. And, by so doing, can reduce the overall application development time.

Furthermore, the users can see something in operation and it will be easier for them to evaluate than mere written descriptions or flowcharts.

The Prototyping Process

1. Identify the user's basic information requirements including desired outputs from the system.
2. Establish realistic expectations.
3. Develop an initial prototype system. The aim is to build a functional interactive system. Inasmuch as the entire program is not being constructed, you should, at first, aim for speed rather than efficiency. The aim is to get something working that the users can evaluate. Therefore, we should understand that our initial prototype will initially be incomplete.
4. Revise and enhance as necessary.

How to Install the System

In the opening portion of this phase, we must determine if the system is acceptable to the user as constructed. While much of this work should have been done during the earlier activities, there is now a complete product. At last, the users will have something definite so they will be able to answer the following questions:

- Is the cost acceptable?
- What is the impact on the organization?

Note: Although many of the same points may have already been covered, some further explanation may be required:

1. The system is not going to be working at full tilt from the beginning.
2. The learning curve effect will slow the production at first.

Types of Installation Procedures

Type and Description	Advantages	Disadvantages
Parallel Operate both at the same time	Safest	Most expensive
Pilot Operate new system with limited capacity	1. Train new personnel without needing two staffs.	1. People are not learning new system as a whole.

(Continued on next page)

Type and Description	Advantages	Disadvantages
	2. Can reconvert to old system at first failure of new. 3. Allows you to work out problems at minimum costs.	2. Two systems are still operating. 3. Organization is incurring the costs of two systems.
Immediate	1. Fast 2. Least costly	1. Major problem if new system doesn't work. 2. Requires quick training.

Systems Maintenance and Enhancement

Any good system should be a living organism. If it is going to work properly, it must be maintained and enhanced as conditions changes.

Maintenance

Systems maintenance equals feedback. Procedures should be installed at the outset to provide signalling devices that all is proceeding as planned. The mechanism can include:

- Statistical quality control procedures
- Internal and operational auditing

Quality control parameters should be established early that will tell you the minimum error rate or amount that is tolerable.

Note: It is often impracticable to look for a zero error rate.

Enhancement

Nothing remains the same. The organization's requirements change. And, various transformations to the state of the art may allow you to perform the procedures required with greater effectiveness and reduced cost. Therefore, it is essential that you continually be aware of indications that new programs, procedures, and hardware should be considered.

- Follow the trends in the technology.

  Attend professional and trade meetings.

  Read the literature.

- Look for changes in the environment, industry, and organization that may portend modified systems requirements.

Note: For a discussion on Top Down Analysis, refer to Chapter 16.

Enhancement versus Replacement

At some point, a decision may have to be made between upgrading what you have and installing a brand new system. Many factors come into play.

- The differential costs. See Chapter 23.
- Qualitative factors such as improved analytical abilities, faster hardware and software, and ease of use.

Systems Development in an EDP Environment

Whether you are considering a manual or an EDP system, the general procedures are the same. However, there are certain factors that are peculiar to computer systems. The following is a list of the various cost factors that should be appraised in contemplating an EDP system:

Hardware

Computer System
Secondary Storage
Keyboard
Other Input Devices
Monitor
Printer
Modem
Cabling
Surge Protector

Software

- Systems & Utilities
- Applications

Data Communications Hardware and Software

Furniture

- Desks
- Chairs
- Lighting
- Filing Facilities

Site Preparation Costs

- Noise Reduction
- Physical Security
- Additional Power
- Communications Outlets

Sales Taxes

Conversion Costs

- Systems Analyst
- Programmer
- Trainer
- Data Entry Clerks

Analysis and Design
Custom Programming
Training

- Trainers Time
- Staff Time

Data Conversion

- Costs of Running Dual

Annual Costs

- Maintenance
    - Hardware
    - Software
- Supplies
- Insurance
- Additional Personnel
    - Data Entry
    - Control
    - Programming

CHAPTER 31

How to Get the Most Out of Electronic Data Processing

Introduction

The next two chapters will cover what you need to know to effectively operate in the EDP environment. They will be generally organized as follows:

Chapter 31—Hardware and systems overview

Chapter 32—Software acquisition and use

Computers are information processors that are able to perform substantial arithmetical and logical functions without human intervention. Because of the many engineered and evolving characteristics, they have become a necessity to almost all professional accountants.

The topics that are presented in this chapter include:

- Types of computer systems
- EDP components
- Computer operating systems
- Understanding and selecting hardware
- Ergonomics
- Internal controls for the EDP environment
- EDP auditing
- Procedures before purchasing
- Becoming an EDP consultant

Types of Computer Systems

Computers are classified by

- The amount of data they can hold

- Their speed
- Their ability to communicate with other systems

Data Storage and Processing

Units of Data: The basic data measurement is a *byte*. A byte is approximately equal to a character. As a rule of thumb, there are 1,000 bytes on a page of text.

Size: The size of a computer is usually measured in bytes where:

1 Kilobyte (K) = 1 thousand bytes
1 Megabyte (M) = 1 million bytes
1 Gigabyte (G) = 1 billion bytes

Capacity: A computer's ability to process data is further measured by Random Access Memory (RAM) and secondary storage.

RAM: Holds the program, the data used, and all the operating instructions while the computer is processing. Since it is part of the operating system, it processes data faster than that in secondary storage.

Note: When the system is shut off, all data in RAM is wiped out.

Secondary storage: Data held on disk or other storage devices. This is slower because it requires mechanical operations.

EDP Components

The ensuing listing and description of EDP components will be built around the following diagram:

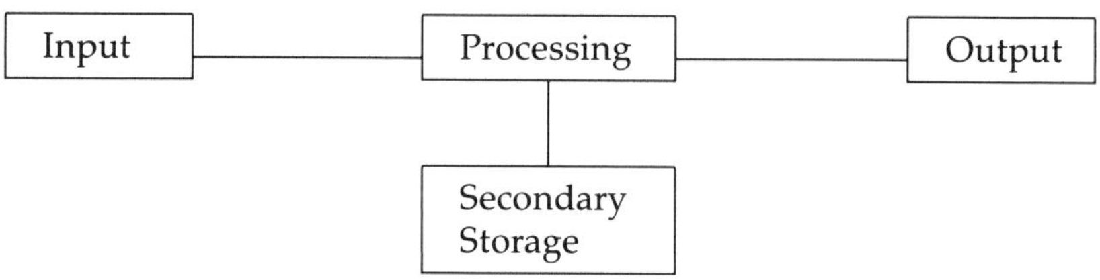

1. *Input*

The following input devices are ways to get the data into the system:

- Keyboard
- Mouse

- Scanner
- Voice recognition
- Optical character reader (OCR)

2. *Processing*

Performed by the computer.

3. *Output*

How you get the information back. It must have the following characteristics:

- Usable format
- Quick delivery
- Quality images
- Monitor
- Printers
- Voice synthesizers
- Plotters

Which Computer Operating System Should You Choose?

The operating system is the particular hardware and software configuration designed to run a particular form of hardware and software.

Attention: Since a computer should be acquired to handle certain applications it is most important to find out if the operating system you are considering will run the applications programs you need.

Many of these applications come in the form of off the shelf software that are only compatible with a specific form of operating system.

Before you get bogged down in their various attributes, make sure you answer these questions:

What are your needs?

What software will fill these needs?

What system will support that software?

Fortunately, while there are many different brands of computers, there are only a few major forms of operating systems:

Name	Runs on	Comments
PC-DOS	IBM Compaq Other compatible systems	Runs most business software. There are over 100,000 applications.
OS/2	IBM	Faster and higher capacity than PC-DOS Limited software available
Apple	Apple Macintosh	For Apple type systems* Good graphics capability
NEXT	NEXT	state of the art system Limited software available
UNIX	Mainframes	

*Apple type computers will accept certain DOS programs.

How to Understand and Select the Best Hardware for You

In this section, we'll cover the specs on the hardware. We will include:

- Central Processing Unit
- Storage devices
- Monitor
- Input Devices
- Printers

In order to be an intelligent consumer, it is necessary to

1. Know what you are looking for
2. Understand what equipment will provide it

This section will help you zero in on the right equipment to do the job you want.

1. *CPU—Qualities:*

- What operating system will it run?
- Speed

- Ease of use
- Expandability

a. *Operating system:* You must determine your needs before you even start to shop. The operating system that best meets those needs is the one for you.

b. *Speed* Speed is measured by the number of machine operations a microprocessor will perform in a second. It is affected by:

Word size or the number of bits processed in one operation.

Obviously, the bigger the word size, the faster the processing. Over its evolution, the microprocessing chip has been improved to expand its word size capabilities.

For example:

Chip	Word Size	Used In
Intel 80286	16 bit	IBM AT
Intel 80386	32 bit	

Internal memory is measured in RAM (random access memory) size. The computer loads the programs into the RAM when it is turned on. The more RAM the system has the faster the processing because, it does not have to draw as much data from external storage.

Example: The IBM-AT uses an Intel 80286 microprocessor. The AT's internal memory is 640K which can be expanded to 4M.

Efficiency of programs

a. *Ease of use:* A computer system should be an efficient integration of software and hardware. If you are not a programmer or expert you should be able to operate your computer as you would your family car—turn the key on and drive. It should therefore be easy to:

- install
- turn on and off
- operate
- backup
- maintain

The seller should provide good documentation. In addition, look for a system that is supported by other books and literature that are readily available at bookstores and libraries.

b. *Expandability:* No matter how much your system is capable of doing when you buy it, there will come a time when you will want more. It should, therefore, be configured to be easily enlarged. An expansion board will plug into the main circuit board and will allow you to add various features as they are needed. These include controller slots and serial and parallel interface ports.

Note: Most computer systems are made up of monitors, keyboards, printers, and other components. These can be easily upgraded when the time arrives.

2. *Portability.* Quite often, portability only means that you can move the computer around without worrying about damaging the hard disk. However, it will still have to be plugged in to be operated.

A laptop, on the other hand, is completely portable. It operates by a battery. It is lightweight and can be easily carried around. However, if this is what you want, check on the battery pack. Some of the packs have a very short life and run out of juice just when you're getting started.

Caution: The lightness and portability of the laptops are often their undoing. They are attractive targets for thieves.

3. *Storage Devices.* These provide offline storage of large quantities of data. When the computer is turned on, their contents are loaded as needed. There are three forms of offline storage that are commonly used.

• *Floppy disk:* This is a flexible plastic surface coated with a ferromagnetic material. They are inexpensive and can be stored and moved easily. However, they are slow compared to other types of media.

Most floppy disks come in two sizes:

5-1/4 inch
3-1/2 inch

The following amount of data can be held in an IBM configuration:

XT – 450K
AT – 1.25M

• *Hard disk:* These use Winchester technology and contain hard disks with multiple platters. While a hard disk is more expensive than a floppy and less movable, they are much faster and can store quite a bit more data. In fact, their capacity ranges from 20M to 2.3 gigabytes

• *Tape drives:* A tape drive is a good backup device. It is relatively inexpensive and can quickly copy everything on the hard disk.

4. *Monitor.* Also called a CRT (Cathode Ray Tube), the monitor is used to enter commands or data and view output. There a number of factors that should be considered by the buyer:

• *Color versus monochrome:* A monochrome monitor portrays the images in black and white, amber, or green. It is more than sufficient to handle accounting, data base, and spreadsheet functions. However, a color monitor provides a more interesting presentation.

Caution: Color monitors do *not* equal color printing.

• *Ability to display graphics.* This is usually established by presence of a graphics card (printed circuit board) in the computer.

• *Resolution.* Resolution standards are usually established by the number of *pixels* that the monitor can display. A pixel is defined as the smallest dot that can be seen on screen.

• *Types of display.*

MGP 720 × 350, one color

CGA 320 × 200

EGA 640 × 400

VGA 800 × 600

• *Brightness.* The screen should be sufficiently bright to avoid eyestrain. Furthermore, the brightness should be able to be varied.

• *There should be minimum flicker.*

• *Characters should not be crowded on the screen.*

• *User interface.* The following should be considered:

Only essential information should be provided.

All data for one task should fit on screen.

Provisions should be made for built in windows, e.g., the ability to see multiple data.

5. *Input Devices.* These get the data into the system. They include keyboards, mouses, and scanners.

a. *Keyboards:* The most common way to enter data. It resembles a typewriter keyboard with the same letter and number configuration. In addition, there are:

i. *A number pad.* Found on the right side of the keyboard and resembles an adding machine.

ii. *Cursor keys.* Used to move the cursor around the screen. They are alternative functions on the number pad. To use them the "num lock" key has to be turned off.

Note: The 101 function keyboard has a separate set of cursor keys which can be used in conjunction with the number keys.

iii. *Function keys* are built in programs which allow you to perform many operations with just one keystroke.

iv. *Control keys* directly command the computer to perform certain steps. They include: control, alt, insert, break, etc.

What Should You Consider When You Buy a Keyboard?

You should try out the various models before purchasing. Look for the following:

1. The feel: Does it enter the characters easily?
2. Configuration: Different versions place various function keys in a variety of locations. Sometimes that placement can hamper your efficiency.
3. The click: How loud does the input of data register?
    a. *Mouse:* This is a device that you allows you to maneuver and manipulate data. It is excellent for working with graphics.
    b. *Scanner:* A scanner is akin to a camera. It takes an image of pictures, graphics, or text and places that image in the form of a collection of bits in the computer's storage.
4. *Output Devices.* The most common way to get information out of a computer is by obtaining hard printed copy. There are two classifications of printers:

Impact Printers: These are similar to a typewriter in that the image is made by striking paper. Most of these are dot matrix printers.

Non-Impact Printer (NIP): An NIP works by transferring images by means of a laser beam or other heat sensitive device to the printer. The laser printer is the most common form.

What to Look for in a Dot Matrix

A dot matrix printer constructs an image by using a print head of tiny pins which are pushed against a ribbon to print a series of dots.

When considering a dot matrix printer, one often has to decide between quality and speed.

Quality is affected by the number of pins the head contains. The 24-pin head, at present, is considered the best.

Speed is a function of the printer used. This is usually quoted in characters per second (CPS).

How to Get Quality and Speed in a Dot matrix printer

Most dot matrix printers allow you to print in normal and near letter quality (NLQ) modes. Generally, NLQ printing is done by double striking the images. This, of course, slows down the process but improves the images.

Laser Printers

These printers operate by using a laser beam to transfer images from the computer into its internal memory and then to the paper. They are generally faster than dot matrix printers and offer greatly improved quality.

Note: Inasmuch as a laser printer does not require a tractor feeder, you can use almost any form of paper plus transparencies, envelopes and labels.

Be careful: The laser printer works on intense heat. The use of stock that does not conform to the manufacturer's specifications may harm the machine.

Printer software support: Many software programs do *not* support all printers.

Ergonomics—The Human Machine Interface

Ergonomics is defined as the science of designing computer hardware and office furniture so that humans find them easier and more comfortable to use. Since a poorly designed workstation may lead to headaches, backaches, and something called the repetitive stress syndrome, you should pay close attention to the following:

1. *Keyboard:* The keyboard should be attached to the system by a long cord. This will enable you to adapt the typing to you rather than the other way around.
2. *Desk:* The work surface of the desk should be at the right height. What is that height? It's where your forearms are approximately parallel to the floor.

3. *Monitor:* The monitor should be able to be tilted and swiveled. It should be placed at eye level and at a comfortable distance.

Note: If you wear bifocals, remember it's the bottom half of the glasses that is used for close work. Make sure you place the screen where you will not have to squint or strain your neck muscles.

4. *Lighting:* Make sure you have enough, glare-free lighting. Halogen lamps are excellent for this purpose.
5. *Noise Level:* Try to situate yourself away from detracting noises. If necessary, you can buy a sound buffer for the printer.
   Note: A laser jet printer is very quiet.
6. *Seating:* When you consider the seating make sure the chair has good back support, arms, and adjustable height and tilt. Also, see that you have sufficient legroom. A footrest helps avoid back strain.
7. *Your Body:* This is the one piece of equipment that cannot be altered or replaced. Here are some things that keep your strain and fatigue level low when sitting at a computer:
   a. Get up and stretch at least once every hour. Take a walk or do some other form of exercise.
   b. Do eye exercises. Take off your glasses and cup your eyes to avoid all light.
   c. Drink plenty of water. It is good for the system, and a good excuse to get up.

Internal Controls for the EDP Environment

Internal controls for a non automated environment are discussed in Chapter 7. We will now cover the particular problems that come into play when data processing equipment is used. We recommend you refer to that chapter in the ensuing presentation.

Overview of the internal control problems inherent to an EDP system:

1. A computer system is self contained. Therefore, many of the functions are performed by one person. And, there is no separation of duties.
2. Something is going on inside the machine. The data goes in and information comes out. The mystery of what's happening keeps many users from trying to understand the workings.

3. Although the hardware keeps getting better, there are still times when it goes down and data gets lost. Without good controls, an event of this kind can destroy a business.

Internal Control Checklist

1. *Documentation.* The following should be chronicled:

a. Tasks assigned to system

b. Write up of procedures to

  collect the data
  input to the computer
  control the output

c. Specific system operating instructions to

  turn on equipment
  enter data
  backup data

d. Hardware description including

  error messages
  help prompts
  maintenance instructions

e. Software documentation

Specific operating instructions
  error messages

f. Persons to contact if something goes wrong with

  hardware
  software

g. Log of errors encountered and action taken

h. Backup log including

  date
  files backed up

2. *Hardware controls.* These are usually built in by the manufacturer and include echo checks and error messages.

3. *Access controls.*

a. Passwords to prevent unauthorized internal access
b. Passwords changed from time to time
c. Internal run data of access times
d. Data entry
e. Passwords to prevent unauthorized access by hackers and computer pirates
f. Write protection to avoid copying over data
g. Clearly defined labels

4. *Input controls*

a. Batch controls before input
b. Batch totals
c. Hash totals

Note: A hash total is a summation of non-monetary numbers. For example, account numbers may be totaled. The computer is also programmed to run a total of account numbers which is compared to your original tape.

5. *Output controls.*

a. Match batch control totals with output results.
b. Determine that output appears reasonable

6. *Disaster control.* When we speak of a disaster we are concerned about the following:

- Breakdown of the equipment
- Loss of data and programs
- Fires and various forms of natural disasters

a. Formal backup procedures should be instituted. These should provide for:

- Regular backup dates.
- Onsite and offsite copies

How often? We answer that by replying: How long will it take you to recapture the data if it is lost?

For example, if data entry is a continuous process, it should be backed up at least once a day.

A Few Hints to Help You Streamline backup

If there is a lot of information stored in the computer, the backup process can be very time consuming. You may want to consider:

- A tape backup system
- A special backup program such as "Fastback"
- Backing up only the files that have changed since the processing
- Automatic backup programs

b. Establish secure offsite storage facilities

c. Document disaster recovery procedures

d. Arrange to use another organization's compatible system while yours is down

e. Provide for adequate insurance

How to Audit an EDP System

If you are called upon to audit a computer based system, you are concerned with the following:

- The degree of compliance with internal control
- The fairness of account balances

Computer audit procedures can be generally divided into the following forms:

Around the computer

Through the computer

Auditing Around the Computer

There are two procedural groupings for "around the computer" auditing:

1. Flowchart the procedures. Use this information to prepare a preliminary internal control evaluation.
2. Compare input to output. What you will do here is take a sample of input data and compute what information it should produce. Then you will compare these expected results with the output data generated by the computer.

Auditing Through the Computer

There are many objectives to your work:

a. To verify extensions and footings
b. To examine records for quality, completeness, consistency, and correctness
c. To compare data on separate files
d. To see that the system properly summarizes and re-sequences data
e. To select audit samples
f. To prepare confirmation requests

When you design the audit program, you should build them around the three legged stool of

audit risk
complexity of system
volume of data

Control the process: If you are going to utilize any of the following methods, it is important that you are in control of the processing every step of the way. You must make sure you:

a. select the data
b. prevent intervention or alterations to the program
c. are there through the entire processing
d. receive all the output including input listings

Through the Computer Techniques

- *Generalized audit software* programs are designed for auditors to help them perform many audit functions on a variety of computer systems and for different clients. By supplying certain parameters, these programs will perform the following tasks:

  a. retrieve requested records
  b. make calculations
  c. create files
  d. produce reports
  e. select samples

- *Customized audit software* is designed for a specific function. While it gives the auditor exactly what he or she may need, the development costs can be very expensive.
- *Utility programs* which are built into a system can be used to help auditors familiarize themselves about how the computer performs its various routines.
- *Test data* consist of created information which can be run through the system to simulate a variety of events. They are used to see:

  a. how the system processes faulty data

  b. how information flows through the system

  c. if the output agrees with the predetermined results.

Caution: When you do through-the-computer auditing the client's computer system will have to be shut down which obviously delays their work flow. So, make sure that you are well prepared before "turning the key".

Be Very Careful: Some through-the-computer techniques may be destructive, i.e. they will write over actual data. Therefore, it is very important to make sure a complete backup has been done before you start your work.

What You Should Do Before You Purchase a Computer System

There are eight steps which should be followed:

1. Needs assessment
2. Determine systems requirements
3. Screen potential vendors
4. Evaluate software
5. Evaluate hardware
6. Select the best hardware and software combination
7. Implement
8. Monitor and maintain

1. *Needs Assessment*

a. *Review priorities:* Do a broad organizational overview.
What is the company's mission?
How are our long-term goals?

How are we moving towards these goals?
What do we need to accomplish them?
How will better information processing help?

b. *Gather data:*
Functions required
Volume of activities
Personnel involved in present processing
Time required to service existing work load

c. *Determine potential benefits:*
Tangible benefits
Labor cost savings
Facilities cost savings
Intangible benefits
Better information

d. *Identify specific applications:*
These may be:
Accounting package
Payroll
Invoicing
Word processing
Data base systems
Spreadsheet analyses

e. *Assess environment:* The top-down analytical approach was covered in Chapter 16. A micro top-down analysis should be performed here.

f. *Estimate costs:* See Chapter 30 for checklist.

2. *Determine systems requirement*

a. *Understand current operations:* A thorough analysis of your current operations is required here. It is necessary to describe:

- The work done
- By whom
- The time required
- Weaknesses in the processes

b. *Determine what should be automated:* In this step you must try to achieve a balance between just automating existing systems and going overboard by buying too many unnecessary features. Try to project your needs to

- Expand volume
- Improve information

The prior analyses will help in this phase.

c. *Research:* Before you contact a vendor and actually start looking at hardware and software, you should do some reading and research to see what is available and whether it will satisfy your requirements.

- Read the computer magazines. They rate hardware and software
- Talk to other users.

Suggestion: Many CPA societies have microcomputer users groups. They can be very helpful.

- Take classes if necessary.

3. *Screen Potential Vendors*

When you look for potential vendors, you are not just trying to find the best price. There are other equally important questions you should ask each candidate:

a. Do you have the ability to deliver what we need?
b. Do you fully understand the system? Try to have a list of questions to ask here. Often, many computer dealers hire people who may have been very good car or carpet salespeople, but their knowledge of computers is limited, at best.
c. Will you be able to train my people?
d. If I am paying for custom designed software, will you provide the source code?

Note: The source code, or the way to get into the system, is very helpful if the dealer disappears.

e. Will you be able to maintain our hardware and software?

Typical Dealer Contract

Price
Terms
Product or service description
Expected delivery date

Conditions:

Your right to reject
Arbitration agreements
Penalty or cancellation clauses
Equipment installation and maintenance agreements
Ownership of source code
In house training
Warranties and guaranties

4. *Evaluate software*

The software must be evaluated and selected before you consider your hardware. See Chapter 32 for detailed discussion.

5. *Evaluate hardware*

6. *Select the best hardware and software combination*

You will want to know:

a. How well does each prospective system satisfy your requirements?
   - will it get the job done?
   - does it require more expertise than you have?

b. Can it handle all your present and anticipated data processing requirements?
c. Can it be adapted to new applications as the need arises?
d. Is it within your budget?

7. *Implementation:* At this point, the system should be ready to go. Schedule and monitor the:
   a. tasks to be performed
   b. time frame required to be operational
   c. sequence of events

d. assigned responsibilities

e. method(s) to phase out of the old system

8. *Monitoring*

It is important to continue to make sure your system is performing as it should. You will have previously established performance goals. You should be able to obtain quick feedback as your work and system evolves.

How to Expand Your Practice by Becoming an EDP Consultant

You will not make any money in this area if people are not aware of your talents. Marketing is the art of recognizing and filling a need. If the need is computer consulting, there are several steps you should take:

- Improve your expertise. There a many courses at the local universities and through your professional societies. It is not difficult to establish a course of study.

Hint: Many CPA societies offer a certificate program in micro computer consulting.

- Be aware of opportunities. You are in an excellent position to see them as you serve your clients.
- Market your services by letting your clients and the public know about you.

Professional marketing can be done in many ways. You can speak at seminars, write for trade and professional magazines, use public relations to get coverage, and buy advertisement. Whatever combination you select, it should only be done in conjunction with your set of goals as expressed in your firm's business plan.

Performing the Consulting Engagement

Much of what I've previously discussed can be used to help you conduct a successful EDP consulting job. Before you begin you should obtain an engagement letter:

Engagement Letter

Pursuant to our discussion, this letter outlines the scope of services to be provided, fees for our services and memorializes the agreement reached between us.

Service

We will provide the following services to you:

1. *Software and hardware evaluation and selection.* This phase involves determining which of the accounting programs and hardware configurations currently available best satisfies your needs. While we make every effort to ensure the most appropriate software and hardware are recommend, we cannot be held responsible for information not revealed by vendors or product manufacturers.
2. *System setup and data conversion.* We will install and initialize the pertinent software on your system. We will assist you in organizing your existing accounting information for input, revising accounting numbers if necessary, determining the optimal cut-over date and drafting the opening journal entries.
3. *Training and on going support.* You and your staff will receive initial training at your office. We will provide continuing support through periodic visits, telephone calls and/or on-line connection with our computer systems.

Costs and Fees

The actual cost of the system depends on the hardware and software you select and the level of assistance you require. Professional fees for this work are billed on the actual time devoted to the job and will be billed at our standard rates of $______ per hour for partner time and $ ______per hour for staff/consultant time plus out-of-pocket expenses. All rates are subject to periodic adjustments. All amounts are billed on a semi-monthly basis. All sums billed and unpaid are due and payable within thirty days of billing, after which they are delinquent. Interest at the rate of % per annum, simple interest, is charged on all delinquent amounts. We reserve the right to discontinue work in the event any amounts become delinquent. We require a retainer of $______ to begin our work. We estimate our professional fees will be as follows:

If circumstances require time in excess of these estimates, your approval will be obtained in advance. We estimate the cost of software plus installation and training will not exceed $

In the event of disagreement, both parties must make reasonable efforts to resolve the matter before initiating legal action including arbitration. If any legal action is necessary to enforce the terms of this agreement, the prevailing party shall be entitled to reasonable attorney's fees in addition to any other relief to which that party may be entitled.

Any controversy between the parties hereto involving the construction of application of any of the terms, covenants, or conditions of this agreement, shall be on written request of one party served on the other be submitted to binding arbitration, and such arbitration shall comply with and be governed by the provisions of the Arbitration Act.

Damages are limited to the total of engagement fees paid. Our firm is not liable for direct or indirect damages, lost profits or damage to the client's reputation arising from this agreement.

This letter constitutes the entire agreement and supersedes all other statements, expressed or implied, written or oral.

CHAPTER 32

How to Select the Software You Need to Get the Job Done

Introduction

The hardware is the part of the system that does the work; the CPU, the input devices, the monitor, the printer. However, the software tells the system what to do. While there are various forms of systems software and utility programs, a discussion of these is better left to technical manuals for computer people. The discussion in this chapter focuses on applications software, the so-called "higher level" programs used for specific jobs.

How to Evaluate Software

Packaged software is acquired for a specific purpose; to process accounting data, to do complex calculations, to process text. Whatever the use, there is a minimum number of steps you should proceed through to:

1. See if its needed
2. Determine which product you should buy

1. *Is It Needed*:

The best way to answer this question is to list both the quantifiable and the non-quantifiable benefits:

Quantifiable:

Time savings

Personnel reduction

Non Quantifiable:

Increased processing

Better analysis

Improved working conditions

Evaluation Questions

In General:

1. Will the program yield measurable dollar benefits?
2. Are there sufficient non quantifiable benefits to justify its purchase?
3. Have you gathered sufficient information to know that you will benefit from this application?

The Publisher: There are a variety of programs published for many applications. These questions will allow you to choose the right package for you:

1. Have you read reviews appearing in various computer publications?
2. Is your system both compatible with and capable of efficiently using the application?

For example, certain programs work with IBM, others work with Apple.

3. Does the publisher have the "staying power" to continue to support its products?
4. Will upgrades, when available, be easily installed at minimum cost?
5. Is the manual easy to understand? Does it provide examples? Is it indexed?
6. Is it widely supported by other publications?

For example, there are a variety of books written about Lotus 1-2-3 in addition to the manual.

7. Are tutorials available?

Specific Features

1. Is the program menu driven? That is, do step-by-step instructions appear on the screen?

2. Are there easily applied help commands and screen messages?
3. Are error messages easy to understand?
4. Are there password controls to limit access to sensitive programs?
5. Can you edit and make changes on the screen?
6. Is the program flexible enough to allow you to custom design reports?
7. Can it be easily backed up?
8. Can you make multiple copies for use of others in your office?
9. Does it provide enough on screen and hard copy data to furnish a good audit trail?
10. Can it be easily expanded?

A Word of Warning

Before you start working with any application program

1. Make sure you read and understand the instructions.
2. Back up all the program disks.

Vertical vs. Horizontal Software

Horizontal

1. Performs specific tasks
2. Can be applied to a variety of users
3. Usually published by major companies
4. Will interface with other programs
5. Examples: Lotus, Dbase, Word Perfect

Vertical

1. Custom designed for a specific application
2. Usually designed by smaller organizations
3. May not be able to interface with other programs
4. Examples: Specific company, industry, applications such as inventory control, sales analysis.

Applications Software

The following is covered:

- Computerized accounting packages
- Tax preparation software
- Electronic spreadsheets
- Word processing
- Data base programs
- Desktop publishing

How to Select and Use a Computerized Accounting Package

Write up software is probably the oldest application for CPA's offices. In the early days, the hardware was large, temperamental and expensive and the software inflexible. But, times have changed. There is now a large variety of accountants packages out there.

Categories

1. *Full featured:* Does about everything, is flexible, and will handle multi-users.
2. *Spreadsheet based:* Built around electronic spreadsheet technology.
3. *Automated/one write* The journal formats are similar to pegboards.

Features

Many good accounting programs are sold as modules. You buy one and add others as needed. Normally, you would start with a general ledger program and than might add the following:

- Check writing/accounts payable
- Payroll
- Invoicing/sales/accounts receivable.

Questions to Ask

1. Will the program service multiple companies? In a CPA firm this is essential. If you are considering software for one client, the feature probably is not necessary.
2. Will it provide better information more efficiently?

3. Will it be able to handle all of your write-up clients without excessive disk switching?
4. Is the program flexible enough to allow you to set up customized charts of accounts and financial statement formats?
5. Will it do more than prepare balance sheets and income statements?

For example:

- Statements of cash flows
- Comparative financial statements
- Divisional and consolidated reports
- Budgets
- Variance analyses—budget versus actual
- Graphing

6. Will it prepare after the fact payroll tax returns, W-2s and 1099s?
7. Can these returns be prepared on pre-printed forms?
8. Can the program be integrated with
   - Spreadsheets for further analysis
   - Word processing for letters and footnotes
9. Ability to make entries. Can the program prepare the following entries?
   - Recurring journal entries
   - Automatic reversing entries
   - Special entries including inventory adjustments and income tax accruals
10. Will it provide detailed general ledgers? Many of the better accounting packages provide detailed analysis in each general ledger account as follows:

Account Number **634**
Name **Office Expense**

Date	**Check #**	**Payee**	**Debit**	**Credit**	**Balance**
6/30					7,432.45
7/1	1056	Blank Papers	12.45		
7/6	1087	Ace Stationery	135.73		
7/9	1943	Pens Plus	9.74		
7/20	2154	Acme Supplies	324.66		
	Total for Period		482.58	0.00	7,915.03

11. Will it provide detailed year-to-date general ledgers?
12. Will the program print out all journals, ledgers, and input registers?
13. Will you be able to view detailed information on the screen?
14. Will it support multiple users?

How to Get Your Accounting Package Up and Running

Converting from a manual to an EDP system is a major undertaking. You have to:

- Set up files for every client
- Convert the information in the files
- Install procedures and controls
- Educate your clients about the new reporting format

Suggestions:

1. Plan to have it installed before your busy season. To keep the stress to the minimum, I recommend the following time schedule:

To evaluate your needs and select a system	3 months
To convert your accounts	3 months
To work out bugs while new system is running	2 months

The following step-by-step procedure will alleviate some of the stress:

1. *Form an accounting package evaluation team.* Make sure it is staffed by affected employees as well as partners. Set time limits and reporting benchmarks. The team's end product should be the parameters of a proposed system, and, the evaluation of at least three likely candidate products.
2. Make selection.
3. Provide time tables for staff training.

Suggestion: If this program is operating at a colleague's office, try to buy some time for familiarization.

4. Push to get clients' bookkeeping up to date in order to gain an early start on conversion.

5. Designate one member of your firm to be responsible for client conversion. Have that member provide the following information:
   - Names of clients' to be converted
   - Expected conversion dates for each
   - Estimated staff time required
6. Prepare flow sheets and other control documents to follow each job as well as EDP logs.
7. Conduct staff training. This should include formal instruction and on the job sessions.
8. Meet with clients to explain new financial reports and ledgers as they are prepared.

Note: This may be a good time to impress your client with your ability to provide better information and discuss fee increases.

9. While financial reports should always be reviewed, you will have to monitor these early reports much closer.
10. Do not return the clients' source data until you've completely reviewed the output.

Tax Preparation Software

Many firms are now preparing tax returns in-house. By converting the work to their own system they are reaping the twin benefits of faster responsiveness while, at the same time, saving costs. But, while the total of tax return processing costs may be cheaper, what you may be doing is substituting fixed for variable expenses.

The following is a brief listing of applicable costs for in house tax return processing:

Computer upgrade

Additional terminals

Tax processing software

Forms

Labor for

Inputting
Printing
Collating
Stapling

Cost Analysis

1. Study the above list
2. Try to derive estimates of one time and ongoing costs.
3. Divide these costs by the number of expected returns to be processed.

If the amount derived is less than your present per return fee, you should consider proceeding.

What to Look for in Tax Processing Software

1. *Can the program process all items by one-time data entry?*

For example, if you have self-employment income, it should be entered only once.

2. *Does it contain built in tax limits and charts?*

For example, medical expenses, sales tax charts, deduction limitations.

3. *Will it process State returns?*
4. *Is it programmed to do non personal tax returns?* corporations, partnerships, fiduciaries
5. *Will the software manufacturer provide regular updates?*
6. *Does it allow you to correct mistakes easily?*
7. *What types of printing options will you have?*

   By batch?

   Continuous?

   On printed forms?

   Preview?
8. *Will the new system overburden your present storage capacity?*
9. *Will your computer run the program?*
10. *Does the manufacturer allow you to make multiple copies so that the program can be processed on other terminals in your office?*
11. *Will the manufacturer provide operating assistance and training?*
12. *Can the features of the program be used for tax planning during the year?*

The Middle Path May Be the Best Way

To ease the transition to full in house conversion, you may consider using a terminal and modem to telecommunicate with your tax return processor. This will save you per item costs and will also improve turnaround time.

Electronic Spreadsheets

Electronic spreadsheets create large displays of two dimensional data on screen. From that point, you can effectively manipulate numbers.

Popular Spreadsheet Programs

- Lotus 1-2-3
- Supercalc
- Excel
- Quattro

Desired Features

- *Easy copying* from portions of files to the full record itself
- *Graphics capability.*

Note: Make sure your CPU has a graphics card.

- *Ability to handle formulas.* These include the normal math plus financial formulas—present value, payment, depreciation, equations, to regression. Certain newer models have linear programming capability.
- *Integration within text.* Certain spreadsheet programs (e.g. Lotus Symphony) have built in word processing capabilities.
- *Ability to Store and handle data.* This feature allows one to build in charts and tables.

For example, tax computation tables can be built into a tax planning or financial statement worksheet.

- *Capability to consolidate files*

How to Use Spreadsheets and Get Rid of Your Workpaper Stationery

In the last few years of my practice, I begin to put all my schedules on electronic spreadsheet. This practice had many advantages:

1. It made computations a lot easier.
2. The formats could be used for other situations and clients.
3. Errors were much easier to correct.

For Example: You are reviewing a client's financial statements and discover an additional adjustment is needed. Consider what has to be done if the work is performed manually:

a. Prepare the journal entry
b. Post the journal entry to the worksheet
c. Extend the worksheet
d. Correct the statement(s). It could affect all three financial statements.
e. Recompute the income tax
f. Math check all the adjustments.

If you use an electronic spreadsheet, all you have to do is prepare the entry.

Tips

1. Make hard copies of all your electronic spreadsheet workpapers. These should go into the client files and be indexed in the usual manner.
2. Keep hard copies of the formula used as backup for your entries.

For example:

Calculating a payment (Regular Format)

Amount owed	50,000.00
Annual interest rate	12.00%
Term (years)	10
Monthly payment	$717.35

Calculating a payment (Formula Format)

Amount owed	50000

Annual interest rate		0.12
Term (years)		10
Monthly payment	@PMT(+ D3,D4/12,D5*12)	

3. Use files as templates.

For example, the loan payment calculation can be saved under one file name. Then, later, it can be retrieved. New calculations are performed. And, then the file is saved under a new name.

4. Generalize equations and cell addresses as much as possible. In this way, information will not have to be reentered and mistakes will be avoided.

Word Processing

Word processing programs store and process text data, edit and format. They make it easier to compose documents because inserts can be made, blocks of data can be moved, and certain print enhancements can be added.

Popular Word Processing Programs

- Wordstar
- WordPerfect
- DOS Write
- MAC Write
- Ami Pro

Desired Features

When choosing a word processing program, ask yourself the following:

1. Will it allow you to easily retrieve and save documents?
2. Will it check spelling?
3. Does it have a thesaurus to find synonyms?
4. Can it print graphics?
5. Can it print mathematical symbols?
6. Can you import other programs?

What About Writing Evaluation Software?

Just recently, these programs have appeared to check grammar, punctuation and syntax. While they won't turn mediocre writers into great ones, they are useful to enhance existing skills.

Data Base Programs

Data base programs are the computer's answer to a filing system. They keep and update records, perform mathematical operations and produce various reports.

Popular Data Base Programs

- DBase 3+, and DBase IV
- Paradox3

Desirable Data Base Features

- Easy entry
- Easy recording
- Easy sorting
- Ability and flexibility to design reports
- Menu driven
- Mathematical abilities

Desktop Publishing

Desktop publishing allows you to set up and print an entire publication. Its features provide for:

- Importing of text
- Graphics
- Pictures
- Changing print styles and fonts

Popular Desktop Publishing Programs

- Aldus Pagemaker
- Ventura Publishing

- Harvard Graphics
- Express Publishing

Special Problems

The major problem is the difficulty learning how to use it. There are many features which have to be applied together in order to utilize the program to its full advantage. Therefore, if you want to get started in this area, make sure you have the necessary time and/or the funds.

Another Warning: Desktop publishing can be addictive. You can spend so much time trying to get things to look just right that other work slips.

Setting Up CPA Office Workstations

A well-designed local area network can

- Link the various members of your firm
- Greatly expand data collection and computational abilities
- Improve time efficiencies
- Increase billings

Possible Applications

1. *Work flow monitoring.* Set up your data base to include the following fields:

    a. Date required
    b. Client
    c. Description of work
    d. Estimated time
    e. Date done

    At any time you can get a picture of what work has to be done:

    - for a client
    - by a certain date
    - for a particular activity

      For example: payroll tax returns

2. *Time keeping.* This has been found to be an effective method of monitoring chargeable and non chargeable time. As work

is done, the time is entered, right on the spot to the computer terminal. At the end of the billing period, these hours at their extended rate become the basis for billing.

Note: The data base timekeeping system that I installed in my office added over 10% to my billing.

Idea: If individual workstations are installed, the administrative partner can get a fix at any time in the month of a particular employee's production.

3. *As a way of accumulating client data.* Assume a client brings in a "shoe box" of information for his or her tax return. Rather than putting this on general ledger or worksheet, set up a data base file to input each individual item. The following fields may be used:

   Account number

   Date

   Payee

   Description

   Amount

   This data can then be sorted, and summarized by account number. The results are then printed out.
4. *For mailing labels.*
5. *For accounts receivable.* Multiple files can be established to account for:

   Balance

   Name

   Billing

   Collections
6. *Write up and statement preparation.*
7. *Spreadsheet analyses.*

Index

J

L

T

U

V